IN SEARCH OF THE DHARMA

Bibliotheca Indo-Buddhica Series–No. 129

IN SEARCH OF THE DHARMA

MEMOIRS OF A MODERN CHINESE BUDDHIST PILGRIM

CHEN-HUA

Edited with an Introduction by
CHÜN-FANG YÜ

and Translated by Denis C. Mair

SRI SATGURU PUBLICATIONS
A DIVISION OF
INDIAN BOOKS CENTRE
DELHI-INDIA

Published by:
SRI SATGURU PUBLICATIONS
A Division of
Indian Books Centre
Oriental and Indological Publishers
40/5, Shakti Nagar,
Delhi - 110 007
INDIA

First Indian Edition : Delhi, 1994.

ISBN - 81-7030-392-3.

Printed in India

In Memorium

HOLMES WELCH (1921-1981)

Mentor and Friend

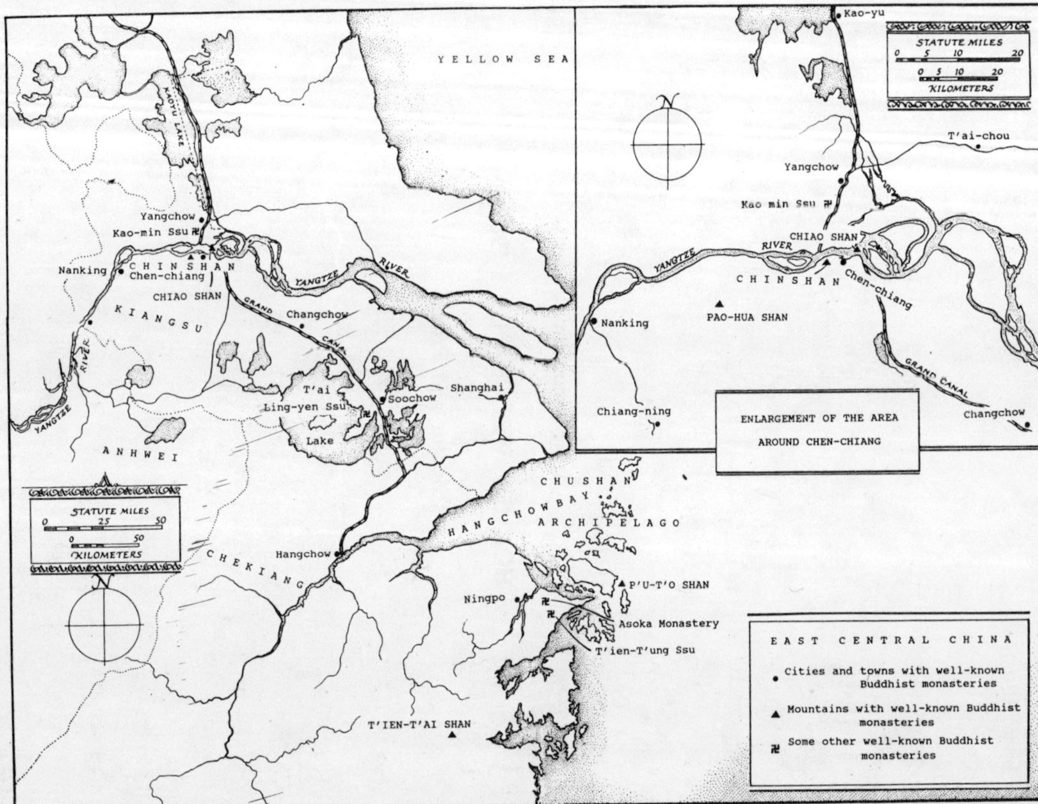
EAST CENTRAL CHINA
Cities and towns with well-known Buddhist monasteries
Mountains with well-known Buddhist monasteries
Some other well-known Buddhist monasteries
ENLARGEMENT OF THE AREA AROUND CHEN-CHIANG
YELLOW SEA
STATUTE MILES
0 25 50
KILOMETERS
0 50
STATUTE MILES
0 5 10 20
KILOMETERS
0 5 10 20
Kao-yu
T'ai-chou
Yangchow
Kao min Ssu
CHIAO SHAN
RIVER
YANGTZE
CHINSHAN
Chen-chiang
Nanking
PAO-HUA SHAN
GRAND CANAL
Chiang-ning
Changchow
KAOYU LAKE
Kao-min Ssu
CHIAO SHAN
KIANGSU
GRAND CANAL
Changchow
T'ai
Ling-yen Ssu
Lake
Soochow
Shanghai
ANHWEI
CHEKIANG
Hangchow
HANGCHOW BAY
CHUSHAN
ARCHIPELAGO
P'U-T'O SHAN
Ningpo
Asoka Monastery
T'ien-T'ung Ssu
T'IEN-T'AI SHAN

Contents

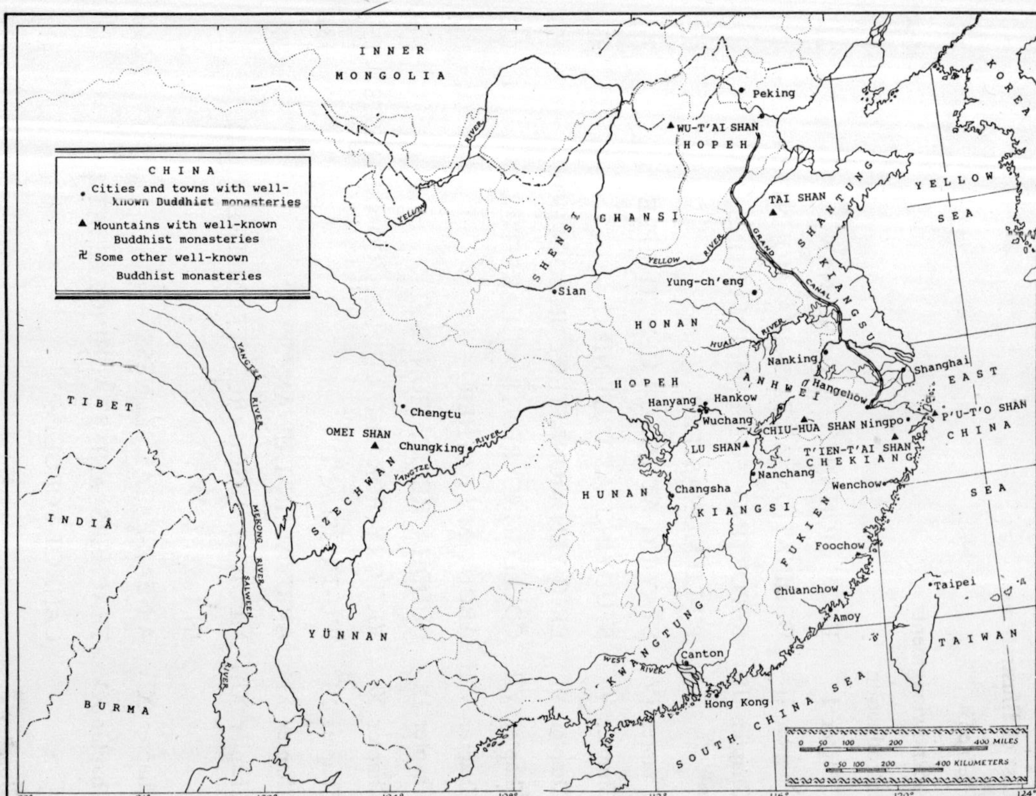
CHINA
Cities and towns with well-known Buddhist monasteries
Mountains with well-known Buddhist monasteries
Some other well-known Buddhist monasteries
INNER MONGOLIA
KOREA
YELLOW SEA
EAST CHINA SEA
SOUTH CHINA SEA
TIBET
INDIA
BURMA
YÜNNAN
SZECHWAN
SHENSI
SHANSI
HOPEH
SHANTUNG
KIANGSU
HONAN
HOPEH
ANHWEI
HUNAN
KIANGSI
CHEKIANG
FUKIEN
KWANGTUNG
TAIWAN
Peking
WU-T'AI SHAN
TAI SHAN
Sian
Yung-ch'eng
Nanking
Shanghai
Hangchow
Ningpo
P'U-T'O SHAN
CHIU-HUA SHAN
T'IEN-T'AI SHAN
LU SHAN
Hanyang
Hankow
Wuchang
Nanchang
Changsha
Wenchow
Foochow
Chüanchow
Amoy
Taipei
Canton
Hong Kong
Chengtu
Chungking
OMEI SHAN
YELLOW RIVER
GRAND CANAL
HUAI RIVER
YANGTZE RIVER
MEKONG RIVER
SALWEEN RIVER
WEST RIVER
0 50 100 200 400 MILES
0 50 100 200 400 KILOMETERS
92° 96° 100° 104° 108° 112° 116° 120° 124°
40° 36° 32° 28° 24°

List of Illustrations

Fig. 1 Portrait of the author, Chen-hua

Preface

One of the most fundamental teachings in Buddhism is that everything in the world comes about as a result of causes and conditions. For instance, although a seed has the potentiality for growth, unless there are present the conditions of sunlight, water, soil, fertilizer, human labor as well as other factors, the seed will not be able to germinate, put out leaves, flower and finally bear fruit. Similarly, if only the conditions of sunlight, water, soil, fertilizer and human labor are present, but no seed is planted, there will likewise be no harvest. Mencius said, "If there is nourishment, nothing will fail to grow, but if there is no nourishment, then nothing will fail to die." What Mencius meant by the word "nourishment" is no different from the Buddhist concept of "causality". Both refer to the conditions which control the growth and decline of things. When the necessary conditions are present, anything one decides to do will invariably succeed. On the other hand, when the necessary conditions are absent, then anything one decides to do will always end up in failure. This is the universal and eternal truth. No one in the whole world can ever alter it. The *Awakening of Faith in Mahāyāna* expresses it this way: "There are causes and conditions responsible for the appearance of every dharma. Only when the causes and conditions are complete, will anything come to pass successfully." Some years ago I wrote the following *gātha* to convey the same idea:

Cause and conditions meet to form events;
No dharma can arise from cause alone.
Just look at the wintry river willows
Turning green after a touch of spring wind.

We should know that causal conditions are the moving forces both in the spiritual and the mundane realms. The reason why my book could undergo two printings in Taiwan and now appear in English translation is entirely due to the workings of causal conditions. It is truly remarkable.

It was over thirty years ago when Master Hsing-yün asked me to write for his journal *Awakening the World* (*Chüeh-shi*) which was published once every ten days. He specifically wanted me to write about my experiences of studying Buddhism as a young monk in mainland China. I had never been very interested in writing. I also had very little confidence in myself as a writer. But he was very persistent in his requests and kept asking me for the manuscript. Finally, with trepidation, I wrote four pieces which I entitled, "A Resolve Made in Ignorance", "A Journey Tearfully Begun", "A Humiliating Stop at A Roadside Temple", and "Trouble on A Dark Road" for the journal. Because they met with good responses from the readers, I was asked to continue writing more installments for over a year. After that Master Hsing-yün decided to publish the series separately as a book. When the book came out, it received several good reviews which praised it for its truthfulness. They gave me much encouragement and made me feel more confident in myself as a writer. This then was the causal condition which made the birth and the first publication of this book possible.

In December of 1977, about ten years after the publication of the book, a writer by the name of Chiang Kuei wrote a review of the book and published it in the overseas edition of a Taiwanese newspaper. A person living in the States read the article and became very interested in reading the book. So he wrote to Chiang Kuei and asked him to buy a copy for him in Taiwan. Even though I was familiar with the name Chiang Kuei, for he often wrote for newspapers and magazines, I did not know who he was. Nor did I read his review. It turned out that Chiang Kuei was the penname of a gentleman who often came to attend my lectures on the *Awakening of Faith in the Mahāyāna* which I gave at the Ten Thousand Buddha Monastery two years ago. But the book was long out of print by that time. Even I myself had only one copy. So when Chiang Kuei came to me for an extra copy, I could not help him. Just then Mr. Ch'en Hui-chien, a lay Buddhist devotee and the owner of T'ien-hua Publishing Company, learned about this situation and offered to reprint the book. I consulted with Master Hsing-yün, the original publisher, who graciously surrendered the copyright without any conditions. In this way, the second printing became a reality.

As to how the English translation of the book came about, it was even more an example of the strange workings of causal conditions. It happened in April of 1977, before the events leading to the second printing of the book took place. I was then living on Mt. Chih-nan outside of Taipei. One day I suddenly received a telephone call from an unknown woman. She said that her name was Chün-fang Yü and explained the reason for the call. Several months ago she happened to find my book at the Harvard-Yenching Library at Harvard University. Because she liked it and would like to have it translated into English, she decided to locate the whereabouts of its author so that she could get his consent. She asked her refuge master Sheng-yen in New York who happened to know me very well. So he told her my address and telephone number. She came to Taiwan to do research, and she would like to meet with me and talk about the translation project. I invited her to come.

The next day she came to visit me with her son, a good-looking boy of four or five. After we exchanged the usual greetings, I said to her right away, "You are to be commended for wanting to have my book translated into English. Not only will I be happy to give you my unconditional consent, but I want to thank you for doing this. However, before you begin this project, you must understand my intention of writing this book. I left the life of a householder when I was only fourteen. During my life I have encountered many difficulties and experienced much suffering. Fame and profit have long appeared to me like floating clouds. For several decades I have relied on the Buddhist sangha for my food and clothing. I naturally have a genuine feeling of love for Buddhism. Therefore, I feel only gratitude but no resentment toward Buddhism. I have no other desire but to practice Buddhism myself and teach others about it. When I criticized persons or things in the book, it was never because I harbored any ill will toward them. Precisely because I loved Buddhism so deeply, that was why I demanded more from its practitioners. I hope you will explain this clearly in the translation. Otherwise, I am afraid that readers may misunderstand me." She answered me with a smile, saying, "Please put your mind to ease, for I will not disappoint you. I took refuge with Master Nan-ting when I was in Taiwan. Later, after I went to the States, I took refuge again with Master Sheng-yen. From the standpoint of a fellow Buddhist, I think I understand the real motivation of your writing this book."

She left for Kyoto soon after our meeting and from there went back to the States the following year. Time went by quickly. Before long five years had passed. I had almost forgotten about this matter when one day, late in 1981, I got a call from Master Sheng-yen informing me that the English translation of my book had already appeared in print. I was very happy to hear this good news. In March 1982 I had an opportunity to go to the States. I visited monasteries in San Francisco, Toronto and New York. I stayed two weeks at the Ch'an Center in New York and received the hospitality of its abbot, Master Sheng-yen. While there Professor Chün-fang Yü came to visit me and presented me with the three issues of the journal *Chinese Sociology and Anthropology* which contained the entire translation of the book. Although I did not know any English, when I looked at the pages of the journal, the English words seemed to wink at me and I could not help myself from laughing.

Now another decade has passed and the translation will be published as a book. This cannot come to pass without the necessary causes and conditions. When Professor Yü asked me to supply a preface to the English edition, I thought it might be of interest to the reader if I reported the circumstances under which both the original Chinese and later English versions of the book came into being. I will conclude with a summary of my recent activities. I have been involved with teaching Buddhism in one form or another for the last ten years. I have gone to the United States, the Philippines, Singapore, Malaysia, Thailand, and Hong Kong to preach. In recent years Buddhism has experienced a revival in Taiwan. As a result, sutra lectures, ordination sessions, and "Buddha Recitation Week" were held in different places almost everyday. As a monk who regards the propagation of the Dharma as his duty and the benefitting of all sentient beings as his task, I feel that I should exert myself to fulfill my obligation as a member of the monastic community. Unless I accept all invitations to participate in the spreading of the Buddhist teaching, I will have failed to create affinities with people everywhere. But a person's mental and physical energy is limited. In the meantime, old age is also creeping upon me. Thus for some time now I have gone on propagating the Dharma in ill health. The last time I went abroad was in 1988 at the invitation of the King of Thailand. To celebrate his 60th birthday, he invited eminent monks from all over the world to receive his offerings. I went to Thailand as the adviser to the Chinese Devotees' Association. After that I have stayed in Taiwan devoting my time to manage the Fu-yen Buddhist Seminary.

Over the years I served in different monasteries as guest prefect, precenter, proctor, manager, and abbot. In Buddhist seminaries I served as teacher, dean of studies, deputy director and director. Aside from these offices, I have also served as secretary, catechist, ordination instructor, ordination abbot, honored witness, and confessor during ordination sessions.

During the forty years since I came to Taiwan I have written a number of articles totalling about one million words. The two books which already appeared in print, *Ts'an-hsüeh suo-t'an* (*Fragmentary Reminiscences of My Search for Knowledge*) and *Hsing-hua tsa-chi* (*Miscellaneous Notes of Practicing and Teaching Buddhism*), occupy a little over one-third of these. I plan to edit the rest for future publication.

I was born a poor peasant boy in north China, entered the monastic order at a young age, and often experienced setbacks in my search for truth. Yet because of certain causal conditions, I can now share my memories and observations with English readers. This is something that I have never anticipated. If this book can help them to get a better understanding of Chinese Buddhism, I will have realized my original intention in writing it.

Fu-yen Buddhist Seminary
Hsin-chu, Taiwan

Chen-hua

Acknowledgments

This book is an English translation of Chen-hua's *Ts'an-hsüeh suo-t'an* (*Fragmentary Reminiscences of My Search for Knowledge*) which first appeared in a serial form in the journal *Chüeh-shih* (*Awakening the World*) for two years starting in 1962. Because of enthusiastic responses from readers, the editor of the journal Hsing-yün, now the abbot of Fo-kuang Shan in Taiwan and Hsi-lai Monastery near Los Angeles, who had asked him to write the series, decided to publish them in a book form. This was done in 1965. It subsequently went into a second printing in 1977.

Preserving the original flavor of the series, *Ts'an-hsüen suo-t'an* has seventy-two sections. There is no chapter division. Instead, it consists of two parts of unequal length: the first and longer part is entitled, "From Honan to Chian-nan [South of Yangtze River]" which describes the author's experiences in visiting major monasteries and studying Buddhism in mainland China during 1945-48; the second and shorter part is entitled, "From Shanghai to Taiwan" which describes his pilgrimages to P'u-t'o and other sacred sites on the eve of Communist revolution, his forced departure for Taiwan as an army draftee, his life in the army, his medical discharge and his reentering the monastic order, covering roughly the ten years from 1949-59.

I happened to read this book in January 1977. At that time I did not know who the author was, but was immediately struck by the lively and forthright manner of his writing. In May of the same year when I was in Taiwan, through the introduction of Sheng-yen, my refuge master and now the abbot of the Ch'an Center in New York, I met Chen-hua at his retreat house in Mu-cha, outside of Taipei. The author turned out to be exactly like his writing, passionate in his devotion to Buddhism, scathing in his criticisms of monastic abuses, a man of strong likes and dislikes, but above all, a man with a good sense of humor. I had long felt the need for more in-depth studies on contemporary Chinese Buddhism, an area left largely untouched except for the books by the late Holmes Welch. When I raised the possibility of having his book translated into English, he readily gave me his consent. He also gave me permission to omit sections and to make other editorial changes to help the flow of the narrative. The English translation is about four-fifths of the Chinese original. What is left out are passages not directly related to the events and personages under discussion. In order to help the reader follow the story, I have also divided the book into 15 chapters.

The English version of the book, entitled *Random Talks about My Mendicant Life*, appeared as three separate issues in the journal *Chinese Sociology and Anthropology*: Fall 1980 (Vol. XIII, No. 1), Summer 1981 (Vol. XIII, No. 4) and Spring 1982 (Vol. XIV, No. 3). I would like to thank Victor Mair who introduced me to his brother, Denis C. Mair, the translator, whose felicity with words matches that of Chen-hua. This project received encouragement and support from Holmes Welch from the beginning, when I decided to go ahead with the translation upon my return from Taiwan in 1978. When the translation was first being prepared for publication in the journal, he read over the entire manuscript with great care, and generously offered valuable suggestions to improve my editorial style. It was all the more unfortunate, therefore, that he only saw the first issue of the journal before he passed away in May 1981. I dedicate this book to his memory.

Since 1982 after the first publication of the English version, I have had occasion to go to mainland China twice and visited most of the monasteries mentioned in Chen-hua's book. Every time I went back to Taiwan, I also visited Chen-hua and talked with him in length. In 1986 when I told him that I would be going to P'u-t'o to interview pilgrims, he immediately asked me to look for his father whom he last saw on the island in 1949. He also asked me to locate and bring back his ordination certificate issued by Pao-hua Shan, a precious document that he left in someone's safekeeping when he was drafted into the army. He gave me names of monks who might lead me to his father and the address of the temple where his father last stayed. In March 1987 I spent the week honoring Kuan-yin's birthday (lunar calendar the 19th of the 2nd month) on P'u-t'o Island. The temple had long disappeared. I did manage to track down one old monk who knew Chen-hua's father. But he could only say that the father had passed away some years ago, not remembering exactly the year. He also told me that Chen-hua's ordination certificate, like so many other religious documents and artifacts, was destroyed during the Cultural Revolution (1966-76). So much has happened since the writing of his book. But some thing has apparently remained the same for the author. At the beginning of the book, as a young man, he left his home and set out in search of knowledge. And now, at the age of 70, Chen-hua is the director of Fu-yen Buddhist Seminary in Hsin-chu, Taiwan, a seminary for nuns.

Bringing the three separate issues together and publishing them as a book has been a long-cherished dream of mine. To see this become a reality, I must thank Douglas Merwin of M.E. Sharpe, Inc. who released the rights and William Eastman of SUNY Press who offered me a contract. Denis C.

Mair, who had been working as a professional translator in China for a number of years, came back to the States in the fall of 1989. To prepare the translation for its second reincarnation, he went over the manuscript once more and made extensive revisions, trying to keep as much the style and flavor of the original as possible. Chen-hua, whom I last saw in Taiwan in January 1990, wrote a preface for the English version of his book. Some years ago, in anticipation of the book's publication, Holmes Welch gave me two photographs from his collection which now become Figures 2 and 3. Figures 4 to 8 were selected from the photographs which I took during my 1983 trip to China. Chen-hua provided original photographs from which Figures 1 and 9 were reproduced. These photographs either illustrate the monasteries where Chen-hua visited or show some typical activities in which monks like Chen-hua would be engaged. I would like to thank Jack Harriett for his expertise in transforming my snapshots into these beautiful photographs. In addition to finding the appropriate photographs, I wrote an introduction, corrected and updated notes, and provided maps showing the places Chen-hua mentioned in the book. I also give the book a new title which reflects its author's intention more faithfully. In the final analysis, throughout his difficult life, Chen-hua was a pilgrim in search of Buddhist truth.

In preparing for the camera-ready copy of the book I received the help of Grace Ahmed and Muyang Yu, both of Rutgers University. I benefitted from the able guidance of Marilyn Semerad of SUNY Press. I am also very fortunate in finding an expert on page layout and type setting. I relied entirely on the technical assistance of Ming-Hsu Tu, also of Rutgers. Throughout the long and frustrating process of preparing the manuscript for publication he was always patient and cheerful. I can truly say that without his help this book would not have been able to appear in print.

Chinese characters for all proper names of persons, monasteries, scriptures, as well as Buddhist technical terms are provided in the glossary. Jean Yap of Rutgers University helped me with the preparation of the Chinese characters in the glossary.

I would like to acknowledge the support of the Research Council of Rutgers University which provided me with research grants to aid the preparation for this book. I have received much help from the above institution and individuals. I have also benefitted from the advice of many "good friends". Any remaining errors are, needless to say, entirely my own.

Chün-fang Yü

Introduction

Chen-hua is a prominent Chinese Buddhist monk now living in Taiwan. In the 1960s he wrote *Ts'an-hsüeh suo-t'an*, of which this book is a translation. He talked about his experiences as a young monk in mainland China with candor. He also offered frank and bold criticisms about monastic abuses which he witnessed personally. Both make this book a very unusual document. Traditionally, Chinese monks have been reluctant to talk about their personal lives. Although there have been some exceptions (the autobiography of Han-shan Te-ch'ing, 1546-1623, entitled *Meng-yu chi*, is one notable example), writing memoirs smacks too much of self-aggrandizement to be a common pursuit of monks who are supposed to have left behind their personal histories together with their secular names when they entered the monastic order. On the other hand, because most of Chinese Buddhists believed that they were living in the age of the decline of the Dharma, Buddhist masters since the 5th century A.D. have often decried the lack of monastic discipline among their contemporaries. However, although this cry of alarm is a leitmotif in monastic discourses, it is very rare indeed that specific abuses connected with identifiable monasteries and persons were made common knowledge to a wide reading public as in the present case.

Chen-hua was very aware of the unorthodox nature of his undertaking. He reiterated throughout the book that his criticisms were motivated not by personal grudge or vendetta, but by his deep love for Buddhism and his commitment to its reform. Instead of following the common practice of "hiding family scandals from the eyes of outsiders", he chose to serve as the conscience and witness of his generation. Thus, what appears as ruthless attacks are intended to serve as pedagogical proddings for improvement. This ulterior motive becomes clear, for instance, when he states at the end of his scathing criticisms about the abuses at Pao-hua Mountain:

> It is true that blemishes on a family's name should not be held up for all to see, but to give examples of the monastic system from which people of the future can select some things and reject others, it behooves me to reveal the dark side as well as publicizing the commendable side of things. Pao-hua Mountain is the establishment

> at which I was ordained. It would seem wrong for me to write about these somewhat unsavory matters, and thus needlessly incur ill feelings of outsiders but, the truth being more important than my personal likes and dislikes, I feel it would be better to make it known to monks, nuns and devotees around the world rather than to bury it in my own heart.

The same commitment to truth compelled Chen-hua to write about his own life with equally unflinching honesty. Even though he used the first person in the narrative, he did not call the book memoirs or autobiography. Instead, he made the four Chinese characters in the title stand for four different activities. In his preface to the Chinese edition, he explained their meanings this way:

> When the book was ready for publication, I asked a fellow monk who was good at drawing to design the cover. I asked him to draw four pictures depicting a monk engaged in four different kinds of activities. In the first picture, he is shown meditating under a tree. This represents *ts'an*, meditation. In the second picture, he is shown reading a book in a room. This represents *hsüeh*, study. The third picture shows him cutting firewood with a big axe. This represents *suo*, performing small tasks. And finally, in the fourth picture, the monk is shown giving sermons dressed in a formal cassock. This represents *t'an*, lecture. The first two activities benefit oneself, while the last two activities benefit others. Together, they constitute the life orientations of a true Buddhist practitioner.

This book is, therefore, essentially about his activities in these areas, his efforts to learn Buddhism and to help others. Because Chen-hua wrote originally for a magazine, he arranged the series around key episodes in his life. Even though they follow a chronological order, the narrative does not constitute a consecutive sequence. In order to prepare the reader for what is being discussed in the book, I will provide some background information about the author and the condition of Buddhism in modern China. Important themes, problems, and Buddhist leaders will also be mentioned whenever necessary. I will center my discussion around two major topics: Chen-hua's personal history and his reflections on the conditions of Buddhism as he saw them. I will thus divide my remarks into two sections, Chen-hua the monk and Chen-hua the witness.

Chen-hua, the Monk

The author refers several times in the course of the book to his childhood, his lay family, his life as a novice and his relationship with his father who, through his urging, eventually also became a monk. But in all the cases, he gives the reader but a brief outline without going into details. In another book of his, *Miscellaneous Notes on Practicing and Teaching Buddhism* (*Hsing-hua tsa-chi*),[1] Chen-hua tells us about his early life. Over the years, I also asked him about his background. What follows, then, is based on his account and my interviews.

Chen-hua was born on February 25th, 1922 in Shan-cheng, Yung-cheng County, Honan Province. His secular name was Liu Fu-yü, but he was also known as Chün-shan to family members and close friends. The Liu family had been one of four prominent families in his home town before his birth. But the family fortune started to decline soon after he was born. Chen-hua's grandfather had three sons and two daughters, his father being the second and the favorite son. Born on the day the Buddha entered Nirvana, Chen-hua was the youngest of six children, coming after four brothers and one sister. Because owls cried all night at his birth, his father took this as an evil omen and wanted to "abandon the baby in the mountain to feed wild dogs." The grandparents saved him by giving the father a severe scolding. But the nex[illegible]y, a blind fortune-teller brought more bad news by saying that the baby was predestined to die of hunger. In order to avert this terrible fate, the grandmother went on a pilgrimage to the Temple of Mt. T'ai (the same temple where Chen-hua later received tonsure), situated on nearby Protecting Safety Mountain (Pao-an Shan) to offer incense, make vows and pray for his safety. She also spent quite a lot of money and asked the fortune-teller to alter the bad fortune. But even though he did not end up dying of hunger, the Liu family nevertheless soon encountered inexplicably one tragedy after another.

The grandfather accumulated quite a lot of property by the time he reached sixty, two years before the author's birth. There were 500 *mou* (about 75.65 acres) of fertile farm lands, four houses, more than ten shops in the city, plus forest land and an empty lot for storing firewood and grains. Because all the children had married, the grandfather decided to divide the property among the sons, keeping only one house and 100 *mou* for himself. But instead of enjoying his old age peacefully as he had hoped, misfortune overwhelmed him. He was forced to sell off 60 *mou* of the land when he was sued through no fault of his own and then a freak fire destroyed all the four houses. This happened when Chen-hua was not yet three years old. As if this was not bad enough, when he was four, during one year, he lost eight of his loved ones. His grandfather and his uncle died within one month of each other. Then, his four brothers and one sister, ranging from six to fifteen years old, followed. Finally, unable to bear the physical abuses from the father, his mother hanged herself. Crazed by the family tragedies, the father tried to kill Chen-hua the second time by abandoning him on the mountain. But he was saved by two distant relatives who handed him over to the grandmother for protection. The father left home in anger and did not come back until Chen-hua was nine. When he did return, he did not stay to take care of the son, but after selling whatever was remaining of his share of the land, he joined the army and left his home for good.

Chen-hua lived with his grandmother in utter poverty until he was fourteen when he lost her as well. He made a meager living by doing odd jobs and almost resorted to begging when the year was lean and no work was available. With the death of his grandmother, he had no family left (he did not mention his father's other brother and sister, who probably could not do anything for him anyway). A kind woman whom he called Auntie Ch'en came to his rescue. A mid-wife by occupation, she was friendly with monks at the Temple of Mt. T'ai. She suggested that it would be best for him to become the disciple of a monk there, emphasizing the good life he would enjoy there. So, wearing a new suit of clothing made by Auntie Ch'en and carrying a huge watermellon (as an offering) weighing more than 20 catties, he went to the temple with her on the first day of the seventh month, lunar calendar, in the year 1936.

Becoming a disciple to a monk, in this case, was clearly a way of making a living for poor children who had no families. It was also clear that no one, including his master, seemed to be conscious of the spiritual significance of taking the tonsure. Without ceremony and ignoring his howling protest, his head was shaven clean. He was not asked to take the vows in the Three Refuges, nor was he given the ten precepts, the normal requirements of becoming a novice. Chen-hua called the temple where he received tonsure "small temple" (*hsiao-miao*), in contrast to the public monasteries, called "forests for the ten directions" (*shih-fang ts'ung-lin*), where he later studied in the south. One major difference between the two was that one could receive tonsure only in the "small temples". One became the heir to the monk who shaved off one's hair. Generational terms, based upon secular lineage usages, were applied to the residents of the temple. Thus, Chen-hua called the monk who gave him tonsure *shin-fu* (literally, "father-master"), monks of one generation above the master, "grandfather-masters", and all the monks belonging to the same generation as his master, "uncle-masters". By the same token, Chen-hua called the monks of his own generation "brother-disciples ", and those one generation below him, "son-disciples". In contrast, public monasteries did not give tonsures. Rather, visitors going there must have already received tonsure elsewhere and undergone some preliminary training. The primary duty of the guest prefect was to make sure that this was the case.

Small temples were the private properties of the dharma families. Abbotship was passed on from father-master to son-disciple. Public monasteries, as the name indicated, theoretically belonged to the entire monastic order. Abbotship was not hereditary, but decided by election or recommendation. Even more important than these differences, monks in the small temples were less knowledgeable about Buddhism and also more lax in their observances of monastic discipline. Before Chen-hua went south to study, he never attended any lectures on Buddhist scriptures. He also did not know how to chant scriptures or perform Buddhist rituals. Most of the residents of the temple were not vegetarians. Instead, the temple kept livestocks for food. In fact, one of the main duties of young novices was to fetch wine and prepare meat dishes for their masters.

Although such small temples were very common in the north, they were by no means only found there. On the other hand, public monasteries, which were all connected with the Ch'an tradition, were mostly located in Kiangsu and Chekiang, the "cradle of Buddhism". Although Chen-hua did not receive any formal training in Buddhism at his home temple, he remembered his master with gratitude, for it was he who provided the chance for Chen-hua to receive an education.

Neither the master nor Chen-hua knew how to read and write. When Chen-hua was 15, his master enrolled him at a private schoolhouse. Although the master's initial motivation for doing so was to make Chen-hua useful in keeping accounts and taking care of other practical matters, he allowed the latter to continue with his schooling when Chen-hua showed promise. It was also the master who made arrangement for Chen-hua, at 24, to set forth for the south to advance his training. If Chen-hua did not become a monk, he would without a doubt have remained an illiterate peasant. In this sense, small temples such as this one did serve useful functions in educating some members of the rural poor.

Chen-hua's story was illuminating in another respect as well. Both in the past and in the modern period, there were probably always people who, like Chen-hua, entered the monastic order not because of religious conviction but as a last resort for survival. The monastic order was indeed the refuge. Because this was the case, the monastic population could be a mixture of good and bad, pure and impure elements. A common saying, which Chen-hua liked to quote, described the situation well, "A monastery is a place where snakes mingled with dragons." However, as Chen-hua himself testified most eloquently, he was profoundly transformed by his monastic training and became a passionate spokesman for the Buddhist tradition. Perhaps more dramatic than others, Chen-hua's case was not an isolated one.

Chen-hua left his home temple in 1945, at the end of the Sino-Japanese war which he called the War of Resistance. In the next four years, he remained in Kiangsu and Chekiang. He received ordination at Pao-hua Mountain, the number one monastery known for its strict discipline. He studied at T'ien-ning Buddhist Seminary for a year, but was forced to terminate his study. He spent six months in Tung-yüeh Temple in Nanking, serving as a funeral specialist. Inspired by the teaching of the Pure Land master Yin-kuang, he went to Ling-yen Monastery in Soochow, the center of Pure Land practice. He intended to spend the rest of his life invoking Buddha's name and practicing Pure Land devotionalism. However, external forces intervened and he was first sent to the countryside to collect rents and then asked to serve as the guest prefect, a busy job which did not leave him much time for personal cultivation. It was also around this time, in 1948, that his father appeared again in his life.

The section describing the reunion with his father requires some effort on the part of the reader to suspend one's judgement, for the father is hardly a sympathetic character. He was a violent and abusive man who drove the mother to suicide and tried to kill Chen-hua more than once. When he came to find Chen-hua, he had become an alcoholic and gambler as well. Harboring prejudices against Buddhist monks, the father had at first no appreciation for Chen-hua's vocation. Instead, he was ashamed of the son who, by becoming a monk and thus unable to produce an heir, had committed the most grievous unfilial act. However, Chen-hua did not turn his back on the father, but tried to convert him to Buddhism. What motivated him was not only Buddhist compassion, but also Confucian filiality. What eventually happened was nothing short of being miraculous. Indeed, Chen-hua credited the father's sudden conversion to the intervention of Kuan-yin, the beloved bodhisattva of compassion.

After the father became a monk, Chen-hua went on a pilgrimage with him to Aśoka's Monastery in Ningpo and P'u-t'o Island, the holy land dedicated to Kuan-yin. But with the defeat of the Nationalists by the Communist forces, Chen-hua was drafted into the retreating Nationalist army in 1949 and taken to Taiwan. He was 28 years old. The Nationalist government was never noted as a protector of Buddhism. Jealous of the temple land holdings and vast monastic buildings, the government tried repeatedly to confiscate the land and turned monasteries into schools or army barracks. Many of the Buddhist reforms of the 20th century, such as the establishment of Buddhist seminaries and the organization of national Buddhist associations were countermeasures adopted by Buddhist leaders against government oppression[2]. But to draft young monks into the army and shipping them to Taiwan in 1949 was truly an unprecedented move, for in traditional China during the imperial times, monks were exempted not only from paying taxes and working as corvee labor but also from serving in the army.

Chen-hua was not angry or resentful toward the government. Any strong feelings he had and harsh words he used were directed against the Communists whom he regarded as the enemy. Instead, he tried to make the best of the situation and see the positive side of the army training. He stayed in the army for three years as a soldier. He kept his vegetarian diet. He helped his fellow soldiers whenever he could. He overcame their initial prejudice and won their respect. When he received a medical discharge from the army at the age of 31 in 1952, he was assigned to work as a janitor in a rural elementary school near Hua-lien on the east coast of Taiwan. He took his new job seriously and received high regards from the principal and other teachers. If he did not quit the job and reentered the monastic order, he would have been promoted by the principal to become a Chinese language teacher. Whether in the army or in the elementary school, Chen-hua always seemed to be capable of adapting himself to the new environment and using it as the opportunity to improve himself. In the Ch'an tradition a true practitioner is supposed to carry on with his meditation wherever he is. Religious cultivation is not limited to the meditation hall. There is a famous Ch'an saying, "In carrying water and chopping firewood: therein lies the wonderful *Tao* (Way)." Chen-hua's philosophy of life would be the logical extension of this attitude toward religious practice. Being a man of humility, however, he did not express it this way. Instead, he would say that he was simply following the proverb: "As long as you are a monk, just go on ringing the daily bells."

One may imagine Chen-hua living the rest of his life in this fashion as a lay person. In normal times, monks in China took the monastic vow for life and would regard returning to lay life as a shameful acknowledgement of defeat. In this respect, it is very different from the Therāvada tradition. In Therāvada countries such as Thailand, monks may return to lay life without suffering any social censure, for many young men would spend sometime in the monasteries as monks before they start a career and get married. Entering the sangha is very much like a rite of passage. But Chen-hua was not living in a normal time. Of the many young monks drafted into the army, those who reentered the sangha probably were the exceptions rather than the norm.

The critical event which turned his mind firmly to Buddhism once more was his near fatal illness (Chapter XIV). He was unconscious for seven days and nights and the doctor had given up any hope for him. In fact, the principal had already had a coffin made in anticipation of his death. But miraculously he recovered after he dreamt of a lady clothed in white who told him that he would get better. In his dream he identified the lady as his mother who died when he was four years old. But surely this must be the White-robed Kuan-yin, the same bodhisattva of compassion to whom Chen-hua prayed whenever he was in trouble. Just as his father was saved miraculously by Kuan-yin earlier from a strange and deadly illness, he himself now benefitted from the same divine intervention. The cult of Kuan-yin has always enjoyed great popularity among monks as well as lay people. It is interesting to note that in the dream Chen-hua unconsciously transformed Kuan-yin into his mother. Since his real mother died when he was very young, it was very likely that he did not remember her very well. On the other hand, he probably had always regarded Kuan-yin as his spiritual mother. Yet in his dream he did not identify her as Kuan-yin, even though the White-robed Kuan-yin was the form of this Buddhist deity most familiar to her devotees.

Chen-hua ended his memoirs by remembering the teachers who influenced him and the Buddhist teachings which made the most profound impressions on him (Chapter XV). In doing so, he deflected the reader's attention away from himself and made one concentrate on Buddhist masters and Buddhist teachings. Although he mentioned a number of famous modern Buddhist masters in the course of the book, he seemed to have the highest regard for five. Three of them were known to him only through reputation and writings, for he was too young to have had an opportunity of meeting them. They were the ascetic Eight Fingers (Pa-chih T'ou-t'o, 1890-1912), the reformer T'ai-hsü (1890-1947), and the Pure Land leader Yin-kuang (1861-1940). With the other two masters, Tz'u-hang (1894-1954) and Yin-shun, a monk who is now in his late eighties, however, Chen-hua had personal knowledge, for he became their student in Taiwan.

Each of these five masters represented some outstanding ideals which inspired him. They emphasized very different aspects of Buddhism. For instance, Tz'u-hang exemplified personal piety, while Yin-shun stressed doctrinal knowledge. Chen-hua did not seem to be bothered by the diversity of views and practices offered by his teachers. On the contrary, he seemed to take delight in this diversity and find the different paths challenging. This openness and tolerance is, in one sense, a major characteristic of Chinese Buddhism. Compared with Japanese Buddhism, Chinese Buddhism has not put too much emphasis on sectarian purity and exclusiveness since at least the Ming dynasty (1368-1644). Although the Ch'an school has been the dominant form of Buddhism in China (and for this reason, all monasteries are identified as Ch'an), individual monks are free to pursue scriptural study, emphasize the invocation of Buddha's name, or devote themselves to the observance of monastic discipline. It is also not uncommon to find someone who tries to combine all these in his endeavors. Chen-hua is in fact such an example. During the years covered in his memoirs, he followed all the paths mentioned above. He studied Buddhist scriptures, practiced Pure Land meditation, endured the rigors of Vinaya training, and followed the circuits of a pilgrim. He can thus serve as a good case study and help us get a sense of the practices and aspirations of Buddhist monks in modern China. Moreover, because Chen-hua was a keen observer, he did not simply undergo his monastic training passively. He was not only a faithful recorder of his experiences, but a passionate critic as well as a defender of the Buddhist tradition in modern China. Let us now turn to him as the witness.

Chen-hua, the Witness

The uniqueness of Chen-hua's memoirs lies in its honesty and truthfulness. Although he clearly loved his father, he did not try to hide the latter's shortcomings or make excuses for his brutality and violence. Similarly, although he was dedicated to Buddhism, he was not afraid to point out the corruptions rampant in Buddhist monasteries. In this book, we are not given just an ideal picture, but the actual conditions found in these establishments. His frank criticisms of monastic abuses and his impartial appraisals of his fellow monks are two features which make this eye-witness account most valuable.

Theoretically, all monks are sons of the Buddha and the monastic order is an universal and egalitarian family. That is why when one leaves the life of a householder, he gives up his secular name and receives a dharma name prefixed by the character *Shih* (Śākyamuni). Unfortunately, as Chen-hua's memoirs vividly testify, this was definitely not the case. Regionalism and factionalism were two powerful factors influencing the interpersonal relationships between members of the sangha. As a corollary, in order to have anything achieved, one must rely on personal connections. The monastic order is a reflection of the society as a whole, for the same three forces have played pivotal roles in forging alliances and creating divisions among the Chinese people as well.

There are many examples about regional prejudices found in the book.

Because Chen-hua was a native of Honan, a northerner, he was given the nickname "Guy with a Northern Brogue" by his fellow monks in the south. Being a member of the minority, he was often subjected to discrimination. The most memorable instances include the collective persecutions by his roommates at P'i-lu Temple, the demeaning ridicule of the Dean of Studies at T'ien-ning Buddhist Seminary, and the unfair treatment he received from the prior of Fa-yü Monastery at P'u-t'o.

Factionalism was another serious problem causing disharmony in the sangha. Chen-hua referred to the animosity between monks in the main halls and workers in the outer sections at Pao-hua Mountain. The former who were better educated looked down upon the latter who did menial work in the kitchen or the fields. Historically, the Ch'an tradition always put much emphasis on physical labor. Early masters who exemplified this ideal were held up as models. For instance, the Sixth Patriarch Hui-neng (d. 713), reputed to be an illiterate peasant, worked as a common laborer in the kitchen of the monastery of the Fifth Patriarch. Pai-chang (720-814), the author of the famous motto, "One day no work, one day no food", insisted on working daily in the field even well into his old age. However, with time, secular values which placed more worth on learning have apparently found their way to the monasteries. Factionalism was also the cause for the differential treatment the wandering monks received on P'u-t'o island from those "native sons". Without exception, all the young monks drafted into the Nationalist army were outsiders who came to the island as pilgrims.

Personal connections provided essential support systems in Chen-hua's monastic training. He could enroll at the T'ien-ning Buddhist Seminary mainly because he was recommended by an influential lay devotee. His small party of pilgrims could receive lodgings at T'ien-t'ung Monastery only after he made it known to the guest prefect that he knew a monk who held an important position in the business office. When he was dismissed from Fa-yü Monastery on P'u-t'o Island as a waiter and had nowhere to go, he was welcomed into Lien-ch'ih Hermitage as a resident through the introduction of a fellow monk who was his colleague in Ling-yen Monastery in Soochow. Finally, when he decided to reenter the sangha in Taiwan, it was chiefly through the help of his old classmates and fellow monks from the mainland that he could find teachers and monasteries to accept him.

Once again, there was a convergence between the secular and the monastic values. In monasteries, just like in society at large, personal relationships and connections formed basic building blocks of the social network. This was such an obvious fact of life that Chen-hua took it for granted and did not think it in any way unusual. From the time he left his home temple and headed south, during his years of traveling from monastery to monastery in China, he usually knew where to go and whom to look up in each place. Most of the time he was accompanied by traveling companions who could provide him with proper introductions. In the few cases when he ventured out without prior preparation and tried to seek shelter at strange monasteries, he invariably was humiliated and treated with suspicion.

Regionalism, factionalism, and personalism could be taken as signs of monastic corruption. On the other hand, since Buddhism has existed in Chinese society for almost two thousand years, it is not too surprising to find Chinese monks hold some of the same social values as their fellow countrymen. As Buddhism became indigenized in China, it also paid the price of absorbing certain Chinese cultural characteristics. How to adapt the religion to the needs of the Chinese people yet at the same time preserve the original spiritual orientation of Buddhism has always been a central concern of all the Buddhist leaders. Chen-hua had the same concern. One reason for his writing the memoirs was to share his reflections on this question with his fellow Buddhists in Taiwan.

Chen-hua did not tell us what, in his view, constituted the ideal Buddhist path. This was perhaps because he wrote the memoirs for a Buddhist journal and he assumed that his readers would have a tacit understanding of what it was. Most of his criticisms against monastic abuses were motivated by his disappointment over his fellow monks' failure to live up to this ideal. Interestingly, regionalism, factionalism, and personalism did not stand out with prominence among the indictments.

Before I turn to the specific monastic practices which Chen-hua condemned, let me briefly indicate some of the general ideals which inspired the Buddhist practitioner. They provide the perimeter of the religious life. Chen-hua measured himself against this model. He castigated his fellow monks when they fell short of it.

When a person becomes a monk, he is supposed to have renounced all attachments. The Buddhist path consists of the three-fold training in morality, meditation and wisdom. Observance of Vinaya, practice of meditation and study of scriptures provide a concrete program in one's spiritual transformation. This is true for all Buddhist traditions, Therāvada and Mahāyāna.

In the case of Chinese Buddhism, due to the Ch'an emphasis on asceticism, Chinese monks have put a high premium on physical austerity and mental concentration. In order to broaden one's knowledge, a young monk should travel to different monasteries to find good teachers. As we read in the book, even in modern times, monks like Chen-hua still traveled on foot, a traditionally favored mode of transportation. By encountering and overcoming hardships while "touring on foot", one gains physical stamina and deepens one's spiritual sensitivity. In order to facilitate the traveling monks, the large public monasteries are obliged to provide free food and lodging. These wandering monks are housed in the hall called, appropriately, "Clouds and Streams", for they are supposed to be as free and unattached to anything as drifting clouds and flowing streams.

After one spends some years in traveling and studying, if one is really serious about meditation, one enters into "sealed confinement". One lives alone in a private cell which can be either set apart in a secluded section within a monastic compound or built specifically for the monk on an isolated location on a mountain. Some monks, like the two venerable Pure Land masters at Ling-yen Monastery (Chapter VI), vowed to spend the rest of their lives in sealed confinement. Other monks, however, usually spend only a designated number of years in this fashion and then resume a normal way of life. While in sealed confinement, a monk does not have to participate in the routines of the community life, but is free to spend his time either meditating or studying according to his own schedule. Very often, in order to gain merit, a lay devotee would put up the money to construct the cell and provide for the expenses for the monk for the duration of his confinement. For example, a wealthy lay woman had a hut built for Chen-hua on the mountain near Nuan-nuan in northern Taiwan and enabled him to practice the sealed confinement for three years (Chapter XIV).

Chen-hua began his memoirs with his departure for the south, in 1945, when he was 24 years old. In the rest of the book, he describes in a very vivid and moving manner his arduous efforts to find the opportunities to receive instructions in Buddhist scriptures and meditation practice. In his wide travels to realize his goal, he visited most of the major monasteries in south China and became acquainted with many famous Buddhist masters. Because in the monasteries he stayed he usually served in one monastic office or another, he could provide the reader with a rare insider's view of the actual conditions of monastic life and practice in some of the most famous monasteries in China. In the remaining pages of this introduction, I will comment on five topics on which Chen-hua the witness seemed to have particularly strong opinions.

(1) *On Buddhist Ordination*

While "leaving home" and receiving tonsure, as we read in Chen-hua's case, is a simple matter, ordination, on the other hand, is a solemn ritual. Although one can choose to have one's head shaven at any small temple, one must go to specific public monasteries, all in the south, to receive ordination.

Pao-hua Mountain, the Number One Monastery of the Vinaya School is the most reknowned monastery granting ordination. In traditional China, before 1911, the frequency of ordination and the number of people to be ordained were decided by the central government. Only those who have been properly ordained receive ordination certificates which, like diplomas or identification cards, confer both prestige and privileges to the holders. An ordained monk has traditionally been granted exemptions from serving in the army, paying taxes and working as conscripted laborer. He can also take up residence at any monastery when presenting his ordination certificate to the guest prefect.

Pao-hua Monastery was famous both for the length of its ordination session and the severity of its discipline. Chen-hua described the harsh treatment suffered by the new ordinands at the hands of ordination masters (Chapter II). The animosity between the two groups became so intense during the fifty-three days that they looked upon each other as sworn enemies by the end of the session. The teachers behaved like high-handed, arrogant and sadistic task masters. On the other hand, Chen-hua felt that the ways of doing things during ordination sessions in other places, such as T'ien-t'ung Monastery where his father went or in monasteries in Taiwan where he himself served as ordination teacher, were too lax and easy going. It probably was very difficult to find a middle way. The purpose of holding the ordination session is to train the monks in liturgy and deportment and instill in them the proper knowledge about monastic precepts. In the Chinese tradition, ordination is consisted of three parts. A person first receives the ten precepts for a novice (*sha-mi*, śrāmenara), then the 250 precepts for a monk (*pi-chiu*, bhiksu), and lastly, the 58 precepts for a bohisattva (*p'u-sa*). Holmes Welch provided detailed description of the entire course of this training at Pao-hua Mountain in his book, *The Practice of Chinese Buddhism 1900-1950*. One can get a sense of the enormity of this task by reading what the monks had to learn just during the first two weeks of their enrollment:

> During the first two weeks, those who were becoming monks and nuns — the clerical ordinands — studied how to eat, how to dress, how to lie when sleeping, how to make their beds, how to pack their belongings for a journey, how to stand and walk, how to enter the great shrine-hall, how to make a prostration to the buddha image, how to receive guests, how to hand over the duty (as a duty monk in the meditation hall, for example), and so on. ...Pao-hua Shan put a high polish on the perfection of their deportment[3].

Chen-hua talked about the hardships of morning devotions and the long hours of kneeling on the stone pavement to receive the precepts. What stood out even more sharply in his memory was the corrupt custom of "cooking small pots" practiced by senior monks at Pao-hua. This was but one of many divergences from the Vinaya found in Chinese monasteries. According to the Buddhist Vinaya rules, monks should not eat after the noon meal and, moreover, they should not eat food different from that prepared for the general community. In China, the observance of not eating anything after the noon meal had long been ignored. Like everyone else, Chinese monks eat three meals a day. (When Chen-hua served as a cook at the Inner Court of Maitreya in Taiwan, for instance, he stated matter-of-factly that he had very little time left to study after preparing the three meals everyday.) On the other hand, it was the norm that everyone ate the communal meal together. Chen-hua was therefore particularly disappointed by the breach at Pao-hua, the supposedly model monastery for Vinaya observance. "Cooking small pots" was the bad practice of preparing special choice dishes for the regular resident senior monks. In carrying out this scheme, their attendants stooped to "rob" the community of the fresh vegetables carried up the mountain from villages down below by diverting them to their private kitchens. They also hoarded the freshly cooked rice and deprived the new ordinands of their fair share. It is such telling details which so starkly reveal the deep divisiveness between the residents and outsiders at the monastery.

(2) *Buddhist Funeral Services and Commercialism of Monasteries*

Performing funeral services on behalf of lay patrons has always been one of the major sources of income for monks and monasteries in China. Chen-hua had to help out by working at funeral services when he stayed at busy urban temples in Nanking and Shanghai (Chapters III, IV). Such services, called either simply, "performing Buddhist services (*tso Fo shih*)", or "chanting scriptures and doing penances (*ching-ch'an*)", were designed to help the dead to have an easier time in their after-life and to achieve a good rebirth. By chanting Buddhist scriptures and mantras and performing the appropriate ritual actions, monks came to serve as indispensible guides to the dying and dead in their journey from death to rebirth. The original intention of such rituals, issuing from the Buddhist compassion for all sentient beings, was to bring spiritual benefit to the donor and his loved ones. Being a very family oriented people, the Chinese became eager patrons of these rituals in their desire to serve their ancestors with filial piety. By providing the Chinese with rituals dealing with death and after-life,

Buddhism filled a real need in the society. Buddhist funeral rituals became so prevalent in the medieval times that the Neo-Confucian thinker Chu Hsi (1130-1200) regarded this as yet another sign of the Buddhicization of China. He tried to replace them with Confucian rituals. But with the exception of some elite families, most people continued to patronize Buddhist monks for their services.

As popular demand for Buddhist funeral rituals increased, more and more monks became professional ritualists and spent their lives doing nothing else. Funeral services could be performed either in the temple or in the home of the donor. It was customary that when someone was near death or soon after someone died, the family would invite monks to come to the house to chant scriptures. Monks who responded to the calls and frequented the homes of secular people became easily influenced by the secular styles of life. Buddhist leaders had long realized the undesirable effects of such practices on the moral and spiritual life of monks. Yün-ch'i Chu-hung (1535-1615), the late Ming reformer, already sounded the alarm more than four hundred years before Chen-hua.

P'i-lu Temple in Nanking and Tung-yüeh Temple in Shanghai, the two temples where Chen-hua was compelled to do his share of working at funerals, were hereditary temples. Since they had no temple land, they had to rely on performing funeral services for their economic sustenance. But even in most large public monasteries, providing such services was an on-going part of the monks' regular activities. Chen-hua was therefore very impressed by the prohibition against performing funeral services at Ling-yen Monastery, a rule laid down by its founder, Yin-kuang. As long as monks were engaged in this kind of commercial activity, it would be very difficult for them to achieve any spiritual progress.

Chen-hua mentioned many examples of the evil consequences of the commercialization of funeral services. Lured by fame and money, young monks who were once serious about their religious cultivation became only interested in worldly pursuits and ended up moral and physical wrecks. Temple managers who were eager to drum up business treated the monks like money-making machines. Professional female agents served as intermediaries between patrons and monks. They set up three categories of monks who were classified not on the basis of knowledge or cultivation, but purely on that of physical appearances and singing voice. Probably for the same crude commercial reasons, scriptural chanting in the regions near Shanghai came to be interspersed with the singing of popular melodies of a decidedly secular nature. The performance of funeral services degenerated into popular entertainment.

The temptation of following the crowd and spending one's days as a funeral specialist must be a real one. Chen-hua was cajoled to take it up as a career. He was ridiculed by the other monks when he refused to do so. When one performed the funeral services, one would receive extra stipend. Otherwise, as a regular resident of the temple, he would only receive a set amount each month, usually far from adequate to meet his needs. Monks were supposed to have transcended the material world. If the reader has any such presuppositions, Chen-hua's memoirs are a needed corrective. Chen-hua was acutely aware of his own poverty. He frequently suffered from hunger. He had no money to buy medicine or see a doctor when he became ill in Shanghai. He was often short of travel money. Just as money made his search for the Dharma difficult, it also influenced the career of many monks and controlled the tradition of many monasteries. Economics has been a potent force in the history of any religion, Buddhism being no exception.

(3) *Pilgrimages and Popular Devotion*

Chen-hua had aspired to a life of religious wandering. If he were not drafted into the Nationalist army, he would have led the life of a pilgrim, going from one holy site to another. When opportunity presented itself, he would then stay in one place to practice meditation or to study under a great master. Such an ideal has had a long tradition in Chinese Buddhism. In the early centuries after the introduction of Buddhism into China, many intrepid pilgrims had gone to India, the holy land of Buddhism. They visited famous Buddhist universities, sought instructions from eminent masters, and went on pilgrimages to the sites connected with the Buddha's life. But as the religion took deep root in China, particular places and monasteries became endowed with traditions of sanctity and began to attract pilgrims. When the Chinese landscape was thus transformed, Buddhist monks from Korea and Japan started to regard China as the new holy land. Chinese monks also began to emphasize the practice of wandering from one pilgrimage site to another, now all located in China, as a spiritually rewarding exercise. Ch'an Buddhism, reaching its maturity in the Sung dynasty (960-1279), provided impetus to this new trend.

Chen-hua described his pilgrimages to Aśoka Monastery and P'u-t'o Island, both in Chekiang Province (Chapters X, XI). The former's fame rested on the legend that it housed the Buddha's relics which were sent by Emperor Aśoka (c. 268-233 B.C.). Chen-hua repeated this apocryphal tradition without comment. His criticism was focused on the commercialism connected with the cult of relics. The worship of relics was considered to be a highly meritorious act. But because not everyone was able to make the pilgrimage to Aśoka Monastery and worship the relics personally, the monastic establishment thought up a scheme to offer a convenient way for the faithful to gain merit and to make money for itself at the same time. Monks who took care of the relics hall were allowed to sell the merit accrued from their own act of worshipping the relics to any donor who was interested in buying it. When the money was paid, the monk would write on a piece of paper the number of years he worshipped the relics and transferred the merit to the buyer. Afterwards the paper would be burned, carrying the message to the appropriate other-worldly authority. This was, in the words of Chen-hua, "a tool for drawing pilgrims and making money."

The cult of relics could also manifest itself in religious frenzy. Some worshippers became inspired by their visions and would burn their fingers as offering to the Buddha. Self-mortification and self-immolation occurred frequently in the history of Chinese Buddhism and these were acts gloried in Mahāyāna scriptures, especially the *Lotus sūtra*. But some over-zealous pilgrims, like the foolish young monk mentioned by Chen-hua, in their eagerness to gain merit, would burn off their fingers without preparing themselves with proper mental disciplines. The result was predictably disastrous.

P'u-t'o Island is one of the four sacred Buddhist mountains in China. Situated in the ocean east of Ningpo, it has been regarded by Chinese Buddhists as the home of Kuan-yin, the bodhisattva of compassion, for the last one thousand years. Since Chen-hua was a devotee of Kuan-yin, it was understandable that he was very anxious to go there as a pilgrim. Through the centuries, many people, emperors and commoners, monks and lay people, literati and merchants, all had made pilgrimages to the island. The island enjoyed a renewed surge of popularity in the 20th century. Modern steamships made the trip from Shanghai, the usual port for most pilgrims to leave for P'u-t'o, much faster and more comfortable. Many Buddhist leaders also liked to come and stay on the island in this century. For instance, Yin-kuang, the Pure Land master, stayed on P'u-t'o for thirty years.

Chen-hua went to P'u-t'o with his father and another fellow monk. Although his stay on the island was cut short by the unexpected draft, one gets a sense that he cherished a very special memory of this sacred island. He related his encounter on the mainland with a solitary monk who had just returned from a pilgrimge to P'u-t'o. He talked about their good fortune of being ferried to the island by a kind-hearted fisherman who did not demand any boat fare. (Since they did not have enough money to pay for the passage, this sudden turn of events was perceived by him to be a blessing sent down by Kuan-yin.) Like a typical pilgrim, he delighted in telling the miracles he learned about the island.

(4) *Buddha Recitation at Ling-yen Monastery*

Although Chen-hua visited a number of small temples and large public monasteries in mainland China, he had the closest relationship with Ling-yen Monastery in Soochow. This was because he participated in the famous Buddha Recitation session there and later served as the guest prefect (Chapters VI, IX). Ling-yen was the center of Pure Land Buddhism in modern China. Chen-hua gave the reader a succinct discussion of the Pure Land meditation practice as taught by Master Yin-kuang who restored the monastery in 1920s and created a monastic code for the monks who followed this practice there.

The "Buddha Recitation Weeks" at Ling-yen ran 77 days or ten weeks. This was modelled upon the intensive meditation weeks of the Ch'an tradition. Both traditions shared the belief that a person could achieve much spiritual progress when he was devoted exclusively to a period of intensive meditation. However, unlike the use of koans and personal interviews with the master in the Ch'an meditation sessions, one was told to concentrate on the calling of the Buddha's name at Ling-yen. The name of the Buddha was used as the focus of one's total awareness. One was not simply to call the name in a devotional manner, but was told to ask, "Who is the one calling the Buddha's name? " With proper training, this question could generate the same sense of doubt as the enigmatic koans found in the Ch'an tradition, and thus propel one into enlightenment. What was found at Ling-yen Monastery was not simple Pure Land devotionalism. Yin-kuang was the modern proponent of the dual practice of Ch'an and Pure Land, a tradition traceable to the 13th century.

In recent decades, it has become very fashionable for monasteries in Taiwan to hold "Buddha Invocation Week" and "Ch'an Meditation Week". Chen-hua was often invited to lead the community during the "Buddha Invocation Week" because of his experiences gained at Ling-yen, the model for such practice. Chen-hua was ambivalent about the popularity of this trend. He was heartened by the strong interests people showed in Buddhism. But at the same time, he felt that "Buddha Invocation Week" in Taiwanese monasteries, like the ordination sessions held there, were conducted without the same single-mindedness and discipline as it was the case in mainland. Despite his criticisms of mainland monasteries, there was a great deal of nostalgia when he recalled the traditions created and kept there.

(5) *Buddhist Education*

A main reason for Chen-hua's coming to the south was to receive education in Buddhism. Therefore, when he finished the ordination session at Pao-hua Mountain and heard the news that Master T'ai-hsü was going to start a seminary at P'i-lu Monastery in Nanking, he jumped at this opportunity. Unfortunately, this turned out to be no more than a rumor, possibly a plot to recruit newly ordained monks to serve in funeral services. He eventually succeeded in enrolling in T'ien-ning Buddhist Seminary at Changchow (Chapter V). The establishment of Buddhist seminaries was the new phenomenon beginning with the 20th century. Realizing that the weak position of the sangha in the modern age was due to the lack of education of the monks, many Buddhist reformers began to advocate monastic education and to set up Buddhist seminaries. T'ai-hsü was undeniably the leader in this movement. He established many seminaries in different parts of China and among them, T'ien-ning Buddhist Seminary was the largest and the most modernized educational institutions for monks. Chen-hua described the three different classes of students, the curricula and the daily schedules at the seminary in detail. Recommended by an influential lay Buddhist, he began his studies there in the elementary class. Although he was very self-conscious at first because he was much older than the rest of his classmates, he managed to excel and was promoted to the intermediate class after only six months. He was prevented from finishing his study, however, because he was forced to leave after he was subjected to humiliating discriminations on account of his northern origin. In this chapter, the importance of lay patronage and the tragic regional divisiveness within the sangha received a most realistic testimony.

One telling observation Chen-hua offered about his seminary experience was the poor quality of its teachers. Because there were not enough good teachers, the monks trained by them were not properly educated. Since this was the case, seminary graduates, some of which became teachers later on, continued to produce even more poorly prepared students. This was a vicious cycle. Seminaries could hire lay people to serve as teachers. The teacher who taught Chinese language and literature at T'ien-ning Buddhist Seminary, for instance, was a lay man. Secular subjects, such as foreign languages, were often taught by lay people. However, traditionally, only monks could teach required subjects such as Buddhist scriptures, Buddhist history and philosophy. This problem has continued to plague Buddhist seminaries even to this day. One constant complaint that any visitor to the seminaries both in mainland China and Taiwan would hear is the lack of qualified instructors. It is perhaps because of this that Chen-hua turned his attention to monastic education in his old age. After spending different periods of his life as a wandering pilgrim, a meditator, and monastic officer of one type or another, Chen-hua finally became the director of a Buddhist seminary for nuns in Taiwan a few years ago. When we meet him at the beginning of the book, he is starting out his life as a student and a searcher, it is fitting that we take our leave of him as a teacher and a guide.

With this short introduction, let us now turn to Chen-hua who will tell us the story in his own words.

NOTES

1. The book was published in 1981 in Taipei, Taiwan, by T'ien-hua Publishing Co. It is consisted of essays the author published previously in different magazines. The long essay, "My Memory" (pp. 135-177), is a detailed account of his family and his early life.

2. Holmes Welch discussed this in detail in his book, *The Buddhist Revival in China* (Cambridge, Mass.: Harvard University Press, 1968).

3. Holmes Welch, *The Practice of Chinese Buddhism 1900-1950* (Cambridge, Mass. Harvard University Press, 1967), pp.287-289. See his Chapter IX "Entering the Sangha" for a full description of the ordination session at Pao-hua Mountain.

Chapter I

From Honan to Chiang-nan

A Resolution Made in Ignorance

Although I renounced lay life at fourteen [in 1934], the havoc wreaked by the Anti-Japanese War forced me to wait until my twenty-fifth year [in 1945] before I received my first master's kind permission to set out in search of spiritual instruction. That was the year of victory against the Japanese, and it was a year when the Communist boss Mao Tse-tung's attempts to seize power were at a frantic pitch. It was an especially difficult time to leave my home district of Yung-ch'eng County in Honan Province: transportation was not convenient and the bandits infesting the hills posed an obstacle. The bandits kept under cover by day and came out at night, often showing up where least expected, so travelers who were not careful could be carried off. After being carried off, victims were stripped of every shred of clothing and beaten half to death or buried alive.

Because I had been born in the North [in Honan], when I went south to seek instruction my fellow students called me "Guy with a Northern Brogue."[1] I did not like the sound of it at first, but as time passed I did not mind. Someone might well want to ask, "Why were you, a northerner, determined to go south to seek instruction?" There were two reasons for this. The first was that in the South there were many large-scale public monasteries like Chin-shan in Chen-chiang, Kao-min in Yang-chou, T'ien-ning in Ch'ang-chou, Pao-hua in Chu-jung, and T'ien-t'ung in Ningpo. All these were giant refining furnaces where men were wrought into accomplished monks. No matter what sort of human scrap metal you were to begin with, you had only to stay several years in such a place, and your every movement and posture would convey that sort of impressive poise that makes people feel: "Here is someone special." This is only external behavior, but in this age of the Decay of the Law[2], if one wants to preside over a place of truth[3] and be a master and example to others, it is necessary to undergo this basic training. The second reason was that the scenic beauty, temperate climate, abundant natural wealth and greater number of "goodly friends"[4] in the South made for an environment where attainment in spiritual study was much easier. For these two reasons, teachers who held high hopes for their disciples would often encourage them in many ways to study in the South, hoping they would become luminaries of Buddhist doctrine and so "bring extensive benefit to men and deities." Although my decision to study in the South was influenced by these two reasons, I resolved to go South without really knowing what was in store for me and without encouragement from my teacher. Owing to my ignorance I tasted quite a bit of bitterness and underwent much hardship, but now, giving it careful thought, I realize this is the one thing in life I can take most comfort in, because my rugged and arduous journey led me, in the end, onto the path of life I wished to travel.

A Journey Tearfully Begun

There was a sobering foretaste of winter in the air on that clear autumn morning when I shouldered my tiny bundle and, with a multitude of feelings welling up in my heart and childishly uncontrolled tears running down my face, bowed farewell to my master and set out on my journey. Buddhism in Honan had been crushed by the "Christian general" Feng Yü-hsiang, and by the time I set out, ninety percent of the province's pristine, solemn places of truth had already become vacant and dilapidated temples, as in these lines:

The old temple, lampless, is lit only by moonlight;
Its triple gate is gaping, sealed only by mist.

The better temples were changed into schools and army camps, their scriptures and images vandalized with impunity and the temple lands divided and taken. Consider for a moment how the monks who depended on temples for a livelihood fared under the circumstances.

Yung-ch'eng is the easternmost county in Honan, and the small temple where I became a monk was on a mountain in the eastern extremity of Yung-ch'eng, at its border with Hsiao County of Kiangsu. Nearby to the southeast was Su County of Anhni. Since ancient days this had been an area "ignored by three provinces". Because of its "advantageous position", the little temple where I took vows was like a fish escaped from a net. Nevertheless, after eight years of depredations by Japanese soldiers, militia members and bandits, there was hardly enough food to live on, let alone money for my travelling expenses. The day before my departure I scurried about trying to put together some money. I did collect a little sum, but no matter how I figured it, it would only get me halfway to my first destination,

Nanking. In order to have a few pennies in reserve for an emergency, I had no choice but to ask for accommodations in temples along the way.

A Humiliating Stop at a Roadside Temple

To "hang up one's bundle" [*kua-tan*] or "hang up one's robe" [*kua-ta*] is used in Buddhist parlance to mean put up for the night. This is because a monk travelling on foot can, with the permission of the abbot, hang his robe and alms bowl on hooks in the monks' sleeping room and take his meals and rest there. (During my search for knowledge, experience taught me that it does not always work out that way.) At that time, since I had just left my home temple and had not yet taken monastic precepts, I had neither a robe nor an alms bowl, and I did not know the slightest thing about the rules for "hanging up one's bundle." Technically I was not in a position to ask for accommodations, but the exigencies of my journey made me give it a try. Fortunately, most of the abbots I met were compassionate elders. Seeing that I was young and determined in spite of all hardships to seek spiritual knowledge, most of them sympathized with me. They opened for me the "door of convenience," received me warmly, and gave me food and lodging. When I took my leave, some of them even gave me dried food to eat along the way. However, there is such a world of difference in the hearts of men, that it is difficult to generalize about them: a person receives widely different treatment at the hands of different people. One thing that happened to me on my southward journey is an example of this.

One day before dusk, the soft and somewhat chilling rays of the evening sun cast long shadows of people, trees, buildings, livestock nibbling on wheat sprouts and everything else that stood more than a few inches above the ground. The shadows were stretched so long I could hardly recognize my own. I was a young monk, braving all sorts of dangers and walking alone in search of spiritual knowledge. With my bundle on my back, facing a cold, desolate wind, I trod toward my oddly distorted shadow until I came to a temple near a village. I had nothing more in mind than eating a meal, staying the night and being on my way bright and early the next day. I went to the gate and took a look. The temple was built facing south, and just inside the gate was a large threshing floor. The temple platform was raised about five feet above the threshing floor, and the whole area was surrounded by a wall of earthen brick. The only growing things around the temple were some tall trees already denuded of leaves, their stark bareness unpleasant to my eyes. A path led from the gate to the shrine hall. There was a chamber on the east side and one on the west. The walls too were made of earthen brick, and the roofs were thatched with corn leaves and wheat straw. The shrine hall, built of red brick and gray tiles, had become terribly dilapidated through age and neglect. In the empty courtyard grew an old locust tree, on which long and short pieces of red and yellow homespun cloth hung flapping in the wind. The flapping motion seemed to dispel some of the desolation of the courtyard, but actually added to the eerie atmosphere of the place. I strode into the courtyard, looking from side to side, but the buildings were quiet and there was no sign of anyone. Not knowing where the guest room was, I put my bundle down on the stone platform before the central hall. I dusted off my clothes, entered the shrine hall, and bowed down to the Buddha three times. When I came out, a monk suddenly appeared at the door of the east chamber and directed a cold stare at me. He was over fifty, of medium stature, and wore a black quilted jacket and trousers. Just as I was about to press my hands together in greeting, he turned quickly and disappeared through the door. Seeing this unfriendly attitude, I thought, "Oh no! It looks as if I won't get a meal and a place to stay tonight." But as the saying goes, "When standing beneath another's eaves, dare you hold your head high?" "All right. To keep my stomach from singing 'The Stratagem of the Empty City,'[5] and because I'm afraid of what might happen if I walk at night, I'll lower my head to him." Thereupon, I picked my pack up and strode bravely into the chamber. My behavior seemed to catch my inhospitable brother of the cloth by surprise. He was hurriedly clearing food and a basket of steamed buns from the table, but as soon as he saw me, he acted as if he did not know where to put the things in his hands. He stood there giving me an ugly stare and holding the bun basket. I calmly put down my bundle, walked over to him, and said, "Sir, are you the head monk of this temple? I would like to impose on you for a night's stay in your precious *caitya*. Please have compassion for me, sir."

I thought these two polite sentences would dispose him to treat me with kindness, as had happened before when I encountered kindly abbots, and that like them he would throw open the door of convenience, receive me warmly with food and lodging, and thus make my predicament "fall away as if touched by a keen blade." Unexpectedly, I was sadly mistaken. Not only did my polite greeting fail to win his goodwill, he gave me a not-so-polite talking to besides. After hearing my request, he put the bun basket down heavily on the stove and said with a scowl: "What business do you have running around the countryside in this time of disorder? I've never laid eyes on you: why should I risk letting you stay the night? It's not dark yet. Hurry up and walk three and a half miles to the east, and you'll come to a temple. It's a big one and there are plenty of people there: you'll be able to put up for the night. I won't have you here." Then he reached into the bun basket and handed me two hard, dark buns[6], saying, "Hey, take these." He took a large brass padlock off the stove and made as if to go out and lock the gate. I put the buns down on the table, pressed the palms of my hands together and said, "Sir, you say that now is a time of disorder, that you don't know me and that you don't dare to let me stay the night. That is understandable, but I plead with you, sir, to trust me. I assure you that I'm not a bad person. Also, I have a good reason for traveling on foot. I'm not just running around the countryside. Please sir, do a good deed and let me stay the night. I'll leave at daybreak tomorrow, all right?" He listened with great impatience and answered, "There is nothing stamped on your forehead that shows whether you're a good person or a bad one. Hmph! Trust you? These days...Enough of your talk; get out! I'm going to lock up. I'm going to lock up."

I have always had a difficult time cultivating the virtue of forbearance, especially in my early twenties, when a few words of disagreement could get me into an argument. This time, however, I showed the utmost forbearance. In spite of the fire of anger burning fiercely in my heart, I heeded the head monk's wish. Shouldering my bundle, I went out into the gloomy night and walked toward the hardships that awaited me.

Trouble on a Dark Road

By that time I had reached Hsiao County in Kiangsu. Although Hsiao County bordered on Yung-ch'eng and the customs of the inhabitants were similar, there was quite a difference between law enforcement in the two areas. As I have mentioned before, my home district was in an area "ignored by three provinces." For many years it had been in continuous turmoil, and the peasants had enjoyed little of peace and tranquility. There were the Japanese devils, the Communist Eighth Route Army irregulars and the bandits — who were almost the same as the Communists. All of these held power over our area in succession. It was as regular as clockwork: when one group left, the next followed close behind. They sucked the people's life-blood dry, until the area was practically in the plight of "nine vacant houses out of ten." Every time a group of armed men moved into the area they set themselves up as kings, and the lives of the peasants fell into their hands. Anyone who dared stand up to them was liable to bring death upon himself. This being so, the approach of twilight found every family locking its doors and no one stepping outside without good reason. If anything stirred outside, they could only blow out their bean-oil lamps and peer through the cracks in their doors.

The situation was much better in Hsiao County, where the county seat was occupied by Japanese devils, but villages far from the city were controlled by anti-Japanese guerilla units. The area controlled by guerrillas occasionally suffered bothersome forays by Japanese devils and the Eighth Route Army, but these, like foxfire flickering in the hills, ended almost as quickly as they began without posing a serious threat to people's lives. However it was, to be sure, a time of disorder, and good men did not have the word "good" stamped on their foreheads, so even though the guerrillas were fighting the War of Resistance for the people's sake, they had to be extremely strict about inspecting travelers to guard against the movements of traitors and Communists. Such an inspection led to my spending a night in a broken-down room with nothing to drink all night but draughts of cold wind.

It happened like this: the curtain of night was gradually falling as I left the little temple, and I could not help thinking of the moral darkness that was also spreading through the world of men. There I was, a young man risking the dangers of the night for the sake of a spiritual quest. Dragging my fatigued body and fighting the pangs of hunger in my miserably empty stomach, I struck out on unsteady legs in the direction of the "large temple with many monks." Before long, a wide riverbed appeared ahead. The water was gone, but the road across the riverbed was piled knee deep with fine sand. When I pulled out my left foot, my right foot sank in; no sooner had I extricated my right foot than my left foot was buried. Dark, dense rushes lined the road. Every gust of wind produced a rustle as if a wild animal were passing through, making the hair on my neck stand up in bone-chilling fear. I wanted to speed up my steps and get across quickly, but the unrelenting sand seemed to be toying with me. The faster I tried to go, the tighter it clung to my feet; the tighter it clung to my feet, the more difficult walking became. By the time I reached to opposite bank, I was panting with exhaustion and could not move another step, so I threw down my bundle and sat down to rest.

I had just sat down when a voice rang out behind me: "Hey, what are you sitting there for?" I turned my head and saw a burly fellow walking toward me. Instinctively I stood bolt upright in a hurry, and he edged up even closer. He looked at me and my bundle and asked, "Are you a monk?"

"Yes," I said.
"Where are you from?"
"From Pao-an Mountain."
"Where are you going?"
"To Huang-tsang Valley."
"Why are you sitting there in the dark?"

"I got tired crossing the riverbed. I'm resting."
"What were you doing today? Why are you walking at night?"
"I planned to stay at the little temple across the river, but the head monk wouldn't let me. He said there is a big temple to the east and told me to go stay there, so I had no choice but to feel my way ahead."
He hesitated a moment, then said, "Hmph. Put that bag on your back and let's go to my unit."

With that he pulled something from his waist and waved it around. I knew it was a gun and realized that anything I said under these circumstances would be useless, so I did as he said. I shouldered my bag and, repeating the holy name of Kuan-yin Bodhisattva under my breath, tottered in the direction he pointed.

"Faster! Faster!" he urged repeatedly as he walked behind me. Hungry, tired, and scared as I was, it was not easy to speed up, but I bore the strain. With my jaw clamped tightly, I hurried forward. We trotted for about twenty minutes and came to a sizeable village; after making a few turns, we entered the courtyard of a large house. By the lamplight that shone from the main room, I saw two men sitting by the door who got up and walked toward us when we walked into the courtyard. "I have a monk for you. Would you like to interrogate him a little?" my gun-toting friend said jocularly and then walked away. The two men shone their flashlights from my head to my toes. They ordered me to open my bag, carefully inspected everything in it, frisked me, and queried me on my destination and home district. I answered all their questions honestly. After more searching, they asked if I were telling the truth. "It's all true." Then one of them said, "All right, since you're telling the truth, we won't make it difficult for you. Take your bag to the west chamber and sleep there, and we'll release you in the morning." With that, they both entered the main room.

Praise be to Kuan-yin Bodhisattva! Their last few words made me feel like a prisoner on death row who has just learned of his pardon!

Contemplating Rain at Sacred Spring

What he called the "west chamber" was certainly not a room complete with door, windows and furniture, but a drafty, thatched lean-to which could not have been in a worse state of disrepair. However, under the circumstances I could only fortify myself with the thought that "since it has come to pass, one should be at peace with it." So I walked into the west chamber, chose a corner in which to place my bag, and sat down against it. I must have been quite fatigued, because I had not sat long before I drifted off to sleep. When I awoke the red sun of morning was well above the horizon. Every muscle and bone in my body was paralyzed with aches and pains; I could hardly bring myself to move. Nevertheless, considering the long road ahead, I had no choice but to brace myself against the wall and stand upright. Once erect I flexed my limbs and put my bag in order; I was just about to take a look outside when my friend of the night before approached me. I nodded to him and asked, "Sir, can I go now?" He nodded briskly and answered, "You can go! You can go! But we put you to too much of an inconvenience. I'm very sorry."

I forced a laugh and said, "Not at all. Not at all. Thank you." With that I picked up my bag and, not even taking time to wash my face, walked out of that west chamber and the courtyard and the gate outside. Well! I had, after a fashion, stumbled singlehandedly through my first difficult encounter.

Having left the front gate, I soon found myself on a small street crowded with traders doing business in wheat and other goods. Such a sight had not been seen in my home district for a long time, and I could not suppress a nostalgic pleasure at seeing it. After walking a few steps along this street, I sat down in front of a food stand and ordered a bowl of hot-and-sour soup, a plate of fried noodles and four steamed buns. After eating my fill, my body immediately felt warm and my spirits lifted. The hunger, cold and fatigue of the night before disappeared like fog on a sunny morning. After paying for the food and asking the road to Sacred Spring Monastery [Sheng-ch'uan Ssu], I turned toward the slowly rising morning sun and pushed ahead one step at a time.

Sacred Spring Monastery is the temple where Dharma Master Chih-tu, presently at Shan-tao Monastery in Taipei, renounced lay life to become a monk. Located on the slope of a mountain northwest of the county seat, it was one of the most famous and scenic sights in Hsiao County. To the rear and on both sides were nothing but high mountains and steep ridges, while in front lay Tai-shan Lake. Inside the monastery grew shrubs and flowering plants that remained green throughout the year, while the environs were planted with pine, cypress, peach, pomegranate, pear and date trees. Such surroundings lent an air of tranquil elegance and solemnity to the monastery. It was truly a rare and sacred place.

A cold, deliciously pure spring issued forth from a stone fissure to the east of the monastery. It is said that men of means from as far away as Hsü-chou often sent people to fetch the water for brewing tea. What is more, regardless of the weather and the time of year, in torrential rain and drought alike, the spring neither increased nor decreased but kept up the same steady trickling flow. Because of these wonders it was named "Sacred Spring." The monastery was built in the vicinity of the spring and took its name from it.

I arrived at Sacred Spring Monastery right at lunchtime. As soon as I said I was from Pao-an Mountain, an old monk welcomed me politely. He called a lay workman to bring me a basin of water, then told me to go to the kitchen and help myself to the food. He treated me as kindly as a member of the family, and I was deeply moved.

After lunch the old monk had something to do in town, so a young *bhiksu* kept me company. We were both young and had never seen each other before, so we sat silently for a while without finding anything to say to one another. Just as I was starting to feel uneasy, he took my bag in his hand and said, "You must be pretty tired. Go upstairs and have a nap." He took my bag to the second floor of a small building next to a place called Embracing Greenery Hall, and I followed him, delighted. He said, "This is the guest room. The bedding is all here. Go ahead and sleep, and I'll call you when it's time for supper." Without a moment's hesitation I took off my quilted robe, ducked my head under the covers and was soon breathing the long, slow breath of deep sleep.

Upon awakening I went downstairs and saw the young monk on the portico of Embracing Greenery Hall, reading a book. As soon as he saw me, he called for a workman to prepare a basin and towel, and grinningly said, "Last night when I went upstairs to call you to supper, I tried several times but couldn't wake you up. I figured you must have been through a lot the last few days, so I didn't dare disturb you any more. Did you have a good night's sleep?"

I was embarrassed to hear this and said, "Just now when I woke up and saw the light outside, I was so mixed up I thought it wasn't dark yet. I had to look out the window before I realized this is the morning of another day." Hearing this, he laughed so hard the tears came to his eyes. After he had laughed his fill, we went to breakfast.

I had planned to take my leave and go to Ching-fan Monastery in Pai-t'u after breakfast, but the monk insisted on my resting another day. "That's what the old monk wants," he explained. Then, pointing at the sky, he said, "Look, it's about to rain. How can you go?" Sure enough, in a little while, a fine steady drizzle began to fail. I laughed, "A long time ago someone told me a story that had this moral: 'When a guest stays on in rainy weather, it is the weather and not his host that bids him stay.' But from the looks of things that sentence should be changed to 'When a guest stays on in rainy weather, it is both the weather and his host who bid him stay." He was delighted to hear this.

Sitting there doing nothing would have made me seem incapable of using my time, so I borrowed an umbrella from the monastery, walked out the main gate and strode alone along a path winding through a grove, quietly contemplating the mist and rain over lake and mountains. Though the original face of the lake and mountains was draped in dense mist and fine rain, when I peered intently a suggestion of the scenery sometimes showed itself, poised between visibilityand invisibility. When puffs of wind stirred the pine and cypress branches, shaking clusters of water beads that fell on the stone slabs at my fee with a wondrous sound, I felt I was walking among "colonnades of trees draped with seven gems"[7]. An inexpressible feeling welled up within me.

Listening to a Sūtra Lecture at Huang-tsang

The next day the rain stopped after breakfast, but the sky was gloomy and threatened to rain at any moment. However, being in a hurry to get underway, I dismissed all misgivings,took my leave of the young monk who had welcomed me so warmly and left Sacred Spring Monastery for Ching-fan Monastery in the town of Pai-t'u. Pai-t'u was about seven miles southeast of the Hsiao County seat. To the east large mountains stretched into the distance; to the west was the vast sweep of the great river. For several miles to the north and south lay level plains. In a time of peace it would have been a quiet and prosperous location. Ching-fan Monastery was built outside the south gate of Pai-t'u on a knoll profusely planted with pines and cypresses. A large ginkgo tree growing within the monastery formed a natural canopy over the front of the shrine hall, setting off the exquisite buildings in a way that made them unexpectedly imposing, tranquil and pleasant to the eye. At my home temple I had often heard the Venerable Ch'ing-yün,the younger brother of my master's master, speak of Ching-fan Monastery. He said that the retired abbot P'in-shan lived there, an ordination brother of old master Shu-t'ang, the deceased master of my master. Before I left for the South, the Venerable Ch'ing-yün took pains to instruct me: "When you go to Hsiao County, be sure to go to Pai-t'u and pay your respects to P'in-shan. While you're at it, you can rest your feet a bit there." However, all things can only be brought to completion under the right circumstances; otherwise, large and small matters alike will,in the end, come to nought. Why do I say this? Because P'in-shan, who never cared much for going out, had gone to another mountain half a day earlier to visit a friend. If that was not a coincidence, what is?

P'in-shan not being in, I was unwilling to idle about looking for something to do, so after eating lunch I hurried on to T'ien-men Monastery, which was only one mountain away from Huang-tsang Valley. I stayed overnight at T'ien-men and hurried to Jui-yün Monastery in Huang-tsang Valley the next morning. Huang-tsang Valley, otherwise known as Huang-sang Valley, was Hsiao County's only large public monastery. At the same time, it was the largest-scale Buddhist place of truth in the Hsü-chou area. Within several hundred miles of Hsü-chou its fame was great enough to compare with Ku-lin in Nanking and Pao-hua in Chu-jung. Surprisingly, the valley's renown completely eclipsed that of its own Jui-yün [Auspicious Cloud] Monastery, which had been the source of its fame in the first place. In the same way, many people know of Pao-hua Mountain but have not heard of Lung-ch'ang Monastery or Hui-chu Monastery.[8] If the reader will permit, I will say something of the state of things at Jui-yün Monastery.

Forgive me for not knowing the dynasty during which Jui-yün Monastery was built, but judging from the ancient objects of art on display there, its history extends back at least a thousand years. It sits at the mouth of Huang-tsang Valley, surrounded by strange boulders, grotesque crags and trees reaching up to the sky. This wild setting gave one the feeling that there was more to this monastery than met the eye. Its courtyards were divided into three enclosures, the layout being similar to that of T'ien-t'ung Monastery in Ningpo: entering the main gate, one climbed successively higher until reaching the dharma hall within the innermost entrance. There were plenty of trees and flowers in the courtyard, but they had not been well tended and were growing in uneven profusion, producing an effect that was jarring to the eye. The shrine hall, the dharma hall and the library had been massive, extraordinary structures but unfortunately eight years of war damage had aged and ruined their once splendid appearance. Nevertheless, I believe that in the hands of a good abbot the buildings can surely be restored to their original state.

At that time a lay devotee named Ch'en lived there. Some said that he had taken a *chü-jen* or provincial degree before the fall of the Manchu dynasty. He was quite learned and came from a rich family, but his wish was to live an ascetic life in a mountain monastery rather than return home and enjoy the pleasures of wealth. In the daytime he often held the *Diamond Sūtra* in both hands, sat on a large rock beside a spring and read aloud, rolling his head to the cadence of the prose. In the evening he expounded the sūtra to a few other devotees who also lived in the temple. He often became so excited that his hands waved about, his feet danced and flecks of spittle flew in all directions. During my stay at Jui-yün Monastery I went to listen every day. I was perplexed, but also quite interested, when he expounded such lines as these: "The so-called Buddhadharma is not in fact the Buddhadharma: in this we have the Buddhadharma." "All forms are illusory. If one sees that all forms are not really forms, then one sees Tathāgata." Whether or not his explanations conformed to reality is a question my knowledge did not equip me to judge. This was because in my ten years since becoming a monk I had never attended a sūtra lecture; what is more, I had not even had the faintest idea that sūtras could be expounded! For this reason I have entitled this section "Listening to a Sūtra Lecture at Huang-tsang" to indicate how pitiful conditions were for young people who chose to become monks in those days.

Because my fellow acolyte Chen-shang served as the village agent for Jui-yün Monastery,[9] the establishment housed and fed me as a guest during my twenty-day stay at Huang-tsang Valley. Instead of attending devotions in the shrine hall or visiting the Buddha recitation hall, I went strolling at my leisure in the mountains after meals. I often climbed to the highest mountain thereabouts — Sheep Muzzle Mountain — and looked out over the valley scenery. Huang-tsang Valley is famous for the variety of its trees. Thus it is said that "all ethnic groups are found in Peking, and every species of tree is found in Huang-tsang Valley." Most amazing were the many old cedars, their trunks so thick it would take two persons to embrace them, which grew out of fissures in the rock. Such places had no soil and probably not much water, but the trees grew to such great size. Was this not a wondrous thing?

Along with the old cedars growing out of stone cracks, other trees contributed their colors to the beautiful scene. The mountains and valley were covered everywhere with yellow-leafed, red-leafed, green-leafed, and purple-leafed trees, as well as some that combined red with yellow or green with purple. Amidst this riot of colors, it was easy to forget how far along autumn really was, but "the sky was high and streams were running dry: frost was settling in the fields on all sides."

My First Train Ride

The reader might wonder why, if my objective was to seek spiritual instruction in the South, I stayed twenty-some days at Huang-tsang Valley instead of continuing on my way after a day or two of rest. There were two reasons for this. First, I should explain that my true motive for going to Huang-tsang Valley was not that I felt drawn to its scenic surroundings or that I coveted the easy life there. Rather, I only hoped that my brother disciple Chen-sheng would put together some money for my travel expenses. However, on the day I arrived in Huang-tsang Valley, brother Chen-sheng was collecting rents in a small village down in the valley called "Earth Basin." When I saw him and explained my purpose for coming he seemed very displeased, but on the strength of our relationship as brother disciples, he finally agreed to do what he could. Nevertheless, he said, "You'll have to wait at least a month." Why was this? He was not willing to say. Though I was as impatient to keep moving as an ant on a hot griddle, I had no choice but to settle down and wait. This was the first reason for my staying over twenty days at Huang-tsang Valley. The second reason was the problem of transportation, or perhaps one could call it the state of national affairs. A few days after my arrival at Huang-tsang Valley, news was released of the unconditional surrender of the Japanese in Nanking. By all rights the common people, after eight years of being trampled upon by the Japanese devils, should have been delirious with joy at this news, but in truth their feelings of unrest and panic were greater than before. Why was this? Because as soon as everyone heard that the Japanese devils had surrendered, they busied themselves with their own affairs. Guerilla resistance groups were no longer in evidence, and the Eighth Army irregulars, who had gotten their start robbing and looting, took advantage of this to move in. They disturbed local peace and order with acts of insane violence, sabotaging the North-South transportation lines and hampering the people's freedom of movement. It was like having a wolf sneak in the back door right after driving a thief away from the front.

Actually, Huang-tsang Valley was quite close to the Tientsin-Whangpoa railway: the Ts'ao Village station in south Hsü-chou was only five miles away. It seemed that if only one could board a train, there should not have been much difficulty in reaching Nanking 700 miles away. No one expected that a few days after the news of the Japanese surrender, the Eighth Army irregulars would sabotage the tracks south of Hsü-chou and north of Pang-fu, leaving them a total wreck. The Central Army worked night and day to make repairs, but whenever they left, the Eighth Route Army came out of hiding, like mice when the cat is away, and ruthlessly set to work pulling up the tracks. In places they even went so far as to level the roadbed. By the time the Central Army got word and hurried to the scene, they had disappeared like frightened rats.

Because of this, I bided my time and waited for twenty-odd days until the state of confrontation had cooled down a bit; then brother Chen-sheng accompanied me and Hai-hsiu to the Huang-shan-t'ou station. (Hai-hsiu was a disciple of my tonsure nephew[10] and had lived at Huang-tsang Valley for quite some time. Though he was a year younger than I, he had already taken his ordination vows and was proficient in the liturgy.) It was no easy matter, but my brother disciple succeeded in buying two third-class tickets to

Nanking. "Riding on this sort of train is mighty cold once it gets moving, but what could I do? There weren't any express tickets to buy," he sighed. He seemed ashamed to make us ride on such a train. But for the two of us, both strangers to the experience of riding a train, this was more than sufficient, especially considering the circumstances.

No sooner had Hai-hsiu and I climbed aboard the train than an ear-splitting blast from the steam whistle rang out, and the train shuddered forward. A clamorous wave of sound rose from the crowds on and off the train, calling up apprehension and bitterness as it dashed against each person's heart, for most of the passengers were cutting family ties and leaving their beloved to find a livelihood in a strange place. After the train left the station and the voices on the platform died away, the passengers took their places and quieted down. Hai-hsiu and I pulled quilts out of our bags and covered ourselves. Then, resting against our luggage and nestling together for warmth, we drew our necks into the collars of our quilted robes, closed our eyes and silently repeated the Buddha's name to the quickening rhythm of the piston rod. We felt none of the discomfort that brother Chen-sheng had predicted.

At that time the area north of Pang-fu was hit by floods. Although we rode on a night train, a vast sheet of water was visible in all directions under the bright moon. Many villages along the tracks were surrounded by water. Looking at this scene, I sadly thought, "They were already beset by the man-made calamity of war, and now, on top of that, comes a natural disaster. How can they go on living?" However, when the train stopped at Ku-jen-ch'iao, I saw vendors carrying lanterns in one hand and balancing trays of roasted chicken in the other as they ran back and forth alongside the passenger cars hawking their wares. I knew then that my concern for them was unnecessary. Nevertheless, I felt sorry for them: "Poor, pitiful people! The hardships you undergo stem mostly from the evil karma you created in the past. There are many ways to make a living: why must you make yours by seeking a fly's head of profit under the blade of a bloody knife?"

All thanks to that train! Running one night and half a day, it carried us safely from Huang-shan-t'ou to Ku-jen-ch'iao; from Ku-jen-ch'iao to Pang-fu; from Pang-fu to Ch'u-chou; and finally from Ch'u-chou to P'u-k'ou, which lay across the river from Nanking. After struggling off the crowded train we took a ferry and arrived at the Hsia-kuan district outside of Nanking's Yi-chiang Gate.

First Days in Nanking

Hai-hsiu and I arrived at Hsia-kuan at around two o'clock in the afternoon. Suddenly seeing the maelstrom of activity before us, we were too bewildered to know what to do with ourselves, and could only walk back and forth on the dock. Hai-hsiu had come to Nanking several years ago on his way to be ordained at Ch'ing-liang Monastery in Ch'ang-chou. By all rights he should have been better at asking directions than I. Unfortunately he had always been the type of person who is unwilling to exchange pleasantries. Pressuring him to make conversation would have been tantamount to threatening his life. Although it was easier for me to start a conversation, I spoke with such a thick local accent that people either did not deign to notice me or snorted with contempt as they walked by. After several such encounters, I no longer had the courage to open my mouth.

Just then a fellow from Shantung walked up with a load of steamed buns for sale on his shoulders. I bought a few buns and asked him the road to Ku-lou. He said, "That's easy. Go through the Yi-chiang Gate and keep going along the same road. Don't make any turns. You'll get there within an hour." Then, looking at Hai-hsiu and me, he continued, "You have luggage. You'd better go by cart. It will only take ten or twenty minutes." When he heard he would get to ride on a cart, Hai-hsiu jumped for joy. Guided by the fellow from Shantung, we found a cart near the city gate, and before we got on he instructed, "You just sit and wait. When he has enough passengers, he'll leave. The fare to Ku-lou is fixed. Don't try to bargain with him, or you'll come out on the worse end." With that, before we had time to thank him, he shouldered his load and walked away with big strides, his head held proudly erect.

Why did we want to go to Ku-lou? When Hai-hsiu and I left Huang-tsang Valley, brother Chen-sheng had said, "When you two get to Nanking, you can go to Tung-yüeh Temple [Temple of the Eastern Peak][11] on Pao-t'ai Street in the east part of Ku-lou. Look for the temple manager, Master Hsi-ch'u. He was a fellow student of mine at P'u-t'o Island,[12] and we lived in neighboring temples before he went to Nanking. When you get there just mention my name; he'll give you a good reception. At the same time, you'll be in a position to ask if they are ordaining monks at Pao-hua Mountain this year. If they are, you'll be in time for the winter session. If not, you can stay there and chant requiems[13] for a while. Then you can be ordained next year." So the first thing we did when we got off the cart in Ku-lou was ask the way to Tung-yüeh Temple. The driver curtly informed us that it was "behind the police station." I was about to ask the whereabouts of the police station when he lifted up his whip and was gone. Oh well. All I could do was harden myself against embarrassment and ask questions of passers-by. I asked until I was blue in the face and, just as at Hsia-kuan, got nothing for my pains. In a burst of irritation, I turned to Hai-hsiu and said, "I'm not going to ask another person, even if we have to look for Tung-yüeh Temple all night." To my surprise, as soon as my outburst passed we found the temple without any further ado. Events in this world often work out in strange ways, do they not?

Tung-yüeh Temple was at the foot of the hill to the right and in front of the North Star Observatory. On the front it was bordered by the police station, to the rear was a small train station, and to the left was a detention center attached to the police station. On the right was a parking lot. The setting was as noisy as could be. The temple had two entrances and three shrine halls. The foremost hall had east and west rooms, each housing a large, lifelike horse statue. One of the horses was maroon-red and the other silver-white. Beside each was the statue of a ghostly boy groom. These horses were, it was said, in preparation for use by the Emperor of the Eastern Peak. The middle hall was devoted to an image of the Emperor of the Eastern Peak. The two wings were shrines to the ten kings of the underworld. In the hall proper were figures of infernal judges, the famous demons Cow's Head [*Niu-t'ou*] and Horse Face [*Ma-mien*], and ghosts who recorded the good and bad deeds of men — everything one could imagine was there. Seeing all of it one shivered even in the heat of summer.

The dense smoke of burning paper offerings and joss money rose from an incinerator in the courtyard before the middle hall and drifted outside, its acrid odor choking those who inhaled it. The central room of the rear shrine hall was in honor of the Buddha, and the left side was partitioned off into four or five rooms for resident monks. On the other side, next to the Buddha niche, was the Hall of Merit, and a little farther back was the Bedroom of the Queen of the Eastern Peak. There were always several shamanesses there shouting, jumping, crying, laughing and carrying on. It was not the most wholesome of places. Nevertheless, quite a few of my fellow monks were not above going inside to perform the "Buddhist rituals of their dreams." Indeed, they were to be admired for their altruistic spirit, for they followed the dictum: "If I descend not into hell, who shall make that descent?"

When Hai-hsiu and I arrived, the temple manager Master Hsi-ch'u and the monks who specialized in performing Buddhist services on request had just finished supper and gone out. Only the lay workman was left to watch the premises. When he heard that we were the temple manager's countrymen, he grabbed our luggage and showed us to a guest room to the left side of the rear shrine hall. Then he brought a basin of water, brewed a pot of tea and asked if we had eaten supper. In order to save him trouble we said we had already eaten. We exchanged a few words, and he returned to the front courtyard. Only then did I shut the door, take out the steamed buns I had bought on the wharf and divide them between Hai-hsiu and myself.

After ten o'clock, the monks who had gone out to perform services came back one after another. We struck up a conversation and found that they were all northerners, and extraordinarily friendly at that. They immediately gathered around us and inquired into the situation up north. Just when everyone was chatting enthusiastically, a fortyish monk with large eyes and beetling brows, holding a white porcelain teapot with a red floral pattern, strode into the room with deliberate pigeon-toed steps. A fellow monk hastened to introduce him, saying, "This is our temple manager." Hai-hsiu and I touched our foreheads to the ground at his feet, got up, and informed him that we had come to meet him at the suggestion of brother Chen-sheng. With lips tightly pursed, he silently ran his eyes over our faces. When he had looked us over to his satisfaction, he rested his gaze on the twelve large, round ordination scars[14] on the top of Hai-hsiu's head and, pointing at him, asked in a coarse voice:

"What relation are you to Chen-sheng?"
"A grandson-disciple," Hai-hsiu answered.
"How many years since you renounced lay life?"
"Nineteen years."
"Nineteen years? How old are you now?"
"Twenty-three years old."
"You left home when you were only four?"
"Yes."
"Where were you ordained?"
"At Ch'ing-liang Monastery in Chang-chou."
"Can you chant and recite well?"
"Well enough to get by."
"Well enough to get by," he repeated.

Then he looked Hai-hsiu over some more and, with the air of someone who has made up his mind, said, "When you get back from taking your young grandfather-master [meaning the author] to Pao-hua Mountain, you'll stay here and help out, all right?" Without waiting to find out whether Hai-hsiu agreed with this, he made his rocking, pigeon-toed way to the front. Looking at his gait, which verged on the ludicrous, I was an inch away from laughing aloud. When he was gone, a few of our fellows said, "'Little Top' is bull-headed, but he is a nice person." After chatting a while, we went to our rooms.

Before we turned in, I asked Hai-hsiu, "They said 'Little Top' is bull-headed. What does 'Little Top' mean? Did you understand them? 'Little Top' means temple manager. Isn't the top part of the first character in the word 'manager' [*tang-chia*] just like the character 'little'?" he answered in an amused whisper. "When I lived at Huang-tsang Valley, people who had been in Nanking often told me that if you want to stay in Nanking and chant requiems, you must first learn some of the jargon used by monks who specialize in that line. Otherwise, everyone will call you 'turnip head.' 'Little top' is one of those expressions. I knew that years ago." Hearing Hai-hsiu say this, I could not suppress a mute laugh. I thought to myself: "Oh no! I have risked my life to travel the great distance to Nanking. Here I am on my first day, learning a slang expression used by funerary monks. Don't tell me I am fated to chant requiems for a living?"

The night passed uneventfully, and we got up for breakfast in the morning. The resident monks went out again to perform Buddhist services. The temple manager invited us to his room for a talk; he hospitably ordered a servant to serve two covered bowls of tea and bring out four bowls of fruit. The three of us sat around a square table set up against the wall and talked, first of common friends at the neighboring temples in our home district, then about traditions at the large public monasteries in the South, and then about such things as the origins and history of Tung-yüeh Temple. The upshot of the conversation was that Hai-hsiu would take me to Pao-hua Mountain and then return to Tung-yüeh Temple to give them help. The manager also expressed his hope that I would return to his temple after my ordination to make some "clothes money" [*yi-tan ch'ien*]. I merely smiled, without indicating my assent or refusal. Then Hai-hsiu and I went out to do some shopping.

A month had passed since the Japanese surrender, but Nanking had not yet recovered its vitality. The area north of Pao-t'ai Street was especially bad — so desolate that it was no different from a rural village. Hai-hsiu and I strolled around the Ku-lou [Drum Tower] area. Storytellers and jugglers were calling for all they were worth to attract audiences, but no one went to hear their stories or watch their tricks. "This desolation and silence is one of the main reasons the Chinese people hate the Japanese," I said softly to Hai-hsiu. "I feel the same way," he replied. We finished our shopping and returned to Tung-yüeh Temple. Then we went on another excursion to the mountain where North Star Observatory had been, and to Chi-ming [Cock's Crow] Monastery. After all that it was time for lunch. After lunch we took our leave of the temple manager and took a small train to Hsia-kuan, our plan being to transfer to the Nanking-Shanghai train and proceed to the town of Lung-t'an in Chü-jung County.

When we got off the train at Hsia-kuan, we saw a monk in his twenties holding a tiny wicker basket and pacing back and forth. He seemed to be quite upset about something. Seeing us, he joined his hands before his chest and asked, "Are you gentlemen headed for Pao-hua Mountain?" We nodded as we walked by him to the ticket booth, where Hai-hsiu watched the luggage while I plunged into the crowd to buy tickets to Lung-t'an. When I returned with the tickets, the stranger was attempting to strike up a conversation with Hai-hsiu, who just stood and listened without answering.

"Are you going to Pao-hua Mountain too?" I asked.

"Yes." Then, like a string of firecrackers, his words came out one after another without pause: "I am from Nan-ch'ang in Kiangsi. When I got off the boat this morning, I ran straight here from the dock to buy a ticket to Lung-t'an. There were too many people buying tickets, and I was carrying this wicker basket in one hand and a large bundle in the other, so every time I tried to squeeze through the crowd I got pushed away from the ticket booth. Just when I didn't know where to turn, a monk suddenly appeared out of the mass of people. He was about thirty. He asked me very cordially if I were going to Pao-hua Mountain to be ordained. I said I was. He was very pleased and said, 'That's wonderful! I'm going there too. I had a friend take my luggage with him this morning. I went to see a fellow from my home district; that's why I didn't get here until now. I was feeling bad about not having anyone to take the trip with. Heh heh, there is truly an affinity from former lives between us!' He showed me a ticket to Lung-t'an and kindly offered to buy one for me. How could I impose on him to push through that crowd to buy me a ticket? Instead I asked him to watch my bundle while I went to buy a ticket, carrying this basket. When I came back, the man was gone, and so was my luggage! I thought maybe he had gone ahead to the turnstile to get in line, but there was no sign of him there either. I've been looking all over, but I can't find a trace of him. I'm only carrying small change. The money for my ordination fee and return fare is sewn inside my quilt, so if I can't find that bundle, not only will my ordination be impossible, but even my trip home will be a problem. What should I do? I'm so worried I'm about to go crazy." Tears welled up and rolled down his cheeks; he had all he could do to keep from sobbing out loud. Seeing the state he was in, I felt terrible for him. To myself I thought, "Could it be that he was tricked in broad daylight in this city that has been a center of civilization for centuries?"

Even the normally taciturn Hai-hsiu chipped in: "No way you'll ever get your luggage back. That guy was a *ma-liu-tzu.*"

"*Ma-liu-tzu*?" That was a novel term as far as I was concerned. Our fellow monk, too, stared at Hai-hsiu in an uncomprehending daze.

"What, then, is a *ma-liu-tzu*?" I asked.

He explained, "*Ma-liu-tzu* are con-artists, but their abilities go far beyond your ordinary con artist. They can tell what you're worth and whether you're an easy mark just by looking at you and hearing you talk. They change their tactics to fit every situation, like a helmsman who turns the tiller to suit the changing wind. They can dress up like monks or change into Taoist priests. They cry and laugh at will. They know jargon from all walks of life and can speak any dialect. They hang around at train stations and docks —any place there are lots of people. When they discover their prey, they latch onto it and don't let it out of sight. When the time is right, they set their schemes in motion and, easy as a snap, the game is theirs." He continued, "The year I went to be ordained at Ch'ing-liang Monastery in Ch'ang-chou, two of my ordination brothers were swindled out of their luggage. I have heard they are especially numerous in Nanking and Shanghai. How could you be so careless?"

When I heard Hai-hsiu say this, something occurred to me. I gave him a meaningful look, picked up my luggage and walked away. He followed along, bewildered. Only when we had reached the turnstile did I put down my bag and say, "Hearing what you just said reminded me of what the head monk of a small temple in Hsiao County once said to me: 'There's nothing stamped on your forehead that shows whether you're a good man or a bad one.' Now he says his luggage was taken. Neither you nor I saw it happen. Who can guarantee he isn't a *ma-liu-tzu* himself? As the saying goes, 'Never think of harming others, but always think of how to guard against them.' We'd better stick to our own affairs. Actually, we're having enough trouble taking care of ourselves. We couldn't help him, even if we did get involved. Let's be on our way and forget about it!" Hai-hsiu did not seem to be in favor of my view, but he kept his thoughts to himself and followed me onto the train.

NOTES

1. *Kua-tzu* means literally "guy with a brogue" and is used as a derogatory term for Northerners.

2. *Mo-fa* is the last stage of the Law in the Buddhist eschatology, coming after the Age of the True Law (*cheng-fa*) and the Age of False Law (*hsiang-fa*). There are different ways of computing these periods, but generally the age of True Law is believed to last 500 years after the Buddha's Nirvana, the Age of False Law another 1,000 years, and the last Age of the Decay of Law 10,000 years. During the last age, Buddhism will eventually disappear owing to people's indifference and neglect.

3. *Tao-chang* (Bodhimanda) is another name for a Buddhist monastery where one can realize truth through meditation.

4. A goodly friend (*shan-chih-shih*) is someone who helps you to become interested in and understand Buddhism.

5. *K'ung-ch'eng-chi* ("The Strategem of the Empty City") is a famous Peking opera telling the story about how Chu-ke Liang cleverly fooled his enemy by making his empty city appear well defended. In modern Mandarin idiom, this expression means to have an empty stomach.

6. *Wo-wo-t'ou* is a pyramid-shaped bun with an empty hole in the bottom. It is made of corn meal and is standard fare for the common people in North China.

7. "*Ch'i-paò hang-shu*" is a phrase in the *A-mi-to ching* (*The Smaller Sukhāvatī-vyūha Sūtra*) describing the miraculous beauty of the Pure Land.

8. Pao-hua Shan is the name of the mountain on which the monastery Lung-chang Ssu is situated. Yet, as the author says here, the name of the mountain has come to stand for the monastery. The reader is referred to the next chapter on "Ordination at Pao-hua" for more information about Pao-hua Shan.

9. Jui-yün Monastery, like most landowning monasteries, hired tenant farmers to till its lands. The monk who is in charge of collecting land rents is called *chuang-chu* or village agent. He usually lives in the village where the farmland is located in order to supervise the tenants, keep an eye on harvests, and expedite the shipment of grain to the monastery. See Holmes Welch, *The Practice of Chinese Buddhism* (Cambridge, Mass.: Harvard University Press, 1967), pp. 26, 221.

10. *T'u-chih*: this means that this monk was the "adopted son" or "tonsure disciple" of the author's "tonsure brother." Among the members of a tonsure family there are various relations corresponding to, and characterized by, kinship terms. We have already seen the term "grandfather-master " which means the master's master. "Brothers" are disciples of the same master belonging to the same tonsure generation. Welch explains the monastic family relationships this way: "The 'family' that owned the hereditary temple was composed of several generations of masters and disciples all of them 'heirs' (*tzu-sun*). The literal meaning of this term is 'son's and grandsons,' but normally there was no blood relationship between any of the individuals involved. It was not like the present system in Japan where priests marry and a temple is usually passed down by the father to his son by blood. In China all these relationships were based on tonsure. When a monk shaved the head of a layman, the latter thereby became a novice, an heir of the monk's temple, and the monk's adopted son, termed in Chinese 'tonsure disciple' (*t'i-t'ou ti-tzu*). Two tonsure disciples of the same generation in the same family were considered 'cousin-brothers' (*shih-hsiung-ti*). They had an obligation to keep up the worship of their 'ancestors.' For example, when their master died, they performed rites to secure him a better rebirth, made regular offerings to his soul tablets, and swept his grave at Ch'ing-ming.... It is worth noting here, however, that the system appears to have been unique to Chinese Buddhism." *Practice*, pp. 129-130.

11. Tung-yüeh, or Eastern Peak, is Mt. T'ai, the most sacred of the five mountains in China. This temple is dedicated to the god of Mt. T'ai, the Great Emperor Tung-yüeh (Tung-yüeh Ta-ti) who is worshipped here together with his consort, Tung-yüeh Niang-niang. He has sovereignty over the spirits of the dead. During the T'ang, under each of the five sacred mountains a temple was erected. However, since the middle of the Sung, temples dedicated to the Eastern Peak began to be built everywhere. The birthday of the God of the Eastern Peak is the 28th day of the 3rd month. The temple in Peking has been better described. According to the entry on "Tung-yüeh Temple" in the *Yen-ching sui-shih chi* (Account of Yearly Events in Peking), the temple was situated some two Chinese miles outside of the Chao-yang Gate. The temple was open on the 1st and the 15th of each month. But in the 3rd month, from the 15th day on, the temple would be kept open for 15 days during which time masses of people would congregate. The activities reached a peak on the 28th day, the birthday of the god. The same temple was discussed by Anne S. Goodrich in *The Peking Temple of the Eastern Peak: The Tung-*

yüeh Miao in Peking and Its Lore. (Nagoya, Monuments Service, 1964.) See also Ting Fu-pao, *Fo-hsüeh ta-tz'u-tien* (Taipei reprint, 1961), p. 1248c. Morohashi Tetsuji, *Daikanwa jiten* (Tokyo, 1955-1959), Vol. 6, p. 177d.

12. P'u-to Shan is the island of P'u-t'o off the coast of Chekiang. It is the main cultic center for the worship of Kuan-yin. P'u-t'o is a shortened form for Potalaka, the legendary home of Kuan-yin. "Her image occupies the place of honor in all the temples on the island. The principal pilgrimage takes place on the 19th of the 2nd month, birthday of the goddess. It is celebrated with stately services, and attended by crowds, some of whom came from the remotest provinces of China." Henry Doré, *Researches into Chinese Superstitions*, translated by Kennelly, S.J. (Taipei: Ch'eng-wen Publishing Co., 1966), Vol. VI, p. 232-233.

P'u-t'o Shan as a pilgrimage center has been described by Reginald Johnson in *Buddhist China* (San Francisco: Chinese Materials Center, Inc. 1976 reprint), and Holmes Welch in *The Practice of Chinese Buddhism*. The story of Kuan-yin as Princess Miao-shan in China is discussed by Glen Dudbridge in *The Legend of Miao-shan* (London: Ithaca Press, 1978). For the cult of Kuan-yin and pilgrimage, see Chün-fang Yü, "P'u-t'o Shan: Pilgrimage and the Creation of Chinese Potalaka" in *Pilgrims and Sacred Sites in China*, edited by Susan Naquin and Chün-fang Yü (University of California, Berkeley Press, 1992), pp 90-154.

13. The technical term is *kan ching-ch'an* (rushing to perform the recitation of sūtras and the saying of penances). Monks are called to the homes of the bereft household and perform *ching-ch'an* for the benefit of the dead. This is one of the main sources of income for monks, especially those living in urban temples. Many leading Buddhist monks have long regarded this practice as one of the chief reasons for the secularization and commercialization of the sangha, and have discouraged monks from doing it.

14. These are called *chieh-pa* (ordination scars) or *hsiang-pa* (incense scars). They are small, round white scars burned into the novice's scalp by moxa at the end of his ordination. They vary in number, ranging from three or nine to twelve and form vertical lines on his scalp. In the *Practice of Chinese Buddhism*, Welch suggests that the practice may postdate the Sung Dynasty. According to one informant he interviewed, "When government control over the issuance of ordination certificates was suspended by the Yung-cheng Emperor (1723-1736), monks were required to burn scars as a

practice began as an offering to the Buddha comparable to the burning of fingers.... Whatever its origin, it was nearly universal for the Chinese sangha in this century" (p. 298). Welch also quoted at length from Prip-Moller's detailed eye-witness account of the application of moxa at Pao-hua Shan. See *Practice*, pp. 298-300.

Chapter II

ORDINATION AT PAO-HUA MOUNTAIN

Lung-t'an was an important town in Chu-jung County, Kiangsu. It was located on the south bank of the Yangtze River in the north of Chu-jung County, abutting on Chen-chiang to the east and Nanking to the west. The Nanking-Shanghai rail line ran through it, and thus it occupied quite an important position. When Hai-hsiu and I left the train at Lung-t'an, people's windows were already aglow with the light of myriad lamps. That night we stayed at Ting-shui Hermitage, a subsidiary temple at the foot of Pao-hua Mountain. Bright and early the next morning we each had a bowl of porridge, took our leave of the temple manager, and started up the mountain.

Most people say that the distance from Lung-t'an to Pao-hua Mountain is six miles, but owing to the ruggedness of the climb, it seems more than ten miles to those who walk it. Hai-hsiu and I had an even worse time of it than most. According to the route that most people took, one had to go through a long pass and across the slope of a foothill in order to reach the proper road to Pao-hua Mountain. The manager had explained this clearly enough, but when we walked to the slope in front of the subsidiary temple and looked up, the mountain did not appear excessively high. What was more, there was a path leading straight up the mountain. Without givingit a thought, we followed the path upward. After half an hour the path became increasingly indistinct, and the thick mountain grass became deeper and deeper. Profuse sweat of exhaustion ran down my face, and a glance upward told me we had only climbed one third of the way. Hai-hsiu was staring blankly at the peak.

"There is no path up ahead. What can we do?" I asked.

"Paths are made by people walking on them," he answered, drumming up his courage to climb further. That being the case, as his nominal grandfather-master, I had no choice but to pick up my sagging spirits and bring up the rear. After an hour of stops and starts, we made it to the top.

Before us were layers of mountain peaks receding into the distance, isolated villages, winding streams, checkerboard fields, and groups of male and female woodcutters shouldering firewood as they hurried along undulating gravel roads. Delighted at the panorama, Hai-hsiu yelled "Namah Amitābha! [Honor to the Amitābha Buddha]" in a voice loud enough to "scare pheasants into flight and rabbits out from cover; send squirrels scrambling for safety and roe deer running for their lives." I lost no time in warning him: "You shouldn't be so loud in a wild place like this. If some dangerous beast heard your voice, it would be all over for us."

"That's no big thing! The worst that could happen is: 'Our reward-bodies [*pao-shen*] having met their end, we will be reborn together in the Pure Land of Amitābha,'" he laughed, seeming quite pleased with himself. Amazingly enough, he was so carried away with being on the mountain that his very personality changed. This goes to show how strongly a person is influenced by his environment.

After a moment's rest on the peak, my body grew cold and clammy from the sweat I had worked up, so I said, "Put your bag on your back so we can find a path down the mountain in a hurry. Otherwise, we'll catch cold." He seemed oblivious to my words, occupied as he was with pointing, gesticulating, and ceaseless chattering. When I lifted my bag to my back and plunged into the dense grass, he finally hurried to catch up. By the time we reached the foot of the mountain and found the road to Pao-hua, we were soaked again with sweat, and every piece of clothing was covered with burrs. We shook and brushed in vain; they would not fall. The only thing to do was pick them off one by one as we walked along. A few young boys herding cows found us so comical they threw back their heads and laughed themselves silly.

The so-called "main road" was by no means a broad, smooth asphalt thoroughfare. Rather it was a rugged, tortuous gravel track which had been scratched through the mountain thickets by generations of virtuous monks. But let us by no means underrate this tortuous road, for numberless great lights of Buddhist doctrine have passed over it before stepping onto the great path of illumination.

Many old khaki-colored tents were pitched along the right side of the road. Inside were Japanese soldiers who had surrendered not long ago. Now they seemed deflated. No longer would they flaunt their might and cruelly kill Chinese people! When they saw a Chinese passing by on the road, even a little child, they stuck their thumbs up in the air and said, "The Chinese are a great people, and you are one of them!" Another hour of steady walking brought us to a small bridge over the stream that flowed at the foot of Pao-hua Mountain. Seeing that it was a picturesque spot, we decided to rest there before proceeding up the mountain. As luck would have it, a large group of women bearing firewood down from the mountain stopped and commenced washing themselves all over. As a result [because a monk may not see a naked woman], we had to climb part way up the slope before stopping to rest again. The laugh was certainly on us, for we no sooner sat down than they shouldered their loads and were on their way. They walked onto the road and ran like the wind with their 150-pound burdens, calling "*yo-ho yo-ho*" to each other all the while. The meaning of all their yohoing was lost on us.

As the firewood carriers departed, three monks appeared walking toward us, each carrying a bundle on his back. We struck up a conversation and found that they too had come to be ordained. One of them was from northern Anhui and the other two were from northern Soochow. They were roughly the same age as Hai-hsiu and I. Though I did not realize it then, their approach was a boon to me. The reason for this was that Hai-hsiu had once said to me: "Grandfather-master! I've taken my precepts long ago, and you're a new ordinee. When we're in the guest department at Pao-hua Mountain, if I sit, you must remain standing. When the usher is about to take you to your quarters, the guest prefect might even make you prostrate yourself before me!" Because I knew nothing at that time of principles such as "treating ordained monks as masters" and "leaving the best seats for prior ordinees," his words put me in a poor mood. To myself I thought, "How would it look for a grandfather-master to prostrate himself before a grandson-disciple? No matter how I explain it when I go home to my home temple, it will give my disciples and disciple-grandsons plenty to gossip about." Because of this I had been feeling ill at ease. On the other hand, I did not know the first thing about guest department protocol: how could I manage without him to accompany me? The arrival of the three monks was a blessing, first, because Hai-hsiu no longer needed to accompany me into the guest department — thus avoiding a disconcerting display of deference — and second, because people are always braver in a group. Thus I was persistent in my efforts to keep up a conversation as we climbed. They too treated me with great warmth. We became absorbed in conversation and, before we knew it, passed through the gate tower on which hung a plaque reading "Number One Mountain of the Vinaya School." At last we saw Lung-ch'ang Monastery, which we had heard of for so long. The beauty of its surroundings did not fall short of T'ao Yuan-ming's[1] description of the Peach Blossom Grotto: "Before him opened a sunlit expanse of level, open land dotted with nicely proportioned buildings, rich fields and beautiful ponds, and groves of bamboo and mulberry." Sorry to say, we four were in no mood to appreciate the beautiful scene.

At the side of Precept Merit Pond I asked Hai-hsiu to remain behind and rest. With my three new friends I walked through the main gate of Lung-ch'ang monastery and headed toward the guest department. We were like soldiers marching stealthily at night or thieves in dread of capture. We moved quietly forward in single file, full of fear and apprehension. Trying to describe this situation to people ordained in Taiwan is like talking to a summer insect about ice: they cannot possibly have a personal understanding of what we felt. To be ordained in Taiwan, one needs only to go to the business office of a monastery. After registering and paying an ordination fee, one can proceed directly to the ordinees' quarters and rest. Even if one must go to the guest department for roll call, there is nothing to be apprehensive about. Times have changed, and everyone emphasizes convenience.

There is no use complaining. It was my fate to have been born in those times and my misfortune to have traveled to such a place for my ordination. From the time classes were opened at the beginning of the session to the burning of ordination scars at the end, we lived a life of "trembling dread, like skirting an abyss or treading on thin ice." From the beginning to the end, the features of the ordination masters were hardened into forbidding masks. For the entire fifty-three day session, I never once saw them give a kind look or say a civil word to an ordinee. Never once did I see an encouraging smile. It was a far cry from the ordination sessions in Taiwan, where the masters find all sorts of things to talk about with the ordinees, in order to establish personal bonds with them.

Having arrived outside the door of the guest department, the four of us did exactly as the rules prescribed. We put our bags down carefully against the pillars on either side of the covered walkway. Then we formed two rows, one on each side of the door. Lifting the foot nearest the door frame, we stepped into the room and then took two and a half steps more. Still standing in two rows, we faced the front of the room and made three prostrations to the Buddha. Then we made a deep bow and stood with our hands joined before our chests, doing our best not to look past the end of our noses. With unrelaxed poise we awaited the coming of the guest prefect. Perhaps the guest prefect had important matters to take care of, or it could be that he was testing our level of endurance. At any rate, we stood there for a long time, but no one came to greet us. My legs were trembling and my hands were cold and aching. I was just considering pulling my hands into my sleeves to warm them when a short fat man in a light-brown, full-sleeved robe suddenly walked past from behind. My eyes turned for an instant to get a look at his face and then immediately went back to looking at my nose, for the gleam in his eyes was like a sharp arrow that threatened to shoot in my direction. One glance at him sent a shudder of fright through my body.

The fat man stopped in front of us and rocked his body from side to side. Five words uttered in an incomparably harsh tone erupted from his mouth: "Prostrate yourselves to the Buddha!" We did as we were told. When our prostrations were completed, the brother ordinee standing next to me elbowed me and said, "Three prostrations for our master, the guest prefect!

[*chih-k'e*]" The four of us got down on the floor again. As to whether or not he was really a guest prefect, only he himself knew. All the older monks at Pao-hua Mountain were qualified to bear themselves this way in front of new ordinees. Such privileges were not limited to ordination instructors and guest prefects. The monk whom we assumed to be the guest prefect said, "One prostration." We answered with an "Amitābha," stood up and made another bow, joined palms before our chests, and stood motionlessly. Without asking us a single question, the guest prefect ordered us to shoulder our bags and follow a young attendant to the guest hall. I thought I had seen the worst of Pao-hua Mountain's monastic code [*kuei-chu*], which was known far and wide for its severity. As it turned out, the facts of the ordination session proved me totally wrong.

The guest hall was located upstairs of the guest department. Everyone who came to the mountain for ordination stayed there temporarily until the session began. The rules were essentially similar to those in wandering monks' halls at most large public monasteries, but there was no hall officer. However, the lay workman there was even fiercer than a hall officer. Nine out of ten of the ordinees paid him all the reverence due a ghost or spirit, but made sure to keep their distance. When the four of us arrived there, we went through the same set of motions prescribed for the guest department. When the lay workman had assigned us our sleeping places, I asked leave and went downstairs to look for Hai-hsiu.

Ordained monks certainly did have things much easier than those who had not yet received ordination. When I left the guest hall, I saw Hai-hsiu sauntering out of the dining hall [*chai-t'ang*], shoulder to shoulder with an old ordination master. He hurried over to me and asked how everything had gone in the guest department. After hearing the details, he said, "Well, then, everything is fine! I'll return to Nanking this afternoon, and when the session is completed, I'll come to get you." He took out the little money he had brought and handed me everything but what he needed for return fare. Then he followed the ordination master to the guest department, and I returned to my quarters. In the afternoon he came to see me again and, having told me to take care of myself, departed for Nanking.

Never having been far from home before, I was not without feelings of loneliness after his departure. Fortunately the three brothers who had come up the mountain with me invited me to go with them whenever they went out sightseeing. This did much to dispel my loneliness before the session began, and at the same time, I made the rounds of all the famous sights and ancient edifices on the mountain. Outside the monastery were such noteworthy spots as Precept Merit Pond, Greenery Encircled Hall, Dragon Pond, Tiger Grotto, Hall of Former Abbots, Precious Pagoda, and the Platform for

Worshipping Sūtras [Pai-ching t'ai]. Inside the monastery walls were the Hall of No Rafters, Bronze Hall, Wei-t'o Hall, Ordination Altar, and assorted shrines and halls too numerous to recall. There was not one of these at which the four of us did not leave our footprints. Once in a while, while resting from chores like carrying water and bringing rice, we went out the main gate to chat with the old truth seekers as they sunned themselves and picked lice from their clothes. If we saw someone in a yellow robe step out the main gate (all monks who served as ordination instructors [*yin-li-shih*] or ordination masters [*chieh-shih*] at Pao-hua wore yellow robes), we were like rats that have spied a cat: we hurriedly followed the wall around to a side gate and sneaked back into the kitchen.

The day we had been waiting for and living in fear of finally came. One morning after our morning meal of rice porridge, the lay workman made the following announcement: "All new ordinees in this hall must shave their heads clean this morning. When you are finished, wait to be called for a bath. After your bath, each of you must pack your bag and prepare to go to the ordination hall." No one dared move slackly in response to this. Soon the room was thrown into busy confusion: we looked like a theater troupe preparing to move to the next town. When everything was in order, the workman led us to the steps before the main shrine hall. He joined his hands in salute and spoke a few soft words to the yellow-robed ordination instructors waiting there before leaving the scene. We stood there like sheep waiting for slaughter, putting up no resistance as the young ordination instructors armed with willow switches did exactly as they wished with us. They were probably influenced by the thought of Confucius, who said, "Does Heaven utter a word? Yet the myriad things are all born from it."[2] As they divided us into groups, they used their switches on the bare head of anyone who met their specifications and motioned him to the right or left without a word. When everyone had been divided into groups on the basis of height, the group leaders wrote down the monastic name and courtesy name of each person and handed the lists to the instructors. Then came the roll call. When the ordination instructor called his name, one brother, who had probably been a serviceman, answered "Here." He was given a few hard lashes on top of his head by the instructor, who warned him: "After this when I call your monastic name answer 'Amitābha,' not 'Here'! Do you understand? " Our ordination brother's features took on a crestfallen appearance as he answered with a slow, unwilling "yes." So funny did this seem to the ordination instructors that they covered their mouths with their hands and twisted their necks from side to side in suppressed merriment.

The ordination instructors at Pao-hua Mountain were the most unreasonable, most unfeeling people I have ever come in contact with in my life. Their attitude toward ordinees was: "When in the right, give them three loads to carry; when in the wrong, make them carry three loads." That is to say, when they beat you and verbally abused you, whether you were in the right or not, your one and only permitted response was "Amitābha": standing up for your rights was absolutely not permitted. Anyone who failed this ran the risk of being beaten [nearly] to death.

I remember that on the first day of the ordination session, an instructor with a billy club in his hand spoke to us: "Since you've made your decision to come all this way and be ordained, you must rid yourselves of all the habits and failings you learned at your small temples. From now on you will walk, stand, sit, recline and do everything else exactly as your ordination instructors tell you. If your instructor says that watermelons grow on papaya trees, you repeat after him: 'Watermelons grow on papaya trees.' If your instructor says eggplants grow on gourd vines, you repeat after him: 'Eggplants grow on gourd vines.' If anyone dares not to do as he is told, or tries to be clever, or says watermelons don't grow on papaya trees and eggplants don't grow on gourd vines, don't blame your instructor if he loses his compassion and beats you to death with a billy club. If that happens, you'll be dragged under your bunk and left there until the end of the session, when all bodies will be taken to the body incinerator for cremation!"

Amitābha! A weak-nerved person would not need to go to such a place for ordination: merely hearing the above tirade would scare him into a horizontal position from which he would be a long time arising. I assure you, none of what I write here is sensationalism: such things had actually happened during the ordination session before ours.

Perhaps the hindrance from my past karma was too great, or perhaps I was just unlucky: at any rate, it happened that a monk named Yen-hua was in my group. On the day groups were formed and roll was called (it was also the first day of the session), as the instructor began calling names from our group, he called the name "Yen-hua." Because he was a southerner and I could not clearly make out what he was saying, I caught only the word "hua" and thought he was calling me. I rapidly joined my hands before my chest and answered, "Amitābha." Hearing this, he raised his head to take a good look at me and then brought his switch down twice across my head. A painful, stinging sensation shot through my head.

"What is your name?" he barked.

"Amitābha. I am called Chen-hua."

"The name I called was Yen-hua. Why did you answer?"

"Amitābha! I..."

"You what?"

Seeing him raise the willowswitch again, I stammered, "I..I..I" but dared not explain my mistake. Finally, I saved myself by repeating "Amitābha."

In recent years, ordination masters in Taiwan have treated ordinees with compassion and consideration. This is a praiseworthy way of doing things. But the way of doing things at Pao-hua Mountain was exactly the opposite. Ordination instructors were especially severe and cruel to ordinees over the age of forty. They felt that a man over forty who received ordination was changing horses in the middle of the stream. The worldly habits of a man who became a monk in middle age were harder to change, and it was especially possible that he might bring them — lock, stock and barrel — into the Buddhist religion. For this sort of man, ordination brought no personal benefit and was harmful to Buddhism, so those responsible had to use drastic means to pound him into shape and make him know the feeling of shame. Only then was it possible for him to remake his externally visible self and wash his heart clean, so he could give his all to studying the true way. Thus, the ordination instructors often said to the older ordinees: "So you've enjoyed your fill of the blessings of worldly life, have you? You can't gnaw through those chicken bones any more, can you? You want to be ordained and come into the Buddhist religion and be an old monk, do you?"

To be fair, I must admit that while the ordination instructors bordered on the barbaric in their treatment of ordinees, they were certainly conscientious about instilling rules in us. They set an unfailingly good example in the four forms of solemn etiquette — walking, standing, sitting, and reclining — and served as excellent teachers in this respect. As long as a person possessed a "root of goodness" [*shan-ken*], he could gain plenty of spiritual benefit during the session. Although the subjects of study were weighted toward matters of form or *chieh-hsiang* [the external manifestations of the Vinaya precepts], the usefulness of this for upholding the Buddhadharma cannot be disparaged. Of course, if they had, in addition to the external manifestations of the precepts, imparted some understanding of the "theoretical doctrine of the Vinaya precepts"[*chieh-fa*] and of the "behavior that stems from the purifying effect of the precepts" [*chieh-hsing*], Pao-hua Mountain would truly have been deserving of its fame as the "Number One Mountain of the Vinaya School." What a pity that, like one who "knowing little, is satisfied" or "having drunk but shallowly, imbibes no more," they became bogged down with external forms.

Aside from this, the most regrettable things about Pao-hua Mountain were its strife-torn atmosphere and the problem of "cooking in small pots." Let me begin by talking about the former. During my stay at Pao-hua Mountain, the most obvious disharmony in personal relations was between monks in the main halls [*tang-li*]and those in the outer section [*wai-liao*].[3] Before the session opened, I once went with my ordination brothers to the kitchen to get rice. A young instructor from Tung-pan Hall [Tung-pan t'ang] was there on the same errand. Because he put his rice bucket down in a place that hindered the rice steward's work, the rice steward fell into a fit of rage. Throwing the rice bucket a great distance, he barked, "Your mother's...! Don't you have eyes?" The young instructor silently picked up the rice bucket and put it in its proper place on the stove. Later I asked a brother who was carrying water in the kitchen, "Why did the rice steward get so angry over such a little thing?"

"This sort of thing happens all the time. You see, the people in the main halls look down on the workers in the outer sections, and the people in the outer sections don't stand for it. It has gotten to the point that they look on each other as sworn enemies."

"Why do the people from the main halls look down on those in the outer sections?" I asked again. He answered, "The hall monks have a saying that goes: 'When they fight, they are stupid monks; in earning their way, they are slavish monks; at scripture readings, they are deaf-mute monks.' They use it to make fun of the workers in the outer sections. The men in the outer sections are a bunch of coarse fellows who couldn't recognize characters if they were written as big as dippers. Naturally they cannot think up any funny sayings or slogans to fight back. They can only resort to coarse words and strong fists as their means of seeking satisfaction."

As for "cooking in small pots," it was, when one thinks about it, a saddening thing. It was, in the words of old residents of Pao-hua Mountain, a "family tradition"[*chia-feng*] with origins dating back over three hundred years. When reading *Recollections of the Dream that Was My Life* [*I-meng man-yen*] by Vinaya Master Chien-yüeh, I came upon the following passage:

When the late abbot San-mei was alive, three eunuchs professed faith in our religion. They were Eunuch Sun, whose monastic name was Tun-wu [Immediate Enlightenment]; Eunuch Liu, named Tun-hsiu [Immediate Cultivation]; and Eunuch Chang, named Tun-cheng [Immediate Realization]. Prince Yu had crossed the Yangtze to flee into the mountains and the late abbot had not yet returned. At this juncture Master Ta-chao performed the tonsure ceremony on the three of them before an image [of the late abbot] he had hung on the wall. When the abbot returned to the mountain, each of the three was living in a private room. On the thirtieth of the ninth month, 1645, Liu Tun-hsiu came before Masters Hsiang-hsüeh and Ta-chao and asked their permission to begin cooking in his own room. Both gave their consent. On the next day, he asked me to his room for tea. The aforementioned masters were already at the table. Tun-hsiu told me of the stove he had built in his room and said, "Master Hsiang-hsüeh already gave me permission; since you are the new abbot, I would like to tell you about it." I said, "Since I am the abbot, why didn't you talk to me about it before? Now here you are letting me know, only after you first got permission on your own. There are three matters of which I should like to inform you. First, when the late abbot was asked to confer ordinations on anyone, he made sure they destroyed any private stoves and pots they might have and ate meals prepared in the main kitchen before he would grant their request. Now it is not yet four months since the former abbot entered nirvana (he died on the fourth day of the sixth month of that year): who dares to cook separately in this establishment? This is taking advantage of the deceased, and I absolutely will not allow it. Secondly, if you must have personal stoves, wait till after my death and you will be allowed to do what you will. (This statement paved the way for boundless harm!) Third, if circumstances call me elsewhere, and I do not remain as abbot of Pao-hua Mountain, then you masters can administer it as you will. As long as I am here, I will not tolerate the ruining of this mountain." When I had finished, I brushed the dust off my sleeves and went out. Masters Hsiang-hsüeh and Ta-chao said nothing. Tun-hsiu had a look of shame and disappointment on his face. I used this incident as a starting point to strengthen Vinaya discipline.

It is true that blemishes on a family's name should not be held up for all to see, but to give examples of the monastic system from which people of the future can select some things and reject others, it behooves me to reveal the dark side as well as publicizing the commendable side of things. Pao-hua Mountain is the establishment at which I was ordained. It would seem wrong for me to write about these somewhat unsavory matters, and thus needlessly incur the ill feelings of outsiders but, the truth being more important than my personal likes and dislikes, I feel it would be better make it known to monks, nuns and devotees around the world rather than to bury it in my own heart. Because of this, I must relate in detail the matter of "cooking small pots."

Pao-hua Mountain has long been notorious for its poor fare. Outsiders might find it difficult to believe how poor it was during the ordination session. People who stayed there used to say: "You are supposed to be eating guest fare, but you get bean curd pressings." The year I was ordained, which was also the year of victory in the War of Resistance, conditions became so austere that outsiders will find it impossible to imagine, and even people who were ordained before us might not believe it. In the past, though the supposed guest fare was not really guest fare, at least there were beancurd leavings to eat. During our session, beancurd with meals was something no one even mentioned, much less making it part of the guest fare. Someone might ask: "Don't tell me you had no vegetables at all with your rice!" There were, but they were only sour, malodorous pickles that had been kept I don't know how many years. Each of us got a pinch of these with our rice gruel — just for embellishment. What is more, during the fifty-three-day ordination session, as I remember we had only four meals of boiled rice (on the first and fifteenth of each month): the rest of the time we ate rice gruel three times a day. However, the ordination masters and privileged elders who lived in personal apartments and monastery officers had boiled rice each day. Their "devotion" (to robbing their brothers) was truly enough to make one throw oneself on the ground and cry out in anger: "Oh Buddha! Who would have thought that your teachings, which prohibit eating separately from the monastic congregation, are being flouted with impunity by the sons of the 'Number One Mountain of the Vinaya School'?"

Well then, where did the ordination masters' rice come from? On, let us say, the first day of the month, there was boiled rice for all. Those who had disciples made them take rice buckets to the kitchens and have them filled. Those who had no disciples carried the rice buckets themselves. When the wooden fish was struck to signal that the rice was ready, the rice steward lifted up a scoop that held 65-75 pounds of rice, dug it into the great copper pot (this pot could boil 1,800 pounds of rice at once), and twisted it a few turns. Then he dished out the rice. Two scoops were just enough to fill the large buckets, which held enough for fifty people. One scoop was more than enough for the small buckets, which held enough for twenty people. After the rice was dished out, each person took his bucket back to his room. By then the fresh vegetables and beancurd in the small pots were ready. The doors were closed, and they sat down to their piping hot food. When the meal was finished, they put away their leftover rice, and when it came time to eat again, they fried some rice in their small pots and had themselves another meal. Because the weather was cold on the mountain, they could eat a bucket of rice for half a month without its going bad. In this way they had boiled rice every day from the first to the fifteenth and from the fifteenth to the end of every month. This method did not work for the ordinees, however. After eating boiled rice on the first, we had to stretch our necks in anticipation and wait until the fifteenth. There were some kindhearted waiters who felt sorry for us and, as they dished out second helpings of rice to us, repeatedly urged, "It's a rare thing for you to eat boiled rice. Try your best to eat a lot!" However, our bellies were, after all, not the rice buckets of the ordination masters. If they had been, we could have stuffed them as much as we wanted. Maybe then we would not have existed for fifty-three days in the living hell of near starvation.

At this point some readers might ask: "If the ordinees ate only malodorous sour pickles, where did the ordination masters' fresh vegetables come from?" In order to answer this, I must say something about the practice of "appropriating vegetables" [*chiang-ts'ai*]. I think that anyone who has been ordained at Pao-hua Mountain knows that there are plenty of outside chores to do. That is why the saying goes: "If you go to be ordained at Pao-hua Mountain, take along a rope and carrying pole." People who do not know the inside story will certainly ask the purpose of taking such implements. The answer is, when you do outside chores like carrying firewood, water, rice and vegetables, these things come in handy. Once I was given the chore of going to Lung-ch'ang (a total of twelve miles down the mountain and back) to carry vegetables. On my return, I had just passed Greenery Encircled Hall when I saw a "privileged elder" [*shang-tso*] waiting expectantly by the road. If a load of tender, juicy vegetables was carried by, he would rush over to the ordinee and say, "Come with me, come with me." Thereupon he would lead the way to his apartment and instruct the ordinee to pile the vegetables in the place he pointed out. Then, looking very concerned, he would say, "It's rough work to carry vegetables for six miles uphill. You'd better go back to your quarters and rest." Just like that. If the business office received fifty loads vegetables out of every one hundred that we carried up the mountain, it was through the intercession of His Grace Wei-t'o Bodhisattva, protector of the dharma and guardian of monasteries. I wondered at the time why the officers concerned in the business office allowed the "privileged elders" to continue their "appropriations" without even looking into the matter. Only later did I realize that all of them were "breathing through the same nostrils."

Some things that happened in the ordination hall were also "not worth telling to outsiders," but in order to give readers an idea of the life of monks during ordination, I feel that a description is necessary. The ordination halls on Pao-hua Mountain were not only much more elaborate than any in Taiwan, but even on the mainland there were none to compare with them. I have heard that when my ordaining abbot, the Reverend Miao-jou, held a "time of arhats" ordination [*lo-han-ch'i*][4] on his sixtieth birthday, over twenty classes of about twenty persons each were formed, yet there was still room to spare. It was certainly not like in Taiwan, where ordination centers must put up bamboo-framed shelters to hold two or three hundred ordinees. Moreover, [at Pao-hua] in the middle of each hall was a small, beautifully constructed altar honoring a solemn Buddha image.

Fig.2 Refectory of a monastery in south China

When ordinees returned to their hall after finishing with Buddhist services for the day, they first lined up to make three prostrations to Buddha, then knelt down in respectful silence to listen to a lecture [*k'ai-shih*] by the hall instructor. (At Pao-hua Mountain the precentor taught the first hall. Instructors were assigned to the second, third and fourth halls according to their seniority and qualifications.) After the lecture, we stood up in unison and bowed to show our gratitude. Then, standing back to back, we quietly pulled off our robes and gowns, folded them neatly, and put them in their proper places. Stepping as lightly as possible, we went to the restroom [*chia-fang*]. When that was finished, we stopped on the walkway outside of the hall to take off our stockings and roll them up in the prescribed manner. Only then could we go to sleep. There were even rules about sleeping. It was not like ordination sessions in Taiwan, where those who want to can sleep, and those who do not can stay up and chat.

When the watchman's board sounded in the morning, there was not even time to rub one's eyes. We had to get out of our beds like lightning and fumble with our clothes in the murky lamplight. (In order to gain time, some monks went so far as to sleep fully clothed.) That done, we rushed to the bathroom, did our business, then rubbed water on our faces on the way back to the hall. We put on our robes, made obeisance to Buddha, then sat on our bunks. The officer in charge poured a cup of water with a pinch of salt for each person. Anyone who had snacks could discreetly take them out and eat them. Those who did not got along with salt water. When the drum had sounded three times, we filed out of the hall to the great shrine hall for morning devotions. This was at about half past three or four o'clock in the morning.

Morning devotions [*tsao-k'e*] were of a length rarely seen at other monasteries. The gatha at the beginning of the *Śūrangama Mantra* [Leng-yen chou] which begins "unmovable Tathāgata, who is subtle, profound, and upholds all things" had to be repeated for thirty to forty minutes. Perhaps because of the cold weather, some of the older ordinees had to ask leave to go to the restroom before the service was over. As the common saying has it: "You may interfere with heaven and earth, but you cannot interfere when nature calls." But during our session, this saying did not apply at all. If you felt a pressing need to go to the bathroom at a time which was not set aside for this purpose, and if you asked an ordination instructor for permission, he would not only refuse you but also "make you an offering of willow noodle" (hit you with a willow switch). Because of this, during devotions and ceremonial rehearsals, even if your need was so pressing that you could not straighten up your waist, you had no choice but to bear it. If you truly could hold it no longer, you disregarded the consequences, blurted out your intentions, and lit out for the bathroom. Naturally you would have to have "willow noodles" to eat on your return.

Actually, such hardships as morning devotions, dining hall fare and chores still had a measure of flexibility. Only the "formal precept-takings at the three altars" [*san-t'an cheng-shou*] were pure, unadulterated misery. What were they? In the first ceremony at the first altar we took *śrāmanera* [novitiate] precepts [*sha-mi chieh*];[5] in the second, *bhiksu* [clerical] precepts [*pi-ch'iu chieh*];[6] and in the third, *bodhisattva* precepts [*p'u-sa chieh*].[7] The three stages were characterized by this saying: "*Śrāmanera* are made to kneel, *bhiksu* are beaten, and *bodhisattva* have scars burned on their heads." Judging from my personal experiences of "kneeling, beating and burning," the most difficult to endure is kneeling rather than burning and beating. Why is this? Because burning and beating lasted only a short time. Also, burning happened only once, and one was not beaten every day. Kneeling, however, was a common exercise. Readers who think I am contradicting myself might ask: "After saying that *śrāmanera* are made to kneel, how can you turn around and say that kneeling was a common exercise?" Actually, people only emphasized the fact that "*śrāmanera* are made to kneel" so they could come up with a clever, easily remembered saying. When we took our *bhiksu* and *bodhisattva* precepts, we kneeled just as we had before. This is just the same as saying: "The sūtras expound *samādhi*, the *vinaya* [treatises on discipline] expound monastic rules, and the *śāstra* [discourses] expound wisdom." Just imagine! In the freezing winter cold of a north wind that pierced like a knife, we knelt on the coarse-grained flagstones in the courtyard before the great shrine hall for at least two hours each time and waited for the end of the ceremony. As the three masters left for their quarters, the ordaining abbot congratulated us on taking the ten *śrāmanera* precepts (or *bhiksu* precepts or *bodhisattva* precepts). We were frozen into corpselike stiffness, and it was all we could do to answer mechanically, "Amitābha."

In closing, I have the following to say by way of criticism: The ordination instructors at Pao-hua Mountain had excellent deportment and were dedicated to teaching monastic rules, but they were overly severe. In fact, they were severe to the point of cruelty. This made the ordinees feel more resentment than respect, more enmity than gratitude. Thus, as the end of the session approached, hot-tempered young ordinees who were lacking in self-control often rubbed their fists in expectation of revenge. Happily, the ordination instructors had the gift of foretelling the future. One day before the ordinees left the mountain, they made themselves scarce. If they had not, the "Number One Mountain of the Vinay School" would have witnessed some mighty brawls!

NOTES

1. T'ao Yuan-ming (365-427), whose name was T'ao Ch'ien, was a famous writer in the Eastern Chin Dynasty. "The Record of the Peach Blossom Grotto" is his account of a fisherman's discovery of a Shangri-la hidden behind a grotto at the mouth of a peach-blossom-lined stream.

2. *Analects* XVII. 19.

3. The outer sections were those that were not connected with ordination, worship of the tablets of earlier masters, and meditation. In fact, except for monks enrolled in meditation hall, usually all the other monks in other departments in a monastery belong to the outer section.

4. *Lo-han ch'i* (a time of arhats), also known as "*ch'ien-seng chieh*" (thousand monk ordination) was held to celebrate the sixtieth, seventieth or the eightieth birthday of an eminent monk. "A much larger number of ordinees than ususal would flock to be ordained under his auspices and the ordination lasted longer." Welch, *Practice*, p. 504.

5. *Sha-mi chieh* are the ten precepts which consist of the five precepts for a layman: 1) not to destroy life; 2) not to steal; 3) not to commit adultery; 4) not to lie; 5) not to take intoxicating liquor. Five more precepts are required of a novice: 6) not to eat food out of regulated hours; 7) not to use garlands or perfumes; 8) not to sleep on high or broad beds; 9) not to take part in singing, dancing, musical or theatrical performances, not to see or listen to such; 10) to refrain from acquiring uncoined or coined gold, silver or jewels.

6. They are the 250 precepts for a monk or bhiksu.

7. They are the 58 precepts contained in the *Fan-wang ching* (*Sūtra of the Brahma's Net*). According to the original Indian Buddhist practice, a monk who has taken the precepts for a *bhiksu* becomes a full-fledged member of the sangha. But according to Mahāyāna practice in China, he still has to take another set of precepts a week or so later. "They were the fifty-eight vows of the *Fan-wang ching*

which imposed a higher stratum of discipline and a commitment to lead all sentient beings into Nirvana before attaining it themselves. Hence they are called 'Bodhisattva Vows'". Welch, *Practice*, p. 294.

Chapter III

REPORTING FOR EXAMINATIONS AT P'I-LU MONASTERY

Now that I have finished with my account of ordination at Pao-hua Mountain, let me move on to my experience of reporting for entrance examinations to the Buddhist seminary at P'i-lu Monastery.

During the ordination session, after all of us had been branded with twelve incense scars and had received ordination certificates [*chieh-tieh*] and yearbooks [*t'ung-chieh lu*], we were like university graduates who have just gotten their diplomas. We were nervous, excited, and at the same time confused about what lay ahead. In groups of threes and fives we discussed our plans for the future:

Some planned to return to their home temples and serve as managers or resident superintendents.
Some planned to go to Chin-shan or Kao-min for Ch'an meditation.
Some planned to go to Ling-yen Shan in Soochow to recite the Buddha's name.
Some planned to go to T'ien-ning Monastery in Chang-chou and chant sūtras.
Some planned to make pilgrimages to the four sacred mountains of Chinese Buddhism.[1]
Some planned to live in thatched huts on Chung-nan Mountain.
Some planned to find work chanting requiems in Nanking or Shanghai.
Some planned to pay honor to relics of the Buddha at A-yü-wang [King Aśoka] Monastery.
Some planned to go to Burma and worship at the Great Golden Pagoda.
Some planned to study the teachings of the T'ien-t'ai school at Kuan-tsung Monastery.
Some planned to stay at Pao-hua Mountain to study monastic rules and discipline.

Fig.3 View of Chin Shan Monastery, Kiangsu

Some had no plan at all except to get by as best they could and take what came their way.

At first I was going to wait until Hai-hsiu came to get me before making my decision, but, urged by a fellow ordinee, I ended up going to P'i-lu Monastery in Nanking, my plan being to test into a seminary and study there. Although I was greatly disappointed when this plan came to nought, it was, after all, a stop along the way in my search for spiritual instruction, so I must give an account of it.

How did it happen that I went to P'i-lu Monastery at the urging of an ordination brother? Well, when the session was beginning to wind down, a fellow ordinee announced an exciting item of news. It seems that someone had written him from Nanking to say that Great Master T'ai-hsü [1890-1947] was soon coming to Nanking and that, on his arrival, he planned to set up a Buddhist seminary at P'i-lu Monastery. The dharma masters who would teach classes had already been hired! Brochures describing the entrance examination were about to be issued. Any young monks undergoing ordination who were resolved to seek knowledge were urged to report for the examination at P'i-lu Monastery at the end of the session. Classes would certainly begin after the lunar New Year. This was a once-in-a-millennium opportunity! It was too good to pass up!

When this news got around, the monk who had spread it suddenly became the man of the hour. Everyone gathered around him and clamored for his attention. The result was that a group of nine people, including myself, made up their minds to go to P'i-lu Monastery. After making my decision, I wrote to Hai-hsiu telling him that he need not come to meet me. I also let him know that I wished to study at a seminary rather than work at funerals.

P'i-lu Monastery was one of the most famous religious establishments in Nanking. It was situated in the vicinity of the Nationalist government headquarters, and its many buildings occupied a huge area. A massive, solemn, and uniquely designed shrine to Kuan-yin injected new life into the monastery's atmosphere of age and decline. After the nine of us had gone through the motions prescribed by guest department protocol, the guest prefect, seeing our newly healed ordination scars and realizing that we had come to participate in the examination, politely asked us a few questions and then personally escorted us to a building at the right of the guest department. The building had three rooms, one with windows and two without. In the room on the right lived a dharma master. The room on the left had a sleeping platform for ten or more people. The wall next to the veranda had a large glass window, in front of which was placed a large square table perfect for writing and studying. Everyone was quite satisfied with the room. We felt that our luck in meeting such a polite guest prefect and getting such a nice room on our first night after being ordained must have been in recompense for what we had gone through.

When the guest prefect had assigned us to our places, we went to the refectory for a late meal and then went on to visit and pay our respects to the Great Shrine Hall [Ta-hsiung-pao-tien], the Kuan-yin Shrine and the Chi-kung Shrine. The board sounded for evening devotions and we were about to join in, but the guest prefect said, "It has been hard on you to come such a long way. Go and rest in your room. Don't perform devotions this evening." His words, like sunlight in the dead of winter, brought rays of warmth to our cold, lonely hearts.

In a few minutes the guest prefect who had received us earlier came to our room in the company of the precentor [*wei-no*] and the proctor [*seng-chih*]. Out of the clear blue sky, the precentor asked if we could chant requiems. Seven of my fellows said they could, but two of us answered in the negative. Hearing this, the proctor gave me a contemptuous look, as if to say: "At your age you can't even chant requiems. You may have been ordained, but you're no more than a rice bucket." However, the precentor and guest prefect spoke to us in comforting and encouraging tones: "That doesn't matter. With a little time you will learn here." Turning to the seven brothers who knew funeral services they said, "The establishment has had many Buddhist services to perform lately. We hope you will resolve to give the establishment some help." The three of them left, and my seven brothers grimaced and stuck their tongues out. "Humph," they exclaimed in unison, "Help out? We didn't come here just to chant requiems. How can they do this to us?" Although they spoke this way at the time, later they obediently did the bidding of the precentor and the guest prefect.

Not long after that accomodating gesture on the part of the guest prefect, precentor and proctor, my seven friends found that they were becoming very busy people. Every day the guest department hung out service assignment plaques that bore their esteemed names. One day they chanted sūtras at the Chang residence; performed a requiem at the Li residence; and "released the burning mouths" at the Chao residence. The next day they released hungry ghosts at the Liu residence, chanted sūtras at the Sun residence, and performed a requiem at the Ma residence. In short, not a day passed without them performing these services. At first it bothered them, and when they came back from a service they would give vent to their discontent by grumbling, "We came here to study. Why do they make us scurry around every day performing services? How can they be so unreasonable?" (My feelings exactly.) However, when they had performed half a month of services, and each of them got a roll of crisp, brightly colored bills, they held them up in front of me and said mockingly: "Guy with a Northern Brogue! Look at these nice bills! Hurry up and learn. When you know how, you'll make some for yourself." In all honesty, when I saw their money and thought of my own difficulties, I was tempted to make an effort to learn the funeral services, to abandon myself to just getting along and be done with it. But sometimes, when a shortage of heads forced the establishment to send me out with a group to fill up space, I thought, "Did I risk my life coming south for spiritual instruction, just to do this?"

I do not remember how many days I had been living at P'i-lu Monastery when one evening Temple Manager Hsi-ch'u and Hai-hsiu came riding on a ricksha to see me. Hai-hsiu asked, "Grandfather-master! How do you find living here?" "Pretty good," I answered.

Hsi-chu looked at the cotton filling that stuck out of my worn robe and said, "I'll say you look pretty good! Why, the fat is oozing out of your very robe." There was a note of reprimand in his voice. He continued, "Little brother, don't be so hard-headed! Come to Tung-yüeh Temple with me. If you don't want to work at funerals, I won't force you. Just do a little bookkeeping, and we'll give you a daily fee (which was equal to the payment for one day of funerary chanting). Everyone at the temple is from up north. Any way you look at it, eating steamed noodles, buns and dumplings is better than eating one meal of old rice and two of corn meal mush every day."

Hsi-ch'u stared at me, waiting for an answer. I replied, "I am grateful for your good intentions, but I cannot possibly accept them. My goal in coming here was to seek knowledge, not to enjoy comfort and make money. The life here is hard, but it is much better than at Pao-hua Mountain. What's more, I can even get a little monthly spending money here. It makes no difference to me whether I wear good clothes or bad. When Confucius' disciple Tzu-lu stood in ragged clothes next to a man wearing fox furs, he still didn't feel embarrassed. Don't tell me someone who has renounced lay life should be afraid that people will laugh at him?"

Temple Manager Hsi-ch'u seemed displeased at this, but he offered no rebuttal. He simply remarked offhandedly: "That's alright too. Since your mind is made up, stay here and discipline yourself." Then he and Hai-hsiu hailed two rickshas and returned to Tung-yüeh Temple.

There is a saying that goes: "When your vision sees through the affairs of this world, the shock of it will go through your vitals; when your understanding penetrates human nature, its coldness will penetrate your heart." Truly, human nature and worldly affairs are frightening things. When you and other men are placed in similar circumstances, when your abilities are comparable or you are worth exploiting, then everything will be fine; but if there comes a time when they enjoy better circumstances than you, when their abilities come into their own or they no longer need to take advantage of you, then their attitude will rapidly worsen, perhaps so much that they will spurn you. Such occurrences are not limited to laymen; those who have renounced lay life are the same. Monks are worse in some respects and in no way better. This is a saddening thought. In saying this, I am not shooting arrows without a target: indeed, I can cite an actual incident to back me up. Look at my account of this incident and see if human nature is not a frightening thing!

Although the eight fellow ordinees who went to P'i-lu Monastery to sign up for the examination with me were southerners, during the ordination session and even for a short time after our arrival in Nanking we not only shared a common sense of purpose, but the feelings between us seemed to grow deeper with each passing day. This was greatly encouraging to me, who had come to seek knowledge among the strange people and unfamiliar surroundings of large public monasteries in the South. Most unfortunately, not long after our arrival at P'i-lu Monastery, my ordination brothers, who had until then shared a common sense of purpose with me, began to use me as a butt for their jokes. When they addressed me, "brother" gave way to "Guy with a Brogue," and their respectful attitude gave way to one of derision. The resulting dissension nearly got the nine of us thrown out of P'i-lu Monastery's gate.

As I said earlier, not a day passed that P'i-lu Monastery did not conduct Buddhist services. Because of this, my seven ordination brothers who were versed in funeral services became daily more fatigued as their wads of money grew ever fatter. Every day after funeral services they ate supper and went straight to bed. According to the establishment's rules, lights were to be turned out at nine o'clock, so I often used the time after supper to study or practice calligraphy. To avoid disturbing their slumbers, I never read aloud. However, this meant nothing to them; whenever they saw me opening a book beneath the lamp, they would shout with complete lack of restraint, "Guy with a Northern Brogue! Go to sleep!" After that would come a click, and the light would go out. At first there was a touch of humor in this. After I asked them politely, they would turn on the light (embarrassing as this admission may be, I was as yet unfamiliar with the mystery of an electric switch) and let me continue reading. Later their tone of voice became threatening and insulting: "Northerner! Go to sleep now! If you don't, I'll smack you." "What in hell are you doing, damn you. You still won't go to sleep, will you. Listen, no matter how hard you study, you'll never get as much money as us." This would be followed by the sound of the light being turned out. Since I knew that under such circumstances pleading with them would have no effect, I tried to reason with them. However, their numbers gave them the advantage, and I got the worse end of the argument. Once I could contain my anger no longer and said, "You've gone too far. When I study, I don't ask you questions and I don't read aloud. If you want to sleep, sleep! Why insist on making things hard for me? The lights-out rule was made by the establishment; I haven't broken that rule. You're making trouble for no good reason. You say no matter how hard I study I can't make as much money as you. Let me tell you, I'm studying to take a test and get into the Buddhist seminary, not to make money. I ask you not to behave like this any more. Otherwise, I will stop being so polite."

I supposed that the rectitude of my position and the sternness of my words would arouse their sense of shame, and that they would no longer torment and abuse me. Everyone would then mind their own business and coexist peacefully. The facts, however, showed me how wrong I was. In addition to tormenting and abusing me as before, they formed a "united front" and tried to railroad me off the premises. When matters came to this pass, I could no longer suppress my "flame of ignorance." An argument ensued between myself and one of them named ___-ch'ing, the one who turned out the light every night as I studied. As he stood at the edge of the sleeping platform, I slapped him soundly across the face. He might have been too much of a weakling, or I might have put too much into the blow, but at any rate he collapsed instantly on the sleeping platform, covered his face with his hands and wailed, "Mama, my mama" for all he was worth. The others who were lying on the bed sat up, pointed accusing fingers at me and bellowed, "You dare to hit people?" I answered, "Yes, I hit him. If you don't like it, come down off there, all of you!" None of them came down off the bed.

When the tempest of anger had passed, all sounds in the room subsided into a stillness punctuated only by the sobs of the injured party. It was so deathly still that even the light bulb seemed covered by black gauze, and a dark foreboding was cast over everything. I was about to return to my place by the window, when the dharma master who lived across from us stepped in the door. I pressed my palms together in greeting. He nodded and looked at me, then looked at the brother crying on the bed, then stood silently facing the sleeping platform.

Seeing the dharma master come in, the brothers, like a group of plaintiffs before a judge, proclaimed my guilt with one voice. After they had their say the dharma master, with the imposing mien of a judge, gave his verdict. First he said to them, "I don't often come to your room, but it's clear to me what's going on here. Since you formed a group to come here and seek instruction, while you're living together you ought to respect, forgive, encourage and cooperate with one another. You ought to help one another to grow day by day in character, knowledge and spiritual cultivation. Only in this way can you be considered true friends and comrades in faith. Bear in mind that for a monk living at a public monastery, the most important thing is to maintain harmonious relations with everyone. The most undesirable things are arrogance and jealousy. You who have recently been ordained and who travel forth in search of instruction have a special need to keep these two sentences firmly in mind. You must constantly say to yourself in warning: 'Arrogance and jealousy are worse than poisonous snakes. They must never be allowed to rise up within my heart.' But from what I have observed, you have no inclination whatever to think this way. To put it frankly, your behavior is a disgrace to your elders and to yourselves." The dharma master turned to point to me, then faced them again and continued, "He came here from far up north to seek knowledge. It wasn't easy. You ought to treat him with the sympathy and encouragement of true friendship, and help him to feel less alienated in this strange place, so he can seek knowledge with an untroubled heart. Rather than doing this, you hinder and mistreat him. I often hear you call him 'Guy with a Northern Brogue,' but I never hear him call you 'Southern Barbarians.' Let me ask you: if one of you went north alone to seek knowledge, and many northerners treated you this way, how would you feel?" (At this point I burst into tears.) He paused for a moment, then pointed at the brother who had been struck: "He who insults others will be insulted by others. Didn't you bring this on yourself? Compare the hearts of others with your own, and all will live in the springtime of peace. I hope you write this sentence down and paste it in a place where you'll look at it every day. Repeat it until it's engraved on your mind, then you won't be struck again." With this he turned to me and said, "You seem to be a good sort. How can your behavior be so crude? You must know that in a monastery exchanging angry words or resorting to violence, regardless of who is right, is punishable by expulsion. If they insult you or abuse you, you can go to the guest department and discuss what should be done, but you must not raise your hands in anger. Haven't I seen you reading *The Sūtra of Buddha's Last Instructions*? [*Fo I-chiao Ching*] Don't you remember this passage? 'The virtue of forbearance surpasses that of monastic discipline and ascetic practices. Only one who can act with forbearance can be called a great and powerful man. If a man cannot delight in tolerating the poison of vilification as if he were drinking sweet dew, he cannot be called a wise man who walks the true path.'" When he had recited this far, he seemed to forget what came next, but, after a moment's thought, he continued, "'Know that a heart of anger is more destructive than the fiercest fire. Guard yourself always against it, let it not gain entrance. Of thieves that rob us, none is worse than anger.'"

At the time I felt a strong urge to answer, "I understand what your Reverence is saying, but sorry to say I just haven't progressed far enough in self-cultivation to 'delight in tolerating vilification as if drinking sweet dew.' What is more, I have endured their vilification more than ten times already. If I had held it inside me and kept on forbearing, they would not have stopped short of shitting on my head!" But I dared not speak out. The dharma master saw that I kept my peace and, apparently supposing that I had already realized the error of my ways, said, "Men are not saints: who can be free from error? To realize one's errors and change them — there is no good greater than this." Then he turned to those sitting on the sleeping platform and said, "Don't go on arguing, or you'll regret it someday." With that, he walked out of the room. Without another sound the nine of us lay down on the sleeping platform.

As I lay there, my emotions churned like the rapid, wind-driven current of the Yangtze River I had seen outside of the I-chiang Gate — turbulent and roaring, the massive breakers rose and fell as they dashed against my heart. For a long time I lay sleepless. I thought, "It's all over now. Tomorrow when the dharma master spreads the news of this to the guest department, the guest prefect may give me a beating with an incense board and then expel me. If it's just going to be a beating, I can live with it, but what if I'm expelled? Going back to the little temple up north would be like a moth flying to a fire for refuge. Going to Tung-yüeh Temple would be like backing away from a cliff and plunging into a ravine." With such thoughts as these running through my mind, I tossed and turned all night, but I could not think of a good way to deal with the situation. What about the others? Having been lectured to by the dharma master, they too seemed to realize that matters had come to a serious pass. All night they shuttled in and out of the room and carried on muttered conversations on the bed, probably in an effort to determine countermeasures. To my surprise, the most self-collected of all of them was the one I had struck. Right after laying down, he expelled a few sighing breaths and before long, his mind tranquil and self-satisfied, began to "dream of the Duke of Chou."[2]

The morrow was the twenty-seventh day of the twelfth month of the lunar calendar. After morning porridge the guest prefect, precentor and proctor assigned chores such as sweeping and placing offerings. Once the work assignments were made, the guest prefect made us stay behind in the vegetarian hall. The precentor, a short young man with a refined manner and a pale, ever-smiling face, looked first at the afflicted brother, whose cheek had swollen to half the size of an apple. Standing before me, the precentor asked, laughing, "Why did you hit Master ___-ch'ing last night?" This question took me aback. I joined my hands before my chest, then pointed to ___-ch'ing and said, "Would the Precentor be so good as to ask him?" This sort of answer to an officer of the establishment was lacking in politeness, but the kind precentor did not mind. He laughed a bit and, without asking ___-ch'ing or questioning me further, he delivered an admonitory lecture that differed only in minor details from the one his fellow dharma master had given the night before. At the end of lecture, he said, "Even the abbot knows of the fight. According to establishment rules for communal living, you should all be expelled. But, considering that you have left your home temples for the first time to seek knowledge, you are spared all punishment. However, you must be sure not to let anything of this sort happen again. Otherwise, not only will you be expelled, but you will first be given a sound beating with an incense board. Now it's almost time to sweep the floors and place offerings. Hurry back to your room and prepare!" Smiling broadly, he walked out together with the guest prefect. The nine of us, in great relief at having been granted this "general amnesty," walked back to our quarters. As I walked, a question came to my mind: "That's strange." Why was the precentor's admonition nearly the same as the dharma master's? Could it be that the dharma master acted as my voluntary defense attorney? Otherwise, why would the precentor have behaved so politely toward a "guy with a brogue" like me? The dharma master, the precentor and the brothers who bullied me are all southerners. I've heard that southerners have strong provincial feelings and are extremely protective of their fellows. Why did this turn into an exception? " Strange! "

Beset by Poverty and Illness

The wheel of time turned unceasingly. New Year's had just passed, and in a wink came the Lantern Festival. The Lantern Festival brought festive joy to the several hundred thousand citizens of Nanking, and it brought promises of glorious possibility to our nation, but it smashed my cherished dream of studying in a Buddhist seminary. Before the lunar New Year, I had often heard the news that the seminary would open right after New Year's Day, but when New Year's passed, the seminary seemed to become a taboo subject, and I began to grow quite anxious. In contrast, P'i-lu Monastery's Buddhist services prospered with each passing day as the holiday season of rebirth and renewal progressed. The income of those who could work at funerals also increased with each passing day. I alone was a hard-luck case. From morning till evening and from evening to morning I lay in bed moaning. Was I suffering from an affliction? One could say that I was, but it would be more accurate to say that I was suffering from boils. They were boils caused by scabies mites — the kind of boils that itch down into one's bones and hurt like crazy.

Mentioning scabietic boils makes me think back to Precept Merit Pond at Pao-hua Mountain. According to tradition, the water in this pond was once "pure and sweet," and it "prolonged life and prevented illness" for those who drank it. Perhaps those in authority were lacking in virtue, or the time had come for the mountain's decline. At any rate "pure" became "turbid" and "sweet" became "brackish." It had become a habit among long-term residents to use the old saying to describe the pond. As to whether drinking the water could or could not "prolong life and prevent illness" (probably not; otherwise they would not have ordered ordinees to carry water from Dragon Pond, which was over a mile distant from the monastery), one cannot know for certain, but to be sure few residents were afflicted with boils. However, among those who stayed at the mountain only long enough to be ordained, nine out of ten of us who drank water from the pond contracted scabies, and some were afflicted with stomach discomfort. Because of this, some said that the pond was a sump for all of Lung-ch'ang Monastery's sewage. This may have been an unkind thing to say, but it was not without reason. Since the monastery was uphill from the pond, when rainy weather came and washed the sewage away, what was to stop it from running off into the pond? When I left the mountain at the end of the ordination session, the beginnings of scabies appeared between my fingers and toes, but they were not so serious as to hinder my movements. During the beginning of my stay at P'i-lu Monastery the weather was still cold and my condition remained the same: I was bothered only by occasional itching. But, right after the New Year, what with the warm weather and the mushrooms and other delicacies I had eaten over the holidays, my whole body erupted with bean-sized purple pustules. Lying down and sitting were out of the question: words cannot convey how painful it was. If it had not been for the kind-hearted verger [*hsiang-teng-shih*] in the great shrine hall who rubbed ointment on me whenever he had spare time, the agony of impatience for the disease to be gone would have driven me out of my mind.

"When you are sick you must take some time to nurse yourself back to health. Why be so impatient?" Although his words made sense, how could a lonely, solitary person beset by poverty and illness not be impatient?

At that time the word poverty could have been applied to me without reservation. As the Tung-yüeh Temple manager had said, fat (that is, cotton wadding) was fairly oozing from the holes in my quilted robe. My short, thin cover, when rolled into a bedroll, was probably not even as big as that of

Vinaya Master Hung-yi (1880-1942) when he went to stay at Ch'i-t'a [Seven Pagoda] Monastery in Ningpo. At least that venerable soul had a frayed straw mat to wrap around his bedroll, while I lacked even that. As for money, although I was not yet, as my teacher Tz'u-hang [Compassionate Voyage] Bodhisattva wrote in his will, "without a penny in my possession," should I have wanted to ride a ricksha to see a doctor, not only would the doctor's fee and money for medicine have been out of the question, but I would not even have been able to come up with ricksha fare.

I still do not know who spread the news of my illness to Tung-yüeh Temple. One wet gloomy day I was lying in pain on the sleeping platform, my eyes wide open, when suddenly I saw Hai-hsiu hurry into the room. Seeing my appearance, which was more ghostlike than human, he broke out in loud sobs. Temple Manager Hsi-ch'u arrived soon after and, taking a look at me, said, "Brother, you asked for your suffering. If you had listened to me and gone to Tung-yüeh Temple, even if you had contracted scabies it wouldn't have been this miserable. Don't be so stubborn. I've already told the guest prefect you'll be going with us to Tung-yüeh Temple by ricksha." I shook my head weakly and said, "It's not certain yet whether or not a Buddhist seminary will be set up here. I'd like to wait another month and see. If they really don't set one up, I'll go to Tung-yüeh Temple to stay with you." This ignited his temper again. He looked around the room to make sure no one was listening and said quietly: "I've lived in Nanking for over ten years. Don't you think I know as much as you? Listen to me! Don't wait here and dream about getting into a seminary. There is no news whatsoever about a seminary being set up here. You say someone here wrote to Pao-hua Mountain saying they would request Grand Master T'ai-hsü to set up a Buddhist seminary here. This simply did not happen. If it did, it was only a come-on to attract you inexperienced young folks to come here and help with funeral services. And good old, honest *you* didn't know enough to turn aside: you butted your head right up against the wall."

Hearing this, I thought back to the morning of my second day at P'i-lu Monastery, when the guest prefect, precentor and proctor had come to our room and asked right out of the blue if we knew how to perform funeral services. "Aha!" A sound of startled realization escaped my lips. "In that case, I'll go to Tung-yüeh Temple with you."

NOTES

1. The four sacred mountains are Wu-t'ai, Chiu-hua, O-mei, and P'u-t'o, which are dedicated to the worship of bodhisattvas Mañjuśrī (Wen-shu), Ksitigarbha (Ti-tsang), Samantabhadra (P'u-hsien) and Avalokiteśvara (Kuan-yin), respectively.

2. In *Analects* VII. 5, Confucius said, "How much I have fallen off from what I was. For a long time I have not again dreamed of the Duke of Chou." In idiomatic Chinese, "to dream of the Duke of Chou" is to go to sleep.

Chapter IV

STAYING AT TUNG-YÜEH TEMPLE

My dream of entering the Buddhist seminary smashed, I had no alternative but to hobble out of P'i-lu Monastery and move to Tung-yüeh Temple, which had struck me from the very beginning as a place with noisy surroundings outside and unsavory goings-on inside. As I was leaving, my ordination brothers treated me with a much better attitude than before. They busied themselves helping Hai-hsiu pack my belongings. Actually I only had a worn quilt and a few cheap, used books. Hai-hsiu alone would have been enough: there was no need whatever for their help. But, since they had come to help of their own accord, how could I refuse them? "Thank you, brothers; thank you, brothers," I said over and over. They replied, speaking as with one voice: "You needn't be so polite, brother. After all, there is an affinity from former lives between us, is there not? We've already lived together here at P'i-lu Monastery for two months. A bit of unpleasantness might have occurred between us, but wasn't that only because we are young and didn't know any better? We are all sad to hear that you want to go to Tung-yüeh Temple. Please forget what is past. The time will come when we meet again. Since there is no hope of pursuing our studies here, each of us will go on his own way."

I answered, "Yes, there certainly is a fated affinity between us. Otherwise, as far apart as we were in the beginning, how could we have gone to the same place for ordination and come here together to seek instruction? But, regrettably, our fated bond seems to have been a bit too shallow. Were it deep, we could study together at the same seminary. Wouldn't that have been even better? Mountains remain motionless always, however much they seem to change to the man who walks a winding course around them. As long as there exists a fated bond, we shall, as you say, meet again. What's past is past. Though it's not easy to forget it completely, I ask all of you not to worry; I will certainly not bear a grudge against you. I only hope that brother ___-ch'ing can forgive me." Then after a few moments of united laughter, Hai-hsiu carried out my luggage, and Master Hsi-ch'u accompanied me to the guest department to take my leave. That done, I limped to the great shine hall to express my gratitude to the kindly verger. Then Hsi-ch'u, Hai-hsiu and I went to Tung-yüeh Temple, each in a separate ricksha.

Having already written of Tung-yüeh Temple's setting in an earlier chapter, I will now say something of the personnel within. Aside from the temple manager there were fourteen resident monks, one cook who doubled as waiter, and two lay workmen who carried boxes of scriptures to where the services were held. With me included, the total came to nineteen persons. Since the temple manager had offered to let me earn a daily fee by doing simple office work rather than working funerals, once I had recovered from the scabietic boils, I did bookkeeping and kept records. It was easy, unhurried work. In my free time, if I was not reading scriptures to myself, I was reciting the Buddha's name. Time certainly did not hang heavy on my hands. A few resident masters thought this was unfair. They often made snide remarks like: "We spend a whole day drawing air in and droning it out, and all we get is our daily fee. You stay here inside where the wind doesn't blow on your face and the rain doesn't fall on your head. You eat three square meals a day and drink fine-leaved tea. You're free to do as you wish, whether it's practicing calligraphy, calculating on the abacus, reading sūtras or reciting the Buddha's name. With no sweat and no fuss, you get your daily fee. Your blessings must come from the good karma you acquired in previous lives." Another of them made even more painfully sarcastic remarks. One day he saw me practicing large, standard characters and said, "With your skill at calligraphy (actually my calligraphy even today is not as nice as a sixth-grader's), once you make it through a seminary —heh —I'd be surprised if monasteries didn't compete with one another for your services as abbot. When you get to be abbot, since we have connections with you, we can be sure of having easy duties and private apartments. When that happens, who will stop us from holding our beards to one side and drinking sesame oil to our hearts' content?" I had no choice but to bite my tongue and laugh at their remarks. Otherwise, I might as well have given up all hopes of leading a peaceful existence at Tung-yüeh Temple.

A Taiwanese saying goes: "The seventh month keeps monks hopping." Nanking was the same. With the coming of the seventh month of the lunar year, service assignment plaques at Tung-yüeh Temple were so densely covered with writing that nothing more could have been written on them. An average of four services were performed each day. The fourteen resident monks were naturally so busy that, whether they wanted to or not, they resembled the superior man described in the *Analects*: "In eating, he seeks not satiety; when resting, he seeks not quietude." The temple manager, too, was as busy as a horse painted on a revolving lantern. He was in and out incessantly, riding in a ricksha. Old Chao the cook was out looking for people to help with services and had no time to prepare meals. Luckily the monks were usually given meals at patron's houses; if not they had to serve the public on an empty stomach. Things were so hectic that even I, who had always been "free to do as I wanted," was not free anymore. Aside from doing normal office work and receiving guests who came to arrange for services and burn incense, I was busy taking care of ledgers and incoming funds: therefore I barely had time to breathe. In short, we were all so busy for the sake of money that we did not know if we were coming or going. We were losing our minds. The temple manager, especially, got more ill-tempered as he got busier. One evening as he was coming in he tripped on the door jamb of the great shrine hall. He turned and fiercely kicked the door jamb twice, then shouted at Old Chao: "Why don't you put a bigger light here in the doorway?"

The next day I came back from a meal of griddle-cakes to find the temple manager in the front courtyard talking with a few monks about the problem of how to get outside help. He said, "The rule in Nanking is that guest helpers are paid double fees. We can't find anyone, even at the rate of two and a half times the normal fee. What can we do? If Old Chao hadn't stood in on last night's 'release of burning mouths,' we would have been obliged to return money that we already had in hand." Then, noticing my presence, he looked like one who has discovered a saviour. He grabbed my hand and said, "Hey, brother! How about this: let me attend to the office work, and we'll ask you to go out with the others and serve the patrons. You know that if only seven men show up for a service that's supposed to be done by eight, the patron will not be happy. If we make the patron unhappy, that's like running a business and offending a customer. If we go on this way, what will we eat?" I answered, "I am unable to beat time, recite or chant. How can I serve the patrons?" He laughed, "That doesn't matter. You ask them if you don't believe me. Is there a single one of them that didn't start out in profound ignorance? But now they're proficient at gongs, chimes and the wooden fish. If you are willing to make an effort to learn, I'll guarantee you that before the year is out, you'll be beating the wooden fish in the ceremony for hungry ghosts." Some of the resident monks added, "In this world there is no such thing as a heaven born Tathāgata or a natural Śākyamuni. If you don't know, learn! Frankly speaking, regardless of what your feelings are toward conducting funerals, if you occupy a funerary position, everyone will say you are a monk who works funerals. Rather than be one in name but not in reality, wouldn't it be a relief to be one in both name and reality? Actually, no monk is willing to throw away precious years chanting '*ma ni hum*.'[1] But we are forced to do it by these troubled times, aren't we?" Then, seemingly forgetful of what they had just said, they yelled in high-pitched chorus: "Take every day as it comes and leave it at that. It's a life too!" They sounded like victims of severe hysteria.

On Working Funerals

Finally, under the press of circumstances, I went out with the other monks to serve the public. That is, I finally became a monk who worked funerals, both in name and reality. I remember clearly that this happened in 1946, on the fifteenth day of the seventh month of the lunar calendar.

Originally, sūtras were the recorded words of the Buddha, and requiems were devised in accordance with the teachings of virtuous men of long ago. For a monk to chant sūtras, conduct requiems or "release the ravenous ghosts" after a person's death, if done properly and honestly, is a "door of expediency" [*fang-pien fa-men*][2] which benefits himself and others: there is nothing to be said against it. The sad thing is that some people view this beneficial door of expediency as a business deal. Because of this, the result of performing funeral services is that others are not benefited and harm is done to oneself and the Buddhist religion. In the half-year that I worked funerals in Nanking, I saw gifted, talented young monks spit blood and die because of bad habits they had acquired while working funerals. I also saw large, respected monasteries which, because they were doing funeral business, fostered a number of degenerate sons and thus brought shame upon their good names. Did these young monks not harm themselves by working funerals? Did the monasteries not harm the Buddhist religion by making a business of funerals? I make bold to say one thing: the demoralization of today's monastic order and the decline of Buddhism are influenced largely by the flourishing of funeral services conducted for money. In hopes of persuading young monks to resolve, "better to freeze and starve to death sitting on a bask prayer mat than to be a funerary monk in this world of men," I do not shrink from "coming forth in person to preach the law" and exposing my own faults, to show the disparity between working funerals as I knew them and the ideal of the sangha.

It happened that on my first day working funerals in an official capacity, I took part in a funeral procession beyond Central Gate. Our group numbered seven monks, all wearing red ritual robes of coarse hemp cloth. The two monks in front clanged large cymbals, while the remaining five carried a hand chime, a small wooden fish, a gong, a bell and a hand-held drum. We marched along in the procession, hurrying to keep up with the coffin. The mischievous coffin bearers appeared to be making a joke at our expense. When they saw that the seven of us were about to catch up, they yelled "*yo ho*" and started forward at a quick run. In order to make a few measly cents, to please the deceased's survivors, to win the temple manager's praise and to keep from being looked down on by the coffin bearers, we had to remain within a certain distance of the coffin. To do this we had to disregard all considerations of the dignity of our station and chase doggedly after the coffin. With our heads exposed to the fiery heat of the sun and our feet treading the searing asphalt road, we stayed close behind, alternately dashing and sauntering. Our red ritual robes bellied out in the wind so that from afar each of us appeared to be carrying a large red ball on his back. We cut a ridiculous figure! At times like this, seeing people staring or laughing at me brought a flash of stinging fire to my face, and I would quickly lower my head, supposing that they were laughing at us for being "social parasites."

When we returned in the evening our clothes were soaked through with sweat. We had just eaten and bathed and were ready to lie down and stretch our legs when the temple manager walked in carrying his ever-present little teapot. With a smile spreading across his face, he said to the group leader: "At eight o'clock there is to be a 'deathbed sūtra reading' [*tao-t'ou-ching*][3] at a certain residence. I'd like to impose on all of you once again." We were eating at his temple, and regardless of how unwilling we all were, we had to submit obediently and "carry out his teachings."

The subject of "deathbed sūtra readings" is an interesting one. A typical episode went something like this: An old gentleman of the Chang residence was lying on his deathbed. At this time a go-between — one of the women who specialized in introducing the services of a temple to prospective patrons — came to the temple to hire a group. People of Nanking addressed monks as "gentlemen monks," but in the eyes of the go-betweens this title was subject to further distinctions. They called upper-level gentlemen monks (men like abbots, resident superintendents and temple managers) "esteemed sir." Middle-level gentlemen monks (quick, alert, young, handsome ones who could wear a Vairocana headdress in the release of burning mouths ceremony) were "so-so" [*ma-ma hu-hu*]. Lower-level gentlemen monks (slavish monks who quarreled with their fists and just mumbled along during sūtra readings) were called "big turnips." Naturally these go-betweens, who depended on Buddhism for the food they ate and relied on monks for the clothes they wore, played up to gentlemen monks of the upper and middle levels. At the same time, they did not deign to notice the "big turnips." The upper and middle level monks, for their part, treated the go-betweens with unflagging respect and "accorded them the honor due to deities." They seemed to be in great fear of "incurring the displeasure of heaven," lest they leave themselves with "no one toward whom they might address their prayers."

The go-between came into the temple and, wagging her voluble tongue, began a head-to-head conversation with an "esteemed sir," telling him the thus-and-so of her mission. When the esteemed sir had given his consent, she called for the so-so monk (the one who led the funerary group) and explained to him the location of the Chang residence and the number of monks needed for the deathbed sūtra reading. The so-so gentleman monk then rounded up a few even more so-so regular monks and, if still more heads were needed, one or two big turnips. Then each person folded a full-sleeved gown under his arm, and the company sashayed over to the Chang residence (occasionally monks were also transported by car or ricksha). The waiter (usually hired temporarily) at the Chang residence had already brewed tea and set out snacks. Thereupon, the so-so monk took the head seat with a great air of self-importance and, crossing his legs comfortably, conversed uninhibitedly with the go-between or the patron. This was a blessed interval for the other so-so monks and the big turnips, because they could convey quite a few desserts into the "temple of the five vital organs." Then the lay workman who carried the sūtra boxes yelled, "Everything is set up. Would the gentlemen monks please open the scriptures?" Only then did it occur to everyone that they were there to read deathbed sūtras for the old gentleman Mr. Chang, who was even then kicking the covers and fighting his last fight.

The power of the Buddhadharma is, after all, incomprehensible. Within fifteen minutes the old gentleman of the Chang family had peacefully breathed his last to the accompaniment of the monks' sūtra chanting and Buddha-name reciting, thus escaping the agony of a deathbed struggle. The old gentleman's filial sons and virtuous grandsons, plus an assortment of distant relatives and close neighbors, gathered like a swarm of bees. Without asking whether "Mr. Eight Senses"[4] — the "master of our life" who is the "first to arrive and the last to depart" — had fled his body or not, some of them wailed and burned paper offerings while others milled around noisily dressing the old gentleman in his best clothes, finding him a hat to wear and putting on his boots. The sūtra-chanting monks were pushed back until they had no place to stand. Backing up one step after another, they found themselves in the rear courtyard with nothing to do but turn their faces toward the sky and count the twinkling stars.

When the corpse had been fully dressed, the deceased's son, accompanied by the lay workman, came to the courtyard and kowtowed three times to the monks. Lest the reader think he did this out of humility or respect toward the monks, I must point out that this was no more than his way of applying pressure on them to hurry them into the spirit hall [*ling-t'ang*][5] so as to keep the newly deceased old gentleman company.

When the filial son had finished prostrating himself, the monks followed him into the spirit hall. All of one accord, they inexplicably made a deep bow to the dead man. Only then did the deathbed sūtra reading begin in earnest.

With the opening of the sūtras, the clamor of voices stopped, and the atmosphere of the spirit hall became chillingly somber. By then the distant relatives and close neighbors had already gone away; the female members of the family had withdrawn; the mourning sons had prostrated themselves before the deathbed and were lying on the floor without a sound; and the joss money in the iron pot, having nearly burned itself out, was sending up green tongues of flame which licked at the edges of the pot. Their ghostly flickerings took on the appearance of old Mister Chang's hand rising out of the joss money ashes to point and gesture to his sons and grandsons about readying a sum of money for a trip to the underworld. The lay workman and the waiter were engaged in a muted but leisurely conversation. Looking exactly like the two impish ghosts painted on the wall at the Temple of the City God as guards of the gate to the underworld, they seemed to be devising a scheme to put the squeeze on Mr. Chang's ghost. What about the monks? They kept up their half-hearted drone, binding precious minutes and hours of their lives to a few stinking copper coins.

It was late at night when the sūtras were finished. The waiter brought a small pot of glutinous rice porridge and four small side dishes. "Would the gentlemen monks please partake? This food cools the internal temperature," he urged courteously. How could he know that the monks, after marching in a funeral procession all day and chanting sūtras most of the night, were so exhausted in mind and body that they could think of nothing but a good sleep? He could have talked himself blue in the face and the monks would not have taken the slightest notice. With the clumsiness of the drunk, each of them folded his robe under his arm and staggered home to Tung-yüeh Temple.

Once there, everyone chipped in to make a sum of several dozen dollars. They shouted at Old Chao to wake him out of his deep sleep and sent him to Pao-t'ai Street to buy a few pounds of machine-extruded noodles at a shop run by a Shantungese. When he got back, he looked around in the kitchen for leftover vegetables from supper. He boiled these together with the noodles, and they commenced eating. Coincidentally, everyone had no sooner taken bowls in hand and started shovelling noodles into their mouths when the other group that had gone out to perform a release of hungry ghosts came back. Without asking any questions as to who had provided the noodles, they filled their bowls and ate, unmoved by the sarcasms and jeers of those who had paid for the meal. Everyone talked, laughed, ate and raised an uproar. When it came time to lie down in bed, they were oblivious to the pale light in the East.

At an hour when everyone was interested in nothing more than continuing their all-too-short slumbers, the temple manager urged them again and again to get out of bed. The group leader rubbed his bleary eyes and roared angrily: "Little top! What are you doing, yelling and carrying on like a ghost so early in the morning?"

The temple manager had this in his favor: as long as services were going smoothly and the money was rolling in, the resident monks could banter with him or direct humorous invective at him, and he took it all in good stride. If, however, there were no services for three days, or there were too many services for the resident monks to handle and no help could be gotten from the outside, then no one dared to make jokes. Otherwise, when he lost control of his bull-like temper, you would end up creeping away with your tail between your legs! His reason for flying into a rage at Old Chao when he tripped over the door jamb the day before was that there had been too many services and no help could be gotten from the outside. The heads of the groups were old hands at Tung-yüeh Temple who had sounded out the manager's temperament until they were totally familiar with it. So this time, when told he was "yelling and carrying on like a ghost," he did not get angry, but walked instead to the group leader's bedside. Pointing at the group leader's nose, he too indulged in a bit of ridicule: "Nice boy. Has sleep befuddled your brain? Didn't the Sun and Li families both hire seven-man groups to read sūtras today? Get up, nice boy. There will be extra alms for sure at this evening's release of the hungry ghosts."

For monks who worked funerals in Nanking, life was like this from morning till night, day in and day out. There was not much variation. If there was any at all, it came when there were no services to conduct. How did we pass the time when there were no services? That depended on each person's interests. Those who had weaknesses for some pursuit were free to go out and look for what they needed. No matter how improper their behavior, they were responsible for their own actions: the temple manager did not concern himself with such matters. Those who had no particular hobby could bury their heads in the covers and sleep the day away. If they felt bored by all that sleeping, they could get together with a couple of congenial friends and go beyond Central Gate to see Ling-ku Monastery, the Tomb of Dr. Sun Yat-sen and the Ming tombs; beyond Chung-hua Gate to see Yü-hua Pavilion and Hsüan-wu Lake; beyond Shui-hsi Gate to see Mo-ch'ou Lake; beyond Kuan-yin Gate to see Yen-tzu Cliff; or below Chi-ming Monastery to see the City of Terraces. Toward late autumn it was even better to go on an excursion to Ch'i-hsia Mountain, if one were so inclined.

The mountains and ravines there were covered with fiery red maple leaves, and there were uncountable vistas and remains of ancient art. There were such things as the beautiful overview of Ch'i-hsia Monastery, the stone caves of Thousand Buddha Cliff, the series of eight murals depicting the Buddha's enlightenment on a reliquary pagoda, the strange old characters carved on a memorial to King Yü, and the "waves of pine trees" on Gauze Hat Peak, not to mention Peach Blossom Ravine, Pearl Spring, the "ray of Heaven" showing between two rock faces, and the "Flying Buddha" rock formation. All of these scenic wonders made the beholder "forget to return in his delight." Wandering at will among these sights would surely have had a cleansing effect on begrimed and narrowed minds, but regrettably, monks who worked funerals had too little interest in such things. If this were not so, why did they resemble old elephants that sink into an inextricable mire?

The most vexing aspect of filling a funerary position was that even when there was leisure time one could not put one's mind at rest and study. Let us say there were no services on a certain day, and you wanted to stay in your room to sit in meditation or recite the Buddha's name or read scriptures. If your roommates did not call you a fanatic, they said you were putting on airs. When you did sit in meditation, they jeered: "Your legs are a perfect sitting position. Why don't you go live at Chin-shan or Kao-min? After three winters and five summers there, you might even find your face as it was before your mother bore you."[6] If you were reciting the Buddha's name, they said, "Why not go to Ling-yen Mountain. Ling-yen is a place of truth where you can devote yourself to reciting Amitābha's name. With your level of advancement, you'll have no trouble getting samādhi after one intensive recitation week." If they saw you reading scriptures, they would say, "Fellow seeker, I think you ought to go to Kuan-tsung Monastery in Ningpo and study doctrine. When you become a dharma master, you'll be the principal lecturer and I'll be precentor. Won't that be much better than being in this racket — beating this gong and chanting '*ma-ni-hum ma-ni-hum*' every day from morning till night?" In short, existing in that environment was like being a moth among wasps. First they "walled you off and buried you — fattening you in seclusion." After a time they were not satisfied until you were transformed into one of them.

Among the fourteen resident monks at Tung-yüeh Temple there were two group heads. One of them was called Le-ch'an. He was a few years over thirty. He was short in stature but distinguished by his features, his speech and his skill in chanting. He had served as precentor for several monasteries at P'u-t'o Island. Because he had been a companion of Hsi-ch'u, on becoming manager Hsi-chu had invited him to return from the island and act as head of a group at Tung-yüeh Temple. When he first arrived, his determination for spiritual work could not have been better. No matter how busy he was with services, he recited the *Mantra of Great Compassion* [*Ta-pei Chou*] a hundred and eight times morning and evening with great concentration and repeated the holy name of Kuan-yin a great number of times. This was his daily regimen. But after less than half a year his spiritual determination plunged like a thermometer in icy water. It plunged so much that smoking opium and drinking liquor took the place of concentrating on mantras and reciting the Buddha's name. His earnings were at least three times those of a normal monk, but he lived so carelessly that, in the end, he had no trousers to wear. I remember once in the seventh month of the lunar calendar, when we went to the foot of Chiu-hua Mountain to conduct rites for universal salvation [*p'u-tu yen-k'ou*]. With the naked lower half of his body covered only by his gown and robe, he went onto the dais. We had chanted to the part that says: "The Great King of Light [Ta-ming-wang] whose name consists of six words,[7] your merit is without bound. Now your pure, clean votaries appear before you, proclaiming your might with one voice." Just then he called softly to the man beating time on the wooden fish: "Friend, I've pissed on myself."

The other group head was called Jen-shan. He was the tonsure brother of Jen-i, the manager of Kuan-yin Temple in Nanking. He was clever and handsome. (I still have a small snapshot of him.) He had a good voice too. He was well versed in all the tricks of the funeral trade that were popular then in Nanking, such as "Sprinkling Flowers" [*san-hua*], "Lamenting the Skull" [*t'an k'u-lou*], "Lamenting Seven-and-Seven" [*t'an ch'i-ch'i*], "Seven Cups of Tea" [*ch'i-pei ch'a*] and "Seven Cups of Wine" [*ch'i-pei chiu*].[8] Because of his excellent qualifications, he began working funerals for Tung-yüeh Temple at fifteen. At seventeen he took his place on the group leader's "throne." The temple manager often called him "precious boy" [*hsiao kuai-kuai*] instead of Jen-shan. The go-betweens, who frequented temples and depended on monks for a living, considered it an honor to adopt him as a godson. As a result he had so many godmothers and godsisters that he himself could not keep the number straight.

In 1946 Jen-shan's tonsure brother, dharma master Jen-yi, fled the troubled conditions in Ssu-yang and went to Nanking. At first he stayed at Tung-yüeh Temple, but seeing his brother's tendency to cave in to circumstances displeased him. He once said to me: "Nothing can be said against a monk who, having left his home temple to seek knowledge, fills a funerary position for a time in order to earn clothes money. But don't ever be so deluded by money that you can't turn around and get out!" Although he was a funerary specialist, his perceptivity enabled him to preserve the demeanor of a true seeker. He "flowed with the current" but did not "mix with the filth." He was indeed a unique flower in the "garden of service" [*ying-yüan*](the Great Master Lien-ch'ih's[9] term for funerary work). Later he went to manage Kuan-yin Temple through the introduction of Monk Chun-ling of P'i-lu Monastery. Before leaving he gave Jen-shan a good talking to, expressing his hopes that Jen-shan would leave Tung-yüeh Temple to study at a Buddhist seminary or else live in a monastery that had an atmosphere conducive to spiritual work. But in the end Jen-shan disappointed him. One could hardly blame him. Day in and day out he conducted himself crudely and self-indulgently in the presence of women. How can you tell a person accustomed to these things to live in a strictly regulated monastery and eat old rice, sit on cold hard stools, eat soup made with foul pickles and sleep on a large mat with many other monks? What was more, he was the key pillar supporting Tung-yüeh Temple's Buddhist ceremonies. The temple manager would never give him up without a flight. Not long after leaving Nanking, I heard that he had received internal injuries while showing off his skills at singing and chanting, and that he often coughed up blood. He went to stay at P'i-lu Monastery for a time but left soon after. After that I never heard news of him again.

Both of these monks were young and full of potential. Because a single covetous thought crossed their minds, they took the wrong road and walked from delusion into greater delusion. They went on justifying their wrongs with even greater wrongs until their humanity, that most precious among the five realms of rebirth,[10] sank into an unfathomable morass of filthy mud. They had no strength to pull themselves out, and others may have wanted to give them aid but were unable. There was nothing anyone could do but stare helplessly as they sank further and further down.

Writing this brings to mind a story about Ch'an Master Kao-feng Miao (1238-1295).[11] Kao-feng Miao was a venerable scholar of the Ch'an school, but in his youth he was proficient in working funerals. One night, after releasing hungry ghosts at a patron's home, he passed through a rural village on his way back to the monastery. Many of the village dogs barked crazily and jumped at him. He was in a quandary as to how to deal with this when he heard an old woman in a thatched cottage ask: "Who could that be, walking about at this hour of the night and making the dogs bark their heads off?"

The he heard an old man answer, "What decent person would be out there walking at a time like this? If it's not a monk coming back from working funerals, it's a robber."

When Ch'an Master Kao-feng Miao heard this he was both angry and ashamed. He thought: "That's nonsense! Why didn't he compare monks with something good instead of lumping us together with robbers?" Then another thought came to him: "Actually, I've brought this on myself. Since I have renounced lay life, I should study the sciptures and spread the dharma, or I should make an out-and-out effort to better myself spiritually — to solve the problem of samsara. Why do I resign myself so willinglyto dissipation for the sake of a career that inverts night and day?" Thereupon, he resolved "rather to die of hunger and thirst on a rush prayer mat than to chant services in the world of men." Later he did indeed go on to become one of the great monks of his time.

Finally, I hope that after reading this story, young brothers of the cloth who are entrapped in this morass and have no strength to pull themselves out will somehow find the strength to jump out of the muck.

NOTES

1. This is a corruption of the famous mantra "*O mani padme hum*" (O, the Jewel in the Lotus!). When this is read very rapidly, one can only catch the sounds of *mani hum*.

2. "Expediency" (*fang-pien*, upāya) refers to the Buddha's ability to adapt his teaching to his audience's level of understanding. This is a highly prized virtue in Mahāyāna Buddhism. The *Lotus Sūtra* provides many examples of the Buddha's upāya. Broadly speaking, any method one employs to make Buddhism more readily accessible to people is *fang-pien*. Therefore, to serve the public by performing *ching-ch'an* is originally one of the ways to make them become interested in Buddhism.

3. *Tao-t'ou* means to put one's head down (to sleep). From the context it appears to mean to recite the sūtra in front of a dying man (who is lying down) to help him die a peaceful death. It has a similar psychological function to the sacrament of supreme unction in Catholicism.

4. According to Buddhism, consciousness is the last part of a man to disappear when he dies and the first to appear when a new life is conceived. Consciousness is divided into eight parts (*pa-shih*): the five senses of sight, hearing, smell, taste and touch; the manovijñāna which coordinates the first five as a sense center; the manas which is responsible for creating the illusion of an ego and thus is called the "I-maker"; and finally, the ālayavijñāna (the storehouse) consciousness which serves as the basis for all the other seven

and from which all seven evolve.

5. This is the room where the corpse is laid out. Close relatives of the dead person keep vigil beside the corpse day and night. Friends who come to bid farewell to the dead and offer condolences to the living also come to this room.

6. This is a very popular *kung-an* used by Ch'an masters at many monasteries. It goes, "Before your parents gave birth to you, what was your original face?"

7. Mahāvairocana, the Great Sun Buddha, is being invoked here.

8. The "tricks of the trade" mentioned here were various tunes the monks sang during funeral services or ceremonies of feeding the hungry ghosts. Even though the melody as indicated by the title of the tune is fixed, monks were free to improvise the words as they went along. The titles of these tunes all have some Buddhist significance. "Sprinkling flowers" refers to the story of the goddess (*t'ien-nü*) in the *Vimalakirti Sūtra*, Chapter 7: When the layman Vimalakirti lectured on the Void (Śūnyatā), the goddess was so delighted by it that she sprinkled heavenly flowers on the assembly. Thereupon, an interesting thing happened. "When the flowers fell on the bodies of the bodhisattvas, they fell off on the floor, but when they fell on the bodies of the great disciples, they stuck on them and did not fall. The great disciples shook the flowers and even tried to use their magical powers, but still the flowers would not shake off." This embarrassed the disciples, for to wear flowers was against the precept prohibiting novices and monks from adorning themselves. It was improper, according to Śāriputra. The goddess proved her superior understanding of Buddhism by saying to Śāriputra, the leader of the disciples, "These flowers are proper indeed! Why? Such flowers have neither constructual thought nor discrimination. But the elder Śāriputra has both constructual thought and discrimination.... Reverend Śāriputra, see how these flowers do not stick to the bodies of these great spiritual heroes, the bodhisattvas! This is because they have eliminated constructual thoughts and discriminations.... These flowers stick to the bodies of those who have not eliminated their instincts for the passions and do not stick to the bodies of those who have eliminated their instincts. Therefore, the flowers do not stick to the bodies of the bodhisattvas, who have abandoned all instincts." *The Holy Teaching of Vimalakirti*, tr. by Robert A.F.Thurman (University Park and London: The Pennsylvania State University Press, 1976), pp. 58-59.

However, even though the tune bears a title which is rich with Buddhist allusions, the words accompanying the tune may have nothing to do with the *Vimalakirti Sūtra*. Similarly, the other tunes usually express secular, instead of religious concerns. "Lamenting the Skull" was a song addressed to the dead person. "Lamenting the Seven Sevens" was a song sung to the dead passing through the forty-nine days before rebirth. Like the *Tibetan Book of the Dead*, these may originally be intended as sermons to the dead person cautioning him against seeking rebirth. The last two songs were secular in nature. This is clear even by the wording of the titles. "The seven cups" of tea or wine refer to the tea or wine (!) offered to the officiating monks, who usually number seven. The tunes were popular in Nanking and Shanghai, as well as other places in Chekiang and Kiangsu. One can see why monks with good singing voices were highly sought after. The performance at *ching-ch'an* was very much like entertainment. In fact, especially in the countryside, large crowds of people would flock to attend Buddhist *ching-ch'an* services and regard them no diffently than theatrical performances. I am grateful to Rev. Sheng-yen of the Ch'an Center at Elmhurst, New York, for the above information. He is about the same age as Chen-hua and shares many similar experiences with the latter. The tunes were popular in Nanking and Shanghai, as well as other places in Chekiang and Kiangsu.

9. Master Lien-ch'ih's full name was Yün-ch'i Chu-hung (1535-1615). He was one of four Buddhist leaders active at the end of the Ming Dynasty. He was famous for his effort to revive the monastic discipline. He was very critical of *ching-ch'an* services, calling monks working at funerals "*ying-fu seng*" (monks responding to calls). See my book *The Renewal of Buddhism in China: Chu-hung and the Late Ming Synthesis* (Columbia University Press, 1981) for more information.

10. The five realms of rebirth (*wu-ch'u, gati*) are gods, human beings, animals, hungry ghosts and beings in hell. According to the karma one creates in one life, he will be reborn in any one of the five realms in his next life.

11. Kao-feng Yüan-miao (1238-1295) was an eminent Ch'an master during the Yüan Dynasty. He was known for his austerity, once shutting himself up in solitary confinement in a cave called "Gate of Death" on Mt. T'ien-mu for seventeen years. He was the teacher of Chung-feng Ming-pen (1263-1323), another famous Ch'an master in the late Yüan. See my article, "*Chung-feng Ming-pen and Ch'an Buddhism in the Yüan*," included in *Yuan*

Thought: Chinese Thought and Religion under the Mongols, ed. by Wm. Theodore deBary and Hok-lam Chan (New York: Columbia University Press, 1982), pp. 419-477.

It is customary to omit the third character in a monk's name; thus he is called Kao-feng Miao here in this book. Usually the first two characters in a monk's name refer to his monastery or the mountain on which the monastery was situated, and the last two characters are his personal name. Thus, Kao-feng Yüan-miao actually means Yüan-miao of Kao-feng.

Chapter V

STUDYING AT T'IEN-NING

After passing another lunar New Year in Nanking, I entered the seminary at T'ien-ning Monastery in Changchow. Though I remained there for only one year, it was a year that made me learn through experience about methods of survival in monastic society. As simple and ordinary as these methods were, if you did not understand them, or understood them but could not apply them, then your life in that environment would be like a journey in a desert with no oases ahead and no villages behind.

For enabling me to enter T'ien-ning Seminary, I am first grateful to Ho-hsüan, the former abbot of Chi-ming Monastery. If it had not been for his encouragement, I do not know when I would have had the determination to leave Tung-yüeh Temple. Next I would like to thank Upāsaka Wei P'u-chi of the Changchow Devotees Club [*chü-shih lin*]. If he had not given his hearty recommendation, there would have been little hope of making it through the front gate of T'ian-ning Seminary for an "Old Guy with a Brogue" like myself. (This was how my younger classmates at the seminary addressed me. Actually I had not yet turned twenty-six.) The circumstances surrounding my admittance are worthy of note.

One day, probably late in the fall of 1946, Ho-hsüan brought a dignified, portly gentleman to Tung-yüeh Temple to see me. I found out from Ho-hsüan's introduction that this was Upāsaka Wei P'u-chi, who had taken refuge with Ho-hsüan. It seems that the Devotees Club over which he presided was involved in land litigation, and he had come to Nanking to pursue the case in the Supreme Court. So why did Ho-hsüan bring him to see me? Ho-hsüan's aim was to have Wei recommend me for admittance to Tien-ning Seminary. Wei was a refreshingly forthright sort who hailed from northern Hsü-chou. Because his older brother worked at Wu-hsi, he too had come south. Later, through the agency of I don't know which supernatural power, he became a "noted personage" in Buddhist circles. He himself had a large number of disciples who took refuge with him. Before we had exchanged ten sentences he promised to help me: "Retired Abbot So-and-so of T'ien-ning Monastery is my master. (I found out later that at least a dozen different masters had administered the Three Refuges to him.) The present abbot is a friend. Two of the dharma masters who teach in the seminary get along very well with me. Don't you fret: I guarantee you'll get into T'ien-ning." My happiness at hearing this was too great to be described.

Sure enough, Upāsaka P'u-chi's assurances came true early in the first lunar month of 1947. He wrote a letter saying he had already made the necessary contacts. He instructed me to go to the Pure Land Devotees Club in Changchow on the twelfth and look him up. After giving me a chance to stay and rest for a day or two, he would accompany me to T'ien-ning Monastery to report for examination. I hurried over to Chi-ming Monastery to let Former Abbot Ho-hsüan read the letter. He seemed even more delighted than I. Excitedly he said, "Wonderful! Wonderful! Hurry back to Tung-yüeh Temple and prepare. The sooner you get to the seminary, the sooner my worries will be over. Go back. Hurry up and prepare. I'll go to Tung-yüeh Temple at noon of the eleventh to see you off."

It shames me to say it, but I have a failing: with everyday acquaintances I can always string together a few polite phrases, but with friends who understand me or people who have treated me with kindness I cannot utter a single sentence in acknowledgement. Common principles of human conduct dictated that I should say a few words of gratitude to someone who had thought so sincerely of my welfare as Ho-hsüan had. However, without so much as an ordinary "thank you," I hurried back to Tung-yüeh Temple.

"Master Chün-shan is going to T'ien-ning Monastery in Changchow on the twelfth of this month!" On the evening of the day I received Upāsaka Wei's letter, the temple manager and the resident monks spread this information as if it were earthshaking news. Though they were not as happy as Ho-hsüan, they did trouble themselves to discuss how to give me a farewell party and what sort of gift to buy me. The temple manager, besides paying for a two-table farewell feast for myself and the resident monks, hired a cart on the day of my departure so that he, Ho-hsüan, Hai-hsiu, Dharma Master Jen-i and a few others could see me off at the train station in Hsia-kuan.

No one in Buddhist circles is unfamiliar with the reputation of T'ien-ning Monastery—that great place of truth. It was not only the most richly endowed public monastery in the whole province of Kiangsu, but it also had a place among the leading monasteries in all of China. Moreover, it was a great refining furnace which forged accomplished monks through its rigorous program of winter meditation and summer study. All young monks considered being allowed to study there a great honor. As a "guy with a northern brogue" who had suffered many hardships and insults in coming south of the Yangtze to seek spiritual instruction, I was filled with mingled joy and apprehension that day, January 16, 1947, as I walked behind

Upāsaka Wei P'u-chi, my bundle on my shoulders and a small wicker basket in my hand, into T'ien-ning Seminary.

The first thing that met my eyes inside the door was a row of neatly dressed monks sitting on a long bench. On the desk before each of them lay a sheet of lined paper. With pens in hand, they twisted their ears and scratched their cheeks in thought. A dharma master walked back and forth before them. I did not have to be told that he was monitoring an exam. He caught sight of us and quickly walked over. When Wei pressed his palms together, the dharma master grabbed his hands and let out a loud laugh. Wei pointed to me and said, "This is Master Chün-shan. In the future please..." Before he finished, the dharma master broke in: "Don't worry! Don't worry! It's enough that he was recommended by such an eminent protector of the Law." Then Wei signaled me to prostrate myself to the dharma master. When I had done so, he directed me to sit down beside another examinee and handed me a sheet of the same paper. He told me to write a composition of at least three hundred characters on "Why I Have Come to Study at a Buddhist Seminary." My heart started pounding uncontrollably at the words "write a composition." Many years ago, while studying in a private schoolhouse, I had written one or two compositions of the "topic and exposition" type, but the heap of classical expressions I threw together rambled away from the topic rather than being an exposition of it. As a result I got a good scolding from the schoolmaster, who said I must have thought I was Chang Fei[1] because I tried to "plow" [homophonous in Chinese with "digress"] all the way back to the Three Kingdom's Period. After that I would rather have turned in a blank paper than write whatever came into my head again. But turning in a blank paper now would embarrass Upāsaka Wei and would expose me to the stares of my fellow examinees. These considerations motivated me to fish nervously in my pocket for the trusty old fountain pen I had brought from up north. Over and over I read the title to myself: "'Why I Have Come to Study at a Buddhist Seminary'...'Why I Have Come to Study at a Buddhist Seminary.'" Poor me! I repeated this silently for all of ten minutes, but my mind was nothing but a big blank. I could not even come up with one sentence to explain why I had come to study at a Buddhist Seminary. The student next to me, seeing that my pen was not moving, though my mouth was working away as if muttering a mantra, whispered, "Go ahead and write whatever comes into your head. You needn't worry about not being admitted." At the time I didn't stop to think of what he really meant. I carelessly dashed off a few sentences and turned the paper in. Later when I thought about what he said, I realized that he was actually making fun of me. But I really couldn't blame him, because I had once again been guilty of "relying on personal connections." Thanks to the compassion of the dharma masters, I was placed in the preliminary class [*hsien-hsiu k'e*] the day after my arrival. Only then did I learn that the seminary students were divided into three classes — the preliminary class, the preparatory class [*yü-k'e*], and the main class [*cheng k'e*]. Qualifications for admission and length of time for each level were fixed by rules, but these were not inflexible. The requirement for admission to the preliminary class was a grade school education or the equivalent; that for the preliminary level was lower middle school or the equivalent; and that for the main class was upper middle school or the equivalent. The length of time for each level was three years. According to the rules, it should have taken nine years to complete the curriculum. In fact this was not the case. Those who made excellent grades in the preliminary class could be placed after one year or even one term in the preparatory class. Excellent students in the preparatory class could, in the same way, be placed in the main class. Excellent students in the main class were absolved of certain curricular requirements so they could delve into subjects of interest to them.

There were thirty to forty students in each class. There were no strict rules with regard to age, but the oldest of us was not over thirty. I was twenty-six years old the year I entered the seminary (according to Western reckoning, I had not yet turned twenty-five). Already many classmates pointed at me and called me "Old Guy with a Brogue" when my back was turned. Fortunately I was promoted to the preparatory class after one semester. Since there were a number of classmates even "older" than I in the preparatory class, fewer people now called me "Old Guy with a Brogue."

T'ien-ning Seminary was an educational institution founded as an adjunct to T'ien-ning Monastery for the purpose of training young monks. The seminary was located on the right side of the monastery. Outside its wall was a river which flowed by the east gate of Changchow and served as a moat. Commercial craft and pleasure boats seldom plied the river, but there were always a couple of medium sized sailboats moored at the bank. These were the boats used by monks from T'ien-ning Monastery on their rent collecting expeditions.

In front of the seminary and close to the monastery's main gate was a road leading to downtown Changchow. Morning and night the cries of vendors hawking their wares rose and fell along this road, but that had no effect on the monks in the seminary and monastery, because T'ien-ning Monastery was a vast complex. Monks born and raised in Taiwan find it difficult to imagine how vast it was. No matter how clever you were, if there were no one to guide you, you would have a difficult time finding your way out. The rear and left sides of the seminary were within the monastery enclosure, but the sounds coming from inside it were no hindrance to our classes. Because of this, people who made tours through the seminary all said it was an ideal environment for learning.

The seminary was housed in a square two-story building built around a central courtyard. Three of the downstairs rooms were the large, well-lit classrooms for the preliminary, preparatory and main classes. The other room was a dining room for student monks which doubled as an auditorium. Two of the four rooms upstairs were used as dormitories. Books were kept in another. I do not clearly remember what the fourth was used for. There were side courts situated at three of the four corners of the building. Two of these had teachers' quarters and one had quarters for waiters [*hsing-t'ang*]. The seminary gate was at the fourth corner. Outside of the gate was the bulletin board of the office of instructional affairs, where notices to the student body were posted. The room just inside the gate had been intended for the preliminary class, but since the class was so small, the rear part was partitioned off as a reading room.

Within the enclosure made by the dining room and three classrooms was a large courtyard. This was where the student monks strolled, chatted and did morning calisthenics. One fair-sized, broad-leaved tree grew in each of the four corners of the courtyard. The dense green foliage imparted life and natural color to the setting.

Behind the main-course classroom was another small courtyard where students washed their faces and rinsed their mouths, hung clothing out to dry, cooked snacks and boiled medicinal herbs when they were sick. All things considered, at a time when monasteries gave little priority to the education of monks, the environment and facilities at T'ien-ning Monastery were passable. On the other hand, the food was poor, and some of the dharma masters who taught there were such that I do not make bold to praise them.

The ancients said, "I have come for the dharma, not for beds and chairs." However, for student monks who "spend their years in persevering study, burning the oil they might have eaten so as to study late into the night," it is not too much to expect adequate vegetables, bean curd and rice twice a day. The alert reader might ask if it were indeed true that T'ien-ning, one of the wealthiest monasteries in China and one committed to the training of monks, did not give vegetables, bean curd and boiled rice to its students. It gave these things all right, but here I must add a footnote by way of qualification to each of these items, lest the reader think me unappreciative.

Truthfully speaking, T'ien-ning's fare was much better than at Pao-hua Mountain during the ordination period. At Pao-hua there were only two meals of boiled rice per month, but at T'ien-ning there were rice and fresh vegetables (or sometimes salted vegetables) every day. There was not much beancurd, but if your luck was good or the classmates who worked as waiters were especially solicitous, your vegetable bowl (soup bowl is more appropriate) might have two or three pieces somewhat bigger than sugar cubes. If your luck was poor — sorry! — you had to pour a bowlful of vegetable soup over your rice. Speaking of vegetable soup, I will use the following conversation between classmates as an illustration of what one could expect:

A: I get nauseated just thinking about today's lunch.
B: Why's that?
A: A waiter refilled my bowl of soup. I picked it up and was about to drink it when I saw a fat white maggot floating on the surface. I didn't want my classmates next to me to see it, so I picked it out with chopsticks and flung it on the floor. When I stirred the stuff around, it was too much: five or six more of them came to the top.
B: What's so strange about that! I picked a dung beetle out of mine!
C: By all means don't blame the manager or the subpriors in the business office for such things, because they eat food cooked in the small kitchen. How are they supposed to know about this?
D: Then whom should we blame?
C: Who's to blame? Hah! We should blame ourselves for having eyes. If we were like the vegetable-washing steward (a blind man), we wouldn't have anything to gripe about.

Veteran monks north and south of the Yangtze have a saying: "The fame of Chin-shan's illicit ham, of Kao-min's incense and of T'ien-ning's stuffed buns [*pao-tzu*] stands supreme over the three rivers." But when I studied at T'ien-ning, those famous buns turned out to be nothing more than a mouth-watering rumor. The monks who took part in the yearly winter meditation weeks were given two dumplings after evening meditation, but these were ordinary vegetable dumplings, no better than those served now at the restaurant in Taipei called the House of Vegetarian Cooking [Su-ts'ai Chih Chia]. Nevertheless, the old rice we ate three times a day could very properly have been said to stand supreme over the three rivers. I wonder if my old T'ien-ning classmates would vote in favor of changing the above saying.

Why do I say that the old rice at T'ien-ning stood supreme? From what I have said of T'ien-ning's wealth, the enormous crop rents it collected yearly can be imagined. Because the monastery collected so much and consumed so little, the rice piled up in mountains. Though everything possible was done to cart it out and sell it, the monks still ate rice that had been stored anywhere from five to upwards of ten years. Those who do not know the inside story might ask why, if so much new rice was collected each year, the monks ate old rice instead of new. Naturally the new rice was easier to sell. The old rice was so moldy it lumped together. Who would buy it? Moreover, those who held authority over money matters in the monastery claimed that old rice, though it tasted somewhat moldy, made people less susceptible to fiery humors, was easy to digest and was highly nutritious. As to whether this claim accords with the findings of nutritional science, I lack the knowledge to say. But it is a fact that after one got accustomed to the old rice, its moldy flavor seemed fragrant and tasty. Perhaps the reason is that "a starving man is easy to cook for." If not, it must have been due to the secret workings of the Buddha!

As for the dharma masters at T'ien-ning Monastery, there were a few who definitely fulfilled their responsibility to "transmit the dharma, teach doctrine and dispel perplexity," but most of them were inferior teachers. Saying this may land me in a position of being scoffed at for being like the young man who "bore witness against his father for stealing sheep." The dharma masters were, in effect, our spiritual fathers. Confucian thought holds that when parents do wrong, their children should remonstrate pleadingly with them. If their remonstrations have no effect, the children should conceal their parents' wrongs from outsiders. Śākyamuni, the great teacher of our faith, also taught his disciples to take this attitude toward teachers and elders: "Contemplate their virtues and do not contemplate their faults; yield to them and do not disobey." Now, instead of concealing the mistakes of my elders, I am examining their faults. Is this not an abominable crime? However, I presume to take this crime upon myself in order to urge masters who are now teaching or will someday teach in Buddhist seminaries not to imitate those inferior teachers who harmed others and themselves. Though I incur ridicule and even curses, I must speak of the teaching methods of those dharma masters and their attitude toward students.

Being a teacher is not easy. Besides teaching through words, there is the even more difficult task of teaching through example. For one who teaches young monks, it is especially important that neither of these two principles be slighted. When young monks complete their studies, they are not going to become ordinary "teaching hacks" who spend their lives just getting by.

On their shoulders will fall the responsibility to carry on tradition and pave the way for the future, to proclaim the Law and benefit living beings. But the dharma master who taught us seemed to be unaware of all this. They always liked to begin class with a few superfluous opening remarks. Rather than say that these were words of exhortation, it would be more fitting to say that they were venting their gripes by saying one thing and meaning another. This usually made the students feel as if they had fallen into a two-mile bank of fog: they did not know what the master was driving at. Only after the dharma master had spoken enough nonsense to suit himself would he open the textbook, pick up a piece of chalk and copy the text word for word onto the blackboard. When the blackboard was covered, he would put down the book and chalk, clap the powder off his hands, and walk back and forth on the podium with his hands behind his back. Occasionally he would stand in front of a student's desk and watch. When the students had finished copying, there was somewhere around ten minutes left until the end of the period. Thereupon he would explain the text according to his textbook notes, avoiding weighty points and dwelling on minor details, until the bell rang.

If the second period were taught by the same dharma master, that was even more fun to watch. I learned not to be fooled by the dharma master's less-than-perfect lecture technique: his ability to spot an opportunity was startling. During the second period, for instance, he might bring up something from his lecture to ask students. The targets of his questions were always dull students or those who had no idea what he was talking about. The ones he asked were often at a loss. Blushing to the tips of their ears, they could not even stammer out a complete sentence in answer. This provoked the whole class into resounding laughter. Then, eyes gleaming victoriously, the dharma master laughed smugly at the "poor creature." With the air of a "cat crying in sympathy for a mouse," he "comforted" the student in a way that was harder to bear than outright abuse. In this way yet another period passed.

Some readers might say that it was right for the masters to direct questions at those dull students who did not know what was going on, because such students must be confronted with problems or they will never have a hope of success. This is correct, and I feel the same way. However, this was not the dharma masters' aim in asking such questions. What were their aims? One was to have a little fun at the dull students' expense, and another was to take up class time so they could keep intelligent students from seizing an opening to ask bothersome questions in front of the class. I remember one occasion in the preparatory class when the dharma master was lecturing on the text *Mahāyāna Discourse on the Door to Knowledge of the One Hundred Dharmas* [*Ta-ch'eng Pai-fa Ming-men Lun*].[2] He had climbed onto the podium and was about to question one of the dull students, but a clever student was a step ahead of him. This student stood up and asked the master to explain the relationship and difference between the ideas of the mind [*hsin-wang*] and its qualities [*hsin-so*] in the *One Hundred Dharmas*. For a moment the dharma master did not know where to begin and was reduced to avoiding the student's point and speaking of something else. Only after that did he begin to treat the "dull" students with any lenience.

Furthermore, as for the attitude of the dharma masters toward their students, the devious and unnatural manner in which they behaved made one uncomfortable just to watch. This was especially true of the dean of studies. The facial expression he wore toward the students was like that of a shrewish stepmother toward her husband's children or a violent ruler toward his subjects. He was both cold and malicious. When students saw him coming, their only worry was not getting away fast enough. Everyone thought it very strange: in depth of learning he could not rival Ta-yüan and Chu-an of the main class, and his bearing left even more to be desired. I do not know what affinity from former lives made it possible for seminary officials to see the worth in him.

The most unthinkable thing was that, besides behaving toward students like a shrewish stepmother or a violent ruler, his strategy for dealing with people was: "Those who submit to me will prosper; those who resist me must perish." In this way he tried to rally some students around himself and oppress others. A few students who had a strong sense of justice were extremely dissatisfied with his actions and often let sarcastic remarks slip out. He simply hated them to death, but unfortunately for him, those upright-minded students were youths of strong ability and impressive backgrounds. There was nothing he could do about them but hate them in the secrecy of his heart. Once, for what reason I do not know, Ta-yüan said to him, "What is so great about you, that you act as if you were preaching to us?" The dean of studies lost no time running to the director and sobbing out his grievances. He told how Ta-yüan had looked down on him and insulted him. He threatened to roll up his bedding and leave if the director did not make Ta-yüan beg for forgiveness before the student body. However, our director was a man of wisdom with a sharp and ready eye. On the surface he seemed to pay little attention to relations between faculty and students, but underneath he understood them more clearly than anyone else. He said a few comforting words to the dean of studies, but he did not make Ta-yüan offer a public confession of his mistakes. Thus he brought an unpleasant incident to an end by leaving it up in the air.

Besides this, the dean of studies had a tremendously deep sense of territorial loyalty. As one of the first steps in assessing students, he divided them into four categories: hometowners, fellow provincials, fellow southerners and northerners. Within these categories he further ranked students by criteria of intelligence and wealth. Then he used different facial expressions, different sorts of eye contact, different tones of voice and different movements in order to handle the students "suitably" according to their ranks. Now I would like to give an example to show how deep our dean's territorial prejudices were.

Besides the dharma masters who taught Buddhist studies, the faculty at T'ien-ning Seminary included a Chinese literature teacher, an English teacher and a teacher of geography and history. These three teachers were all laymen with abundant teaching experience. Moreover, they were all men of scholarly manner, who seemed stern and remote at first but proved warm when one got to know them. This was especially true of the Chinese literature teacher, Mr. Wu. Although he was nearing the age of seventy, he was bursting with good spirits. His lectures were clear and precise: not a sentence was muddled. He had acquired his knowledge when eight-legged essays were the prescribed examination form, but in his teaching there was not a trace of pedantry. Once he made every student in the seminary write an in-class composition on the topic "Filial Son Kuo Searches for His Parent." (Though the seminary was divided into levels, some of the classes, like the one in Chinese, were held en masse.) This is the name of a story from the novel *The Grove of Scholars* [*Ju-lin wai-shih*], which Mr. Wu had included in *Choice Selections from Chinese Literature*, a book which he had personally compiled. Because the students had expressed special interest when he lectured on this reading, he assigned the above topic and told us to evaluate the special characteristics of the filial son Kuo's behavior. Without stopping to think, I wrote a composition of over one thousand words during the allotted time. What I wrote in that essay was this: to journey thousands of miles in search of one's father was a filial act ordinary sons could have managed with effort, but to care in secret for the father who had become a monk and refused to recognize Kuo as his own son would have been extraordinarily hard for most filial sons.

On the day the compositions were returned, Mr. Wu stood at the lectern and said, "Which of you is Chen-hua? " Hearing this gave me quite a start. As I hurriedly stood up, I thought: "Oh no! Something is dreadfully wrong with my composition and the teacher wants to make a fool of me." But when I stood up he gave me a long look through his old wire-rimmed glasses and motioned me to the podium. When I stopped before the podium he handed over my composition without a word. Then he passed out everyone else's compositions. This slight act made my heart jump and came as quite

Fig.4 Modern day young students studying at the Beijing Buddhist Seminary

a surprise to my classmates, because when passing out papers in the past, the teacher had usually handed them to the class leaders, who then passed them out to their classmates. This usually proceeded from the main to the preparatory to the preliminary class. This time he had unexpectedly singled out an "old guy with a brogue" like me and called me up front. Naturally everyone felt this was a bit extraordinary. I had just left the podium when a classmate grabbed my paper out of my hands, glanced at it and yelled out, "Ninety-nine! Chen-hua got a ninety-nine on his composition!" A swarm of classmates gathered around him and craned their necks to see. After a moment another classmate began to walk around bobbling his head and shaking his behind as he repeated over and over: "Strong in both style and content: your realm of thought surpasses the ordinary! Strong in both style and content: your realm of thought surpasses the ordinary...."

When everyone had made enough noise, the composition was returned to my hands. I went back to my place, sat down and read the corrected composition carefully. When I got to the last page and saw the two big, red nines and the comment which had sent my classmate into such paroxysms, I was actually so happy that tears began to flow. This sort of behavior may seem namby-pamby, but were I to write of my experience during the two short years I studied in a private schoolhouse, I am confident the reader too would brush a tear aside for my "moment of glory," such as it was. Nevertheless, it is not my intention to inspire the reader's tears, so back to the subject.

I was reading my handiwork over and over with great relish and self-satisfaction when I looked up and saw the dean of studies standing before me, a thin smile stretched across his hard-set features. I immediately perceived the expression of abhorrence for me on his face, but I made an effort to keep the smile on mine. I lowered my head and continued reading, paying him no attention.

But our dean of studies seemed to be satisfied with nothing less than flinging a dipperful of cold water on my head. He edged slowly up to my desk. First he let out a mirthless little chuckle, then asked, "What sort of essay is worth getting so happy over? Let me see it!" I had to hand it to him. While reading it, he pursed his lips like the waist of an oversized pair of pants to show his contempt. When he had finished, he put it down heavily on the desk and clasped his hands behind his back. "If this *thing* you've written can be called an essay, people who can really write essays would die of shame! Let me tell you: don't let it go to your head. If Wei P'u-chi hadn't recommended you, would you have been qualified to get into this seminary? Open up your eyes. How many northerners are there in this seminary?" (There was one other besides myself.)

What kind of talk was this? Was this what an upstanding dean of studies should have said to his student? The last few sentences, especially, made me feel that arrows were piercing my heart. I stood rooted to the spot in anger — as paralyzed as a wooden chicken. When I came back to myself, the dean had disappeared. Most of the students had gone to the courtyard for a stroll. The few left in the classroom looked at me with various expressions on their faces, and soon they too left one by one. The group of them amused themselves outside, laughing and talking animatedly. How free of care their happiness was! Meanwhile I staggered back to my room like a wounded soldier and toppled onto the bed in agony.

Dejection

No matter how the dean of studies went out of his way to find fault with me and make life hard for me, there were still many classmates who sympathized with me and were indignant for my sake. Once the officers of the monastery decided to send two seminary students to the countryside to collect rents. Since a reward equivalent to the price of 420 pounds of rice was given upon return from a collecting trip, quite a few people wanted to go. A few well-meaning classmates, seeing that I relied on others for financial assistance, used their connections to win support for me among the higher ups. They gained the consent of persons in authority, but their solicitude came to nothing, because the dean of studies secretly obstructed me. Because of this, the classmates who had sought to win support for me often said privately that he was "worse than a beast." However, events in this world often take unexpected turns. A few days after the rent collectors went into the countryside, two of them died at the hands of bandits who were in collusion with tenants. One of them was a seminary student and one was a guest prefect. On the day that the establishment brought their bodies back in a rent-collecting boat, every master and student wept for the martyred classmate. Although I was glad that the dean's secret obstructions had kept my own life intact, the sorrow in my heart was no less than anyone else's when my eyes fell on the classmate who had been shot by the bandits. Originally he had been unwilling to go rent-collecting. But a T'ien-ning Monastery prior who was his master's tonsure brother wanted him to render some service to the establishment and thus ensure himself a place in the future. In the face of the prior's insistent urging, the student finally gave in and went, only to die before rendering service. Later, the establishment gave him the posthumous office of secretary to reward him for "sacrificing his life for the monastic community," but the students and teachers in the seminary still sighed over his death. Naturally his master's tonsure brother experienced an inexpressible pain even stronger than ours.

After the tragic rent-collecting incident, everyone seemed to feel the presentiment of a coming storm, and interest in studying fell off. Some students who had not gotten along with the dean of studies and the dharma masters withdrew from the seminary on various pretexts and left. Later, when I met Chu-an in Soochow and Ta-yüan, Hsiu-wu and other fellow students in Ningpo, we all lamented the T'ien-ning Seminary's poor selection of personnel.

Not long after several of the students withdrew, Jui-kuang, who was nicknamed "Little Guy with a Brogue," was called back to Nanking by a letter from his master. That left me, the "Old Guy with a Brogue," feeling even more alone. In my loneliness I felt that I was living in a desert with no oases ahead and no villages behind. In spite of this, I set my jaws and bore it until winter vacation, so that I could live up to former Abbot Ho-hsüan's enthusiasm and Upāsaka Wei P'u-chi's assistance. Then, giving the reason that I would go to the devotees' club to help Wei conduct charitable activities during the winter season, I left the seminary.

When I had nothing to do at the Devotees' Club, I sat down and wrote "dejection grows within my heart" on strips of paper scattered about my desk. One day, Wei P'u-chi saw them and asked in surprise: "What do you mean by writing this?" I laughed a bit and said, "I have become discouraged about studying at T'ien-ning Seminary. I'd like to find a place to recite the Buddha's name and make an end of life and death!" I did not expect what Wei P'u-chi said in reply: "I don't oppose your leaving the seminary, but you needn't go somewhere else to recite the Buddha's name. There's an empty building east of the club here. You can move in and live here permanently. I have an entire set of the Tripitaka. If you so resolve, I'll provide everything for you to study the scriptures for three years. You needn't worry about food, clothing or any necessities. What do you think?" Seeing that he spoke in all earnestness, I answered carefully and seriously: "I am grateful for your generous intentions, but my karma does not merit such a blessing. I have been ordained less than three years, and I have quit my studies midway. I am a mute, slavish monk [*ya-yang seng*] with little learning or attainment in meditation, and even less in wisdom and virtue. If I allow you to provide for my material wants, it will be a wonder if I don't come back in my next life with fur on my back and horns on my head! What is more, I've received a lot of alms from you over the past year. I am upset as it is because I have no way to repay you. How could I dare to add debt on top of debt?" He did not agree with my way of looking at things: "The sangha is a field on which men sow charitable deeds and reap blessedness.

It is only right for lay disciples to provide for monks. (I am not sure it was right for him to be provided for by the disciples who took refuge under him.) It will be enough if you say the Buddha's name once for my sake (but not necessarily!); why talk of paying me? To tell the truth, living in a monastery is good for spiritual work, but the life is just too hard. Saying this may be a sin, but the food they give you to eat is worse than what people give to beggars. (It would not have been a sin to say it was worse than what dogs were fed!) If you're willing to remain here, I'll tell them (his nephew's wife and a female disciple did the cooking) to serve you three well-cooked meals a day. Then your body will be healthy. Your body must be healthy before you can put your mind at ease and study scriptures or recite the Buddha's name. Otherwise, you might as well forget about doing anything. Didn't Great Master Yin-kuang once say, 'Only after the body is properly cared for can one's spiritual health flourish'? And don't foreigners say that health is the basis of all successful undertakings? I wish you would accept my expression of sincerity and not cling so stubbornly to your principles." But then I said, "I came from far away at the risk of my life to seek out learned men and study the Buddhadharma. How can I sit back like a country squire and let you provide for me? Good sir, your sincere intentions are moving, but forgive me for being unable to accept them." With this thought uppermost in my mind, I reluctantly spent the New Year at the devotees' club and then left Changchow.

Before I left the club, many of my classmates came to see me. One classmate told me that not long after I left the monastery an amusing thing happened between a student and a monastery officer. It seems that a few of the wounded soldiers quartered in the monastery had died, and the proctor asked the faculty to send thirty seminary students to help bury them. He also prescribed that everyone wear shirts and trousers and not wear caps. When they showed up at the public cemetery behind the monastery, the proctor discovered that one of them was wearing a loose robe. In a very uncivil tone the proctor demanded of the student: "Your instructions were to wear shirts and trousers. Why are you wearing a loose robe? Take it off!" Instead of taking it off, the student said in the same tone of voice: "According to instructions, none of us are to wear caps. Why are you wearing a cap? Take it off!" When I heard this, I could not help laughing out loud and asking, "Was our scabby-headed proctor able to stand such a counterattack? " (Because his head looked a mess due to a chronic favus infection, he kept his cap on year round.) My classmate said, "He couldn't take it off, so he ran crying to the abbot like the dean did last time and wanted to resign. He wanted to have the abbot make the student beg forgiveness in public so he could save face, but the student would rather have been expelled than beg forgiveness." I sighed, "The proctor was too authoritarian. A measly matter of face kept him from setting an example for others. Why should he have blamed our classmate? This certainly is a time when the rich and mighty are allowed to set fires, while peasants are not even allowed to light lamps. If people don't do something to change this mentality, it will pose a great obstacle to the advancement of Buddhism." My classmate nodded so much at this that he looked like a chicken pecking rice.

NOTES

1. Chang Fei (d.220) was a famous hero during the Three Kingdom period. He helped Liu Pei fight Ts'ao Ts'ao and become ruler of Shu (Szechuan).

2. This is an important text of the Yogācāra school. It was written by Vasubandhu and translated into Chinese by Hsüan-tsang in one volume (T. 1614). It has many commentaries, the more important being *Pai-fa ming-men lun-chieh* in three *chüan* by Kuei-chi (T. 1836), and *Pai-fa ming-men lun-shu* in two *chüan* by P'u-kuang (T. 1837).

Chapter VI

Ling-yen Monastery in Soochow

Since I was disheartened with studying at T'ien-ning Seminary, and I was unwilling to accept long-term support from others, tarrying longer in Changchow would have been a waste of time. One day, in a small room of worship upstairs at Upāsaka Wei P'u-chi's house, I saw the *Writings of Dharma Master Yin-kuang* [*Yin-kuang Fa-shih wen-ch'ao*]. After getting Wei's permission, I took it to my room and read it. Until then I had been standing at a crossroads, in a quandary about what to do next, but upon reading this, I was given a direction for my efforts. In the deepest way I gained an appreciation of Great Master Yin-kuang's keys to helping self and others — sincerity and reverence. The ten *gāthas* in his letter to Devotee Wu Pi-hua, for instance, often move me to tears when I recite them aloud. Although these add up to only 160 words and have nothing in the way of intricate philosophical concepts, they go a long way toward expressing the "Causes and Conditions of the Great Matter" which the Buddha came to preach. I copy them out here for the benefit of readers unfamiliar with the *Writings of Dharma Master Yin-kuang*:

The mind and nature of common man
Do not fall short of the Buddha's own;
Illusion leads us all astray,
We spin through endless life and death.

Tathagata, moved by pity,
Preached the dharma to receptive hearts:
To each and every living thing,
He pointed out the homeward road.

Enlightenment has many doors,
But two of them stand at the fore:
Ch'an and Pure Land are their names —
The simplest roads to reach release.

With Ch'an there's no one but yourself,

While Pure Land borrows Buddha's strength:
When these are on a balance weighed,
Pure Land seems suited to our need.

As crossing over boundless seas,
No man without a trusty craft
Can swiftly reach the other shore,
His mind and poise still undisturbed.

For men in times of Law's decay,
This way alone can meet the test;
Else missing opportunity,
Our fruitless labor comes to naught.

Develop the enlightened mind[1]
Let faith take root within your heart;
Hold firmly to it all your days,
Dwell only on the Buddha's name.

Recite until, all motive gone,
To dwell [Amitābha] on Him is not to dwell!
In this the awesome truth of Ch'an
Is borne out to its deepest core.

Then when the end of life looms near
With help from Buddha's guiding hand,
Ascend straight to the highest plane[2]
And learn the patience of birthlessness.[3]

I give you now the key to every door:
Use every ounce of strength to live
With sincerity and reverence —
The fruits are marvelous indeed.

Reading Dharma Master Yin-kuang gave me a direction for further effort, so I was naturally unwilling to sit back and enjoy the undemanding comforts of the lay club. Early in 1948 I said goodbye to Upasaka Wei P'u-chi and a few close classmates, shouldered my bundle and left Changchow for Ling-yen Monastery in Soochow. Some teachers and students who knew me were quite shocked to hear of my decision. They thought that I must have absorbed a certain amount of new ideas in the year I spent at T'ien-ning

Monastery. Most people who have new ideas about Buddhism think those who recite the Buddha's name are "fanatics." I was leaving the seminary to become a Buddha-reciting fanatic: no wonder they felt shocked. Actually, my aim in studying at the seminary was to understand the principles of Buddhism better, so that I could later apply them within the limits of my native ability and strength. My hope was simply not to betray my initial resolutions to renounce lay life and seek knowledge. There was no distinction between the new and the old in my thinking. Naturally it was impossible that I would come and see men who earnestly recited the Buddha's name as fanatics.

The preface to *A Short Account of Ling-yen* explains the origin of the place's name: "It was a place of many grotesque rocks, among which the 'spirit fungus' [*fomes japonica*] grew in profusion. Thus it was named Ling-yen ['spirit-crag']." The same preface goes on to say: "Beautiful landscapes abound in the region of Wu. A few miles southeast of the city tower many mountains, arrayed like a protective wall. The wondrous valleys are filled with beauties of nature, and water coming from pure secluded springs gurgles over rocks. Looking from the peak, one sees distinctly the encircling mountain ridges: the view from Ling-yen is especially grand. The mountain is 3,600 feet high and covers 1,800 *mu* of land."

Again, the "Famous Sights" section of the same book gives the following narrative of the founding and rebuilding of Ling-yen Mountain Monastery:

"Ling-yen Monastery is located on the old site of the Kuan-wa Palace built by Fu-cha, king of the ancient state of Wu. During the Chin dynasty a minister of public works named Lu Wan donated his home as a monastery. During the T'ien-chien period (502-519) of the Liang it was expanded and named Hsiu-feng Monastery. One of its marvels was a painting of the metamorphosis of Bodhisattva Chih-chi[4] [Jnanakara], so the court bestowed a plaque naming it the 'place of truth which manifests Chih-chi Bodhisattva's transformation.' In the T'ang it was named Ling-yen Monastery. In the Sung dynasty Han Shih-chung, the Prince of Ch'i, conducted ceremonies in gratitude of ancestral blessings and renamed it Hsien-ch'in Chung-pao Ch'an Monastery. In the Hung-wu period (1368-1398) of the Ming dynasty, it was first made a public monastery and given the name Pao-kuo Yung-tso Ch'an Monastery by imperial decree. It was renovated in 1413, only to be destroyed in the Hung-chih period (1488-1506). During the Ch'ing dynasty monks renovated it again in 1650, and the court bestowed upon it the name Ch'ung-pao Ch'an Monastery. In 1674 the provincial governor, Mu T'ien-yen, rebuilt the shrine hall, which was destroyed again in 1861. In 1874 Monk Nien-ch'eng repaired the major buildings. In recent times [after 1920] the shrine hall has been rebuilt, the main gate widened and calligraphy for the name plaque done by Dharma Master Yin-kuang. This was when the monastery was again given its former name — Ling-yen Monastery."

From this description of the site as a place abounding in grotesque boulders, the reader can imagine the magnificence of the craggy peak capped by the splendid-looking monastery. It was indeed magnificent: looking upward from the east, the mountain's dark green layers made it look like a jade pagoda; from the south it seemed a massive, towering fortress of stone (Ling-yen Shan is also called Stone Fortress Mountain); and from the west it looked like an elephant (Elephant Mountain is another of its names) carrying on its back a dazzling crown which seems to turn as it glitters in the sunlight. Yet another grand view awaited those who climbed to its peak. In front of the mountain was Lake Tai's watery expanse. East and West Mt. Tung-t'ing were faintly visible in the middle of the lake, riding the swells like two approaching steamers. From the rear one could see T'ai-p'ing Mountain, home of the Sung statesman Fan Chung-yen. A circuit of the mountaintop showed vistas of Shih-tzu Mountain to the east and Ch'iung-lung Mountain to the west. What is more, there were checkerboard fields, intersecting waterways and a spider's web of roads and villages laid out like gardens. One needed only to let one's eyes wander to discover patterns as fascinating as constellations of stars or positions on a chessboard. In view of all these excellent qualities, it would not be excessive to say that it was designed and created by heaven and earth as a perfect Buddhist place of truth.

Patriarch Yin's Precious Heritage

Patriarch Yin was Great Master Yin-kuang, the thirteenth patriarch of the Pure Land School. He was not only the well-known pillar of the Pure Land School, but also a great scholar whose knowledge embraced both Buddhism and Confucianism. Nevertheless, he was never one to be impressed with his own attainments. All his life, his secret for benefiting himself and others was no more than: "The utmost in sincerity and reverence, holding to monastic vows, and reciting Amitābha Buddha's name." Because he held to this throughout his life and because his words were consistent with his deeds, these simple words were looked on by thousands of laymen and monks as principles for spiritual cultivation and growth in virtue. Thus many people who had never seen him cried like orphaned children on hearing the news of his death [in 1940].

Fig.5 Approach to Ling-yen Monastery, Soochow, Kiangsu

Fig.6 Entrance to Ling-yen Monastery

To better understand the tradition Yin-kuang established, it is necessary to speak of the rules that he added to Ling-yen Monastery's code. These were:

1. The criterion for abbotship will be deep faith in Pure Land doctrines and strict adherence to monastic discipline rather than affiliation with any school. In order to curb the practice of dharma-family favoritism, offices will be transmitted on the basis of personal merit [*ch'uan-hsien*] and not of relations within a lineage of dharma transmission [*ch'uan-fa*].

2. In order to avoid having mediocre men take precedence over men of superior talents, the position of abbot will be given on the basis of rank, not of generation.

3. In order to avoid distracting influences, ordinations and public lectures will not be given. Lectures will be given daily within the hall, but outside persons will not be invited to listen.

4. Since our purpose is to recite Buddha's name with complete concentration, our monks will conduct only Buddha recitation weeks [*ta Fo-chi*] and will not be on call to perform any sort of Buddhist service.

5. No one in the monastery is permitted to accept tonsure disciples. The penalty for infraction of any of these five rules will be immediate expulsion.

These five rules seem simple and unpretentious, but after studying them carefully we can see that each one was directed against the corrupt practices rife in large monasteries of mainland China at that time. Let us throw open the windows and let the light of honesty shine upon our subject! Of monks who have lived in large monasteries on the mainland, who does not know that the great majority of famous places of truth were ruined by "dharma family favoritism"?[5] Master Yin-kuang's democratic policy of transmitting only to men of merit rather than to dharma disciples was not just the main reason for Ling-yen Monastery's becoming a great place of truth in little more than ten years, but was also the best prescription to bring Chinese Buddhism back to life. The pity was that at that time the elders who held authority over large monasteries were mostly a complacent and selfish lot. None of them paid attention to Yin-kuang's reforms. As a result the famous monasteries that had been founded through the backbreaking labors of the original great monks became personal paradises for complacent, selfish men and battlegrounds in which their disciples and grandson-disciples schemed to win fame and personal advantage. Even in the midst of all this they shamelessly mouthed phrases like: "Abiding by the proper chain of dharma transmission, we extend the life of the Buddha's wisdom." Stop to think: if the proliferation of such a strange state of affairs in major monasteries does not eventually cause the Buddha dharma to die out completely, it will be fortunate indeed, and yet they turned around and used such phrases. Was this any more than deceitful, self-deceptive babbling?

The rule stating that "the position of abbot will be given on the basis of rank [*tzu-shu*], not of generation [*tai-shu*]" was an innovation that showed Yin-kuang's unique insight. The significance of this rule is intimately related to Rule Number One. In monasteries which gave preference to dharma transmission, the abbot's throne had to be passed on to his "dharma son," regardless of whether he was worthy or not.[6] Otherwise, wrangling among rival claimants would ensue and spread a miasma of confusion through a once fine monastery. From this we can see that giving the office of abbot on the basis of rank rather than lineage is not only a way to avoid "mediocre men taking precedence over men of superior talents," but is also the best strategy for doing away with the struggles for fame and personal advantage among dharma disciples.

The rule stating "ordinations will not be given" conformed to the "three prohibitions" which Master Yin-kuang upheld throughout his life. The three prohibitions were:

1. Indiscriminately accepting disciples is prohibited.
2. Indiscriminately conferring ordinations is prohibited.
3. Indiscriminately long stays by wandering monks are prohibited.

Indiscriminately accepting disciples means to perform the tonsure ceremony for anyone who comes along. In order to strengthen the "line-up" of their [future] dharma families, some masters perform the tonsure ceremony on the strength of a single convivial conversation, without carefully looking into a person's background and motivations. The end result of this is terrible indeed. It is important to realize that the monastic order is the main pillar of the Buddhist religion and a source of guidance for the human and spirit worlds. If one uncritically agrees to perform tonsure for someone, and that person does something despicable, does not Buddhism in its entirety suffer thereby?

To confer ordinations indiscriminately means to set up an altar and ordain anyone who comes along. This is even more harmful to Buddhism than the practice just mentioned. There are certain people who can still behave themselves and abide by the rules after renouncing lay life, but simply let them receive ordination and, right away, before the ordination scars heal on their heads, they believe themselves to be full-fledged *bhiksu* [monks], or *bhiksuni* [nuns], or even dharma masters. This leads them to an arrogant and overweening sense of self-importance, and they suppose themselves to be above their masters and elders. This sort of person does much to bring on the decline of our religion and to hasten the demise of the Buddhist Law.

Indiscriminately permitting stays by wandering monks means opening the wandering monks hall to any and all comers and allowing them to stay as long as they wish. In the past many public monasteries with indiscriminate policies of "convenience" and "compassion" did not interfere with the coming and going of monks. Because of this, many monks who were ordained did not meditate or recite the Buddha's name; nor did they listen to lectures or study doctrine. Instead they spent their time in carefree travel. Everywhere there were places to put up for the night, so there were no worries about food and shelter. They devoted their lives to such enjoyment and never tired of it. This practice was largely responsible for the common notion that monks are rice buckets or parasites.

In summary, Master Yin-kuang was an enlightened being who returned to earth. If we carry out his code of rules or his three prohibitions to the best of our ability, though we may not be able to remove all traces of indiscriminateness, we may keep certain evils from getting out of control.

Two Virtuous Men

Within the Buddhist religion there are many people who claim to be engaged in spiritual exercises, but those who can truly lay aside selfish considerations, root out all entangling affinities and treat spiritual work as a matter of life and death are fewer than few. Though I am a man of little ability, I once wore out two pairs of straw sandals in my travels on the mainland, visiting quite a few large monasteries and paying my respects to eminent monks, but I never met anyone so able to see through this world's illusions, to put aside desire and striving, and to devote themselves to spiritual work as the two old dharma masters Te-sen and Liao-jan.

Both Te-sen and Liao-jan were from Kiangsi Province; both had been in the inner circle of Great Master Yin-kuang's disciples; both had been instrumental in assisting him to spread Pure Land doctrine; and both had entered sealed confinement [*pi-kuan*] at Ling-yen for the duration of their lives. Their knowledge, virtue and experience at Ling-yen were at least equal to those of Abbot Miao-chen. Moreover, they possessed the deep faith in Pure Land doctrine and strict adherence to monastic discipline required by the code that Yin-kuang had drawn up for Ling-yen. According to the custom of most public monasteries at the time, after Great Master Yin-kuang passed into nirvana, they should have been equally eligible as Miao-chen for selection as abbot. But instead of competing with Miao-chen they were happy to assist him in the capacity of rank-and-file monks. This made Abbot Miao-chen esteem them even more, whereupon he had a private cell [*kuan-fang*] built for each of them and provided for all their needs. These two admirable old men then resolved to enter sealed confinement for the remainder of their years. Their strength of commitment was much like that of Śākyamuni when he sat down beneath the *bodhi* tree and resolved not to arise until he had attained enlightenment. Because I often accompanied visitors when they knocked on the wicket and asked for advice, I came to know something of the words and deeds of these two great men. I am confident that the reader will be glad if I share a bit of what I saw.

Te-sen lived in the East Cell, which was near the memorial hall to the Venerable Master Yin-kuang. The surroundings were quiet, and it was a fine place for getting down to the business of religious work. Because he had often lived in Shanghai in the past, the people who knocked on his wicket and asked for advice were much more numerous than those who visited Liao-jan's cell. However, he never felt vexed or troubled by the large numbers of people who went to see him. On the contrary, no matter who called on him and regardless of the time of day, he always received them with a hearty welcome and patiently answered all their questions. Although his Kiangsi dialect was not easily understood, he spoke with such warm concern that people were often able to grasp the meaning of his words from the attitude he projected. I remember once when a few old women whom I had heard of but not seen arrived from Shanghai. It was already dusk when they reached the mountain. Jabbering loudly, they walked into the guest department and demanded to go to the cell and visit Dharma Master Te-sen. I was on duty in the guest department that day, and in keeping with the duties of my post, I had to give in to their request, even though I found their conduct irritating. When I led them through the outer door of the cell, I ran right into the cell attendant. This gave him a start, but seeing it was I, he joined his hands before his chest and said, "What is the guest prefect's reason for coming to the cell so late?"

I pointed to the old women: "They would like to see the dharma master."

The cell attendant replied, "The old dharma master is not feeling well today. He has finished his evening devotions and now he is resting. Would you ask them to come see him tomorrow?"

The old women had already filed in the door, and hearing the attendant say they would have to come back in the morning they turned their voices up to full volume and yelled, "That won't do at all. We have to go down the mountain first thing in the morning. We have to see the dharma master this evening, no matter what." The attendant looked at me in chagrin, and I looked helplessly back at him. During our moment of hesitation the impossible old women had already rushed over to the cell. As I hurried over, the familiar emaciated face appeared at the wicket. Matters having come to this pass, the attendant and I could only exchange rueful smiles, stand silently off to one side and listen to the old gentleman's unvarying message. "Where are you from? What business is your family in? What does your husband do for a living? How many years have you been a practicing Buddhist?" After the people answered his questions he would always say, "Good! Good! Recite 'Namah Amitābha' as much as you can..." After their interview the old ladies said, "The dharma master's accent is hard to understand, but hearing him speak sure does make you feel good inside." They felt that they had not come in vain, and the next day they returned to Shanghai in good spirits. Unfortunately for all who could have benefited from meeting him, he passed peacefully into the Western Paradise in 1962 on the twenty-sixth day of the eleventh month, at the advanced age of eighty.

Liao-jan lived in the West Cell, which was about three hundred meters distant from the East Cell. Its setting was even more beautiful and roomy than that of the East Cell. In the courtyard outside the cell was a natural stone spring. More than a hundred goldfish of various sizes and colors glided through the crystal-clear spring water, giving every appearance of joyful ease. On all four sides of the spring, stones were arranged in the shape of terraced cliffs. Various types and colors of potted plants had been placed at each level with a marvelous eye to arrangement. Most striking were the exotic miniature peach trees. Though they stood little over a foot tall, they each bore several ruddy, egg-sized peaches. Looking at them, one felt an intimation of something beyond the ordinary. Those who did not know thought a master landscape artist must have been in charge of planting and trimming, but actually this was the work of Liao-jan himself.

Not long ago I remarked to my old brother of the cloth, Dharma Master Ching-nien: "If someone proposed an election to choose the fourteenth patriarch of the Pure Land school, I would cast my vote for Dharma Master Liao-jan." Why? Because in many ways Liao-jan's words and actions were much like those of the Venerable Master Yin-kuang. He had originally been a Ch'an practitioner who meditated on such questions as "Who is it that recites the Buddha's name?" and "What was my original face before I was born?" But after getting to know Master Yin-kuang he threw himself single-mindedly into practice of Pure Land. Because the old man adhered so strictly to monastic discipline and recited Amitābha Buddha's name with such fervor, many round crystalline *sariras*[7] appeared on the altar, on sticks of burning incense and on the lampwick in his cell. I have seen these *sariras* with my own eyes, and I am sure that anyone who lived on Ling-yen Mountain in the years 1947 and 1948 saw them also. Besides this, Liao-jan's self-mastery left most people's far behind. I recall a certain devotee named Chao Chieh-sang who fled disorder in his home province of Anhui and came to Ling-yen Mountain. Because he was the Venerable Master Yin-kuang's Refuges disciple, had been a commissioned officer during the warlord period and was fairly learned, Abbot Miao-chen hired him as Chinese instructor at the Buddhist seminary. In 1948 his family also fled to Soochow, where they stayed in Pao-kuo Temple, a subsidiary temple of Ling-yen. All the expenses for their support were taken care of by Abbot Miao-chen. Chao not only proved to be an ingrate, but even accused Abbot Miao-chen of mistreating his family. Later he insisted on receiving a certain sum of money to get started in business, or he would show the abbot how tough he could be. Naturally Abbot Miao-chen would not satisfy his demands. At this Chao asked Liao-jan to intercede with the abbot. Liao-jan answered with a laugh: "Devotee Chao, this establishment's money and rice were given by lay believers to provide for monks. From the karmic point of view, it was not strictly proper for the abbot to take your wife and children into the temple. How can you expect him to give you money to start you in business as well? You understand the moral causation that all of us work under. The best thing would be to give up this idea of yours." Hearing this only incensed Chao all the more. Slamming his hand on a table, he roared, "Liao-jan, you're a damned good-for-nothing yourself." Liao-jan smiled at him and said, "If you want to sit here and let it out of your system, that's all right too, but I haven't finished my devotions yet. I cannot keep you company." With that he went to prostrate himself to Amitābha. Chao kept cursing until he was exhausted and his throat was hoarse, and then he finally left the cell.

NOTES

1. Bodhicitta (*p'u-t'i-hsin*) is the enlightened mind. To give rise to and develop this mind is one of the first requirements in one's becoming a bodhisattva.

2. According to the Pure Land sūtra, *Kuan wu-liang-shou ching* (*Sūtra on the Contemplation of Boundless Life*), there are nine different kinds of rebirth in the Pure Land. They are divided into the three chief gradations of superior, middle and inferior. The three are further subdivided into three, e.g., superior-superior, superior-middle, superior-inferior and so on. Depending on one's religious cultivation and moral quality, one is reborn in any of these nine ways. *Shang-p'in* is rebirth in the superior grades. A person who will be reborn in the highest form of the superior grade must be one who, first of all, wishes to be born there, and second, have the "true and sincere thought," the "deep-believing thought," and the desire to be born in the Pure Land by "bringing one's stock of merit to maturity." His reception in the Pure Land is spectacular. "He will see the Buddha's (Amitābha's) form and body with every sign of perfection complete, and also see brilliant rays and jewel forests and hear the bodhisattvas propounding the excellent Law." See the *Amitayurdhyana Sūtra*, tr. J. Takakusu, in *Buddhist Mahāyāna Texts*, F. Max Muller, ed., *The Sacred Books of the East*, Vol. XLIX, p. 189. See also my book, *The Renewal of Buddhism in China: Chu-hung and the Late Ming Synthesis* (Columbia University Press, 1981), pp. 126-127.

3. *Wu-sheng-jen* refers to a bodhisattva's realization that phenomena are neither born nor destroyed, for everything is void (*śunya*). Therefore, he gains the endurance or patience of no longer being worried about birth or death. Depending on sources, this realization occurs either at the first stage (*ch'u-ti*) or during the seventh, eighth and ninth stages of a bodhisattva's career.

4. His name literally means "accumulation of knowledge." He appears in the *Lotus Sūtra*, a bodhisattva in the retinue of Prabhatratna.

5. The author uses the expression "*fa-chuan ssu-shu*" (favoritism toward one's dharma family). See Holmes Welch, "Dharma Scrolls and the Succession of Abbots in Chinese Monasteries," *T'ung Pao* 50. 1-3: 93-148 (1963). The system was largely limited to the lower Yangtze basin.

6. The author's views expressed here were not shared by many senior monks Welch interviewed. He reports that an unworthy "heir" was sometimes passed over. Welch, op. cit.

7. *Śariras* (*she-li-tzu*) are crystalline bodies which are found in the ashes of cremated saintly monks. The fact that *śariras* formed spontaneously in Liao-jan's cell while he was still alive was special proof of his virtue.

Chapter VII

COLLECTING RENTS AT LAKE T'AI

My original aim in going to Ling-yen Monastery was to enter the Buddha recitation hall [Nien-fo t'ang] and recite Amitābha Buddha's name, but being dominated by a chain of causation that conflicted with my aim, I was dragged out of the hall only three days after entering it and sent to a place on the bank of Lake T'ai called Heng-chin. After collecting rents there for two months I returned, only to be pressed into service a few days later as guest prefect in the guest department. These unexpected events make a long story.

When monks seek to enter a public monastery for instruction they must, unless they have personal connections, be interviewed by a guest prefect in the guest department before they are shown to the guest hall by the guest prefect or usher. Because I had no personal connections at Ling-yen, I had to sit through a lecture delivered in the guest prefect's "bureaucratese ", just like hundreds and thousands of other monks, before I was admitted to the guest hall.

The guest hall, also called the "wandering monks hall" or the "hall of clouds and streams,"[1] was a place in which the common and the saintly mingled, and dragons were found in the company of snakes. Within the hall every member of this chance assemblage was treated as a guest. Moreover, aside from the prohibition against discussing the rights and wrongs of national politics, we had unlimited freedom of speech. That is to say, if you enjoyed doing so, you could speak in the most outrageously expansive way about all matters past and present, and no one would interfere. One often heard such foolish nonsense as: "Don't let my tender years fool you. I've stayed three winters and five summers in each of the seventy-two thatched hermitages on Chung-nan Mountain." Two or three years before, when leaving the North, I had put up for the night several times along the way, but that had always been in small temples without a guest hall. After receiving ordination I had gone to P'i-lu Monastery in Nanking and T'ien-ning Monastery in Changchow but in neither place had I passed through the guest hall. As soon as I arrived in the guest hall at Ling-yen Monastery, I met so many interesting people, heard so many interesting stories and saw so many interesting things that I gave up my plan to ask for entrance into the recitation hall after one day's rest and ended up staying in the guest hall for half a month. If I had not accompanied a few newly arrived "guests" to honor the remains of the Venerable Yin-kuang in the new reliquary pagoda and on the way encountered Master Ching-ch'ih, who had served as water bearer in the meditation hall of T'ien-ning Monastery, I am afraid my entrance into the recitation hall would have been postponed until the "year of the donkey."

Master Ching-ch'ih was also a native of Hupei. Because his master's brother disciple did double duty as assistant instructor [*t'ang-chu*] and financial subprior [*fu-ssu*] at Ling-yen Monastery, he had not been there a year when he was given the post of assistant subprior [*wai fu-ssu*]. When he learned that I had already stayed in the guest hall for half a month, he seemed as anxious as a monkey juggling hot iron as he urged me to enter the recitation hall with all possible haste. He said, "No matter how long you stay in the guest hall, you won't be considered a resident of this establishment. Since you've resolved to come to Ling-yen Mountain and recite the Buddha's name, the sooner you enter the better." Without indicating my decision, I pressed my palms together before my chest and went on to Patriarch Yin's reliquary pagoda with the newly arrived guests. Unexpectedly, after I had eaten porridge and returned to the guest hall the next morning, the hall master handed me a note on which was written: "Master Chün-shan (the name I went by while at Ling-yen Mountain) is requested to bring his luggage to the guest department."

When I obeyed the summons and went to the guest department, I found Master Ching-ch'ih talking and gesturing enthusiastically to a few guest prefects. Without giving me a chance to put a word in edgewise, he collared me and dragged me before the guests prefects. He had me bow to them while he "blew loudly on the Conch of the Law," proclaiming all the things I had done while studying at T'ien-ning Seminary and how deep his friendship with me was. Though I detested the old bodhisattva's worldly-wise unctuousness, my only choice was to let him go on with his exaggerations. Otherwise, the loss of face for him would have been considerable, and my entrance into the hall might not have proceeded smoothly. Thus, like a solely chosen *chin-shih* [doctor of letters], I alone was sent into the recitation hall by the guest prefect.

Owing to Master Ching-ch'ih's excessive praise, Abbot Miao-chen called me to his quarters on my third day in the recitation hall. After I had bowed to him, he got straight to the point: "I just got back from Shanghai yesterday, and I heard Ching-ch'ih say you were a good buddy of his at T'ien-ning Monastery. He is leaving to collect rents at Lake T'ai tomorrow, and hopes you'll go with him. You look like a decent fellow. How about making your mind up to go?" His mention of rent collecting immediately brought memories of the tragedy at T'ien-ning to mind, so I said, "Abbot, have compassion on me. I came to your mountain to devote myself to reciting the Buddha's name. Going to collect rents after only three days in the hall would be letting myself down. Also, I am inexperienced in such matters; even if I go, I won't be any help. Please have compassion on me. Ask someone else to collect rents. I would like to remain in the hall and recite the Buddha's name for a few years." I bowed down in apology, but he was obviously quite displeased: "A public monastery is made up of monks who come from far and wide. Anyone who stays here has an obligation to do his part for the establishment. You came here to recite the Buddha's name. Is there anyone who didn't come for the same reason? If you give your all to reciting the Buddha's name, and I do the same and everyone else does it, then who will see to the needs of the establishment? You say you have no experience in such matters. That's no reason; it's an excuse. You should know that experience comes from doing things. If you do nothing, you'll never gain experience. The most important thing for young men travelling in search of instruction is to do what they are told. Even travelling to each of the four sacred mountains won't do a person much good if he doesn't do as he is told." Seeing that I held my peace, he continued: "Go back to the hall, get your luggage together and go with Master Ching-ch'ih to collect rents tomorrow. When you get back you can enter the hall again and settle down to reciting the Buddha's name." In a subtle way Abbot Miao-chen's words pointed out the two roads open to me: one was "do as you are told" and the other was "roll up your bedroll." There being no way out, I was forced to choose the first alternative.

Lake T'ai was a paradise for fishermen, but it was also a hotbed for bandits. At a time when the nation was beset by the double pressures of foreign and domestic crises, the activities of bandits became increasingly fierce and cruel. Because of this, murder, arson and robbery were frequently heard of in the Lake T'ai area in 1947-48. This brought much suffering and fear to the honest, hard working citizens of the area.

The green willows were putting forth their first yellow flowers when, under the leadership of Master Ching-ch'ih, I set out together by sampan with another monk, a lay devotee and two workmen from Mu-tu.[2] Under the touch of the gentle spring wind, the trees on either bank were bursting with new life, but the villages along the way had a lonely, desolate look. Occasionally we stepped onto the road and saw small groups of farmers and village women carrying the vegetables they had grown with their own sweat and blood to market, but not a trace of happiness showed on their faces. All we could see were the marks of distress and brooding sorrow. "What is happening here? Are their distress and sorrow caused by the bandits, or do they feel this way out of sympathy for their compatriots in the North?" Pointing at the pedestrians on the road, I asked this question of Master Ching-ch'ih. Quite a while passed without his making answer, so I turned to look. There he was, sound asleep against the gunwale. I looked at the others and found that they too were all dozing. Even the boatman was no exception. I could not restrain myself from giving him a swat on the shoulder and saying loudly: "Hey! You're taking our lives into your hands. How can you sleep?"

It was already afternoon when our boat reached Heng-chin. Everyone scrambled to move our supplies from the boat onto the bank and then to the house that had been rented for us beforehand. It was almost dusk by the time we had gotten everything in order and eaten supper. After everyone had rested a bit, Master Ching-ch'ih told the monk to go outside with one of the workmen to buy a few necessary articles. He took the devotee and me to see a few tenant families. The remaining workman stayed behind to watch our possessions and clean up.

The nominal purpose of our going to the tenants' houses was to visit them, but actually we seemed to be telling them: "Hey! We've come to collect rent. We hope you prepare to pay immediately." The tenants looked simple and honest on the outside, but inside they were as cunning as could be. When they saw us, they did not bother to show us the politeness a host should show a guest, and they immediately let us know by the looks on their faces how unhappy they were to see us. Whenever we brought up the real object of our visit, they answered knowingly with a none-too-subtle hint that our presence was no longer welcome: "We'll talk about it more in the tearoom tomorrow."

At house after house we heard the same sentence. I was as mystified as one who tries to identify a statue by feeling it in the dark but cannot reach its head. "Why do they insist on discussing it further at the tearoom tomorrow morning?" I wondered aloud. The devotee explained that saying this was a time-honored Soochow custom. It may have been familiar to him, but to me it was a novel and amusing incident. Since everyone had expressed a desire to talk further at the tearoom, we could only adopt a democratic policy and accede to majority opinion. We returned empty-handed to our lodgings, washed our feet and went to bed.

Before dawn the next day Master Ching-ch'ih was already ordering the workmen to get up and cook breakfast as he discussed with me and the devotee how to handle the sly tenants at the tearoom. As the saying goes: "If three stinking tanners put their heads together, they can devise the strategies of a Chu-K'o Liang."[3] The results of our discussion were two hypothetical measures. First, if some of the tenants were to say, "The harvest was poor last year; we have no way to pay all our rent right away," our strategy would be to say: "If you really cannot pay all at once we won't make things hard for you. How about paying eighty percent first?" If the tenant could not come up with eighty percent, we would tell him to pay seventy percent first. But no matter what, we would not settle for less than sixty-five percent, and we would add the condition that the remainder be paid in full before this year's harvest. Second, what should we do if the tenants refused to see us or resisted paying rent *en masse*? Our proposed strategy was first to utilize connections with influential citizens and have them urge each tenant to pay. If that did not work, we would get the other monk in our party to carry his wooden fish to the homes of those who refused to see us or who resisted payment as a group. Once there he would beat on the wooden fish and recite "Namah Amitābha" without stopping until they promised to pay. If that did not work, we would furl our banners, quiet our drums, recall our soldiers and return to the mountain.

Our strategy fixed, we got out of bed and washed up. We kneeled down together before our hastily improvised altar, recited Amitābha for ten breaths and repeated our daily Refuges vows. After eating morning porridge our little party of three monks and one layman went to the teahouse agreed on the day before, carrying writing supplies and an abacus.

The teahouse was an old-fashioned two-storied building. Though both floors were filled with seats, only a few people were there having tea. The four of us sat down at an upstairs table next to a window overlooking the street. The waiter brought a red porcelain Yi-hsing tea set and asked us if we would like any snacks. Master Ching-ch'ih shook his head, and the waiter walked away grinning. Each of us poured a cup of tea. We had just filled our stomachs with porridge, and though the tea's pure fragrance was a delight to sniff, none of us took a sip. We simply set it in front of us for appearance's sake.

We sat there as vapidly as wooden chickens for about two hours before the tenants stumbled up the stairs. From the looks of them they had not taken morning tea, but had taken plenty of morning wine instead. They lurched into the room and, before they had even sat down, began babbling away in their dialect. The devotee who had come with us was a native of Soochow, so he acted as interpreter between the tenants and Master Ching-ch'ih. We conversed this way until after twelve o'clock before reaching the figure the three of us had agreed to settle for during our discussion earlier in the morning. Just as we were about to go back for lunch, a few tenants we had not yet seen began filing upstairs. Luckily they said right away that they would pay their full rents in one payment. Otherwise I do not know how long we would have had to negotiate before coming to an agreement. Collecting rents was terribly exasperating — like pecking about in the dust for pennies.

As I have said, Ling-yen Monastery was a recently revived establishment that had no large landholdings.[4] What I did not know was that besides the tenants at Heng-chin, Ling-yen also had quite a number of tenants at East Tung-t'ing Mountain. Thus, as soon as he had agreed with the Heng-chin tenants on the time and amount of rent payments, Master Ching-ch'ih took the lay devotee with him to East Tung-t'ing Mountain. The other monk and I found a layman to act as our interpreter. Every morning we carried an abacus to the teahouse and waited for the tenants, who were so fond of "morning tea." Unexpectedly, Master Ching-ch'ih and the devotee returned to Heng-chin empty-handed after three days. Master Ching-ch'ih shook his head emphatically and said, "There is no way — no way at all." When I asked him what had happened, he said, "The tenants on East Tung-t'ing Mountain are uncivilized. They are so bad you simply can't deal with them. Not only did they hold back on the rent, they also used their fists. We saw that things weren't going right, so we stayed in a temple for three days, not daring to show our faces. Then the temple manager said to us, 'You two had best go back, or you'll come to harm at the hands of those banditlike tenants.' So the two of us slipped back here when no one was watching us." This brought back memories of the tragic incident at T'ien-ning Monastery, and I said with a sigh: "Going out to collect rents in these times is like gambling with our lives." But the other monk would not resign himself to this: "I'm not afraid. Tomorrow I'll take the wooden fish there and beat on it. If they don't pay, I won't leave. What can they do about that?"

Master Ching-ch'ih turned to him with a sardonic smile and said, "You won't leave? If you don't leave, they'll throw you into the lake to feed the snapping turtles." This monk's jaw dropped in fear as he thought of this.

Carrying Money in Disguise

Since the tenants on East Tung-t'ing Mountain were too savage to deal with, we decided to lay aside our plan for collecting rents and focus our energy on working at Heng-chin. But worldly matters are never resolved as smoothly as one imagines. The more unbearably anxious we became, the more nonchalantly those slippery tenants behaved. If you pressed them a bit too hard, they would ridicule you so mercilessly you felt like looking for a hole to crawl into. And so, though we worked hard day after day, we were still far short of the amount we had counted on. I repeatedly proposed to Master Ching-ch'ih that we gather up our band and return to the mountain, but he always postponed our departure by saying, "Let's wait a few more days and see." What with one postponement after another, we ended up tarrying for two whole months before collecting something over 200 *tan* [14 tons] of rice.

One day, when we were about to rent a larger boat to transport the rice back to Mu-tu, Master Ching-ch'ih received an express letter from Abbot Miao-chen that went something like this: "In the past few days banditry has been rampant in the Lake T'ai area. It is imperative that you wrap up the business of collecting rents immediately. However, in order to avoid unforseen circumstances, it is my wish that you sell all grain where you are and return immediately with the cash and all members of your party. Please carry out these instructions with all urgency." After this urgent warning, we were at a loss as to what to do next. Some said that since the situation was so bad and we could not easily sell off the grain in two days, we should just leave the grain in storage and return empty-handed. Some felt that "there are certain orders which the officer on the spot cannot obey" and favored our original plan of renting a boat and taking the rice back to Mu-tu. Master Ching-ch'ih thought that the best thing would be to follow the instructions in the letter. He was a subprior and the leader of our party, so we had to go along with his suggestion. But the next day when he returned from selling 150 *tan* [10.5 tons] of rice at grain shops in town, he said to me in secret: "Before I received the abbot's letter, I could see that a lot was going on behind the scenes here, but I never noticed how terrifying it really is."

"What is terrifying?" I asked.

"This morning when I went to the center of town to do business at the grain dealers, I felt that people were watching me. In a situation like this it would be dangerous to wait until we've sold all the rice and then return together by boat...."

"Then what should we do?"

"I would like you to put on workman's clothing tomorrow morning and take the money I made selling rice today back to the mountain with you. Tell the abbot what our situation here is. We'll wait until we have sold the rest of the rice and then figure out some way to get back. What do you think?"

"It sounds all right, but it would be dangerous to carry all that money with me. Besides, I don't know the road to Ling-yen Mountain. If I stumble into the bandits' hideout, won't we be in a worse mess?"

"Naturally there is some danger to it, but it won't turn out as badly as you imagine. After you leave Heng-chin walk northwest a little way and you'll see Ling-yen Mountain. As long as you don't turn and walk off in the opposite direction, you won't stumble into a bandit hideout." After a pause he addressed me by name, speaking with added earnestness: "Master Chün-shan, no matter what happens, you have to take this risk for the sake of the establishment. Truthfully speaking, I know that I can trust you to carry out this hazardous mission." (In lay life Master Ching-ch'ih had served as an army adjutant. Often he unintentionally used military expressions in his speech. Also, he spoke in tones that an officer would use toward his subordinates.)

The common saying has it that even Yen-lo, the ruler of the underworld, is susceptible to flattery. Once Master Ching-ch'ih had lightly placed that high hat labeled "trustworthy" on my head, I had no heart to utter the unwillingness I felt. All right! If I can live so as to win the trust of others, what is wrong with dying? Moved by thoughts like these, I agreed without reluctance. The next day, while darkness still blanketed the earth, Master Ching-ch'ih woke me and the other monk up. He made me put on a pair of light gray workman's trousers, and then he tied a bagful of money flat against my stomach. After winding a long strip of cloth tightly around my torso, he covered it with a loose robe. On top of that he added a sweaty quilted jacket. The other monk took a pair of straw sandals and bound them tightly on my feet. The devotee put his worn conical hat on my head. Somehow Master Ching-ch'ih had gotten hold of an old bamboo basket full of fresh vegetables. After prevailing on me to put it on my back, he said, "Now you look like a hayseed!" It was still so dark outside that I could not see my fingers. According to tradition this was the time of day when Chu Hung-wu, the onetime monk and founder of the Ming dynasty, had set out to steal a pot and boil himself some beef. As Master Ching-ch'ih pulled me outside, he said, "Now is the perfect time to leave. It won't do to start at daybreak." With carefully placed steps he led me out of Heng-chin. Just before we parted I whispered, "Old Ching, if you don't see me at the mountain on your return, do not think for a minute that I have run off with the money. If I don't show up it will be because the money has been stolen by the bandits and I have been killed. Please don't forget to ask the abbot to hold a plenary mass to take me across to my next life."

My fear seemed to affect him for a moment, but then he said, "Old Chün, that won't happen. Put your mind at rest. I'll see you on the mountain."

After parting with Master Ching-ch'ih, I walked for a mile and a half before dawn lit up the sky. South of the Yangtze, early summer is supposedly a time when "warm winds lull the traveller into rapture." But such was not the case for this "hayseed" carrying his basket of vegetables through the mist in the faint morning light, slipping and lurching on the narrow, slippery paths between paddies. When the dew soaked my sandals, my feet felt as if they had stepped into icy puddles, and the cold penetrated straight from my feet to my vitals. The morning wind blowing on my face made me feel that a layer of skin had been taken off with a razor. Though the physical discomfort was dispelled in a while by the warmth of my exertions and the force of my will, I still shiver to think of it.

Thank Amitābha! After suffering groundless dread I arrived safely at Ling-yen Mountain and turned the money over to the financial subprior. I did not fail Master Ching-ch'ih after all. Upon my arrival, as I was passing from the guest department to the business office, I encountered a clerk whom I knew but who did not recognize me. Seeing my bedraggled, mud-splattered appearance, he grabbed me and asked, "Who are you looking for?" I have always had quite a temper, and what was more, I had just walked hard for three or four hours and hunger was burning in my stomach. His grabbing me and speaking to me in that tone of voice made my temper flare. "Is it your business who I'm looking for?"

He answered loudly: "I am an officer in the business office. Why shouldn't it be my business? Get out! Unauthorized persons are not permitted in this office." I was about to sport with him some more, when Assistant Instructor Yüan-an happened to walk out of the business office. At first he looked at me angrily, but when I had taken off my hat, pressed my palms together and explained the whys and wherefores of my strange outfit he laughed heartily: "O Bodhisattva! O Bodhisattva! For a minute there I thought you were a madman!"

Serving in the Guest Department

After I had counted out the money from 10.5 tons of rice to the subprior, I borrowed a full-sleeved gown and went to the abbot's quarters to report my return. Later, Assistant Instructor Yüan-an told the abbot of what I had gone through bringing back the money. The abbot spoke very highly of me and told me to stay in the honored guests' quarters for a few days until Master Ching-ch'ih and the others returned, at which time I could enter the Buddha Recitation Hall. In deference to the principle of "doing as one is told," I entered the honored guests' quarters on the evening of my return. Mentioning this makes me think of the various buildings at Ling-yen Monastery which were maintained for the purpose of extending hospitality to special guests. While we are awaiting the return of Ching-ch'ih and the others, it will not hurt to list these:

1. The honored guests' quarters consisted of simply furnished guest rooms. Officers from neighboring mountains and former officers of the establishment were usually housed here. Food, tea and water were provided by the guest department. Residents were not required to attend devotions in the shrine hall or go to the refectory for meals. Their time was completely at their own disposal, but they had to ask leave of the guest department before leaving the monastery.

2. Hsiang-yen [Fragrant Majesty] Chamber was built opposite the honored guests' quarters. Its setting and furnishings were both superior. In front of it was a small courtyard lush with flowers and shrubs. Standing in the middle of the courtyard, one could let one's gaze wander over distant mountains, nearby groves, smoke from quiet villages and neatly laid out fields. Most lay patrons were put up here. The guest department was also responsible for bringing meals here.

3. Hsiang-kuang [Fragrant Light] Chamber, also called Great Dharma Hall, was behind To-pao [Many Treasures] Pagoda. The front room was dedicated to a painting of Chih-chi Bodhisattva and the rear was dedicated to a stone image of the Venerable Yin-kuang. On the two sides were guest rooms. The furnishings were of a graceful traditional design, and the setting was tranquil. This was used to house venerable, learned men and important personages who came to see the sights. Meals were sent there by the business office, while the guest department was responsible for entertaining the guests. When necessary the abbot also came here to keep guests company.

4. The East House was on the left side of the bell tower. It was a modern building with Western style doors, windows, tables, chairs and baths. On a clear day one could look out the window and see Hu-ch'iu, where Master Sheng had preached the Dharma;[5] the city of Soochow; and Han-shan [Cold Mountain] Monastery which lay outside the city wall and of which the T'ang poet Chang Chi wrote in his poems. The sad thing was that, though this was a wonderfully inspiring place for poets and writers, it was usually occupied by rich gentlemen and young ladies from Shanghai. Although small groups of literary men sometimes asked to sit awhile inside, they stopped only long enough for tea or to have a meal before going back down the mountain. Few ever stayed overnight. Meals and entertainment for guests were handled the same way as in Hsiang-kuang Chamber.

Some people might find this objectionable on the grounds that all guests, regardless of wealth or status, should be given the same impartial treatment. Why should guests have been divided into so many different ranks? Was this not the same sort of snobbishness which distinguishes "sit down," "please sit down" and "please take the honored seat" or, "serve tea," "please serve tea" and "please serve some of our excellent tea," according to the wealth and prestige of the person spoken to? Actually, this was not entirely the case. In order to make each guest fit in where he felt most comfortable, it seems that things had to be done this way. For example, if a few country bumpkins coming to the mountain for a night's stay had been taken to Hsiang-kuang Chamber or the East House and treated as exalted guests, they would surely have felt uncomfortable and out of place among all the expensive calligraphy scrolls, rare antiques and fancy furnishings. On the other hand, if wealthy men accustomed to living in mansions had been shown to rooms in the Hsiang-yen Chamber or the honored guests' quarters, they would have felt slighted. I am not saying this to cover up Ling-yen Monastery's faults, much less to indicate my own agreement with this policy. I am simply saying that in this age of the Decline of the Law, when people's wishes take precedence over the Dharma, doing all this is necessary to insure survival of the monastic establishment. If everything must be done according to the strictest orthodoxy and no exceptions are tolerated, it would be impossible for monks to eke out a living.

On my third day in the honored guests' quarters, Master Ching-ch'ih and the others returned safely from Heng-chin. The results of the rent collecting expedition had not been as good as expected, but Abbot Miao-chen was happy at our safe return, and so the next day he instructed the small kitchen to prepare special dishes and held a welcoming dinner for us in the guest department. Aside from the abbot himself, the assistant instructors Hua-tung, Lien-yin, Yüan-an and P'i-lin, as well as the senior guest prefect Ti-huan, joined us at table. After the meal Abbot Miao-chen announced some news which nearly frightened me into insensibility:

"Though the rent collecting expedition did not meet our expectations, we owe their safe return to the intercession of the Three Treasures and the protection of Heaven. Subprior Ching-ch'ih and the others risked their lives for this establishment and for everyone in it. They worked hard for over two months without the slightest complaint. I feel great happiness and reassurance at seeing such forbearance and determination in the face of adversity. So that Master Ching-ch'ih, Master Chün-shan and Master So-an-so can continue contributing their efforts to this establishment and those within it, I would like to ask them, respectively, to assume the positions of assistant instructor, guest prefect and grounds prefect [*chih-shan*]. Are the assistant instructors in agreement with this?"

The four venerable assistant instructors answered in their commanding tones: "Agreed! Agreed!" The one named Lien-yin even began clapping his hands. I looked beseechingly at Master Ching-ch'ih, but the feeling that "all's well with the world" showed on his beaming face. He was murmuring into the ear of the senior guest prefect, T'i-huan, who looked at me, nodded and now and then forced a smile. Master Ching-ch'ih was like a blind man who looks but does not see: he took no notice of my anxiety. I had no choice but to drum up my courage and stand up, thinking to explain why I could not serve as guest prefect. However, at that very moment an accursed waiter ran in, pressed his palms together and said to the abbot: "That devotee's car has been at the foot of the mountain for some time. He told me to ask if you still want to go to Soochow."

"I'm going! I'm going! Tell him to wait a bit; I'll be right there." With this he stood up and said to the assistant instructors: "A letter came from the Hung-hua Hui [Association to Uphold the Buddhist Transformation][6] this morning, saying my presence is required. I'll go have a look and come back tomorrow. Let's leave the personnel appointments for the day after tomorrow." Then, like a man hurrying to catch a train that has already begun to move, he walked out of the guest department, his short pudgy frame rocking to and fro. The assistant instructors also left one after another to return to their quarters, while I stared at their backs in a daze.

"Congratulations, old buddy!" Master Ching-ch'ih walked up to me and spoke. I stood motionless and did not say a word.

"Now that we're co-workers I hope you'll give me plenty of help," chipped in T'i-huan, the senior guest prefect. I still stood motionless. After smiling bitterly for the sake of politeness, I returned to the honored guests' quarters. Back in my room I thought: "Even Ling-yen Monastery, a place known far and wide for its religious atmosphere, cannot accommodate my single-minded search for enlightenment. What place in the whole world can enable me to seek the truth I wish for?" Great sadness rose up within me, and unable to help myself I wrapped my arms around my head and cried.

The next day Abbot Miao-chen returned from Soochow, and on the day following a notice of appointment was hung under the porch of the refectory:

Master Ching-ch'ih is hereby appointed assistant instructor. Master Chün-shan is hereby appointed temporary guest prefect. Master So-and-so is hereby appointed temporary grounds prefect.
Effective this day the ___th of ___, 1948.

In this way I entered the Ling-yen Monastery guest department and began doing work that had to be done whether I liked it or not. At first there were three guest prefects in the guest department, but a few days after I assumed my position a guest prefect named Kuang-hui left without prior notice and ran off to Ch'iung-lung Mountain to live in a thatched hut. The other young one resigned and went elsewhere because of illness. In this way all the duties of the guest department fell on the shoulders of myself and T'i-huan.

Before assuming my new position I had thought that the duties of a guest prefect consisted of no more than asking questions of monks who wished to put up temporarily, receiving lay guests, and accompanying lay patrons on tours of monastery buildings and scenic lookouts. How was I to know that trivial matters kept one so busy from morning to evening that there was barely time to breathe? These duties included mediating disputes among rank-and-file monks in the outer sections; arranging meals for guests; accompanying patrons as they made offerings [*shang-kung*], attended plenary recitations of Amitābha Buddha's name [*ta p'u-fo*], or transferred merit [*hui-hsiang*]; scheduling work for waiters; and dealing with officers of the establishment asking for leaves of absence or reporting back to work. Luckily the abbot soon appointed two more guest prefects, or I might have followed the steps of Kuang-hui and struck out for parts unknown without so much as a "by your leave."

NOTES

1. It is called the *Yün-shui t'ang* (Hall of Clouds and Streams), because wandering monks were supposed to be as unattached as clouds and streams.

2. Mu-tu Chen was the name of the district. Mu-tu was a tower on the shore of Lake T'ai.

3. Chu-ko Liang (181-234 A.D.) was a hero of the Three Kingdoms whose ingenuity put Liu Pei on the throne of Shu (Szechuan). As we read earlier, the Peking opera "Strategem of the Empty City" is based on a story of his life.

4. The monastery was actually very old (see Chen-hua's account of Ling-yen in the previous chapter), but it had often been destroyed, last by the Taip'ings. Before 1949 it owned about 3,000 *mou* of rented farmland. This was small in comparison with some famous monasteries in Kiangsu. See Holmes Welch, *The Practice of Chinese Buddhism* (Cambridge, Mass., Harvard University Press, 1967).

5. Hu-ch'iu is Tiger Hill in Soochow. Master Sheng was Tao-sheng (d. 434), who was famous for his doctrine of universal salvation. He taught that all beings possessed Buddha-nature, including the *icchantikas*. This doctrine was revolutionary at that time, for it contradicted the translation made by Fa-hsien of the *Mahāparinirvāna Sūtra,* which appeared in 418. But Tao-sheng was convinced that he was right despite the strong attacks of his critics. He believed that Fa-hsien's translation was incomplete. He was vindicated when a new translation of the sūtra made by Dharmakshema appeared soon after 430. The new text confirmed Tao-sheng's view of universal possession of Buddha-nature. Tao-sheng was also reported to be a great preacher. He was supposed to have preached the Dharma to stones which would respond by nodding.

6. This was a lay Buddhist group in Soochow. Lay associations often invited monks to lecture and direct their activities.

Chapter VIII

ABOUT MY FATHER

Urging My Father to Renounce Lay Life

My family had once been fairly well off. We had been thought of as one of the four major families in the market town where I was born. But when I was four years old my grandfather, uncle, mother, older sister and four brothers all died within the space of a year. The next year the only son of my father's elder brother died of a sudden illness only three days after his wedding. In the wake of these misfortunes my father changed from the respected son of an educated farming family to an alcoholic and a gambler. Before many years had passed our fields were all sold for cash, and our house went to a new owner. My father was forced to enter the army, and I was cared for by my aging grandmother. By the time my father came back from the army, grandmother had already released her grasp on this world, and I had become a monk with the help of a neighbor, Mrs. Ch'en. All this was too great a blow for my father. His sorrow at grandmother's death was compounded by the feeling that he had not been a filial son. My becoming a monk was to him the most unfilial of all acts, especially since I was his only survivingchild: I would not leave any progeny to carry on his line. His state of mind became even more abnormal. He sold the twenty *mu* of land that had supported grandmother in her old age and opened a tavern in town. Month in and month out he led a drunken mess of a life, until the Japanese devils marched into our home district and shot the son of my father's younger brother. Then my father turned the tavern over to someone else and took part in resistance work for a few years. In the year of China's victory in the War of Resistance I heard, after arriving in Nanking, that he had disentangled himself from worldly matters and gone to the my little home temple to live a peaceful life. Naturally I was overjoyed to hear this, but I did not realize that his only purpose in going there was to live peacefully and that he was just as unreceptive to Buddhist truths as ever.

Then in the early winter of 1948, unable to bear the treatment he had received at the hands of Communists up North, he came south by train to find me. Once my father came, I could not allow him to "return empty-handed from the mountain of treasures." I resolved to urge him to renounce lay life, in hopes that he could — in the words of Great Master Lien-ch'ih [Chu-hung 1535-1615]— "leave the world of dust and dirt."

On the day after my father's arrival at Ling-yen Mountain, I was about to take him to the West Cell to visit old Dharma Master Lian-jan. I found a full-sleeved gown for him, but he refused to wear it, saying: "I'm not a monk. Why should I wear this?" Coincidentally two lay devotees who had entered the Buddha recitation hall walked by at that moment. I pointed to them and told him: "Dad, look! They aren't monks, but they're wearing them." I put the gown on him, but he did not seem happy about it.

When we arrived at the cell and saw Dharma Master Liao-jan at the wicket, I told my father to press his palms together and make a prostration with me. He gave me a reluctant look, but I pretended not to see and pulled his sleeve downward as I knelt. With this bit of prodding he went through the motions of touching his head to the floor in front of Dharma Master Liao-jan. When I had told Liao-jan about my father's escape from the North, he gave my father a few words of advice, and we went back to the guest department.

On the way back my father looked as if he had suffered a great wrong. With tears glistening in his eyes he said, "Since your grandmother died, I haven't kowtowed to anyone. I've lived over fifty years, and here I am kowtowing to a monk I don't even know."

I lost no time in pointing out his mistake: "Dad, you shouldn't think that way! You should know that prostrating yourself to a pious monk can erase much bad karma and bring many blessings. That is why many high officials and wealthy men..."

My father interrupted angrily: "Don't say any more. I don't believe in such stuff. If you try to make me kowtow again to this, that and the other monk, I'd rather go beg on the streets than stay here."

This scared me so much that my tongue lolled out of my gaping mouth. My wish to have my father become a monk had little hope of being realized. That evening I said to another guest prefect: "What can I do? My father got in a terrible fit of anger because I had him kowtow to Dharma Master Liao-jan. Will my wish for my father to become a monk come to nothing? Friend, can you help me think of a way to make my father change his mind?"

My co-worker said, "Since he doesn't understand the Buddhadharma, why use the Buddhadharma to persuade him? I think you should wait for the right opportunity to talk with him about unfortunate matters in your family's past and at the same time work in some Buddhist ideas of karmic cause and effect. This way you can move him and make him receptive."

This was good advice, but my father and I had lived through too many misfortunes. Where was I to start if I wanted to move my father? I thought all night, but I could not think of any past event the mention of which could move my father. This is not to say my father lacked feelings: rather, his feelings were so hardened that when someone spoke of a past event that would reduce others to tears, my father could listen without a trace of emotion. I was particularly clear on this point, but I was still determined to persist in my efforts. I was willing to suffer his blows and abuse if only he would renounce lay life. That is why I did not abandon what seemed an impossibly difficult plan.

One day father and I were in Hsiang-yen Chamber having a conversation when I inadvertently brought up the eight deaths that had happened in our family in one year. My father sighed deeply, shook his head and said, "If such a calamity had not descended on our family, I would not have been reduced to such a state, and you would not have become a monk."

I felt that the right time had come. "Dad, in this world, success and failure, calamity and blessing all come about through cause and effect. None of it has permanence. Why trouble yourself thinking of things that happened twenty years ago? You have undergone many hardships in the last twenty years, but you never knuckled under to the evil acts of the Japanese devils or the cruelty of Mao and Chu's Communists. You deserve to take some solace in this. As for my renouncing lay life, you need not feel sad about that. Didn't you just say that over one hundred people in our town died because of Communist-instigated political struggles? If I hadn't become a monk, wouldn't I have met the same fate as all those innocent young people? And come to think of it, if our family hadn't met with that terrible calamity twenty years ago, you and I wouldn't be sitting here having a leisurely conversation. The principles of misfortune and blessing, of cause and effect, are inescapable, but they are difficult to foretell. Why should you resent heaven and blame your fellow men for your misfortunes?"

Having spoken this far without disturbing the tranquil expression on my father's face, I continued: "Dad, there is something I have wanted to say to you for a long time but didn't dare for fear you'd get angry. Think about it: all your family members have died. Who is there left for you to worry about? That is why I think the best thing would be to renounce lay life, because..."

"What? You want me to renounce lay life?" My father stood up and shouted, his face livid with anger. Realizing that the situation had taken a turn for the worse, I stood up silently and prepared to submit to a tirade of curses. However, my father did not curse me. He only walked one circle around the living room. Then, returning to his seat, he asked, "How could you think of such a thing? Don't you know what a tongue-lashing my two sisters-in-law gave me after you became a monk? They said, 'Now that you've taken your only child to a temple to be a monk, how will you face his mother after your death?' Actually, you became a monk when I was still in the army. When I returned and found out, I wanted to get you back, but you'd have died rather than go back home. What was I to do? But all my neighbors and friends put every bit of blame on me. My two sisters-in-law ridiculed me mercilessly. They filled me with a shame that there was no hiding from. Now you want me to become a monk. If I really do as you say I would be unable to face your grandparents, let alone your mother." He got up and paced in circles around the room. I stood as motionless as a wooden figure, but inside I was grasping for something to say that would rid my father of his erroneous views.

After a pause, when I saw that my father's agitation had subsided, I found the courage to say: "It makes me sad to see you get so angry before I even finish what I wanted to say. Why do I want you to become a monk? Because I am all that is left of your family: I am the only person you have to worry about. Naturally you are the only family I have left and the only person I worry about. Since this is the case, we two, father and son, should stay together as if our lives depended on it. But how can we stay together? It is only possible if you renounce lay life. Why do I say this? Because I have already renounced lay life and come to live in a monastery. Although you are my father and I want very much to go on serving you, circumstances do not permit me to do so indefinitely. If you will renounce lay life, I can not only serve you, but I can be at your side no matter where we go. We can live and practice religious exercises together; we can travel on foot together; and we can make a pilgrimage to the four sacred mountains. If the political situation clears up, we can go back north to have a look. Wouldn't that be wonderful? As for what others have said or may say to berate you, it shows nothing but their own banality, and you should not let it affect you. There is a saying: 'When a son attains enlightenment, all his kindred will rise to heaven.' Although I haven't attained enlightenment, I am even now progressing in that direction. If the spirits of my grandmother, grandfather and mother could be aware of this, they would not be angry at you; they would be overjoyed. If you could resolve to renounce lay life, they would be even..."

A thunderous yell from my father cut me short. Once again I had to stand stock still. This time my father did not pace about the room, nor did he sigh. His fury gave way to mirthless laughter as he poked my forehead with a trembling finger and said things that left me between tears and laughter. But I had to listen patiently, because he was my father.

"I nearly starved sitting on the train for two days and a night to come to Soochow and find you. Now, not three days after my arrival, you're pushing me to become a monk. Is it because you grudge me the few days' worth of free food I've eaten here at your temple? You good-for-nothing, inhuman thing! I'll tell you the truth. I didn't come here because I worried about you, but because the Communists pushed me too far and I had to get away. I thought you could give me a little money so I could work as a street vendor in Nanking or Soochow to support myself until the troubles up north blew over. Who would have expected that all you talk about is how learned this dharma master is and how virtuous that monk is. Then you make me bow down and kowtow to people. I've put up with it to keep you from losing face, but now that I'm giving you an inch, you're trying to take a mile by forcing me to become a monk. I never thought that you would become such a fanatic in only two or three years."

Seeing that I stood through all this without stirring or making a sound his anger seemed to subside a bit, but he continued: "Didn't you know that at home I don't go a day without a drink? Have you bought me a single bottle since I got here? I won't dwell on this, because none of you here drink, but a person has to have cigarettes! You haven't bought me a single one. You treat me like this, and yet you say you want to serve me from now on. What good is that? I've had enough! Even if you feasted me on ambrosia and nectar I wouldn't stay here with you people. Hurry up and give me some money: I'll go to Nanking tomorrow."

Tears fell from my eyes like pearls from a broken necklace. I was not crying because my father's tirade had hurt me, but from my pain at not being able to change his mind. Then in an agony of frustration I said thoughtlessly: "All right, if you put it that way, I won't urge you to renounce lay life anymore. However, I have no money to give you." With that, I walked out of Hsiang-yen Chamber.

A Prayer to Kuan-yin

After returning to work in the guest department I spent the rest of the day in a confused and preoccupied state. Not long after morning devotions the next day the servant who waited on my father rushed into the guest department and said, "Master Guest Prefect! Your father is ill. Please go take a look right away!" The servant's words fell on me with the force of a club. I was on the point of falling over in a faint, but I pulled myself together and ran to my father's room. In the early morning darkness, by the light of a kerosene lamp, my father's features looked as flushed as they usually did when he was drinking. His forehead was hot to the touch. I called his name twice in a soft voice, but there was no response. He was sleeping soundly and did not seem to be in pain, but judging from his color and body temperature, there was no doubt that he was ill. I told the servant to watch over him while I went to ask for the services of Assistant Instructor Ta-ch'eng, who was fairly well-versed in medicine. After examining the patient, Ta-ch'eng bought a few packets of powder and a dozen pills and told me when to administer them, without so much as explaining what the illness was. He spoke a few comforting words: "Don't you worry. When he finishes all the medicines he'll be better." But this was the opposite of what happened. After my father finished all the medicine, his illness grew even more severe. When I, my co-workers and the officers from the business office crowded into Hsiang-yen Chamber to ask after his health, he did not speak or moan. His only response to well-wishers' questions was to shake his head feebly.

When I spoke of my father's condition to Abbot Miao-chen, he said, "Hsiang-yen Chamber has guests coming and going every day. It is terribly inconvenient for you. Won't it be much better if you take him to the subsidiary temple and nurse him there?" Regardless of whether the subsidiary temple was preferable or not, I was in no position to disobey the abbot's instructions, so I moved my father down to the small temple at the foot of the mountain on the third day of his illness.

For four or five days after the move, my father let forth occasional sighs, but he neither spoke nor ate nor drank. He passed all his time in a deep sleep. I was desperate over my inability to do anything for him. One evening after the prayer for transfer of merit in the recitation hall, I put on my robe, picked up twelve tiny cones of incense and stole quietly to the sculptured island behind the great shrine hall. After making three prostrations to Kuan-yin, I rolled up my sleeve, placed my left arm on the altar and placed the pieces of incense in three rows on my arm. After using a small candle to light them, I chanted the holy name of Kuan-yin as I watched the twelve little pillars of fire change into ash.[1] Then I knelt down, took out the prayer that I had written beforehand and read:

Your disciple, *Bhiksu* Chen-hua, carries a heavy burden of sinful karma. When I first emerged from my mother's womb, a seer predicted evil fortune. [According to my grandmother, a blind fortuneteller said I had been born to die of starvation.] Just one month after my birth my family's fortunes declined. When I was barely four years of age, my kindhearted mother passed away. When I was nine my father went to war; when thirteen my grandmother left this world. Thenceforth I stood alone. The next year Mrs. Ch'en took pity on my lot and arranged for me to become a monk. At fifteen, upon entering a private schoolhouse, I first learned to read 'one' and 'two.' At nineteen I passed tests to enter a 'foreign academy' [At nineteen I was admitted to the Hsiao County Normal School. Because of my grandfather master's opposition, I was unable to take up studies there. In my district, public schools were called 'foreign academies.']; at twenty I became a schoolmaster. Absurdly enough, at twenty-three I marched to battle in my black monk's robe. [That year half of my home temple had been burned to the ground by Japanese soldiers. I resolutely set out to take part in the War of Resistance to wash away this outrage, but after a short time I was found and brought back by my grandfather master.] At twenty-four I left my hometown and went south for ordination and study. After visiting famous mountains and places of truth in the Nanking area, I went to Ling-yen in Soochow, where I was ordered to assist the guest department. Helping in the guest department did no harm; reciting the Buddha's name is not limited to the Buddha hall. Though I am your disciple, the weight of evil karma bears down upon me, so much that my father was forced to flee from home. This was cause for grave concern, and so I came to the decision that the best course would be for my father to renounce worldly life. First, so I could in a small way fulfill my duty as a son, and second that my father might better see into his own mind and thus repent of his past sins. Who could have foretold that no sooner did I express this wish than my father became ill from anger? For seven days and seven nights he has lain in a deep sleep; all the doctor's art avails him nought. In my confused and worried state, I know not what to do. I kneel down and beg for compassion; in devotion and reverence I burn incense on my arm. I pray that my father's sickness will soon heal, that his mind will be clear and bright, and that he will become a monk. These three things would be the answer to all my hopes.

Having finished the prayer, I made three more prostrations to the bodhisattva before returning quietly to my room and lying down in my clothes.

Like Waking from a Dream

The next day as I walked down to the subsidiary temple, my heart heavy with worry, I thought: "As serious as the old gentleman's illness is, what will I do if he should pass away? If I have his remains cremated and take the ashes up north, the relatives and friends of my lay family will curse me to the heavens. Having him shipped home in a coffin is beyond my power. What can I do? May the compassionate Kuan-yin intercede to make my father better soon! Otherwise, how can I possibly stand such a terrible blow?"

As I was walking through the gate of the subsidiary temple, the temple manager saw me and shouted from a distance: "Master Guest Prefect! You came at just the right time. I was just about to send someone after you."

"How is my father? How is my father?" I asked as I ran toward him. Seeing me in such anxiety he grabbed my hand and laughed: "Calm down! Your father is taking a turn for the better. He called for me very early. That seemed strange to me: how could a man who has been unconscious for seven days know that I am the temple manager? And how could he know he is in the subsidiary temple? I thought he was entering what people call the 'last brightness at sunset.' As soon as I ran to his room he asked, 'Are you the temple manager?' His voice was weak but very clear. I told him in a whisper that I was indeed the temple manager. Then he said, 'I have made trouble for you by staying here. I feel much better today. Please send someone up the mountain to call Chün-shan. Can you?' I thought he wanted something but was embarrassed to ask, so I told him to ask for me if he wanted anything. He shook his head and said, 'I don't want anything. Just send for Chün-shan, please. I have something to say to him.' Then he closed his eyes peacefully and slept. He did not look at all like a man who has not eaten or drunk for seven or eight days."

Scarcely able to believe my ears, I walked to my father's room, tiptoed to his bed and called, "Dad." Praise be to Kuan-yin! It was truly unbelievable. At the sound of my voice my father straightened himself and sat up as straight as a pen. In a warm, kindly tone (which my father had never in his life used before) he said, "Chün-shan, I'm feeling better. Don't you worry. There is something I want to tell you. You must agree to it, or I'll stop eating and wait for death."

I quickly knelt before his bed and said, "I know what you want to tell me. Please don't worry. No matter how great the difficulty, I will put together the money for travelling expenses. When you have recovered, I will take you back home."

Shaking his head and waving his hands, he said, "Get up, get up! What are you kneeling for? Chün-shan, you misunderstand me. I didn't want to tell you to collect the travelling expenses to take me home. I want you to find an ordination fee [*chieh-fei*] so when I recover you can take me to be ordained."

"Ordained." I was so unprepared for this that all I could do was repeat the last word. I stood up in fright and, in the tone of one begging for mercy, said, "Dad, don't get angry again. I won't urge you to renounce lay life any more, much less urge you to receive ordination. Don't get angry again. When you've recovered, I'll take you home."

To my surprise a faint smile appeared on his lips. He patted the edge of the bed and said, "Chün-shan, calm down. Sit down and listen to me. It is true that I became ill out of rage at your urging me to become a monk. However, I've come around to thinking you are right, so I have decided to become a monk as soon as I recover. After that I'll go to T'ien-t'ung Monastery in Ningpo for ordination. Then we two will go on a pilgrimage to P'u-t'o Island and then come back here. We two will live and practice religious exercises together forever. We needn't go anywhere else. What do you think?"

Praise be to Kuan-yin: I was nearly wild with joy at hearing this! But I still had trouble believing such words had come from my father's mouth. Forgetting for a moment his weak condition, I embraced him with sudden force. "Dad! Do you really want to become a monk?"

Seeing that I had nearly lost control of my movements, he stroked my shoulders with his trembling hands and said feelingly: "Chün-shan, today is the first time I have thought of you as a son since you became a monk. You are the person in the world who cares about me the most, son. Would I trick you? I think the only way to stop us from worrying about each other is for me to become a monk. Only if I become a monk can both of us find true happiness. I don't know how I could have been so stupid in the past. If I had come south with you in 1945, I wouldn't have suffered through those years of living hell." (Meanwhile I was thinking that if my father had felt the same way seven days earlier, he would not have gone through seven days of painful illness.)

At this point the temple manager walked slowly into the room. He looked at my father, then said to me: "The old gentleman just got better, and he hasn't eaten for seven or eight days. He shouldn't talk too much or sit up too long. Let him lie down and rest."

But my father's spirits seemed even better upon seeing the temple manager. He told the manager to sit and said, "I'm not tired. It feels wonderful just talking about what's on my mind." He repeated what he had said to me for the temple manager's benefit.

The temple manager looked at me in astonishment. I told him laughingly: "Not only has my father recovered from his physical illness, but the illness in his heart has gotten better too. That is why he is in such good spirits after his great illness."

The temple manager laughed and asked my father: "Didn't you fall ill because you were angry at our Guest Prefect for urging you to become a monk? How is it that right after getting better you want to become a monk? When did this notion come into your mind?"

In answer to this my father told us a dream: "Last night I dreamed I walked into a large temple and saw many monks seated in a large room eating. I felt very hungry, so I walked in, sat down and prepared to eat. But when I had taken the bowl in my hand, an old monk appeared before me and said, 'Are you willing to renounce lay life?' I nodded yes without thinking. The old monk said with a smile: 'This food is for monks. Only the monks deserve to eat it. Since you are willing to become a monk, go ahead and eat.' The old monk left, and I woke up feeling comfortable and happy. I think that the old monk must have saved me. How else could I have gotten better so fast? I want to become a monk so as not to deceive the old monk in my dream."

Father and Son Together

After hearing that my father had entered such a realm of thought in his dream, the temple manager praised him for having a deep root of goodness [*shan-ken*]. Then he turned to me and said, "Your father's illness is better and he is willing to renounce lay life. Now you can cast away the weight that pressed on your heart! Today you need not go up the mountain at lunchtime. In order to celebrate your father's new life and your filial behavior, I will buy some vegetables for you two and 'make an offering to the monastic community [*kung-chung*].'"

I couldn't suppress a laugh at this. When he asked me why, I answered, "I'm laughing at your amusing choice of words. To 'make an offering to the monastic community' means to offer sustenance to the monastic community at large. It hardly makes sense to apply this term to my father and myself."

He laughed even louder: "So the guest prefect is starting to find fault with my choice of words. I'm afraid you wouldn't have been in the mood for this yesterday. Hah hah. All right! Since you tell me to offer sustenance to the monastic community at large, that's just what I'll do. Anyway, there are no more than ten people in the subsidiary temple. Making one offering to the monastic community won't send me into the pawnshop." With another roaring burst of laughter he went out to send someone to Mu-tu to buy food.

Actually, this was only an expression of goodwill on the part of the temple manager. My father could not eat food prepared with oil while he was taking the first steps of recovery from a major illness. And it was not all that easy for me to get such food down either. My mood was not as relaxed as the temple manager imagined. Why was this? For one thing, my father was still a long way from complete recovery, and for another, the matter of my father's becoming a monk after his recovery was not going to be resolved simply by talking about it. With these two matters pressing on my mind, how could I stretch my stomach and gorge myself on the rice and vegetables he offered?

After the temple manager left, I asked my father to lie down and rest. I paced to and fro in the courtyard as I looked up toward Ling-yen Mountain and turned these matters over in my mind: How ideal things would be, if only they could work out as father hopes! He has told me: "I've decided to become a monk as soon as I've recovered. After that I'll go to T'ien-t'ung Monastery in Ningpo for ordination. Then we two will go on a pilgrimage to P'u-t'o Island and later come back here. We two will live and practice spiritual exercises together forever. We needn't go anywhere else." If we could do that, we would be like a pair of wild cranes, one young and one old, soaring freely in the boundless sky. When tired of flying, we could land anywhere — atop mountains or beside rivers, among graves or in treetops — and go to sleep. When hungry we could eat whatever we find, be it sour, sweet, bitter or peppery; hot, cold, fragrant or malodorous. Then we could fly back to our starting point, Ling-yen Mountain, lay aside the myriad entanglements of karma, and put forth our ultimate effort to make a place for ourselves in the Western Paradise, on the Nine-Tiered Lotus that floats in the Pond of Seven Treasures. That is everything I wish for; I need not seek elsewhere.

My father's temperament had always been extremely obstinate. I had never seen him get along with another person or do as another person said. But, after recovering from this illness, the old gentleman underwent a 180-degree change. No matter what anyone said, he expressed agreement in a most unaffected manner. This "abnormality" of temperament bewildered me with joy, and at the same time it filled me with much apprehension. However, my apprehension vanished as he recovered full health.

After my father regained his health, the senior instructor performed the tonsure ceremony in Dharma Master T'an-hsü's stead, after having written for permission. Many people were overjoyed at my father's decision and praised him highly. I too was glad that my father could honor one of the great luminaries of our age as master.[2] My father himself was even happier. From the day of his tonsure ceremony, if he was not having me teach him to read sūtras he was asking me to explain the rules for traveling from temple to temple and putting up for the night, or even to teach him how to make prostrations to the Buddha. Even more amazing was the fact that, when he saw everyone doing morning and evening devotions, he followed along of his own free will; when everyone entered the recitation hall, he followed along and recited Buddha's name with everyone else. In sum he was immersed body and mind in the sea of the dharma. In such a situation how could others fail to praise him? How could I not be glad? How could my father be anything but happy? Praise be. I thank the Bodhisattva for making my own and my father's life complete.

NOTES

1. This was a common form of self-mortification. The pain was intense.

2. T'an-hsü was a famous contemporary monk. He wrote a memoir called *Ying-ch'en hui-yi lu* (*Recollections of Shadows and Dust*, Hong Kong, 1955) in two volumes. See also references to T'an-hsü in books by Welch, who interviewed him in Hong Kong during the 1960s.

Chapter IX

BUDDHA RECITATION WEEK

Now that I have given an overall account of my father's renunciation of lay life, I will move on to the subject of Buddha recitation weeks at Ling-yen Mountain. For the past ten or fifteen years most temples and monasteries here in Taiwan have conducted recitation weeks every year around the time of Amitābha's birthday for purposes of celebration. Actually one can only say that these encourage beginning believers to plant the root of goodness by reciting Amitābha Buddha's name a bit, but they cannot really be called Buddha recitation weeks. And the gatherings held by invited masters so that the initiators could get their hands on small sums of money are not even worth mentioning. Well then, how were the recitation weeks at Ling-yen Monastery conducted? Don't be impatient: I'm coming to that.

In this Age of Decay of the Law, when factional struggles run deep, Ling-yen Monastery truly deserved to be called an ideal place of truth for those who sought to lead a religious life. I could illustrate this by comparing the Ling-yen monastic community's way of life with that of monks at other public monasteries, but for fear of digressing too far, I will stay on the subject of recitation weeks.

The daily regimen in the recitation hall at Ling-yen Mountain lasted for six sticks of incense (one and one-half hours per stick). On top of that were morning and evening devotions and the transfer of merit chanted at the end of the day. Thus, an average day's practice took up to twelve hours. Hearing this will scare the wits out of people who have newly resolved to renounce lay life. Don't let this scare you. In the eyes of the old hands at Ling-yen Monastery, this was as commonplace as a home-cooked meal. Did we not take solemn vows to "be paragons among men" and "break away from life and death"? If we cannot even stomach this mild hardship, how can we fulfill our vows?

Someone may ask: "Your normal practice was twelve hours long. Don't tell me that during recitation weeks you even recited Buddha's name while eating and sleeping?"

Yes, that is right. During intensive recitation weeks we repeated Amitābha's name silently while eating and sleeping and even while going to the restroom. I would first like to talk of matters that were to be kept in mind during recitation weeks, and then speak of the aim of recitation week and the proper method of recitation.

The key to a smooth, properly conducted recitation week was in the hands of the precentor [*wei-no*], the monitors [*chien-hsiang*] and the percussionist [*ch'iao chien-ch'ui*]. If the precentor was thoroughly familiar with recitation week rules, the monitor serious about keeping watch over the participants and the percussionist able to move his hands in perfect response to his thoughts, then the recitation week would without a doubt be an excellent one. However, if the precentor did not understand the rules; if the monitors were lax in discharging their responsibilities; and if men who could not even recite "Namah Amitābha" in the prescribed rhythm were asked to beat time, then the recitation week would be a slipshod one. Therefore, in advance of recitation week the precentor, monitors and percussionists had to get a clear idea of their respective functions, so they would not harm others and themselves. In Ling-yen Monastery's *Ceremonial Rules for Recitation Week* [*Fo-chi yi-kuei*], the section "Points to Keep in Mind" has this to say about precentors:

"The precentor is the monastery's pillar of discipline. On him depend the spiritual fates of all the monks. His duties are not light: he must bear up under resentment and arduous work. At normal times, of course, he must be conscientious, but during intensive periods his presence must impart even greater solemnity to the proceedings, so that all may rise out of the dust and transcend the worldly. Unless pressure is kept up by the rhythm of the wooden fish, the work of the participants cannot follow its proper course. Seek instantaneous realization and watch over the participants with compassion: only then can you yourself find true attainment."

The points to keep in mind for monitors included these: "The Dharma never arises in isolation: it comes into being through causation. Getting down to the business of spiritual work is not difficult, but one must rely on outside protection [*wai-hu*]. Those who give such assistance are classed among beneficial friends of the spirit, because they give support for the process of transformation and assist in efforts at singlemindedness. Since the aim of advanced work is an advanced spiritual plane, we must borrow the help of causal affinity [*chu-yüan*] to make it happen. What is more, we are seeking instantaneous realization, so we must naturally rally the strength of the group to give succor to its members. The monitor in the recitation hall helps others toward attainment."

The points to keep in mind for percussionists were these: "The community's spiritual work depends upon a measured rhythm for chanting. This is a matter of utmost significance. The loudness and tempo of the bell and wooden fish should be moderate. Never be careless; never change hands in the middle of a measure. You must keep perfect rhythm — never unsteady or irregular...."

The "Intensive Sessions" section discusses the true aim of a recitation week and the proper method of recitation. The aim of a recitation week is: "In order to make our minds whole and undisturbed [*yi-hsin pu-luan*], we must do intensive spiritual work. The purpose of conducting an intensive recitation week is to allow participants to gain good karma, thus discharging all karmic debts and enabling them to be reborn in the highest plane [*shang-p'in*]...."

The method of reciting Amitābha's name during recitation weeks (of course it would be better if this could always be practiced) was this: "...All must feel strongly the dilemma of life and death, put aside all affinities and dwell only on one thing. When reciting Buddha's name, one must draw the six senses inward. Mind and sound must be united; pure thoughts of Amitābha must succeed one another without interruption, like a son thinking back on his mother. In walking recitation, walk with a slow, stately gait to allow connectedness of mental effort. Sit straight in the lotus position so that your vital force and spirit are not hindered. Recite with undivided mind before sleeping and hold Amitābha within yourself as you fall asleep. Resume immediately upon awakening. The sound of your recitation should be soft and heartfelt. Do not recite so loudly so as to do injury to your vital force; do not inflame your vital force so that emotions are awakened; do not heat your blood with silent vehemence; do not relax and allow other thoughts to be present; do not lapse into quietude or drowsiness. Enunciate the six syllables clearly and distinctly; never interpose the four syllable 'Amitābha' alone; and never recite in an oily, affected manner."

Now let us look at what had to be done at the opening of a recitation session. Recitation sessions can run anywhere from seven days to seventy-seven days. At Ling-yen Monastery the session began after repetition of vows on the evening of the fifteenth day of the tenth lunar month and concluded on the twenty-fifty day of the twelfth month — in all seventy-seven days or ten recitation weeks.[1] Before the opening of the session everyone from the abbot to the vergers had to bathe thoroughly and put on clean new clothes. The period from the first day of the session to the twenty-sixth day of the tenth month was called "Adding Incense" [*chia-hsiang*]. That is, aside from our normal morning and evening devotions, we added a stick of incense to the length of both, and the transfer of merit in the evening was lengthened by one hour. During the Adding Incense period special monitors

Fig. 7 Monk doing meditation in Fa-yüan Monastery, Beijing

and percussionists were assigned. After evening devotions on the last day of the Adding Incense period, when everything was running smoothly, each participant went individually to the abbot's quarters and asked leave to depart from the round of birth and death [*kao sheng-ssu-chia*].[2] Then everyone assembled at the great shrine hall to perform a plenary recitation of repentance and to pray that the Trikāya [*san-fo*][3] guard us from demonic hindrances during the session and that our deeds would enable us to enter the Pure Land. After repentance we went to the recitation hall for the lighting of incense, thus formally beginning the intensive portion of the session. From the twenty-seventh day of the tenth month — the day on which Great Master Yin-kuang acted out the onset of affliction[4] — to the fourth day of the eleventh month, the day on which Yin-kuang acted out his entry into nirvana[5], was the recitation week devoted to Yin-kuang's memory. From the fifth day of the eleventh month to the twenty-fifth day of the twelfth was the special intensive period [*ching-chin*]. During this period participants held their attention exclusivelyon the six mighty syllables, being excused from all other religious duties except chanting the *Amitābha Sūtra* [A-mi-t'o-ching][6] once in the morning, calling on the name of Amitābha after meals and performing a transfer of merit in the evening. This was not like recitation weeks in modern-day Taiwan, where in a single day one must sing incense hymns, chant several chapters of scripture, repeat a certain number of mantras, recite the chants for transfer of merit before the plaques of longevity [*ch'ang-sheng wei*] and rebirth plaques [*wang-sheng wei*],[7] and listen to lectures by the monk in charge. Sometimes the lecturers in Taiwan start "turning the wheel of the Dharma" and speaking on scriptural subjects which have nothing at all to do with recitation week. Even more amazing are the monks in charge of recitation weeks who give elaborate talks, as I have heard, on the story of Monkey raising an uproar in the Jade Emperor's palace. Good heavens! The moon could become an inferno and the sun could turn into ice before this sort of recitation week could enable participants to attain the *samādhi* of Buddha recitation.

Inexpressible Wonder

The reader might ask: "You say that most recitation sessions in Taiwan are not properly conducted and participants cannot possibly attain the *samādhi* of Buddha-recitation [*nien-fo san-mei*]. Since the recitation weeks at Ling-yen Monastery were conducted with such attention to the rules, is it true that all the participants attained *samādhi*?" Excuse me for not presuming to shoot my mouth off. You see, the *samādhi* of Buddha recitation is something only those who have attained it can know. I have not attained it, so I do not presume to say. However, during every recitation session at Ling-yen Monastery there were always unbelievable occurrences. I know of the following cases.

Sitting Transformation. Dharma Master Ching-nien, who now lives in Tainan, knows more about this than I. I can only give a brief account. An old hand at spiritual exercises lived in the recitation hall at Ling-yen Monastery. Even brothers who had lived with him for years knew nothing of his personal history. He seldom spoke or laughed in daily life. When spoken to, he would answer with Amitābha's name. After a time everyone became familiar with his personality and no longer tried to involve him in idle conversation. Of course this was perfectly suited to the old practitioner's wishes. Every day from morning till night he did nothing but recite Amitābha's name. Had the sky fallen about him he would not have paid the slightest heed. One year during a recitation session when the transfer of merit had been chanted at the end of an incense period, everyone stood up at the sound of the hand-chime to prostrate themselves toward Amitābha, but the old man sat motionless as before. Thinking that he had entered perfect absorption, no one dared to disturb him, and everyone went about their own business. However, when the next stick of incense began and he still sat erect and motionless, the precentor walked up to him and patted him lightly, but there was no response. When the precentor put his hand before the old man's mouth and nose, he finally realized that the old man had stopped breathing quite some time ago.

Supernatural Powers of Vision. If the reader's memory does not fail him, he will remember the incident of the young monk from Kiangsi who was swindled out of his luggage by a *ma-liu-tzu* on his way to ordination at Pao-hua Mountain. This young man, whom I had almost mistaken for a confidence man, later became my ordination brother and ended up at Ling-yen Monastery as a verger in the recitation hall. Even more unexpectedly, he suddenly attained supernatural vision [*t'ien-yen-t'ung*]. His monastic name was Tsao-wu. Though he looked a bit dull, he had excellent motivation for spiritual work. He ate only one meal a day and never slept lying down. One day while sitting in the hall during a period of silent recitation, he saw a monk from the western section of the hall moving his bowels without washing afterwards, and then walking into the recitation hall. "Hey! Are you entering the recitation hall without washing yourself first?" he shouted.

The monitor happened to be right before him and, thinking that Tsao-wu had been touched by demons, rapped him with an incense board. Tsao-wu opened up his eyes and only then realized that he was still sitting in the recitation hall. He himself was mystified. How could he have seen the man in the bathroom through several walls? When the stick of incense burned out, the precentor asked him what he had been shouting about. He told exactly what he had seen. The precentor went to the western section and asked the monk whether such a thing had happened. The honest rank-and-file monk blushed scarlet, pulled his neck down between his shoulders and said, "That is true."

Emittance of Brilliant Light. One morning the gatekeeper was roused out of meditation by the sound of a crowd milling outside the gate. Upon opening the gate and peering through he was surprised to see a large number of people. He wanted to quiet them down, but before he knew it they had rushed through the gate and were asking excitedly:

> "Master, did the fire in your monastery do much damage?"
> "Fire? What fire?"
> "Uh, wasn't there a fire here at the monastery last night?"
> "Who told you that?"
> "Nobody told us. We saw it with our own eyes. Last night at around ten o'clock we saw a fire lighting up half the sky. We couldn't very well make the long climb in the dark, so we came up this morning to look."

Shaking his head like a peddler's drum, the gatekeeper mumbled:

> "Don't you people have anything better to do than come up here early in the morning and put a jinx on Ling-yen Monastery?"

Seeing the gatekeeper shake his head and mutter, the crowd disregarded him and swarmed into the monastery. When they had seen for themselves that the buildings were all in good shape, they walked down the mountain in a state of utter amazement. Later, news of this spread from mouth to mouth, and the monks all knew it. Everyone thought that the light had appeared because of the chant for the transfer of merit, which had been performed at around ten o'clock. There are grounds for this explanation. In the text for "The Great Transfer of Merit" [*ta hui-hsiang*] under the sentence "May there be no obstacles at the moment of death," there is a note reading: "This sentence has proved its power with miraculous events down through the ages. Sometimes extraordinary signs are seen at the moment when it is truly taken to heart. Sometimes Amitābha comes in dreams and emits brilliant light. Miraculous phenomena are too many to list. Only those who give their all to carry out their practice believe that such things are not unreal."

If the "fire lighting up half the sky" was not Amitābha emitting a brilliant light, what could it have been?

Inexpressible Wonder. Speaking of the above miraculous events makes me think of the modest little thought-realm that I attained during the recitation session at Ling-yen Monastery. In the eyes of long-term practitioners my little thought-realm would not even have merited a laugh, but it gave me no less joy than that felt by a lost child who has finally found his mother. Since I have brought it up, I should describe it further, but this modest little thought-realm was one of inexpressible wonder. It was "like a man drinking water — he alone knows the warmth or cold of it." How can I describe it? My little thought-realm was not the "treasure of the eye of true Dharma"; nor was it the "wonderful mind of nirvana." Even if I were to speak of it, the reader would not smile wordlessly in understanding like Mahākāśyapa.[8] With all respect I must inform the reader that the thought-realm of Amitābha recitation is known only by those who actually recite Amitābha's name. If your faith is deep, your will is strong and you perform this with sincerity, at the moment of death Amitābha will receive you into the Pure Land even though you are still laden with karma [*tai-yeh wang-sheng*]. Whether or not you experience a certain thought-realm is beside the point. Some may think that breaking out of life and death could not be so simple. In his letter to Upāsaka P'u Ta-fan, Great Master Yin-kuang addressed this problem most admirably: "The Dharma of Pure Land must be looked at with different eyes; it cannot be ranked among ordinary teachings. Had Tathāgata not opened the way to this dharma, no one could be found to break out of life and death in this age of Decay of the Law."

He was so very right: Pure Land should not be ranked among ordinary teachings.

NOTES

1. The length of seventy-seven days, however, was not necessarily always the rule. Informants from Ling-yen told Holmes Welch that "seven recitation weeks were held each winter." Readers may compare Chen-hua's account with that found in *Practice of Chinese Buddhism*, pp. 90-100. Just as Chin Shan was the model for Ch'an meditation, so was the prestige of Ling-yen among the practitioners of Buddha invocation.

2. According to monastic rites, a monk must ask leave from his abbot whenever he is not participating in the daily routine of monastic life. When he enrolls in the recitation session, his purpose is to leave *saṃsara*, the round of death and rebirth. So he asks formal leave to be engaged in this endeavor.

3. The Threefold-bodies of the Buddha are the Dharmakāya (the Body of Truth), the Sambhogakāya (the Body of Enjoyment), and the Nirmāṇakāya (the Body of Transformation).

4. This meant the day Yin-kuang became ill.

5. This meant the day Yin-kuang died.

6. *A-mi-t'o ching* (*The Smaller Sukhāvativyūha Sūtra*, T. 336) is one of three basic scriptures for Pure Land believers. The other two are the *Wu-liang-shou ching* (*The Larger Sukhāvativyūha Sūtra*, T. 363) and the *Kuan-wu-liang-shou ching* (T. 365). This sūtra is the shortest of the three.

7. They are the wooden plaques on which the names of the living and the names of the dead are written. Through the ritual of the transfer of merit, monks can pray for the long life of the living or the rebirth into the Western Paradise for the dead.

8. This refers to the famous legend about how the Ch'an school started. Once at Vulture Peak the Buddha Śākyamuni gathered the assembly of bodhisattvas, arhats, monks, nuns and lay people. But instead of preaching the Dharma as he usually did, the Buddha held up a flower without saying a word. Everyone except Mahākaśyapa was puzzled by this. Mahākaśyapa smiled and by doing so he showed the Buddha that he had understood. In this way, the Dharma was said to be transmitted wordlessly from the mind of the Buddha to that of Mahākaśyapa.

Chapter X

VICTORY FOR THE CHINESE COMMUNISTS

The Rolling Red Tide

The unfolding of political events set the once-rock-steady hearts of several hundred monks at Ling-yen Mountain adrift like gourds bobbing on water. First, some of the more timid student monks in the seminary fled to places they thought safe, ignoring the pleas and advice of the dharma masters. Then, one after another, the rank-and-file monks in the recitation hall, menial officers and lay workmen ran off to who knows where. Abbot Miao-chen was quite alarmed at this. He called together all officers for an emergency meeting at the East Pavilion. At the beginning of the meeting, Abbot Miao-chen said, with tears running down his face, "Ling-yen Monastery is a public establishment, and those who have gathered here from every corner should resolve to preserve it. Now people hear how bad the political situation is, and they run off to fend for themselves. How can we allow this? You gentlemen are either elders responsible for the resurgence of this Monastery or pivotal officers. Today I ask all of you, in consideration of the great pains Patriarch Yin [Yin-kuang, 1861-1940]took in founding this monastery and of my authority as abbot, to resolve as a group to set an example for the monastic community in preserving our place of truth until this difficult time is past. We must stay at all costs. As for providing necessities in the future, you need not trouble yourselves: no matter how difficult a task it is, I will take complete responsibility."

After Miao-chen's speech, everyone sat silently for a long while before an old instructor stood up to speak: "The abbot's intention to preserve this place of truth certainly deserves our admiration. However, we must consider whether all of us can preserve the establishment by remaining here once the Communists come. If we think it is possible, then everyone should remain on the mountain together and take the bad with the good: if we think it is not possible, we must ask the abbot to be compassionate and allow everyone to stay or leave as they wish."

Another officer said, "The Communists are like a scorching, ruthless torch. Whoever comes close to them dies or gets seriously hurt; there is no hope of escaping through mere luck. The day before yesterday I heard someone talking about the head monk of a certain temple in the vicinity of Peking. Because he believed that all groups of armed men were the same, he was not willing to leave the temple he presided over. Soon the Communists arrived. First they searched out and confiscated every article of value in the temple. Then they insisted that the head monk had buried a cache of gold under the foundation stones of the shrine hall. They told the old monk to hire laborers to dig up the floor. When the old monk said there was no gold, he was beaten cruelly and forced to dig up the foundation. When the excavations were completed, the shrine hall collapsed, but there was no gold to be found. The Communists said the old monk was holding something back. Not allowing him to speak on his own behalf, they locked him inside a small room and warned him that if he did not produce the gold they would starve him to death. Because he recited Amitābha's name singlemindedly, the old monk was still in good spirits after four days, though he had not touched a drop of water or a grain of rice. When the Communists interrogated him about the gold, he kept reciting to himself and did not say a word. After seven days of this he still had not starved to death. Most people would say that after treating a harmless old monk with such cruelty they should have left well enough alone, but the inhuman Communists did not think this way. Seeing that the old monk was still alive after seven days, they laughed malignantly and said, 'You've recited Amitābha for seven days, but Amitābha hasn't come to rescue you from this little room and lead you to the Western Paradise. Hah hah hah. It looks like we will have to give you some help!' So saying, they stabbed him to death with a knife."

When the officer had finished telling this story, he turned to the abbot and continued: "The fire of Communism cannot burn long, but while it is burning fiercely, the best thing for us is to hide from it. This is why I think that those who wish to leave the mountain should be urged to do so by the abbot."

Upon hearing this speech, Abbot Miao-chen's already scarlet face turned purple. With a painful mixture of expressions showing on his face, he forced out these words: "I admire your perceptive opinions, but from my point of view it would be better to meet that old monk's fate than to leave Ling-yen Monastery. Nevertheless, in view of what you have said, I will not interfere with any of you who wish to leave the mountain. But if you wish to stay, I will not put pressure on you to do otherwise." With this his eyes swept over the whole assembly, and he moved his squat frame back to his room. Everyone hung their heads as they too returned to their rooms. When I, the very last to leave, stepped out of the East Pavilion, I was intercepted by the officer who had described the Communists as a blazing torch. "Are you leaving or not?" Without a moment's hesitation I replied, "I'm definitely leaving." He smiled and walked off in the direction of the refectory.

Fleeing South Kiangsu

After the assembly at East Pavilion, all the monastery officers engaged in heated discussion, but no consensus was reached. Some wanted to share the fate of Abbot Miao-chen and Ling-yen Monastery, whatever it might be; some could not leave the mountain soon enough; and some passed their days in blissful unconcern, preferring to "wait and see what develops." As for me, I wanted to put a great distance between myself and Ling-yen Monastery right away, but various considerations held me back. I had to have my "grandson disciple" Hai-ch'ao accompany my father to report for ordination ceremonies at T'ien-t'ung Monastery in Ningpo. I set busily to work clearing up the paperwork in my department, so that I could ask for leave to go down the mountain. I hardly expected that right after I saw my father off, Nanking would be thrown into a panic. Tidal waves of refugees were meeting head on. I say this because people from Nanking, Chen-chiang, Ch'ang-chou, Wu-hsi and Soochow were fleeing east to Shanghai, while people from Shanghai, Soochow, Wu-hsi, Ch'ang-chou and Chen-chiang were fleeing west toward Nanking. Suddenly the people of these regions were like a directionless swarm of locusts, fleeing at random for all they were worth. Actually none of them had seen the slightest sign of the Communists. Observing this sort of mass panic reminded me of the same situation during the War of Resistance. Someone might see a man at the east end of one village raise his arm, and everyone in that village would run wildly toward the west, carrying their children and leading their livestock, as if the Japanese devils were breathing down their necks. The people of the next village did not bother to ask if there were a good reason for this: they too joined the stampede toward the third village. Naturally the people in the third village ran like everyone else. In this way scores of villages might be emptied out in no time at all. Finally when inquiries were made, it would be discovered that the villager who had raised his arm had only been stretching his back, and everyone had mistaken this to mean that he had seen the Japanese devils and was signalling them to flee.

The panicky flight from Shanghai and Nanking was the same as the flights from the Japanese army in rural areas of the North during the War of Resistance. These were mostly blind, groundless panics. If everyone had remained calm, the southern half of our motherland would never have fallen into Communist hands so quickly. Perhaps it would not have fallen into Communist hands at all. Still now, when I close my eyes and think back on those heartrending scenes, I am deeply saddened.

The nation was like a tottering skyscraper, and most people were too busy running to think of doing anything else. How could the strength of one man or a few men hold it erect? Each person's mind latched onto the notion of the safety he could find somewhere as he followed the waves of fleeing humanity. Even now I can hear the clamor of wails, shouts and blows that penetrated to the farthest corner of every train station and dock. But this did not intimidate the waves of humanity. Instead, the hearts of the scrambling people grew more frenzied at the din. The M.P.s and police who were supposed to keep public order could only stand and watch from afar as waves of struggling people dashed toward the boats or trains.

Push! Push! Push! In the end it was the strong, young people who elbowed their way onto the train or boat. The old, weak and very young looked enviously at the grinning victors. What to do? Waiting for the next run was the only choice. Heaven only knew if the young, strong ones who were yet to come would let them step easily aboard when the next train came.

Three monks were caught up in the waves of humanity that dashed against one another at the train station in Soochow. Two had come from a thatched hermitage on Ch'iung-lung Mountain and were named Yi-chen and Lung-p'ing. The third one was myself. Lung-p'ing had once served in the guest department of the Ling-yen Monastery, which made us colleagues. Yi-chen was a veteran practitioner of spiritual work who had lived in a hermitage, and some affinity had caused us to run into each other several times. The three of us met by chance in Ling-yen Monastery's subsidiary temple. The original plan of my two companions had been to follow the Yangtse River upstream and go to see a brother in Nan-ch'ang, Kiangsi, before continuing westward. They wanted to enter the mountain fastnesses to the West and live as hermits. But then they changed their minds and went with me to Shanghai. The route I had planned was from Soochow to Shanghai, then from Shanghai to Ningpo. In Ningpo I would await the end of my father's ordination and then make a pilgrimage with him to P'u-t'o Island. If the political situation cleared up, I would go first to T'ien-t'ai; then on to Hangchow and vicinity to do some sightseeing; and then back to Ling-yen Mountain. Otherwise I would stay put on P'u-t'o Island and leave everything to Kuan-yin. So the three of us went to Soochow by boat. Once there we fought our way through the crowds and bought three train tickets. (Actually we could have just climbed on the train without tickets, but we were unwilling to do something so akin to thievery.) We pushed our way onto the platform, but no matter how hard we struggled, we could not get aboard the train.

The train was jammed full with people. Every space that offered handholds on the top and outside of the train was covered with people. The locomotive was belching thick black smoke and seemed to be building up steam to get moving. Yi-chen, Lung-p'ing and I realized we had to do something. We were in no position to concern ourselves with maintaining solemn deportment. Putting our strength together, we pushed our way through to the side of the train. I kneeled down to let my friends step on my shoulders and climb onto the roof. I handed up our knapsacks and then, with the help of my friends and much desperate scrambling on my part, I made it to the roof of the car. We had climbed up all right, but the top was not flat and there were too many people. Of course standing up was dangerous, but sitting down was not a whole lot better. Everyone was wondering what to do when a loud voice rang out: "The train is about to start! Everyone put your luggage in front of you and sit on the crest of the car roof. Join hands with the person facing you to prevent an accident!" Sure enough, we were much safer when everyone straddled the crest of the car and joined hands.

The steam whistle let out a long blast and the train began moving. But the train seemed hardly able to move under its great burden of sadness. It let out a series of disconsolate wails as it crawled forward like an injured black dragon. For those who watched, it must have presented a poignant, heart-wrenching spectacle.

I — a young monk worn down by hardships encountered in seeking knowledge--turned my head every few seconds to gaze at Ling-yen Mountain and the towering pagoda on its peak. Softly I said to myself: "Goodbye, Ling-yen Mountain! No, goodbye South-of-River!"

A Night in Shanghai

I arrived in Shanghai — that huge bustling center of commerce — in February 1949 on the top of a train with my two friends. After the waves of people had deposited us outside the train station, we looked at each other and suddenly burst into loud laughter. We laughed so hard that tears rolled down our faces. What was so funny? Well, our dignified visages had been blackened by smoke from the locomotive, and we looked like three images of Lord Pao, the judge of "iron-faced impartiality."[1] In a spoofing, self-justifying tone I said, "In order to enlighten all human beings, Kuan-yin appears sometimes as the Buddha, as one of the Buddha's immediate disciples [*sheng-wen*], as a *pratyeka* Buddha [*yüan-chueh*],[2] or as a Vajra-holding spirit [*chih chin-kang shen*].[3] She wanders to all countries and preaches the Dharma to all men. All three of us have now appeared as Judge Pao. To whom should we preach the Dharma?"

They looked at me silently, shook their heads and smiled ruefully as they said, "Bodhisattva! You are about as absurd as they come. Don't you realize how bad the times are? Haven't you looked around and seen the situation we are in? No — you're still getting a charge out of your own sick jokes." With that they shouldered their packs and said, "If it's in our fates, we'll meet again!" They turned and walked toward Jade Buddha Monastery [Yü-fo ssu],[4] while I struck off in the direction of Chüeh-yüan [Garden of Awakening] on Ho-teh Street.

The atmosphere of war pervaded Shanghai. In the vicinity of the train station there were foxholes every five steps and pillboxes every ten steps. Large numbers of fierce, proud-looking soldiers, sporting arms and ammunition belts, walked in endless streams. They looked ready to enter the fray and sacrifice their lives if necessary to defeat the Communists.

Why did I have to go to the Garden of Awakening when I reached Shanghai? The reason was that a famous personage in Shanghai named Huang Chin-jung had organized a Dharma assembly at Chüeh-yüan Monastery that was to consist of a seven-week recitation session. Besides asking Abbot Miao-chen to preside over the session, he had brought forty-nine veteran practitioners from Ling-yen Mountain to lead laymen in reciting the Buddha's name. Before Abbot Miao-chen's coming to Shanghai, I had explained to him that I wanted to go to T'ien-t'ung Monastery in Ningpo to see my father. At the time he had given permission without a moment's hesitation, but just before leaving for Shanghai he said to me: "Most of the old guest prefects have gone. How can you do this to me? I'll go to Shanghai first and have a look. If the political situation looks really bad, it won't be too late for you to go to Ningpo then. (The logic of this sentence was strange indeed, because when he uttered it the political situation was already bad enough, though the disaster that threatened had not yet actually come.) Otherwise, you can stay here until the recitation session is over and we all come back."

In the end the old man's refusal to forget the establishment for even a moment had an effect on me. That is to say, I gave in to his request. Then, only three days after he left, the national situation darkened to the point that even the sun and moon seemed blotted out. I had to go to Ningpo to take care of my father. To explain my reason for not remaining on the mountain longer, I first had to look for the abbot at Chüeh-yüan Monastery.

It was dinnertime when I found the place. After I had seen Abbot Miao-chen and told him the details of my coming down from the mountain he said resignedly: "Since things have gotten this bad, of course I won't force you to go back. But I hope that if the crisis takes a turn for the better and you have seen your father, you'll go back and report for work right away." He gave me a five-dollar gold certificate and told me to buy a boat ticket to Ningpo. Then he had a servant show me to a pleasant, quiet room to rest. Because the servants were all brought from the guest department at Ling-yen Monastery, they treated me with special hospitality. In a moment Instructor Hua-tung and a lot of rank-and-file monks crowded in to ask what had happened since they had left the mountain. Feeling that it is "better to roil up the waters of a thousand rivers than disturb the mind of a man intent on the Path," I simply told them: "Things on the mountain are about the same as when all of you left, the only difference being that refugees on the Nanking-Shanghai railroad are more numerous every day. This has influenced the monks on the mountain and made them less able to focus their minds on their religious work." As I spoke, Devotee Tu Ts'un-wo walked in. Tu was a native of Hsü-chou whose devotion to Pure Land had become stronger with age. Because he had often stayed overnight at Ling-yen Monastery and because my birthplace and home temple were not far from Hsü-chou, we had gradually come to view each other as fellow countrymen, even though we were from different provinces. He spoke the usual polite words of greeting and then asked me to tell him everything I had seen and heard along the way. His sentiments were those of a man inquiring nostalgically about his hometown. I repeated what I had just told the others, and in this way time passed until the clapper signaled the lighting of incense for evening devotions. All of them filed out to the shrine hall. After I had taken the bath prepared by the servant, I blew out the lamp and lay down to sleep.

Not long after lying down I entered the land of dreams. I dreamed that I was with Lung-p'ing, Yi-chen and many other people straddling the crest of a railroad car. As the train started moving, I saw people with wild hair flying, their faces covered with grime. Some were so emaciated their bones protruded like dry sticks, and their clothes were in tatters. Some wore expressions of agony and cried out in torment. Some cried for their fathers and mothers with wailing sobs. I was terribly saddened by all this. Turning toward Lung-p'ing and Yi-chen, who were reciting Amitābha's name with closed eyes, I said, "Hey! Don't you see the pitiful state these people are in?" I heard Yi-chen answer: "So what. All phenomena produced by causation are like dreams, like hallucinations, like bubbles, shadows, dew or lightning — one should view them in this way."

I disagreed strongly with this, so I protested in a loud voice: "You, brother, are about as absurd as they come! Don't you think about how bad the times are? Haven't you looked around and seen the situation we are in? Is it right for you to talk this way? These suffering people are really here, right before our eyes. Look how pitiful they are! How can you view them as dreams, as hallucinations, as bubbles, shadows, dew or lightning?"

No matter what I said [in the dream], he and Lung-p'ing went on reciting Amitābha's name with eyes closed. They were not paying the slightest attention to me. This filled me with anger and impatience. In order to express the sympathy I felt, I suddenly stood up. I was thinking of going to comfort those pitiful people, when a false step sent me falling headlong from the roof of the car. When I heard myself shout in fear, I knew it was a dream. I heard people outside the window talking softly. When I rubbed my eyes and looked, it turned out that everyone was outside my room washing up and getting ready for morning devotions. I hurriedly got up, washed and joined the others, but all through devotions the heart-rending images from my dream still hovered before my eyes.

Looking for My Father at T'ien-t'ung

The T'ien-t'ung Ch'an Monastery is a place of truth with over one thousand years of history. Its setting is secluded and its architecture massive. It has produced many luminaries and pious monks like Eight Fingers [Pa-chih],[5] who gave his life for his religion; Great Master T'ai-hsü, who reformed the Buddhist religion; Great Master Yüan-ying, who proclaimed the teachings of the *Leng-yen sūtra*; and Great Master Yin-shun, whose learning was as vast as the sea. Some of them served as abbots at this monastery, some served as officers and some received ordination here. In short, these and many other outstanding figures were all fostered by the "local spirit" of the place.

T'ien-t'ung was in the area of the Ssu-ming Mountains. Tradition has it that during the Eastern Chin a Ch'an master named Yi-hsing built a thatched hut there and practiced meditation. His efforts moved the Emperor of Heaven, who changed the planet of Venus into a young lad and sent him to earth to provide Yi-hsing with food every day. Later Yi-hsing's fame spread far and wide. The thatched hut expanded into a public monastery. In memory of this extraordinary event, he changed the name of the mountain to Venus Mountain [T'ai-pai shan] and named it the Monastery of the Heavenly Lad [T'ien-t'ung]. Because of the miraculous

Fig. 8 Monk serving as meditation patrol in T'ien-t'ung Monastery, Chekiang, holds the incense board, the symbol of his office

circumstances of its origin, incredible things have never stopped happening at this famous monastery over the past thousand years. Unfortunately I did not stay there long. If I had, this chapter might not have turned out so empty of incident.

After crossing a few ridges and following a few turns in the rugged, winding path, I reached Dragon Pavilion. When I saw the rows of old pines on either side of the road and the crystal-clear, babbling stream, I thought of lines from poems by Eight Fingers: "A five-*li* pine-shade road/With rest stops long and short/Stream flowers tinge the ravine blue/Forest birds sing the woodsmoke gray." "The ten-*li* road of pine shade is not far..." "Ten *li* of great pines green up to the gate." At the time I did not know what he meant by "rest stops long and short," but when I reached Tiger Pavilion I put two and two together. Actually, Dragon Pavilion is not a long-distance rest stop, and Tiger Pavilion is not a short-distance rest stop. The reason that Eight Fingers used "long" and "short" instead of "Dragon" and "Tiger" was probably that dragons and tigers differ greatly in length!

It was marvelous walking on this "live-*li* pine-shade road." Pines shaded the road like a canopy, and the cool wind blew refreshingly. Though it was still early summer, many songbirds were hopping about and warbling in the branches. From deep in the woods wildflowers sent whiffs of tantalizing fragrance.

The road was paved with rough-hewn stone slabs of uniform size. Every five steps a lotus was carved in the stones. Each time I stepped on a lotus, I repeated silently: "This flower sprang forth from the earth, and my body was born of this flower." What with walking, saying my little prayer and seeing the sights, I soon arrived at the main gate of the monastery without feeling the least bit tired. Eight Fingers' "The ten-*li* road of pine shade is not far..." was so true!

I walked through the gate and into the guest department. After greeting the guest prefect politely, I explained my reason for coming. An usher led me• to the wandering monks' hall. Right after I had been assigned my sleeping place, a brother of the cloth walked over to greet me, addressing me repeatedly as "Master Guest Prefect." I waved my arm to stop him and asked softly: "Bodhisattva, how should I address you? Why do you call me that?"

Instead of answering me he asked with a laugh: "Aren't you the guest prefect at Ling-yen Monastery? When I went to Ling-yen last year, it was you who interviewed me before I was put up in the guest quarters. Have you forgotten?"

I laughed in return and said, "This is the wandering monks' hall of T'ien-t'ung and not the guest department at Ling-yen. Let's just call each other bodhisattva, all right?"

He seemed to have something else to say, but at that very moment Hai-ch'ao, who had brought my father here for ordination, walked in and said, "Grandfather-master, if you'd have come any later the old gentleman would have worried to death!"

"Worried about what?" I asked.

"Yesterday a monk came from Hangchow. He said that Nanking has already been occupied by the Communists, and the Nanking-Shanghai rail line has been cut. The old gentleman was so worried he didn't sleep well all night. This morning he cried and said, 'If anything happens to Chün-shan, my ordination will be meaningless.' He also said, 'After ordination I'm going right back to Soochow. If he dies, I'll die with him.'"

Without stopping to eat, I said a few words of greeting to the hall master and then went with Hai-ch'ao to see my father. On the way we saw many new ordinees walking back and forth. They looked at us veteran ordinees as if we were not even there. They did not press their palms together in greeting, and they did not make way for us. Thinking back to the very different situation at Pao-hua Monastery, I said to Hai-ch'ao: "The ordination session at Pao-hua was so severe it bordered on the barbaric. Here, it is so lenient it borders on laxity. Unless a middle ground between severity and laxity is found, in either case the ordinees will be confused about what to accept and reject."

We were discussing this when I heard a voice from behind: "Chün-shan! Chün-shan!" I was overjoyed to see that it was my father. Both of us ran quickly toward the other. Without any preliminaries my father asked, "I heard that Nanking has been taken by the Communists and the Nanking-Shanghai rail line was cut. How did you come?"

"That was only a rumor. The Communists haven't taken Nanking, and rail traffic between Nanking and Shanghai is flowing freely. Otherwise how could I have come to see you?" I went on to tell about the recent state of affairs at Ling-yen Monastery as well as some trivial matters I had heard of in Shanghai. Then I asked how he had gotten along during the ordination session.

"With Master Hai-ch'ao's help, everything has been fine. But I worried about you all the time. Last night when I heard the rail line had been cut, I was so anxious I couldn't sit or lie still. All I could think of was going back to Soochow to look for you. Now you're here, and there is nothing to distract me! You couldn't have slept all night on the boat. Go to the guest hall and rest. We'll save our conversation for this evening." With that he walked rapidly after the new ordinees toward the rear courtyard. Hai-ch'ao took me on a tour of the monastery buildings, after which I returned to the guest hall and Hai-ch'ao returned to the waiters' quarters. He had already gotten a position as waiter and was serving the new ordinees.

In the eyes of most itinerant monks, T'ien-t'ung Monastery's guest hall was a most convenient and ideal place. Except for required attendance at offerings in the wandering monks' hall and devotions in the shrine hall, everything was arranged to suit your pleasure. If you resolved to read scripture while staying there, the bookcase behind the Buddha niche had everything you might want. If you wished to meditate, you were free to enter the meditation hall and meditate for as many periods as you wanted. When you saw the couplet on the door which read: "In this examination hall for Buddhas/ The empty mind is the successful candidate," you might perceive then and there your original face before you were born. If you wanted to bow down before the Buddha or recite Amitābha's name, the guest hall was spacious and, as long as you did not impose on others, you could prostrate yourself or recite day and night, and no one would interfere. If you did not care to read, meditate or recite, and you only wanted to chat or climb mountains and have a little fun, you were invited to step onto the porch behind the hall or climb any of the surrounding mountains. The kindly hall master would never stand in your way. Besides all this, the best part was that, as long as you did not break hall rules, you could stay indefinitely. It was not like other monasteries, where you were asked to roll your bedding and hit the road after two meals and a night's sleep.

I put up for over ten days in the guest hall. Except for going to devotions, eating meals and seeing my father, I passed most of my time walking among the scenic wonders and ancient buildings in the vicinity. I recall that one day I went walking with a few brothers who could best be described by the lines: "His bowl filled by rice from a hundred homes/ A solitary man on a never-ending trail." We visited the reliquary pagoda of the Enlightened Patriarch Mi-yün. Mi-yün had been the man who brought T'ien-t'ung Monastery out of decline and gave it new life. The pagoda was built near the old monastery site. Within the monastery was a quiet room where Mi-yün's personal effects were on exhibit. On our way back to the monastery we passed Eight Fingers' Cold Fragrance Pagoda. Amid the fresh green cedars and bamboo grew numberless plum trees. Unlimited respect arose within me for the great teacher, who had loved his faith, his country and the beauty of plum blossoms. Before I knew it, my feet had carried me inside the pagoda, where I silently paid my respects. It is said that the Cold Fragrance Pagoda was designed by Eight Fingers and built under his own supervision. One of the walls bore a poem written in his own hand:

I have broken forever with the human world;
In cold mountains there is also glory.
Lonely smoke dims as sunset comes,
Then brightens as a ghost of moon appears.
At void's edge we peer in vain for shadows;
In incense smoke a certain feeling grows.
This is what I have longed for all my life,
May it fill the remainder of my days!

Later I found two more poems on Cold Fragrance Pagoda in "The Poems of Eight Fingers." One of them was:

The Buddha's lifetime knows no bound;
Should not my span, then, have a beyond?
Mind passed from finger to the moon,
Bones buried under a million plum blossoms!
Caves for spirit to rest in red cliff,
Guests to come visit my green mountain:
Resting in this tower someday soon,
I shall be here with mist and rainbow clouds.

There are several poems about plum blossoms in the same book. I shall copy two of them here so the reader can understand the meaning behind the name "Cold Fragrance Pagoda." The first is taken from a series of twenty-one poems called "Moved by Events":

All things return to the realm of extinction;
White clouds hurtle vainly toward green peaks.
Frosted bell tolls down the mountain stream's moon;
Only plum blossoms are fragrant in the cold.

The other, entitled "Shown to Everyone on New Year's Eve" is as follows:

Mountain families bustle on New Year's Eve,
The monastery bell joins in festive song.
Seekers of the way drink no spiced wine
But savor the cold fragrance of plum blossoms.

After we had toured Cold Fragrance Pagoda, we talked about the great teacher's life all the way home. Eight Fingers was orphaned at an early age. Because of his poverty he was forced to work as a cowherd and janitor and cook in a schoolhouse. For a time he was ordered around as a slave while he worked as a servant for a rich family. One day when he saw beautiful peach blossoms blown to the ground in a storm, he was choked by violent sobs. At this moment he made his mind up to become a monk. Soon after he went to the Fa-hua Monastery in Hsiang-yin to become a disciple of Elder Tung-lin, after which he went to Chu-sheng Monastery at Nan-yüeh to receive ordination.

For five years after his ordination the great teacher stayed at a mountain temple and practiced austerities. When he had free time he accompanied the rest of the monks in seated meditation, so he gained fairly deep insight into the meaning of Ch'an during this period. Once on a trip to visit his maternal uncle at Pa-ling, he climbed Yüeh-yang Tower and looked out upon the scale-like flecks of light on the vast blue expanse of Tung-t'ing Lake. Suddenly a line popped into his mind: "The waves of Tung-t'ing's carry a lone monk here." Soon his fame as a poet was widely proclaimed. He then wandered to all the famous monasteries in the Kiangsu and Chekiang regions, visiting learned and pious men wherever he went. Both his poetry and meditation advanced rapidly to a high realm. The autobiographical essay in his *Collected Poems* has the following paragraph:

"Finding myself among valleys and crags that bore no sign of human presence, I sang and uttered wild cries. When thirsty I drank from springs and nibbled on cedar leaves. I enjoyed chanting loudly the *Leng-yen Ching* [*Sūragama Sūtra*] and the *Yüan-chüeh Ching* [*Sūtra of Perfect Enlightenment*], with a bit of *Chuang Tzu* and *Li Sao* thrown in for good measure. People looked on me as a lunatic. I once climbed through the snow to the Hua-ting Peak of Mt. T'ien-t'ai. The sea of clouds sent a thrill through my breast, so I flapped my sleeves in the wind and howled. A sleeping tiger stood up in alarm and ran toward me growling furiously. I looked at him with compassion and his fury dissolved. Once, deep in the mountains, I encountered a huge serpent riding on the wind. Its head was as large as a basket, and its flickering tongue shot out over a foot. I kept fear at bay by reciting Amitābha's name. When I returned to nurse an illness in Kao-t'ing Mountain, I was awakened one night by the sound of claws scraping on the door. I opened the door and saw nothing but a still, moonlit scene. This happened several times. One night I waited for the sound and quickly threw the door open to see a black furry body leaping crazily. Several dogs and I gave chase. At the foot of the mountain I yelled fiercely: 'I am a poor monk. I don't bother you: why do you bother me? Do you think I am afraid of you?' I then recovered from my illness almost immediately."

From this we can glimpse something of Eight Fingers' unique spiritual life. Alas! It has been sixteen years now since the mainland fell into

Communist hands. I wonder if Eight Fingers' Cold Fragrance Pagoda has remained unharmed?

Putting up at Aśoka Monastery

On the day of my visit to Cold Fragrance Pagoda, I received a letter from Abbot Miao-chen at Garden of Awakening in Shanghai. The main idea of the letter was that the situation in Shanghai had improved somewhat. At the end of the recitation session he would lead his monks back to Ling-yen Monastery. Concluding the letter was that same old sentence: "At the end of the ordination session, I hope you will return to the mountain and report for work." I related this to my father and Hai-ch'ao. My father expressed his view: "During a crisis like this, you have to take one day at a time. You can't decide anything in advance." Hai-ch'ao said, "No matter what happens, we should go stay for a few days at Aśoka [A-yü-wang] Monastery[6] after the ordination session. After we worship the holy relics there for a few days, we'll make a pilgrimage to P'u-t'o Island. If things get better while we're there, we'll go back to Soochow. Otherwise we can stay put on the mountain and wait." Anything at all was fine with me. My father had finally received ordination, and this had been my only wish. As for everything else, I was happy to "pass the seasons going where my karma led me." What is more, Hai-ch'ao's suggestions agreed perfectly with the plans I had made when leaving Ling-yen Monastery. So the day after my father took his Bodhisattva Vows, we went to Aśoka Monastery.

We really did not have to put up in the wandering monks' hall, the reason being that a dharma master named Hua-ti lived there. He had once stayed at Ling-yen Monastery, and we had become good friends. After he returned to Aśoka, he often wrote and told me to visit him. I wrote that I would certainly go see him if I had the chance. Now that we had arrived at Aśoka, I needed only to bring up Hua-ti's name when we entered the guest department and, though we would not necessarily have been received as exalted guests, we would at least have been excused from performing devotions, eating with everyone else and crowding onto a sleeping platform in the guest hall. (Aśoka Monastery was partly a hereditary and partly a public monastery.[7] Hua-ti was a young and able member of the family of tonsure disciples there. He was also financial subprior and a man to be reckoned with at Aśoka.) But in order to let my father gain experience, to avoid relying on connections and to see how things were done at Aśoka, I decided to put up in the guest hall. However, I did plan to visit Hua-ti in the business office before we left. Strangely enough, something went wrong in my attempt to put up for the night, and we were nearly driven out the front gate by the guest prefect. In the end I had to mention Hua-ti's name after all. It happened like this:

I led my father and Hai-ch'ao up to the door of the guest department. Having put our luggage down left of the door, we stepped over the right side of the threshold. There sat a monk who seemed to radiate well-being as he drank tea and conversed cheerfully with two prosperous-looking women. Experience told me that this was probably the guest prefect.

The common saying has it that "in the eyes of a mouse, a kitten is thousands of times more mighty than a tiger." In the same way, the most powerful person to a wandering monk wishing to put up for the night was the guest prefect. Though I had served as a guest prefect myself (and never gave wandering monks a hard time), now that I was playing the part of a wandering monk, I could not help being nervous. Without allowing myself to lapse into casual self-assurance, I prostrated myself to the Buddha, sat down carefully on a stool on a right side of the room and waited quietly for the guest prefect to "interview" me. Soon he walked out from the room where he had been having tea and, according to the usual rule, looked out the door at our luggage. Then he sat down in his chair at the head of the room. My father, Hai-ch'ao and I stood up, at which I cried out, "Kowtow to the guest prefect!"

Who would have expected the guest prefect to be so impolite as to say "One prostration!"? (According to rule, he should have said, "A bow will be fine.") My father and Hai-ch'ao did as he said, but I only bowed and returned to my seat. I sat on my stool, still as a wooden puppet, and did not look past the tip of my nose. Perhaps my actions caused him to lose face in front of the ladies. At any rate, he walked up to me and yelled brusquely: "Where did you receive ordination?" (He should have asked, "At what establishment did you receive ordination?")

"At Pao-hua Monastery."

"If you received ordination at Pao-hua Monastery, why do you know so little about rules for putting up for the night?"

"I know the rules for putting up for the night. It is the guest prefect who does not understand them!" I thought he would not stand for this, but as soon as he heard it, his unreasonable attitude softened instantly.

"I'm sorry," he said with a laugh. "I thought you were one of the new ordinees from T'ien-t'ung. I didn't know you were an old hand. Anyway, I'm sorry. The guest hall is already filled with people who have come to the mountain on pilgrimage. Please go put up in some other temple." Without waiting to see our reactions, he went back to drink tea with his guests.

"A fine fellow he is! He wants to drive us right back out the gate," I thought to myself.

"What are we going to do?" Father and Hai-ch'ao asked in desperation.

I suddenly stood up and said loudly to Hai-ch'ao: "You two stay here. I'm going to the business office to find Hua-ti."

The guest prefect was taken aback. He walked hurriedly over to me and asked, "Do you know Hua-ti?"

I answered in a somewhat surly tone of voice: "What? You didn't let me put up for the night, and now you're going to interfere with my seeing a friend in the business office?"

As he held me back, he said, "I would never do that! Why didn't you say sooner that you're Hua-ti's friend? Sit down; I'll send for him."

When Hua-ti came and introduced me as a guest prefect from Ling-yen Monastery, the guest prefect's face blushed as red as Lord Kuan's.[8]

Paying Respects to a Holy Relic

The worship of holy relics is an amazing phenomenon. The *śarira* at Aśoka Monastery was brought to China during the reign of Emperor Aśoka two hundred years after the Buddha's death.[9] King Aśoka was both an enlightened monarch and a great protector of Buddhism. He used supernatural power to pulverize gems and then mixed the powder into fragrant paste. In the space of a single night he built 84,000 stupas and placed a *śarira* of the Buddha in each. Then he asked the elder Ye-she [Yaśas], who was gifted with magical powers, to send down 84,000 rays of light. He ordered ghosts and spirits to bear the stupas to the most beautiful, auspicious places on the southern continent, so that all men could make offerings and plant the seeds of goodness for themselves. It is said that there were nineteen places in China which were "most beautiful and auspicious." The site of Aśoka Monastery is one of these places. Any place which has a stupa for the Buddha's holy relics is one and the same with the Buddha's Dharma Body, and all men, gods and demons "should gather there reverently to strew flower essences." But this is not the way things were for us. Perhaps this was due to the karmic hindrances and scant blessings of men in the Age of Decay of the Law.

On the afternoon of our arrival at Aśoka Monastery, after we had been assigned our places in the guest hall, we put on our robes, took articles of worship in hand, and went in the company of some other guests to worship the *śarira* in the Śarira Shrine. In answer to our requests the senior verger brought out the *śarira* reliquary and placed it on a table on the porch behind the shrine. He told us to make three prostrations and then kneel with hands joined and eyes closed. We were to recite "Homage to Śākyamuni, the Original Teacher," a certain number of times and then open our eyes and look at the *śarira*. According to the verger, people's perceptions of the *śarira* differed according to their fundamental abilities. Perceiving the *śarira* to have a golden color was best, while perceiving it as gray-black was worst. Being anxious to prove my fundamental ability, I stared at the place in the tiny jewel-crusted reliquary where the *śarira* was kept. I looked until my eyes ached, but I could not see where it was. Fortunately the somewhat irritated verger picked the reliquary up in both hands and held it in front of my face. I finally saw the *śarira*, which was smaller and blacker than a black bean. Afterward I asked my father, Hai-ch'ao and the others. They had all seen it, but their impressions of its size and color differed. Some said it was yellow, some said it was red and some said it was rainbow-colored and as large as a watermelon. I had to admit that the verger had been right in saying that different people's impressions of the *śarira* differed. However, I would not go so far as to praise the old man's beggarly manner when he reached out and asked for money from patrons.

The verger of Śarira Shrine appeared to be over sixty. By all rights he should already have laid aside the myriad entanglements of human affairs and gotten down to the business of life and death. But for the sake of money the old man with his neat brown gown and his imposing string of large rosary beads ran mindlessly after the patrons, his mouth constantly babbling about the great benefits of worshipping the *śarira* and all the merit one gained by making offerings to the *śarira*. There was nothing wrong with extolling the benefits of worshipping the *śarira*, but he irritated people by following them and talking ceaselessly. If there were no benefit or merit to be gained, who would be willing to travel a great distance to worship and make offerings? When the patrons handed him a bill or two out of pity, his hand would dart out as he repeated the Buddha's name and smiled broadly. The wrinkled lines on his face got even deeper when he laughed, but of this he was oblivious.

The proverb says: "Clear wine reddens people's faces; money tempts their hearts." Some old practitioners who had made worship of the *śarira* their lifelong devotion were seized with covetous thoughts when they saw the unending flow of money which ended up in the verger's pockets. A bright idea came to them; they conceived of the method called "selling śariras" to fill the yawning chasm of their desire.

"Selling śariras" does not mean that they dared to sell the *śarira* itself but that they sold the merit acquired by worshipping the *śarira*. For instance, if I had worshipped the *śarira* for ten years, I could sell the merit thus gained to whoever wished to buy it. However, after the price was agreed upon and before the sale was made, I had to write my name and the years of earned merit on a piece of paper and affix my thumbprint. The purchaser then folded the piece of paper, carefully placed it in a yellow envelope marked "Proof of Merit," and consigned it to the flames. In this way my merit was transferred to him, while his cash was transferred to my pouch. This sort of transaction was enough to make people laugh themselves to tears.

Besides this there were a few irrational individuals who, after seeing people burn off the end-joint of a finger to the Buddha in requital of their parents' kindnesses, blindly decided to "join in the merit" [*sui-hsi*] without stopping to consider whether they had the strength to bear up under the bone-piercing pain. In the end the pain was so great that they jumped about screaming like ghosts and howling like wolves. I once saw a brother of the cloth die after burning off a finger to the Buddha. When I and many others gathered about to recite the Buddha's name and speed him on his way to his next incarnation, his face was still contorted in a rictus of agony. I am afraid that if the Buddha himself saw people do such things, hoping to get something without the necessary self-cultivation, he would condemn it as foolish.

NOTES

1. Lord Pao was Pao Cheng (999-1062), a Northern Sung official noted for his astuteness and fair-mindedness in passing sentences. He was the prefect of Kai-feng during the reign of Jen-tsung (1022-1063) and once held the titular post of Auxiliary Academician of the Lung-t'u Pavilion. In the late Ming a collection of stories with Lord Pao as the hero appeared under the title of *Lung-t'u kung-an* (*The Cases of Lung-t'u*). Early complete editions in the Ch'ing carry one hundred stories. Later editions have a much smaller number of stories and have more popular titles, such as *Pao-kung an* (*The Cases of Lord Pao*).

2. Pratyeka Buddhas are also called private Buddhas. They were the ones who achieved enlightenment by themselves without the help of any teacher. They also do not teach others or help them to achieve enlightenment. This is why they are called "private" Buddhas.

3. Vajra-holding spirit is a bodhisattva represented in the Mandala of the Diamond Realm in Tantric Buddhism. He holds a vajra or thunderbolt staff with one, three, or five prongs. Vajra symbolizes the indestructible power of wisdom.

4. The Jade Buddha Monastery was among the most famous in Shanghai. Its name was derived from the beautiful white jade Buddha, a gift from Thailand.

5. Pa-chih was an abbreviation for his sobriquet, "Pa-chih T'ou-t'o" (The Eight-fingered Ascetic). His name was Ching-an and his courtesy name was Chi-ch'an. He got his alternate name because in his youth he had burned off two fingers as an offering to the Buddha. Welch mentions him in *The Buddhist Revival in China* (Cambridge, Mass., Harvard University Press, 1967), which shows his photo on p. 36.

6. Aśoka (A-yü-wang) Monastery was one of the most famous monasteries in China. It was named after the famous Indian monarch, Emperor Aśoka, who was the grandson of Chandragupta Maurya, the founder of the Mauryan dynasty. He reigned from about 274 to 232 B.C. and spread Buddhism in India, Ceylon, and other neighboring countries. The monastery is situated in Ningpo, Chekiang. The founding of the monastery went like this: in 281, the site of an old stupa was discovered on the mountain and it was taken to be one of the 84,000 stupas Emperor Aśoka had established. The Aśoka Monastery was founded in 435 and rebuilt in 540 under the Buddhist Emperor Wu of the Liang. He named it Aśoka Monastery.

7. For the distinction between "hereditary" and "public" monastery, see Welch, *Practice*, pp. 129-141, 282-285.

8. Kuan Kung, or Lord Kuan, is the god of war and is portrayed as having a red face. His name was Kuan Yü, a general who helped Liu Pei in establishing the Kingdom of Shu. He died in 219 B.C. and was made a god in 1554 A.D. by Emperor Wan-li of the Ming Dynasty His deeds are immortalized in the popular novel *Romance of the Three Kingdoms* (*San-kuo yen-i*). He is the patron of pawnshops and antique dealers. His image is placed in the first hall of most Buddhist temples and worshipped as a guardian spirit of Buddhism. Many temples are also specially devoted to his worship.

9. This story about how Emperor Aśoka sent the Buddha's relic to the monastery is apocryphal. Śākyamuni Buddha's dates are usually given as 563-483 B.C. Buddhism was first introduced to China in the Later Han or about the first century A.D. But according to this account, the Buddha's relic was brought to China in the third or the second Century B.C., one or two hundred years after the Buddha's death.

Chapter XI

P'U-T'O ISLAND

On a Trek with My Father

Seeing the covetousness of the verger, the asinine behavior of those who "sold *śariras*," and the grimace of the man who died burning off his finger made me feel terribly distressed with Aśoka Monastery. Because of this I spoke frankly to Hua-ti on the eve of my departure for P'u-t'o Island. "The fame of your monastery is known far and wide, because you have a *śarira* of the Buddha. Those who hear of it consider themselves fortunate if they can come here to visit and worship. This is an honor that reflects on every one of the virtuous monks who live here. Each virtuous monk ought to cherish this honor. But, judging by what I have seen after a few days at your monastery, it seems that no one pays the slightest attention to the *śarira* except to make it a tool for drawing pilgrims and making money. Since the verger of Śarira Shrine always tells people of the great benefits and merit to be gained by worshipping the *śarira*, why doesn't he seriously seek the same benefit and merit for himself? If things go on this way, pilgrims who come here full of enthusiasm will go away sadly disappointed, and nothing could do more damage to the good name of your monastery. Brother, you are a virtuous, capable, perceptive young monk. You may very well become the future leader of this monastery. I think you ought to take it upon yourself to do away with these practices, so that future pilgrims to this monastery will not feel they have come here in vain."

Hua-ti seemed a bit displeased, but after a moment's thought he sighed and said, "This problem has been around for a long time: it's not something that can be gotten rid of all of a sudden. But if the day comes that it can, I'll do everything in my power." We ended the conversation by urging each other to "take care of yourself." Early the next morning my father, Hai-ch'ao and I left Aśoka Monastery and began our journey on foot.

After walking a mile or so we saw a barefoot brother of the cloth walking toward us with a tranquil, detached air. He was wearing a broad-brimmed straw hat and a wide-lapeled, sleeveless under-robe. The wicker baskets he bore on either end of his carrying pole had feet on the bottoms so he could readily set them down. He carried a metal-tipped walking stick in one hand and a yellow-cloth bag at his waist. The four corners of the bag bore the characters for earth, water, fire and wind, while "Buddha" was written in the center. There were also red seal marks in several places.[1] When he was five or six steps from us, I pressed my palms together, but he seemed not to notice. I asked in a loud, clear voice: "Bodhisattva, have you come from P'u-t'o Island?" But he continued walking slowly forward without paying me any heed. At this I asked Hai-ch'ao in a low voice: "Isn't it a shame? Is it right for a man as blind and deaf as this to be traveling afoot?"

No sooner were the words out of my mouth than the supposedly blind and deaf brother lightly set down his carrying pole, laughed mildly and said, "My reaction time may be a bit slow, but my hearing and eyesight aren't as poor as you think, Bodhisattva." After a pause he added, "What was your purpose in asking if I had come from P'u-t'o Island?"

I was embarrassed at my rudeness. Pressing my palms together again, I said apologetically: "Bodhisattva, I'm sorry to bother you for no good reason. We're making a pilgrimage to P'u-t'o Island. I'm afraid of taking the wrong road, so I thought I'd ask you."

He gave me a long look and spoke words fraught with deep meaning: "Yes, I've come from a trip to P'u-t'o Island, but the turns I took were mistaken time after time. My route is not necessarily the right one for you."

"If your route was mistaken time after time, how did you reach P'u-t'o Island?" I asked.

This provoked three bursts of loud, wild laughter. "Because I was not afraid of mistakes — because I realized my mistakes and corrected them. Since you are afraid of making mistakes, I said that the road I took might not be the best one for you."

Though his tone of voice made him seem somewhat daft, I found his words quite encouraging. At the same time I grasped the truth of what he said. I thought to myself: "Life in this world is always like traveling on a strange road, is it not? If one shrinks back for fear of mistakes or makes mistakes and will not repent of them, then what possible attainment can there be? I have traveled thousands of miles in search of knowledge without fearing anything. Now that three of us are walking together, I am suddenly afraid of taking the wrong road. That shows how weak and incapable I am, doesn't it?" When my thoughts reached this point, I pressed my palms together and said, "Bodhisattva, I very much admire your courage to risk making mistakes and correct the ones you make. Now we are going to emulate you!" With that I glanced at my father and Hai-ch'ao as if to tell them to begin walking again.

Unexpectedly our brother monk said, "Bodhisattva, don't be in a hurry.

In order to avoid wrong turnings, you had better let me tell you how to get to P'u-t'o Island."

"The bodhisattva has been there before: we'd better listen to what he says," my father and Hai-ch'ao said in unison. They took off their backpacks and sat down at the side of the road. I stood by my father, my backpack still on my back. Our brother monk rested on his carrying pole and said in a long, drawn out manner: "Follow this road and you can reach Ch'uan-shan by evening. In Ch'uan-shan is Hui-chi Monastery. When you get there, just mention that you are making a pilgrimage to P'u-t'o Island, and your food and lodging for the night will be taken care of. Rest your feet there for the evening. In the morning go from there to Shen-chia-men. If it's still early when you get there, you can hurry on to P'u-t'o Island. Otherwise you can stay the night at Chu-t'ien Temple. However, only fire and water are provided there."

"How many miles is it to Ch'uan-shan?" asked Hai-ch'ao.

"About twenty," he answered.

"Twenty miles is nothing at all," said my father. "Why, before I became a monk, walking sixty miles in one day was a normal thing." Hearing my father's confident boast made me happy, but, for a reason I myself could not explain, I was also moved to sadness.

Before we parted from our brother monk, I pointed to his legged carrying baskets, which appeared to weigh at least 100 pounds, and asked, "Bodhisattva, don't you feel that carrying such a load is an inconvenience?"

"Now that I'm used to it it's not so inconvenient. Except for taking out my alms bowl once a day and putting up at temples, I seldom ask anything of other people, because I have all my own daily necessities." With that he patiently took out his possessions one by one and showed them to us. He had images of the Buddha and bodhisattvas, sūtras and Vinaya texts, the three regulation garments,[2] a mat, an incense burner, a walking stick, an alms bowl, a water-bottle, a hammock, flints, a knife, tweezers, handkerchief, a cloth bag for filtering water, a willow twig, and soap.

Having seen each one of his treasures, I couldn't help exclaiming: "Bodhisattva, it is truly amazing for one so young to follow the ascetic rules so correctly."

"Don't embarrass me! How could I possibly have what it takes to practice asceticism. I'm just carrying these things about for appearance's sake."

The more he spoke this way, the more admirable I thought he was. As we walked our separate ways, I turned my head repeatedly to gaze at his receding figure until it disappeared in a thick bamboo grove.

My father, Hai-ch'ao and I had such a pleasant time walking, seeing the sights, talking and laughing that we forgot for a time the pervasive strife in the North and the impending war south of the river. We hiked thirteen miles in half a day without even feeling tired. But then, when we stood up and started walking after a short rest by the side of the road, our legs suddenly ached and threatened to give out. Every step was an effort. Thus sun above our heads seemed to get hotter, and the packs on our backs seemed to get heavier with every step. Our stomachs, which we had stuffed with two bowls of porridge in the morning, were beginning to feel very empty. But what could we do? Though we passed several villages along the way, there was no one selling water and tea, let alone solid food. We managed to endure until we reached Ch'uan-shan, where food was available, but in order to save a little money, we had to tighten our belts, drum up our sagging spirits and bear our hunger, thirst and fatigue until we could cross over one last mountain and arrive at Hui-chi Monastery.

Hui-chi [Wise Help] Does Not Help

Having done our best to bear the pangs of hunger and thirst, we hardly expected that we would almost be refused entrance at the front entrance of Wise Help Monastery. This was truly "running into a rainy spell just when the roof is leaking" or "being caught in a flood just when the boat needs repair."

We arrived at Wise Help Monastery just as the sun was setting behind the mountains, but the main gate was already shut tightly. I knocked a few times, but there was no response. I called out, but nothing stirred inside. "The people inside might be eating supper right now, or they might be doing evening devotions. Let's put down our packs and rest awhile before trying again." So we put down our packs, sat down in the moonlight and absorbed ourselves in watching the shadows that had been "gathered up by the setting sun and brought back by the moon."

After a long wait we suddenly heard footsteps within. "Someone is coming to open the door," I whispered in a burst of happy anticipation as I shouldered my pack and got ready to run inside and solve the problems of hunger, thirst and fatigue as quickly as possible. But as I stood with my eyes fixed intently on the door, I heard the steps stop for a moment and then move in the opposite direction. The door still stood locked as tightly as before. My urgency at this point was no laughing matter. I lifted my fists and hammered them against the door with resounding blows. "Please open up! We're making a pilgrimage to P'u-t'o Island. Our route brought us to your monastery, and it's too late to go on. We'd like to impose on you for a night's stay."

My hammering and shouting had the desired effect: a voice from inside asked, "Who are you?" I repeated what I had just said. The voice inside said, "We can't put you up here. Go to Ch'uan-shan."

I knocked on the door twice more and said, "Shouldn't monks place compassion above all else when dealing with one another? We have been walking all day; we're hungry and tired. We really can't walk another step. Would you please open the door and let us put up for the night?"

My words moved the man within the gate to pity. The gate opened with a creak. Since the man stood inside the door and carried no lantern, we could not see the expression on his face, but we pressed our palms together as we walked in.

We walked to the shrine hall, put down our packs and prostrated ourselves to the Buddha. A look around showed that all the buildings were cavernously dark, and the deserted stillness gave them a air of desolation. Still, the problem of hunger was uppermost in my mind, so I implored the brother who had let us in to find us something to fill our empty bellies. He shook his head without saying a word. We could not tell if he was refusing us or admitting his inability to meet our request. He went into the shrine hall to light a candle and then showed us to a room piled high with various objects. He said in a quavering old voice: "There is straw outside. Bring some in and lay it down to sleep on it." So saying, he put down the candle and left.

Hai-ch'ao and I brought a few armloads of straw to put on the floor. We got our quilts, and I told my father to sit on one and rest. Hai-ch'ao and I took the candle and felt our way toward the kitchen, hoping to find some hot water to wash our feet with before going to bed. Looking around, we discovered a pile of dried taro strips on the floor and some leftover vegetables and soup in the cupboard. As the flames of hunger leapt up fiercely within us, I thought to myself, "When a person leaves home to become a monk, the temple becomes his home. There is food here, and we are going to eat it. We'll discuss the matter with them after we've eaten." My mind being made up, I told Hai-ch'ao to start a fire and heat the pan while I washed the taro strips and threw them in. Then I added some leftover rice and vegetables. Then I quietly led my father inside, and we all sat down to this sumptuous repast. Just then the brother who had opened the gate suddenly ran in the door with the two other monks. "We were saving these leftovers to eat in the morning. How can you...?"

Without letting them finish their shouted question, I walked over to them and said with a laugh: "Have a little compassion, bodhisattvas! The proverb says: 'A portion of food should go to each *arhat*. If the *arhat* doesn't come, the food won't come.' We ate your portion; never fear, the gods who protect the Law will give you two portions in return." They stared at us in sullen anger, but did not interfere. Perhaps they were thinking: "Since we've met with this sort of tough-skinned friar, we might as well let them do as they please."

To P'u-t'o Island

Having eaten a supper of sorts and gotten a night's sleep at Wise Help Monastery, we took our leave of the head monk at daybreak and set out for the dock in Ch'uan-shan.

Though the situation in eastern Chekiang was peaceful and quiet at the time, quite a few people appeared to have been thrown into a panic by rumors. When we arrived at the small, remote dock, it was already crowded with a bustling mass of humanity. They were in the same state of panic and desperation I had seen at the train station in Soochow. The unnerving thing was not the large number of people but the small number of boats headed for Shen-chia-men. There were only two runs per day in an old passenger holding fifty or sixty people at most. Though fishing boats frequently appeared at the dock looking for passengers, few of them found any takers because the price was too high. Hai-ch'ao, my father and I had a total of six silver dollars between us, so naturally we did not dare express an interest.

Then the inconceivable happened. Just as we were pacing forlornly on the dock, a middle-aged fisherman walked up to us. After glancing at our packs and looking us over from top to bottom, he asked if we were making a pilgrimage to P'u-t'o Island. Thinking he was trying to make a deal with us, we nodded our heads in a preoccupied manner and did not answer. But he seemed to divine what was on our minds. He pointed to a small fishing boat resting on the bank and said, "Get aboard. I'll take you to Shen-chia-men for free." I could scarcely believe my ears. "At a time when everyone is out to earn easy money, is there really such a good man?" I thought.

What happened eased my doubts. The fisherman jumped into the boat and began sculling it as he beckoned to us and shouted, "Come aboard. I'm leaving now!"

Homage to Kuan-yin! Who can say this was not a blessing she sent in answer to our needs? We boarded the fishing boat, which was no more than twenty feet long and only a few feet wide, and left the dock. Seeing the vast, open sea before us, we began to regret accepting his offer. "It's dangerous riding in such a small boat when the waves are high and the wind blows so hard," my father said in a low voice.

"That doesn't matter. Just recite 'Kuan-yin' singlemindedly and everything will be fine!" Actually, when I saw the little boat being tossed now back and forth, rising and falling on the huge waves like a leaf adrift, I was frightened into a cold sweat. I forced myself to act calmly to comfort my father. Luckily the fisherman was an expert seaman, and he kept the boat close to shore. Though we suffered three or four hours of needless fright, we arrived safely at Shen-chia-men a little after one in the afternoon. When we learned there were no more boats going to P'u-t'o that day, we expressed our gratitude to the kindly fisherman and went to Chu-t'ien Temple.

I am not clear whether the "Chu" of Chu-t'ien Temple was the "*chu*" that means "various" or the one that serves as a family name, but I do remember that it was a folk temple filled with the atmosphere of heterodox faith. The man living in the temple was neither a monk nor a Taoist priest but a layman who believed in *Li-chiao*, a religion devoted to pure living that had been founded by Yang Lai-ju in the early Ch'ing dynasty. Everyone addressed him as "Curate" [*miao-chu*]. He was over seventy years old. His benign face and snow white beard reaching to his chest gave a "breath of faerie" to his appearance. The bottle gourds of all sizes hanging in the guest room added a Taoist flavor to the place. When he first saw us, he got straight to the point: "Two monks from Shanghai just went out to buy vegetables and rice. If you want to stay here, you had better go out and buy some too. We only provide water and a cooking fire here." Just then the two brother monks came in with their arms full of groceries. When they learned that we had not eaten lunch (or even breakfast for that matter), one of them said, "Don't go buy food: we bought plenty. Eat our food for this meal, and we'll eat yours for breakfast tomorrow." Without allowing any polite refusals, they grabbed us like old friends and pulled us into the kitchen. Each of us got to work at a separate task like rinsing rice, washing vegetables or heating up the pan. Everyone pitched in busily and fixed a four-course meal with soup and deliciously fragrant white rice. For Hai-ch'ao, my father and myself this was a veritable New Year's feast.

After breakfast the next morning we went to the dock with our brother monks from Shanghai, hoping to reach P'u-t'o Island before noon so we could do some unhurried sightseeing before putting up for the night. It may have been coincidence or it may have been a divine response to our need: at any rate, we had no sooner arrived at the dock than we saw a monk standing in a small boat who waved to us and shouted, "Bodhisattvas, come aboard. Let's go together." The five of us climbed aboard and, without spending a penny, soon arrived at the place we had longed to see for so long.

P'u-t'o Island is located off the southeastern coast near Ting County of Chekiang Province. Its peak is over a thousand meters above sea level. Few succulent plants or lush groves thrive there, but there are many spring-fed streams. Tradition has it that before the Later Han dynasty, P'u-t'o Island was still a wild, uninhabited island. After the Emperor Kuang-wu revitalized the Han ruling house, a hermit named Mei Tzu-chen retired to the island and was never heard from again. During the Chen-ming period (915-921) of the Later Liang dynasty, the ship of a Japanese monk named Hui-o passed by the island on its way back to Japan. Numberless iron lotuses suddenly appeared on the face of the waters and kept him from going further. Hui-o shivered with fear at this sight. "I have committed no odious sin in this life," he thought. "Why has such an evil befallen me?"

But when Hui-o, at his wit's end, begged the Buddha for succor, he recalled something which enabled him to understand perfectly. What did he recall? It so happened that earlier, when Hui-o had made a pilgrimage to Wu-t'ai Mountain, he had stolen a pristine, solemn image of Kuan-yin, which he wanted to worship once he returned to Japan. But how could he have known that the bodhisattva would not permit him to take what did not belong to him. "Since the bodhisattva is unwilling to go to Japan, and I cannot go back without her, the best thing would be to leave my boat and build a hut on that mountainous island, so that I can spend the rest of my life in China with the bodhisattva." As soon as this thought came to him, the iron lotuses disappeared. This deepened his faith even more. So he left his ship, built a hut on the island and spent his days practicing austerities with the bodhisattva before him. The proverb says: "If a man shows one part sincerity, the bodhisattva will repay him with ten parts blessing." How much more would the bodhisattva respond to Monk Hui-o, a man who could forget himself in his devotion to the dharma. Owing to enthusiastic publicity by local fishermen, believers began to come to the island in increasing numbers. The hut was expanded again and again. Hui-o named his hermitage "Kuan-yin Who Refused to Leave." Thus Hui-o became the first patriarch of P'u-t'o Island.[3]

Cooking Dried Beancurd

Anyone who has been to P'u-t'o Island has probably heard the phrases "exotic traditions" and "realm of *arhats*." The former means that the rules at P'u-t'o were different from those of public monasteries on the mainland. When a monk stopped for a time to seek instruction or put up for the night in a monastery on the mainland, his every act, from eating and sleeping to heeding the call of nature, had to be done in accordance with the rules. Not the least laxity was permitted. When a rule was broken one was, in minor cases, made to kneel for the period of one incense stick as a warning, and in serious instances one was expelled outright. Things were much different at P'u-t'o Island. As long as you did not transgress the four basic vows, you were free to do what you liked. It did not matter if you smoked cigarettes, drank wine, begged for alms, cooked your own food, played majong or slept all day.

What about the "realm of *arhats*"? This means that you were not to look for flaws or turn up your nose simply because of the external appearance of any person or thing at P'u-t'o Island. For example, if you were walking along and you suddenly encountered a drunken, ragged monk who cursed you with filthy language and shook his fists, you did your best to see him as a great *arhat* who had "resolved the problem of earthly existence and gotten beyond future karma." In no case was one supposed to curse or strike in return.

If you were walking on the island and you saw a monk under a thatched lean-to boiling some fatty meat in a pot, you were not to revile him as a "flea on the lion" or a reprobate Buddhist. Instead, you were to press your palms respectfully together and say to him: "Light of virtue, your religious commitment is truly amazing. Rather than going down to the monastery to eat the food already prepared, you stay here and cook dried beancurd."

Why, when it was as clear as day that someone was cooking meat, was one supposed to say that he was cooking beancurd? There was a reason for this. The story goes that toward the end of the Ch'ing dynasty there was a high official from Hunan named P'eng, who was nearly as famous as Tseng Kuo-fan and Tsuo Tsung-t'ang. Because of the influence of scholars like Han Yü (768-824) and Chu Hsi (1130-1200), he viewed Buddhism as a heretical, evil teaching and monks as transgressors against Confucian morality. It was his fervent wish to carry on the work that Han Yü set out to accomplish when he wrote: "Force their adherents to resume lay life; burn their books; and turn their temples into ordinary dwellings." One day a certain matter took him to P'u-t'o Island. He was seized by an urge to make an excursion and enjoy the landscape. Looking at the green mountains and the azure sea, he felt himself somewhat cleansed of the vulgar preoccupations that had been clinging to him. This made him think: "It's a pity that such a wonderful place has been overrun by a bunch of monks — people who don't know wheat from barley and live off the offerings of others. They never lift a finger to produce for themselves. What I'll do is pay close attention to their conduct. If they obey every rule and uphold their Buddhist tenets, that will be the end of it. Otherwise I'll drive every last one of them off this mountain."

He walked along thinking such thoughts and peering about until he reached P'u-chi [Universal Salvation] Monastery, where his deserved comeuppance awaited him. It happened that this eminent Mr. P'eng saw a raggedly dressed, dirty-faced monk staggering through the main gate as he carried a large, juicy piece of pork. P'eng puffed out his cheeks in rage: he wanted nothing more than to have the monk brought before him and beaten. But another thought held him back: it would be much better to send someone after the monk to find which room he lived in and what he was doing with the meat. Then P'eng could go into the monastery and lay down the law to the abbot. In the face of testimony and material evidence, the abbot would have to admit that his establishment was guilty of breaking the rules. With this in mind, P'eng sent a man to follow the monk inside. In a few minutes the man came back and reported: "The monk who was carrying meat lives in a room just inside the main gate. He's in there now with his rump sticking up, blowing on a fire and boiling the pork."

Mr. P'eng was overjoyed to hear this. He sent a man to bring the abbot right away. "Are you the abbot here?" he asked with a harsh tone and fierce expression. The abbot took note of P'eng's overbearing manner and thought to himself: "Even the emperor had some regard for my dignity when he granted me an audience. Am I to fear this sort of official?" So he simply smiled at P'eng and nodded his head.

Seeing the abbot do no more than nod his head confidently infuriated P'eng all the more, so he asked loudly: "If you have authority over this monastery, why don't you take severe disciplinary action against monks who violate the rules of purity?"

"Every monk in this establishment is a good one: none of them has ever failed to observe the rules of purity," replied the abbot with an unworried smile.

P'eng laughed coldly and dragged the abbot to the room where the monk was "sticking his rump into the air and blowing on a fire." P'eng pointed at the unsuspecting monk and said to the abbot: "You say that none of your good monks ever fail to observe the rules of purity. Would you ask him what he is boiling in the pot?"

The abbot had no choice but to ask, but the busily cooking bodhisattva, who had been frightened into a little ball by the approach of the official and the abbot, was even more frightened by the abbot's question. "I...I...I'm cook...cook...cooking dried beancurd," he stammered.

P'eng was enraged. "Nonsense! It's plain that you are boiling pork, yet you say you are cooking beancurd. Someone open the pot, and we'll see what he's cooking in there." In the twinkling of an eye an underling lifted the lid. P'eng walked over to look, and got the surprise of his life. "That's strange. How can pork change into tough beancurd?"

Only then did the abbot and the monk realize what was up. The abbot turned to P'eng with a smile and said self-righteously: "As I said, every monk in this monastery is a good one. You did not believe me. Now you know I was telling the truth."

By this time P'eng was disgusted with the turn of events, but he could only swallow his pride and say a few superficially polite words to the abbot: "I'm sorry. I accused you wrongfully. To make up for my mistake, I'll do whatever I can from now on to protect this island."

After that remarkable incident, anyone who bent over the fire with his rump sticking up might be an *arhat* in human form. Therefore some good-for-nothing types used this for an excuse. If they were boiling meat in a pot and someone asked what they were cooking, they might answer, "I'm cooking myself a little dried beancurd." In this way "dried beancurd" became jargon for "meat."

Nevertheless, the reader should not assume that everyone on P'u-t'o Island eats "dried beancurd." Like any other place of truth, it is a place in which snakes mingle with dragons, and the sacred is found together with the profane. The good should not be lumped together and criticized with the bad. Masters Yin-kuang, Ti-hsien and T'ai-hsü are excellent examples of the good monks of P'u-t'o Island.

Waiting on Tables at Fa-yü

For the first ten or so days of our stay, we looked on P'u-t'o Island as a paradise "free of hardship and full of joy." When we were not climbing mountains to look at ancient relics, we were listening to the stories of veteran monks. The political turmoil of the time had completely slipped our minds. But soon we had seen all the relics and heard the stories so many times we were tired of them. Just when we were about to settle down and get to work on matters that concerned ourselves, a series of frightening rumors came out of nowhere. The spread of these rumors shook the sea-girt island and the hearts of every monk and layman on it.

One unbearably hot summer afternoon I sat facing my father on the porch of the guest hall at P'u-chi Monastery. I was holding a copy of "Morning and Evening Devotions" and teaching my father to chant the "Śūrangama Mantra," when the two brother monks from Shanghai ran panting into the courtyard. When they saw us they said, "Brothers, something terrible has happened. The Communists have taken Ningpo!" This gave me such a start that my book of devotions fell to the ground. I hurriedly stood up and asked, "Where did you hear this news?"

"We heard it outside the gate from a man who just came from Shen-chia-men," they answered.

They went to pack their bags, saying they would return to the mainland. "Where will you go after you've crossed over to the mainland?" I asked.

"After we reach Shen-chia-men, we'll see which way the wind blows," they said.

When they heard this news the veteran monks in the guest hall, whose hearts had always been as placid as still water, could not remain calm. Within two hours, more than half of them had left, amid intermittent shouts of "Let's cross over to the mainland!"

"Everyone is crossing over: what should we do?" I asked my father.

"Since the Communists are already in Ningpo, our avenue of escape is already cut off. We will be better off staying here on the island than crossing over to throw ourselves into the net." Though Hai-ch'ao and I agreed with his point of view, we could not set our minds at ease. After a few days various rumors were spread from Shen-chia-men. Some said that Ningpo was still intact but that Shanghai had fallen to the Communists; some said that Ningpo and Shanghai were still controlled by Nationalist forces, but a fierce battle was raging in Shanghai; while others said that the booming of cannon from Chen-chiang could be heard in Shen-chia-men.

Life in the temples and monasteries had always depended on the support of pilgrims who came to the mountain from many places, but who would dare come during such a time of upheaval? The rumors in the air threw people into confusion, and posed a threat to the income of each temple and monastery. As I mentioned earlier, my father, myself and Hai-ch'ao had only six dollars between us. We had used two dollars for our two meals at Chu-t'ien Temple. When we arrived on the island, we spent two more for rosaries and memorabilia. The remaining two were used up on small purchases. Just when we were totally strapped, a brother recommended me for the job of waiter at Fa-yü [Dharma Rain] Monastery. The monthly allowance was two dollars in silver certificates. (At that time gold certificates had already been taken out of circulation. The value of silver certificates corresponded to that of silver coins.)

Fa-yü Monastery was one of the three major monasteries on P'u-t'o Island. Though not as large in area as P'u-chi Monastery, it was ten times better as a setting for spiritual work. Because Great Master Yin-kuang had practiced there in anonymity for thirty years, the customs there were less unfamiliar than at P'u-chi Monastery. But anyone so heavily laden with karmic hindrance as I could not be privileged to enjoy such a setting for long: after staying there for almost three months, I was kicked out by the guest department on the pretext that I was a "new arrival."

Waiters occupied one of the forty-eight positions[4] in the monastery system. Most of the hard luck cases who filled this position were "slavish monks" who only mumbled during scripture readings. Though my abilities did not surpass theirs to any remarkable extent, I had after all spent a few days in a Buddhist seminary and had served for a time as a guest prefect. Thus, when I entered the waiters section, my co-workers did not look on me as one of them. No matter how I tried to blend in with my surroundings and become one of them, they kept at a respectful distance from me. When working, however, they treated me with special consideration. They did not want me to do any heavy work like carrying rice and water: instead they had me do light tasks such as dishwashing, setting and clearing tables, and cleaning the dining hall. But I had always been proud by nature, and their special treatment struck me as a patronizing sort of pity, so after a few days of light work, I began carrying water and rice like the others. (Actually I had carried water at my home temple, but the buckets had been smaller.) For this reason my co-workers gradually took kindly to me. Naturally I was happy at being able to "fulfill my mission."

One day while carrying two wooden bucketfuls of water weighing over two hundred pounds up some steps, I lost my footing and slipped. The buckets were smashed and I got sopping wet. This incurred the wrath of the proctor standing nearby, who berated me as a "damned zombie" and a "rice bucket." I have always been notorious for my hot temper, and I was not about to stand for such insults. I raised the carrying pole to club him, but my mind changed at the last moment and I said to myself: "Under these circumstances, violent action would do me no good whatsoever." I put down the carrying pole to brush the water off my clothes, then picked it up again and said defiantly: "Within a month I'm going to ask you to take back the names you called me."

Seeing me holding the carrying pole in barely suppressed rage, he walked away without making a sound. Another time, when he saw me run up a flight of steps carrying two buckets of water without missing a breath or showing strain, he shouted, "So you're showing off your ability, are you?" I laughed coldly and answered, "The proctor is mistaken. I don't presume to show off my ability: I only want to let you see what a 'damned zombie' can do."

From then on I was the cinder in his eye and the thorn in his flesh: his constant wish was to "pull me out." Behind my back he often asked my co-workers in the waiters' section: "That guy with a northern brogue from the front monastery [P'u-chi Monastery] has such a hot temper and a sharp tongue. Can you people get along with him?" When I asked how they had answered him, they said, "We all said that you are very nice, but he seemed displeased to hear it." "The proctor is probably going to have me expelled," I sighed.

Sure enough, after ten-odd days had passed, the guest prefect called me to the guest department, kindly bade me be seated and said, "The financial situation of this monastery is like a stream of water that has been cut off from its source. When we use a dipperful, that's one dipperful less; when we use a drop, that's one drop less. It's possible that it will soon dry up. That is why the establishment has decided to require all newcomers to leave the monastery on their own within three days. Though you show strong determination in your work, the fact remains that you are a newcomer here. (Since I was the only newcomer there, the proctor's underhanded plot was obvious.) I'm truly sorry. Please find another place to stay within three days. If you fail to do so, don't blame the guest department for not giving advance notice."

These superficially polite but fundamentally cruel words left me trembling. The perceptive reader will be able to imagine what difficulties I faced finding a place to stay now that Fa-yü Monastery, one of the three large monasteries on P'u-t'o Island, was in such desperate financial straits. Could I go back to P'u-chi Monastery? Impossible! P'u-chi Monastery had already made a rule "granting permission to any monk who wishes to leave and denying it to those who wish to enter." Fo-ting Mountain offered no hope either, because it was not allowing overnight stays either. What was I to do? I decided to leave. I was not about to beg the guest prefect to take pity on me, even if it meant starving to death outside of Fa-yü Monastery! With these thoughts in mind I pressed my palms together and walked silently out of the guest department.

Boat for a Drowning Man

After returning to the waiters' section to pack my pathetically simple luggage, I bade farewell to the co-workers I had lived with for not quite three months and trudged uncertainly through the gate of Fa-yü Monastery, my eyes filled with tears. In my disordered thoughts I could see myself changed from an ebullient youth at the morning of life to an old man bowed under the weight of approaching night. Outrage and fear of hardship stole over me and plunged me into dejection. Turning to look at the white clouds floating over Fo-ting [Buddha Peak] Mountain, I said a silent prayer: "O compassionate, merciful, all-knowing Kuan-yin! Help your disciple in his hour of need, or he will die a victim of adversity in your own place of truth."

After my prayer I turned my uncertain steps in the direction of P'u-chi

Monastery with the idea that, no matter what was to happen, I had to see my father first. To my surprise, I had just crossed the bridge before the gate when an approaching monk pressed his palms together in greeting while still at a great distance. Looking carefully, I saw that he was Master Hsing-wu, who had struck the great bell at Ling-yen Monastery and had been a devoted reader of the *Lotus Sūtra*. When he was near me he knelt down by beside the road and began to make a prostration to me. I took a quick step toward him and pulled him to his feet. "I don't deserve this. When did you come to this island, Master Hsing-wu?" I asked.

He answered with a question for me: "Where do you plan to go with that knapsack, sir?" I replied that I was going to P'u-chi Monastery to talk with my father about crossing over to the mainland and going to T'ien-t'ung. He flapped his arms anxiously and said, "Ting-hai and Shen-chia-men are swarming with soldiers. Full-scale warfare is liable to break out at any moment. What makes you even think of crossing over and going to T'ien-t'ung?"

"I don't want to cross over, but there isn't even enough extra ground on this island for me to stick an awl into." Then I told him everything that had happened in Fa-yü Monastery.

Strangely enough this sent him into a fit of loud, handclapping laughter. "This is excellent! Marvelous!"

At first I thought he was taking pleasure in my misfortunes, but when he had explained himself, I was so moved I could not restrain myself from grabbing his hands and saying, "Master Hsing-wu, I don't know how I can ever thank you enough!"

What was it that had moved me so deeply? Master Hsing-wu had said to me: "I came to the mountain half a year ago, but I have never left Lien-ch'ih [Lotus Pond] Hermitage, where I've been staying. Yesterday an errand took me to P'u-chi Monastery, and I ran into Master Hai-ch'ao. When I heard you were a waiter at the Fa-yü Monastery, I felt very badly. When I got back to Lien-ch'ih Hermitage, I told the manager everything about you and took the liberty of getting a place for you in the recitation hall. The temple manager was happy to do as I asked. He even urged me to hurry over here and invite you to live at Lien-ch'ih Hermitage. I came here today expressly for this reason. You could have left sooner or you could have left later, but you picked this very moment to leave Fa-yü Monastery. Isn't it excellent? Isn't it marvelous?"

After a pause he continued: "Lien-ch'ih Hermitage belongs to Monk ____, the present abbot of P'u-chi Monastery. A number of years ago he was fortunate enough to receive a special endowment. At a cost of several million silver dollars he built a five-story foreign-style building with balconies and a rooftop gazebo. There are several hundred elegant guest rooms for important visitors and wealthy pilgrims, but because of the present turmoil, there are no signs of life in the upstairs rooms but spider webs and bird droppings. There is nothing to distract the residents of the recitation hall."

Then he told me about the quality of life and the spending allowances at his monastery: "The temple manager likes to take good care of his monks, but his territorial loyalties run deep. We get three dishes and a soup for a midday meal, and there are four side dishes with the morning and evening porridge. The meals are a bit better than usual on the first and fifteenth of every month. Our monthly allowance is two pecks of rice. (At that time silver certificates had become like gold certificates of the year before; the paper currency one got from selling a cow in the morning was not enough to buy a chicken come evening. For this reason, many people who did mental or physical work for others figured the value of their services in pecks or *tan* of rice rather than money.) Sometimes visitors give alms as a way of striking up affinities that can lead to future salvation, and this provides us with enough spending money for our needs. Each person has a room to himself, complete with table, chairs, bed and mosquito canopy. The lighting is more than sufficient. In short, I can guarantee that you won't find a more ideal place now on P'u-t'o Island than Lien-ch'ih Hermitage."

Just when I was feeling like the weary traveller who "amid a waste of streams and hills, begins to doubt the road ahead," I suddenly saw "the shady willows and sunlit flowers of yet another town" open out before me. I felt like a drowning man on a wave-tossed sea who suddenly meets with a rescue boat. Of course I was deeply moved.

After Master Hsing-wu led me to Lien-ch'ih Hermitage and I was assigned a room and a place in the recitation hall, we went to P'u-chi Monastery together. When they heard that I had entered the hermitage, my father and Ching-ch'ih jumped for joy. Even the head of the wandering monks' hall rejoiced for my sake.

There were five monks including myself in the recitation hall at Lien-ch'ih Hermitage. Except for morning and evening devotions and three incense periods of recitation each day, we were free to arrange our time as we saw fit. Not long after settling in, I established a devotional regimen to which I adhered strictly, hoping to reach the level described in the *Sūtra of the Buddha's Last Instructions*: "Learn and practice diligently the dharma of goodness throughout the day; do not miss a moment. Do not stop your work, even in the late night and early morning. Rest in the middle of the night by chanting sūtras. Do not allow your life to be wasted away by the conditioned cause of drowsiness." My karmic hindrances must have been too great. Why else, when it was time to "chant sūtras in the middle of the night," would I either slip into drowsy wool-gathering or spoil the whole undertaking by falling fast asleep? Master Hsing-wu, on the other hand, could keep himself in a state of constant wakefulness.

Once, just as I felt myself entering the realm in which mind and truth are one, the demon sleep stole upon me. I made a great effort to do battle with it and emerged victorious, but there was no way to recapture that realm. I was more frustrated than if I had been told to "scare an oriole into flight without causing it to cry out first on the branch." My feelings were a mixture of three parts envy, three parts shame and four parts jealousy when I asked Master Hsing-wu: "What is your method for using your time so well?"

"Methods of spiritual work differ according to people's fundamental natures: there are no easy generalizations. However, the one key to all such efforts is press forward intrepidly."

"What if you feel like sleeping when you're trying to press forward intrepidly?" I asked.

"If you feel like sleeping, then you are not really pressing intrepidly forward. If it's the real thing, you won't feel like sleeping. You see, pressing intrepidly forward and wanting to sleep are like light and darkness; they cannot possibly exist at the same time. If you are trying hard but still feel like sleeping, you should quickly meditate on your impending death. If you still feel like sleeping, think of yourself plunging into hell after your death."

Afterward, I followed his advice and found it quite effective, but as the days wore on, the demon sleep came back with overwhelming strength. Sometimes I slept even longer than I had before pressing intrepidly forward and contemplating my death and descent into hell. And I behaved like Tsai-yu, whom Confucius scolded for sleeping during the day with the words: "Rotted wood cannot be carved; a wall of dried manure cannot be trowelled." Oh hateful sleep! From time immemorial you have dragged so many people down into oblivion.

Then something happened that I could not even have dreamt of. I was living uneventfully in the recitation hall at Lien-ch'ih Hermitage, minding my own business, when misfortune struck like lightning from a clear blue sky. This misfortune forced me to leave my aging father; it forced me to lose for a time my qualifications for belonging to the *sangha*; and it nearly cost me my life. In view of the fact that "the ordinary man shares responsibility for the rise or fall of his country," my sudden misfortune may not mean much, but, in view of my aspirations and way of life, this was the cruelest blow of all.

One day after breakfast I was sitting in my room reading *Essentials for the Practice of Samatha-Vipaśyanā Meditation* [*Hsiu-hsi chih-kuan tso-ch'an fa-yao*] by Great Master Chih-i (538-597) of the T'ien-t'ai School. I was reading as follows: "Though I have made but negligible progress in my search for truth, my alms bowl receives the charity that will bring blessings to my benefactors. Why give rein to earthly desires and lapse into the passions of the five senses? Once you renounce the joys of the passions, abandon them and do not turn around to look at them again. If you still wish for them, you are like a fool eating his own vomit. Desires are painful when unfulfilled. When fulfilled they bring uneasiness and fear. When the object of desire is lost, there is anger and spite. There is nothing joyous in any of this. These being the evil effects of desires, how can we renounce them? If we experience deeply the joys of meditation, we will not be tricked by desires." Just then the temple manager walked quietly into the room. He stood before me, sighed heavily and said, "I can't tell you how respectful and happy I feel to see you studying like this, but it looks as if the present turmoil is getting worse. I don't know if we'll be able to go on living together." With this he handed me a note and fixed his gaze on me as if to observe my reaction.

The note was a message from the fellow who was nicknamed the "headman of monks" [*ho-shang pao-chang*], telling Master Hsing-wu and myself to attend a meeting at Hsing-shan Temple at two o'clock. There was no explanation of the reason for the meeting. I looked at the manager in astonishment and asked, "For a month or two there has been talk of drafting monks from this mountain into the army. Could this notice have anything to do with that."

The manager listened nervously and answered, "I'm not the headman of monks; how should I know?"

"You're not the headman of monks, but you're a member of his group. I don't believe that you weren't notified about the reason for this meeting," I said with a slight laugh.

"Maybe they are conscripting laborers to build the airport near Tai Mountain."

I shook my head in disagreement. Just then I saw Master Hsing-wu standing silently outside the door. I motioned to him, and he walked in with quiet, measured steps. I handed the note to him, and he read it at a glance. He waved it back and forth with an air of utmost misery. Then, after a long pause, he spoke in a voice on the verge of breaking into sobs: "Master Chün! This note is enough to cut short our dharma bodies and our life of wisdom. It may send us both into a hell of knives and spears."

Hearing this saddened me deeply, but I suppressed my misery and comforted him: "Master Hsing-wu, why do you look at this problem as if it were the end of the world? If our country needs us, we should do what we are asked to do, keeping in mind that we will be entering hell so that others need not do so. As long as we don't lose our faith, even if we do become soldiers and die on the battlefield, Amitābha will take pity on us and receive us into a new life in the Western Paradise." He listened in surprise as great, bean-sized tears rolled down both sides of his nose. Then he sighed deeply and walked silently out of the room.

That afternoon Master Hsing-wu and I arrived promptly at Hsing-shan Temple to find forty or fifty monks sitting in a large, poorly lighted room. Some were from Fo-ting Monastery; some were from P'u-chi and Fa-yü Monasteries; and others were from various temples and halls on the island. All were between twenty and thirty years old, and there was not a layman in the lot. Moreover, all of us were wandering monks from other places; there was not a son of P'u-t'o Island among us. As I wondered what was going on, a brother with a Szechuan accent walked in shouting the headman's name. "He is an apostate who wears the Tathāgata's robe while breaking the Tathāgata's laws. He received special favors from the county government and monetary gifts from each temple, so he is only interested in protecting the sons of this island. He thinks nothing of betraying us wandering monks. When I become a soldier, I'll come back here someday and put him in front of a firing squad!"

Just as the old bodhisattva was voicing his outrage in grand style the headman of monks approached, along with a middle-aged army officer and eight or nine rifle-toting soldiers. Like a rat that has seen a cat, the monk scuttled away from the doorway and shrank into a corner, hardly daring to breathe for fear of being heard. Everyone tittered at his frightened trembling, while Master Hsing-wu and I looked on in detached silence. After strutting self-importantly into the courtyard at the head of the army officer and nine soldiers, the headman whispered a few words in the ear of the officer and disappeared in a flash. The officer then gave an order in a low voice to the soldiers and strode toward the room. The soldiers walked back and forth in the courtyard holding their rifles. At last everyone realized the gravity of the situation.

The officer stopped at the door to look at the group of poor, ignorant, useless monks. Then, walking over to a broken table inside the room, he spoke to us in tones of authoritarian certainty: "I have been ordered to come for all of you. From now on you will act in obedience to my commands. Otherwise you will suffer the consequences." He then ordered us to form a line and follow the soldiers.[5] After going out the main gate of Hsing-shan Temple and passing through P'u-t'o Island's only marketplace, we arrived at the district office of the county government. Herding us like sheep, the soldiers drove us into the upstairs of a small, wooden building and locked the door behind us.

A Blot on the Name of P'u-t'o Island

We spent the rest of the day and all of that night locked in the building near the county office, looking at one another uncomprehendingly. We had neither food to eat nor water to drink, and we were deprived of the freedom to relieve ourselves. It was no different than being thrown into prison! Some impatient brothers stuck their heads out of a window at dawn the next day and demanded answers of the guards below: "Hey! Hey! Which law have we violated? You lock us up without food or water: don't tell me you want to starve us to death." But the guards went on performing their duty without heeding them in the slightest.

In a moment the officer who had come to take us away walked upstairs and said good-naturedly: "Would you gentlemen calm down a bit and watch what you say? Though you haven't broken any laws, we must inconvenience you somewhat to accomplish our mission smoothly. I ask your forgiveness for this. Right now there are some old masters outside the gate demanding to see you, but you must wait calmly, or I'll have you taken to the boat at gunpoint and sent to Ting-hai immediately." He hurried downstairs and everyone quieted down. His words about the old masters and the plan to take us to Ting-hai kept ringing in my ears.

We waited and waited: each minute seemed a century. After at least two hours, the officer walked upstairs again and announced, "You gentlemen may now go downstairs and see the old masters. However, there are three things you must keep in mind: First, you may not talk longer than one hour; second, if you have business to take care of, hurry up and ask the old masters to take care of it for you, because we may leave here at any moment; and third, while talking with the old masters downstairs, you may not take it upon yourselves to..." Without waiting for him to finish, some of the monks swarmed past him and ran downstairs. I pulled Master Hsing-wu and ran downstairs also. As I walked out the door downstairs, I spotted my father and Hai-ch'ao looking anxiously into the small crowd. I leapt to my father's side and burst out sobbing.

I cried for a long while before hearing my father say, "Don't cry. The Communists have made such a mess that if you young people don't become soldiers, there won't be a decent future in store for you. Go with your mind at ease: don't worry about me. I can still take care of myself."

Dharma Master P'in-yi was from my home district and had helped me a great deal during my stay on P'u-t'o Island. He now lived in Hung-fa [Vast

Raft] Hall. He walked over and consoled me: "Don't worry at all, Master Chün. As long as I have food, your father will not go hungry."

I prostrated myself before Master P'in in wordless thanks. Right at that moment the manager of Lien-ch'ih Hermitage came, unobtrusively pulled two heavy red envelopes from the waist of his robe and handed them to Master Hsing-wu and me, then said in a low voice: "Each envelope has five silver dollars. Three dollars are your monthly allowance and the other two dollars are a gift from me. It's just a trifle. Please accept it! Yesterday afternoon when I heard that you were locked up in the county office, I ran everywhere looking for the headmen, hoping he could figure something out, but I searched half the night without finding a sign of him. I was frantic."

When the temple manager said he had looked in vain for the headman, the words of thanks on the tip of my tongue were forgotten in anger. Having wiped the tears from my face, I was about to tell him how the headman had betrayed us when Master Hsing-wu, of all people, laughed coldly and made an attempt at wry humor: "I hear that we wandering monks have the headman to thank for our good fortune in being able to become soldiers. Hah hah hah! You were going to have him figure something out to help us? Did you want to tear down the glorious banner he had raised for P'u-t'o Island? It was a lucky thing you looked all night without seeing a sign of him. Otherwise, aside from undertaking a thankless task, you would have gotten yourself into plenty of trouble as well."

The temple manager listened in astonishment and said, "Is this really true? " Master Hsing-wu only smiled. I took advantage of his silence to tell the manager what the Szechuanese brother had told us at Hsing-shan Temple the afternoon before. "This is a blot on the name of P'u-t'o Island," he said over and over.

This was a good place to break off the conversation with the temple manager. I opened the red envelope he had given me, took out three silver dollars, and placed them lightly in my father's hand. "This is the last monthiy allowance I'll get on this island. Take it so you will have money to get back to Ling-yen Monastery in Soochow when the turmoil blows over," I said, tears welling up in my eyes again. My old father, too, looked at me through a mist of tears, his lips quivering. He might have been struggling to say something, or perhaps he was on the point of weeping, but before he could open his mouth, the middle-aged officer blew a blast on his whistle and shouted, "Attention everyone! You have exceeded the time allowed for conversation. Now we're going to serve you a meal. Everyone from outside leave immediately. All those who stayed upstairs last night gather in front of me."

My father, Hai-ch'ao and the others were forced to walk out the main gate of the county office as the soldiers wrenched and dragged us to form two rows in front of the officers. "Count off!" the officer ordered. Everyone stared at him vacantly. "You don't even understand 'Count off'?" he asked with an ill-suppressed laugh. Everyone still stared at him in ignorance, so he counted us one by one with his finger. That done, he said, "When I saw all of you talking with the old masters today, I cried and sniveled out of sadness for you. However, when we get down to the heart of the matter, isn't this all because of that treacherous Mao Tse-tung?" When he said this, everyone wailed and wept aloud. It was such a distressing scene that I cannot bear to write about it further.

NOTES

1. These characters and seals showed that he was a model wandering monk.

2. The "three garments" (*san-i*) were the long gown (*ch'ang-shan*), the full-sleeved gown (*hai-ch'ing*), and the *chia-sa* (kāsāya) or formal monk's robe, which did not cover the right shoulder.

3. The best source on P'u-t'o is Ernst Boerschmann, *P'u-t'o Shan: die heilige insel der Kuan Yin, der gottin der Barmherzigkeit* (P'u-t'o Mountain, the Sacred Island of Kuan-yin, the Goddess of Compassion), Berlin, 1911. Reginald F. Johnson in *Buddhist China* gives an account of P'u-t'o and the Kuan-yin Cult in Chapter 11. The history of the island and its founding myths are discussed in my article, "P'u-t'o Shan: Pilgrimage and the Creation of Chinese Potalaka." For additional information on P'u-t'o, see Note 12 in Chapter 1.

4. See Welch, *Practice*, Appendix II.

5. Monks have traditionally been exempt from military service and corvée labor in China. The year 1949 was a watershed in this respect too. See Welch, *Buddhism under Mao* (Cambridge, Mass., Harvard University Press, 1972), Chapter 3, note 59.

Chapter XII

ARRIVAL IN TAIWAN

When the officer blamed our misfortune on Mao Tse-tung's treachery, we all felt there was truth in what he said. However, if it had not been for the weak-willed vacillators who believed the divisive rumors spread by the Communists and insisted on President Chiang's resignation, our country would not have been reduced to such a state (See "The Collected Speeches of President Chiang," Vol. 19, page 54), and we peaceloving monks would not have fallen victim to the [Nationalists'] "brilliant idea" of conscripting monks. It was only human that such considerations would fill us with outrage at the times and the workings of fate. But there was nowhere for us to vent our sadness and outrage. All we could do was weep together.

The officer felt badly at seeing us cry so miserably, but he was, after all, "under orders" to take us back. He could not release us out of compassion simply because of our chorus of weeping. In spite of our weeping, he carried out his duty: that is to say, he and the soldiers marched us to a boat and took us to Ting-hai that afternoon. Not only that: he gave us a harsh, intimidating lecture at the county office before we left for Ting-hai. He held a pistol in his hand throughout his lecture, the gist of which ran: "We are about to set out. Follow one after another along the road. No lagging behind will be permitted; nor will talking among yourselves; nor will leaving your place to relieve yourself while on the march. I'll tell you what will happen if you don't obey: I recognize you, but this pistol doesn't recognize you, and neither do my men's bayonets!"

Everyone was good and frightened at this. "This morning he spoke so politely, and he was sad to see us cry. What's wrong with him? All of a sudden he's turned so cruel," we thought. But some people understood what he really meant: he was trying to strike fear into our hearts to prevent us from deserting. If someone had fallen behind because of a bad leg or stepped out of the ranks to relieve himself, the officer would not have lifted his revolver and fired; nor would the soldiers have slashed the offender with bayonets. Actually, the officer was wasting his time worrying about such things: now that we had resolved to leave a glorious mark in the history of Chinese Buddhism, we were not so shameless as to desert our unit and make traitors of ourselves.

We were marched aboard a small army steamer which left P'u-t'o, stopped at Shen-chia-men for two hours, and then went straight to Ting-hai. For some reason they divided us at Ting-hai into two groups. The twenty-one people in my and Master Hsing-wu's group were sent to a dilapidated temple in the suburbs of Ting-hai, and the other group was, according to what we heard, sent to the county office building. However, we did not see a sign of them when we were taken by boat to Taiwan in a contingent of some seven hundred new soldiers. Even now I have no idea what became of them. For this reason I wonder about them, just as I wonder about my father, whom I have not seen or heard from in seventeen years and whose fate is unknown to me.

The ship that took us to Taiwan reached Keelung and sailed slowly into the harbor. After it had coasted up against the dock and dropped anchor, the officers in charge sent men to the appropriate units to arrange for temporary quarters and ordered the recruits to pack up and prepare to go ashore. In an instant the quiet ship turned into a noisy marketplace, with everyone milling about in nervous confusion. Seeing the tumult they made, the officers shook their heads resignedly and said, "The recruits in this batch are civilians through and through." Once ashore, we were marched to a square in front of a railway station, where we sat down to rest. The officers went to make arrangements for the noon meal, while armed soldiers watched over us from the perimeter.

In 1949 there were bullet marks and signs of damage everywhere we looked in the port of Keelung. The lively bustle of urban life had been stilled, and there were few people on the streets. As we sat in the square, many of us who had gotten seasick during the crossing still felt their bodies were heaving, the earth moving and the surrounding buildings revolving. Because we had not eaten, slept, bathed or changed clothing for a whole day and night aboard the ship, we looked more dead than alive. After sitting awhile, some recruits fell to the ground asleep. The citizens who gathered around to watch us thought we were captives from the Eighth Route Army, and we, seeing their bare feet and wooden clogs, mistook them for foreigners. Actually we were all children of China and descendants of the Yellow Emperor, but the mountains and water between us had created a lack of mutual understanding. Like the clan of dragons that were dispersed by the flooding of the Dragon King's palace, we did not recognize our own kind.

It was almost twilight by the time we finished our lunch, which did double duty as supper. We boarded a passenger train and set out southward for Taichung. From the moving train we frequently saw, by the light of the moon and the stars, night travelers pedaling unhurriedly in twos and threes along the road below. We envied them, and at the same time we were moved, because we had not seen such a peaceful scene since the War of Resistance broke out.

The train stopped at every station along the way. All were exhausted from the long trip, and they fell into oblivious slumber on the wood-backed seats. Only my and Master Hsing-wu's eyes stayed wide open: we were not in the least sleepy. He asked me in a whisper: "Master Chün, do you know that when we arrive in Taichung, we'll be sent to a camp for basic training. I'm afraid we'll be separated."

"I heard that at the railway station in Keelung. But don't worry! We two will be together," I said.

"I hope I'll be able to stay with you, so we can look out for each other. But I'm afraid that when the time comes to assign us to our units, we'll be assigned to different places."

"Relax! That won't happen. If we sit together as we are now, we won't be assigned to different units," I said confidently. My reassurances seemed to make him feel better. However, the facts proved me wrong, because the officers who brought us over to Taiwan had already compiled a list of names. Though Master Hsing-wu and I sat together when units were assigned, we were nevertheless sent to separate units.

We reached Taichung and, while luckier souls were lying in bed dreaming pleasant dreams, we and the officers in charge were exposed to half a night of chilly wind at the Taichung train station before we went to the barracks outside of ___ ___, where we cooked a meal and went right to sleep. As I remember, the barracks were situated in a clean, quiet area. Quite a few officers made friendly conversation with us as we sat and rested in a grove. When they talked to our group of twenty-one monks, their friendliness was mixed with amazement and sympathy.

After we had eaten, the officers blew whistles and had us fall in. Our names were then called in the order they appeared on the roll that had been drawn up beforehand. When the officer called the names of us monks, one brother answered "Amitābha!" The officer struck him a light blow on the chest and said laughingly: "From now on when I call your name, answer 'Here,' not 'Amitābha!' From this day on you are a member of the revolutionary army — not a monk living in a temple and reciting 'Amitābha.'" The brother answered "Here!" in self-correction and took three big steps forward.

Sometime after one o'clock, the seven hundred of us had been assigned to two different detachments. One detachment remained in the barracks outside of ___ ___ and received basic training there, while the other was marched to Lu-kang. I was assigned to the latter detachment. Later that day we reached Lu-kang and settled down for the night in the school where we would be stationed for the duration of our basic training. Early the next morning we got to work cleaning up the area, setting up beds (or rather floor mats), shaving heads and bathing, and changing into uniform. That night, after a hard day's work, the broken-down school and its messy surroundings had been transformed into a clean, orderly place. At the same time, our group of out-and-out civilians had taken on something of the proud bearing of soldiers. Looking at what we had done, I thought: "No wonder that when we arrived yesterday, the leader of our detachment hung a sign outside the gate with the words 'Stand with dignity between heaven and earth: carry on the past and pave the way for the future!" It is true! Men working together in the army have the power to accomplish great things."

"Recruits have a tough, nerve-racking time of it during basic training," a recruit said to me one day in his thick Chekiang accent. "I just can't take it any more!" He was absolutely right about the strictness and tension of life in boot camp. The treatment was so severe that one dared not be careless about anything, and the tension was such that no one dared put anything off. What was more, when one person slipped up, his companions were punished along with him.

Once, when we were learning to stand at attention, our group leader came up behind me unawares and kicked the back of my knees with all his strength. I instantly fell to my knees on the gravel-strewn ground, and blood flowed from where the sharp stones had pierced my knees. Still the group leader roared at me, saying that my legs were not close enough together and my heels not planted firmly on the ground. Then each member of our group got a kick on the back of the legs. Fortunately I had served as a cautionary example, and no one else fell over from the kicking. However, the back of each man's knees bore a deep red bruise from the group leader's big leather boot.

As for tension, an example will show what I mean. When reveille was sounded in the morning, we had five minutes in which to dress, make our beds, go to the bathroom, wash our faces, and clean our teeth. If we could not do all these things in five minutes, we would be late for drill. The punishment for being late was, if one were lucky, listening to the tiresome admonitions fo the officer of the day or, in more serious cases, being made to stand motionless with a rifle at arm's length, march in place, or perhaps do fifty push-ups in a row. Thus it often happened that, as the officer of the day began to shout "Attention!...Right face!...About face," the slow-moving men would throw down their mugs, hitch up their trousers, and bolt for the drill area, only to find themselves already late. Though they might be only a few steps away when the "right face!" order was given, it did them no good to take their places once the order had left the officer's mouth, since they would nevertheless be dragged from the ranks and made laughing stocks.

However, such a challenging, tense experience is good for young people. It can instill responsibility and punctuality and, at the same time, can bring out an ability to think on one's feet and the sort of purposefulness that makes excellence possible. I had always been a muddleheaded weakling, but after a month of basic training my dull mind became quick and my frail body became strong. (I hope the reader does not suppose that this came from gorging myself on meat.) Because of my experience I strongly believed Tseng Kuo-fan's maxim —— "The spirit comes forth as we avail ourselves of its richness: wisdom shines brightest when adversity threatens." Furthermore I feel that, among all the assemblages of people in this world, the army is the nearest thing to an ideal assemblage. Between officers and soldiers, or between soldiers and soldiers, there is honesty and directness, but not hypocrisy and treachery. The blows and curses and talk and laughter are all truthful: nothing happens that is not truthful. Think for a moment: where in this increasingly degenerate and immoral world can such a scheme of human relations be found?

I remember: on November 1, 1949, I left the detachment of recruits and was transferred to the second Company, _ Battalion, _ Regiment, _ Division, _ Corps of the infantry, in which I was given the rank of private, second class. That is to say, I officially took my place in the Revolutionary Army of the Republic of China and began to fulfill my sacred duty to "fight to save our country and our people."

For the first few days it was hard to adjust to life in my company. In my earlier detachment everyone had been a recruit and had come to Taiwan on the same ship. It had been easy to work out interpersonal problems by talking things over and helping each other out. Even in official matters such as training on the drill ground, everyone had cooperated to make things easier. But it was a different story once I arrived in my new company. The whole company was made up of strangers, and they were all battle-hardened veterans. To them blows and curses were everyday things, and punishments like prolonged standing or confinement to quarters were not enough to make them raise an eyebrow. Seeing that I was a recruit and a monk besides, they gathered around and used disgustingly coarse language to get a rise out of me. Though officers who saw or heard such things berated them for it, this did not faze my fellow soldiers at all. During this period I thought to myself: "These tough old customers are boorish to the point of savagery. Just living with them will be the end of me. Why worry about anything else?"

There was another problem which was extremely hard to deal with — that of eating vegetarian food. While I was with the detachment of recruits, the detachment leader saw that our group of seven or eight monks (the other monks had been assigned to a different detachment) refused adamantly to eat from the community pot, so he ordered the quartermaster to set aside our mess allowance to buy peanut oil, fresh vegetables, and beancurd. He also had the cooks fix special dishes for us. In this way the problem of diet was taken care of very smoothly during basic training. But in my company the tenor of life was different, and I was the only monk. Since the circumstances offered no prospect of fulfilling my wishes, I unconditionally gave up my share of the mess allowance and soaked my rice in salty water to make it palatable. When the captain learned that I poured nothing but water over my rice, he urged me to give up my "vegetarianism."

"I eat vegetarian food out of compassion — not because of 'vegetarianism,'" I answered.

"What happens to your compassion if we go into battle? Would you fire your rifle at the enemy?"

"I would," I answered without a moment's hesitation.

"Doesn't that run counter to your idea of compassion?"

"A soldier is duty-bound to kill the enemy in order to protect his country. Since I am a soldier, that is my duty too. At the same time, killing one man in order to save one hundred is, in Mahāyāna Buddhism, an act of expedient mercy. If we kill a small number of evil men to save a large number of good men, we are not acting contrary to compassion," I replied.

The captain listened with great interest and said, "I thought monks could only strike the wooden fish and chant sūtras. I never imagined that they did any thinking!" One day the captain pointed to me and said to the quartermaster: "Liu Fu-yü (my lay name) has taken monastic vows. Let's not be too hard on him. Set aside his share of the mess fund and let him use it as he sees fit." From then on I went to the quartermaster's office every day to pick up my seventy-cent food allowance, which I would use to buy a piece of beancurd or some peanuts to eat with my rice. When they saw this, the savagely boorish old veterans stopped having fun at my expense.

At the end of 1949 my unit was ordered to move from its original encampment at Hsing-kang to Pei-pu near Hua-lien. In Pei-pu we underwent thirteen straight weeks of advanced training. Besides reviewing basic drills, I learned such combat skills as the use of machete and bayonet, riflery, outdoor survival, distance running, obstacle course running, pole climbing and gymnastics. Since I knew a few written characters, the veteran soldiers often asked me to write requests for passes or read letters. As long as I had free time I was happy to help them. Thus the veteran soldiers gradually became kinder to me, while the squad leader and assistant squad leader came to value me. This provoked my fellow monks from other companies to say, when they ran into me, that I had the ability to fit into my environment and at the same time change it. Actually, I had no such special ability. I simply said what was appropriate to the situation and got along, doing what I should, like a monk who rings the monastery bell every day.

But then, as I singlemindedly practiced combat skills with my comrades in arms, preparing to show my mettle on the battlefield as soon as our army attacked the mainland, I — due to my heavy karmic hindrance — received a serious unexpected injury while throwing a hand grenade. This injury was not inflicted by any weapon, but it was more painful and harder to heal than any wound. I had been a combat-ready fighting man, but I suddenly became weak, unfit, and only half a soldier. And because of this I sank once again into the abyss of dejection. This is how it happened. One afternoon the officer of the day ordered everyone in the company onto the drill ground to practice throwing hand grenades. The first platoon was to throw first, then the second platoon, then the third platoon, and then the artillery platoon. When my squad's turn came the squad leader, thinking to win a little glory for himself, warned us again and again: "The throwing distance must be no less than forty meters, and you will have to be accurate. Otherwise, I'll have you do two hours of individual calisthenics." Most young people want to be winners. No one would be willing to do two hours of calisthenics for not measuring up, unless there were absolutely no way out! Naturally, I was no exception. On the count of three I used all my strength to throw the dummy grenade forward. At the moment I released it, I fell to the ground. To the officer of the day and the squad leader, it looked as if I had broken my arm through excessive use of force. After the two of them carried me to the clinic and a medic looked me over, we learned that I had dislocated a joint. The pain being more than I could bear, I repeatedly asked the medic to think of some way to put it back in place. But, perversely enough, the old medic did not know the first thing about orthopedics. He jerked and pulled at my right arm half the night, but, even though I fainted away several times from the pain, it did not go back into place. When the medic could think of nothing else, he called a medic from the division hospital who put my arm back into place within three minutes of his arrival. However, he warned me as he left: "Don't do any more strenuous exercise when it gets better. Otherwise, the first time you're not careful it will dislocate again." "It's all over," I thought with a sigh.

As the saying goes: "When the scab peels, the hurt is forgotten." I stayed in the clinic for a day and then rested in the company barracks for a week. The swelling had gone down, and the pain had disappeared. I reported back to duty and took part in exercises on the drill ground, thinking that, since the bone had gone back into place so well, it would not pop out again. But when I gripped the horizontal bar with my two hands and lifted myself forcefully, I felt pain shoot through my right shoulder. My hands loosed their grip, and I fell to the ground again. My shoulder was dislocated this way four times in one year.

The mental agony of a handicapped soldier who stays with his squad but cannot join in training exercises is indescribable. For example, the squad leader might assign a task which I was incapable of completing because of my injury. Even if my squad leader did not complain, my fellows would mutter under their breath. Anyone would find this hard to take. Luckily this mental suffering only lasted one year, after which I was transferred to the company headquarters to handle paperwork. Otherwise, I would have lost my mind for sure.

As a first-class private and secretary, I was much less confined than I had been in the squad, and the work was quite a bit easier. Still, I did not presume on my freedom to the point of losing my self-discipline and becoming negligent. I felt that since my injury ruled me out for combat duty, I should take advantage of my time to do more reading. By bettering myself in this way, I hoped to keep my injury from making me a useless person and a dead-weight to my country. At that time interest in reading had become widespread throughout the armed forces. Besides the political textbooks which were issued to each soldier by the Ministry of Defense, there were all sorts of books, magazines and newspapers in the Sun Yat-sen Room (the reading room). I whiled away all my time there after work and on holidays. Never once did I go out with my comrades to have a good time walking the streets or watching a movie. Because of this I was ignorant of the existence of Tun-ching Monastery, which lay only a stone's throw away, even though I was stationed in Pei-pu for over two years!

Man is an emotional animal. When men who enjoy talking to each other are together for a time, friendship naturally develops. During the period that I worked as a secretary, I was often together with the company officers. As the days passed, their understanding of me deepened and their attitude toward me changed. The more their attitude changed and the more they understood, the kinder they were to me. In our personal relations we gradually became close friends and confidants.

Chapter XIII

MEDICAL DISCHARGE FROM THE ARMY IN 1952

Sometime around the end of 1951, the Ministry of Defense initiated a plan to discharge old, weak and disabled personnel so as to streamline the armed forces. The plan included provisions to place discharged soldiers according to their skills and abilities, so they would be able to support themselves. On hearing this news, I asked my captain several times if he would report my name to his superiors. I hoped to leave the army soon, not wanting to take up space in the army and wastefully consume the rice that was meant for fighting men. At first he refused, saying, "You're not in bad enough shape to be reported as handicapped." Only later, when I asked again, did he give in, but he added, "I'll report your name, but if my superiors don't approve your request, don't bother me again!" To my surprise, a physical examination showed me to be "weak and unfit for military service," for which reason I received my discharge papers in the spring of 1952. The captain had not expected this, and neither had the other officers. They had thought that though I was unfit for rigorous activity, there was nothing weak about me, and they wondered how I had obtained a discharge so easily. A few comrades who had also signed up for a discharge but not received it were especially amazed. They thought I had cast a spell on the eyes of the medic who had given me the examination. Fearful of being overheard, they asked in low tones: "When the medic gave you that physical, we saw your mouth moving. Were you mouthing incantations?"

When they heard that I had gotten a discharge, some of my close friends were happy for my sake, some were sad and some worried over the problems I would face. As for me, my mind was filled with vagueness and confusion, which I could call neither happiness nor bitterness. I did not have the faintest notion of what to do after my discharge.

When I left my unit, a comrade-at-arms named Kuo Tzu-heng shouldered my knapsack and saw me to the airport several miles from our base. He found a patch of grassy ground for us to sit on and grabbed my hands lingeringly. For a long time he sat there, with shining tears flowing from his valiant, tiger-like eyes, before he said his slow, deliberate farewell: "Brother Fu-yü, it's been nearly ten years since I left home, but I've never met another person who understands me as you do. Now that you've gotten your discharge papers, I should give you my blessing and be happy for you, but when I think of you having to make your own way in a society of strangers, I can't help but feel sad. Wherever you go and whatever work you find, please write and tell me about it. Though I am an ignorant soul who cannot write characters, I'll ape the people who can and put something down on paper to send you." With this he reached into his pocket, pulled out five ten-dollar bills and said, "This is the prize money I won in the division-wide footrace the day before yesterday. It won't do me any good to keep it. I know you don't have money. Take it!" He stuck the money in the neck of my shirt and made off with large strides, as if afraid I would catch him and return the money. I stood on the grass strip near the airport and stared at Kuo Tzu-heng's receding figure until it disappeared at the end of the runway. Then I carefully put away the money, shouldered my pack and went to report my arrival at the regimental farm nearby.

Why do I write at such length on this matter? Because my comrade-at-arms Kuo was *too* good to me! In a rich man's eyes, fifty New Taiwan dollars may have been worth no more than the hair on an ox, but for a soldier this was a substantial sum of money. I was a private second class then, and my pay was nine dollars a month. He was a private second class, so he drew twelve dollars per month. This meant that fifty dollars was equivalent to four months and five days of his pay or five and a half months of mine. What was more, he had won the money by exerting every ounce of his strength on the running track. I have kept in touch with him, so as not to let such a good friend down: he is now my only good friend from army days. He is no longer an uneducated person who must imitate letters written by others, but a literate second lieutenant. In 1961 when he came to spend his spring leave in Lo-tung, where I was presiding over a Buddha recitation session, he said, "Someday, after we've retaken the mainland, I want to be a monk too!" "Good," I said. "When that time comes, I'll be glad to have you live in the same monastery with me." He opened his mouth wide and laughed for joy.

Why did I have to report to a farm when I left my unit? Because my superiors had ruled that each soon-to-be-discharged soldier should serve for three months on the regimental farm, then undergo two weeks of training before he could receive his discharge and begin life as a civilian. However, because I was elected to the mess committee, I did not take part in such honest-to-goodness work as planting, weeding, irrigating and harvesting. Instead I wrote more than ten articles, at the urging of an officer, for publication in *Pure Loyalty*, a magazine put out by a unit I now forget, and *Ocean Roar*, put out by my own regiment. I was remunerated not with money but with towels, soap, toothpaste and other useful articles. When I passed out these insignificant items among my buddies, they were delighted.

Most of the men on the farm were old veterans who had shed blood for their country. Some had participated in the Northern Expedition; some in the War of Resistance; some in "extermination campaigns" against the Communists; and some in campaigns to suppress rebellions. Most of them were sergeants, but there was a small number of privates as well. They had lived through glorious episodes that deserve to be sung and lamented: for their country's sake they had performed acts of tragic heroism embodying the ultimate in purity and beauty. Now they were about to remove their armor and return to the fields, to live out their allotted spans in peace. They lived together happily and treated one another with kindness. Gone was the carousing and troublemaking of their younger days.

Some readers may wonder why I, a private, was elected to the mess committee. There was a good reason for this. On the day of my arrival I found a five-dollar bill outside the door of my sleeping quarters and immediately turned it over to the detachment commander. During roll call that evening he asked if anyone had lost the money. Nobody had, so the commander gave the money back to me. It happened that I was sent to town on procurement duty the next day, so while I was there I bought a five-dollar ticket to the Patriotic Lottery. During lunch I announced: "I used the five dollars I found yesterday to buy a lottery ticket. If I'm lucky and win a prize, I'll divide it equally among everyone, no matter how much it is. If I don't win, we can write the five dollars off as a contribution to our country." I handed the ticket over to the commander for safekeeping. Everyone entertained hopes of the ticket winning a $20,000 prize, which would give each messmate a few thousand dollars to stuff into his pouch.

Strangely enough, the ticket really did win a prize — of a hundred dollars rather than twenty thousand. At that time, however, one hundred dollars was nearly a full year's pay. Because of this, everyone suggested that I keep the money for myself. Their reason was that my rank, and therefore my pay, were the lowest, and that I could use the hundred to buy a suit of clothes when I got out. But I firmly refused to go against what I had said beforehand. In the end I used the money to buy one hundred coolie hats — one for each member of the detachment. Because of this little matter I was elected three months in a row to the mess committee, a position which gave me plenty of time to practice writing. Another result was the warm regard my fellows felt for me. On the day that I left the farm to report to division headquarters for training, the commander patted my shoulder and said, "You were a good monk and a good soldier, and now you're going to be a good citizen."

A Change of Occupation

The division implemented the training of retired and discharged personnel to allow them to make their way in society as conscientious, law-abiding citizens. It was hoped that they would make a good impression on society. Because of their concern over the difficulties unskilled veterans would face in making a living, the officers of the division arranged with various government-owned institutions such as telecommunications offices, post offices, sugar factories, paper factories and schools to give janitorial jobs to veterans. The training given by the division was intended to help the veterans make the transition to their new jobs.

Three hundred and sixty veterans out of the whole division underwent this sort of training. When the training was concluded, those who had friends or relatives to stay with or had found better jobs themselves were free to go once they obtained consent from the officers in charge of the training program. The rest were sent to the offices of the Hua-lien County government, where final arrangements for employment were made according to their wishes.

On June 1, 1952 I received my discharge certificate, and on the same day I was sent to the Hua-lien County courthouse. Yang Chung-ching, the county commissioner, gave us a pep talk to build up our courage. "In the army you were distinguished and gallant fighters. All of you are heroes who protected your country and your people. You will surely receive a warm welcome as you make your way in society. If you encounter any difficulties with your new jobs, just let me know, and I'll do everything possible to solve them...." However, our later experiences showed us that once we arrived on the job, not only was there no warm welcome awaiting us, there was no welcome of any sort. When we had difficulties and required the commissioner's help, he did not even give us the pleasure of seeing his face, let alone helping us solve our problems. This led to frequent discord and even litigation between veterans and the people in charge at their workplaces. My veteran friends felt this way: "I am a soldier of the revolutionary army who shed blood and sweat for our country. Damn it! Who in hell do they think they are, that they order me around like some cat or dog?" But those in charge took this line of thinking: "You may have shed blood and sweat for our country, but now that you're a janitor in our institution, we have a right to order you around just as we would any other janitor."

Thanks to the intercession of Kuan-yin, the principal and teachers at the school where I served as janitor treated me politely, and the grade school students even addressed me as "teacher." Nobody ordered me about like a cat or dog, and nobody looked down on me. When the principal or teachers asked me to do something, they always said, "Please." It was always: "Please come here a minute, Old Liu," or "Old Liu, would you please bring me some paper?" At that time Shen Ting-yi, who is now the principal of Ta-fu Elementary School in Hua-lien, was principal of the school and my new boss. He treated me as a friend in those days and still does now. When I went to Hua-lien in 1960 with Dharma Master Kuan-yü (now at Shan-tao Monastery in Taipei) and Brother Sheng-ming (now at Chu-lin retreat in Hsin-tien) to see him, he was overjoyed. He took me to his living quarters and pointed to a large frame on the wall. "In order to honor you, my wife put the picture you sent us last year in the center of all the others." Some people may ask: "What special ability did you have that let you to get along so well with the principal, teachers and students?" To tell the truth, I have no abilities. I simply try to say what is appropriate to each situation and follow this proverb: "As long as you are a monk, just go on ringing the daily bells."

I reported for work at Ch'eng-ch'iao Elementary School on a weekend. The principal and teachers were not there; only a few students were playing on the playground. As I walked toward the office, I saw a young lady disappear soundlessly into a classroom when she caught sight of me. In a moment she came out to the front of the office, where I was standing not knowing what to do with myself, and said forthrightly: "Where are you from? Why are you here?" When I had told her, she laughed a bit and said, "So you're the one the county was going to send? Well, wait here for a moment please. I'll ask the principal to come."

After about an hour an energetic young man came and, without wasting any time on preliminaries, said, "I am the principal. Do you have a letter from the county office?" I nodded and handed him the letter. "Good," he said after a quick look. He pointed at the girl. "She is also a janitor here. Now I'll divide the work up between you. If there's anything you don't understand, you can ask her." My share of the work turned out to be ringing the bell for classes, caring for flowers and trees on the school grounds and mailing documents and letters. The girl was to serve tea, do mimeographing and sweep the office. After a month or so of this sort of work, the principal had me handle official correspondence, cut stencils, file documents and watch the office at night. Jobs like ringing the bell and mailing letters reverted to the girl janitor. Besides my regular monthly salary, I was given a monthly bonus of ninety New Taiwan dollars, much to the displeasure of the girl janitor. She objected several times to the principal, saying that he was playing favorites, but he shrugged this off with a laugh.

One Saturday afternoon the principal and the teachers all went into Feng-lin to see a movie. I was sitting alone in my room reading when the girl janitor suddenly walked into my room. She had nothing much to say, but she tried to strike up a conversation anyway: "It's Sunday. Why don't you go out to have some fun and watch a movie? What's the point of sitting here all alone?" I looked up and shook my head to show that I did not wish to go out and I did not wish to talk to her. But this did not faze her. She sat down before the window and started asking questions like a census taker: "Which province on the mainland are you from? Are your father and mother still alive? How many brothers do you have? Do you have any sisters? I heard that you were a monk while you were still on the mainland. Is that true? How many years were you a monk? Can monks get married?" Her questions struck me as both irritating and laughable. Closing my book, I asked her in return:

"Why do you ask me all this?"

"We're co-workers. What's wrong with asking?" she said laughingly.

"There is no harm in asking, but right now I'm reading. I have no time to chat about trifles. Please go out and have a good time." With that I opened my book again. My announcement that she was an unwelcome guest discomfited her, but she sat there with no intention of leaving. After a moment of silence she asked again: "The teachers say you know a lot. Why do you keep reading? Do you want to be a teacher someday?" Seeing that I ignored her in favor of my book, she went on talking, more to herself than to me: "A janitor can never become a teacher, no matter how much he knows. Don't read any more. Go out and see a movie. Have some fun!" I could not refrain from laughing at this. "What are you laughing at?" she asked.

"I'm laughing at how you underrate yourself. If you have learning you can not only become a teacher, even becoming a principal is not out of the question. I want to be a principal someday; that is why I put effort into reading. You've finished lower middle school, haven't you? Why don't you keep on studying?"

"That's a laugh! Who ever heard of a janitor becoming a principal?" Just then the principal walked into the room. He laughed, amused at finding me talking with the girl, and asked her: "Didn't you come to ask Old Liu if he would go to a movie?" "Oh no, no," said the girl, directing a coy laugh at him as she answered, and then she ran out the door. The principal turned toward me, laughing again, "She treats you pretty nicely!" he said. He laughed yet again, this time with more than a trace of the conspiratorial in his manner. After he had gone, I said to myself: "Whatever the principal had in mind, that was certainly a strange laugh."

Chapter XIV

A NEAR-FATAL ILLNESS

Time passed swiftly. Suddenly the closing month of 1952 had passed, and the first days of 1953 had crept stealthily up to take its place. One day as I was cutting a stencil in the office, a sudden chill passed through me. I stood up shivering, my legs turned rubbery and I fell unconscious into a wicker chair. At that time I was living in a school-owned Japanese style house, together with the principal and three teachers who called themselves "old bachelors." When I regained consciousness, I was lying on my own bed in our living quarters. A look around told me that no one else was there. "That's strange," I thought. "Wasn't I just in the office? How can I be lying here?" I felt no discomfort except for a dry, bitter taste in my mouth and an overpowering thirst. Since the living quarters were situated in a courtyard over two hundred meters from the school building and classes were in session, I knew that no one would come for quite a while. But I could hardly lie there and allow myself to die of thirst! With great effort I pulled myself out of bed and lifted a foot to walk toward a water bottle in the kitchen.

Thud! I fell head first on the floor. A bump the size of an egg began forming on my head immediately. Luckily I did not pass out. I struggled several times to get on all fours, but it was wasted effort. There was nothing to do but lie spread-eagled on the floor and stare at the ceiling as I helplessly awaited a summons from the grim reaper.

In a little while I heard the sound of people removing their shoes in the vestibule. The principal led a doctor, whom I recognized as the director of the local health clinic, into the room. The principal asked why I was lying on the floor, and I told him what had happened in a raised voice. Even so he asked, "You're not talking. What is wrong with you?" I heard the voice of the clinic director break in: "Don't bother asking him. He can't talk."

I told him how wrong he was: "Nonsense. I'm talking as this loud and you still can't hear me. And then you say I can't talk! Both of you are deaf! What a laugh. Ha ha ha..." For five days I lay in this sort of delirium before I came back to myself. But I still could not get out of bed or eat rice. The only things I could keep down were water and rice gruel. Blood ran from my painfully burning nose. Four or five purple pustules the size of peanuts formed on my upper and lower lips. My tongue was stiff, and my throat was on fire. My rumbling, writhing insides felt like a pot of water that had just come to a rolling boil. Numbness and a dull ache pervaded my body; I could not have moved an inch if I wanted to. My eyes were sealed with dried mucus; for a long time I could not open them. But, at any rate, I had regained consciousness. Fighting back the pain, I managed to get my eyes open. There was the principal sitting at the window, still looking at me. He sprang to my bedside at my call. I moaned faintly before I found my voice and said, "Sir, I don't know how to thank you enough." After a few more moans I asked, "How long have I been asleep?"

"Five days and five nights."
"Did I eat or drink anything?"
"Not a thing."
"Did the doctor see me?"
"He came every day to take your temperature and give you a shot."
"What illness did the doctor say I have?"
"He didn't really say."
"Did he say there's still hope of my getting better?"
"Oh, you'll get better, but..."

"Sir!" Several moans escaped my lips before I could continue: "If there is no hope that I'll recover, please don't keep me in the dark. You see, there is an important favor I'd like to ask you to do for me."

Seeing my composed air, he finally told me the truth: "Old Liu, you renounced lay life in the past: I think you are able to view the matter of life and death with detachment. According to the director of the health clinic, your illness is very serious and its causes are multiple. You have symptoms resembling both typhoid fever and malaria, but his diagnosis showed that what you have is neither. He has told me repeatedly there is nothing he can do, so yesterday I told a carpenter to cut down the tree in the backyard. If by any chance the unfortunate should happen, we'll have it made into a coffin. We will take you to the Kuang-fu Public Cemetery, because you said your friend who died while in the army is buried there."

I felt comforted instead of saddened by the principal's words. "If I can really be buried in the Kuang-fu Public Cemetery after my death, I will be able once again to seek the truth together with Master Hsing-wu," I thought. After resting awhile, I spoke to the principal again: "Sir, you are too good to me. I thank you from the bottom of my heart. I would still like to impose on you to write what I am going to say now on a piece of paper. When the mainland is retaken, send it to my home district." When I had recovered my breath I dictated the following: "I was born in the town of Shan-cheng in Yung-ch'eng County, Honan. I became a monk at the age of fourteen; received ordination at twenty-four; came to Taiwan as a soldier at twenty-eight; was discharged from military service at thirty-one; and died of illness at thirty-two years of age at Ch'ang-ch'iao Elementary School in the village of Wan-li-ch'iao, Feng-lin Township, Hua-lien County, Taiwan. My remains are buried in Kuang-fu Public Cemetery in the same county."

Having written this down carefully, the principal read it back to me. Then he brought me a cup of boiled water. I took a couple of sips and found it bitter and brackish, so I shook my head in refusal. When he took it away, I sank back into a torpor, never once thinking of repeating the name of Amitābha. One evening, while lying somewhere between sleep and wakefulness, I suddenly saw an old man carrying two baskets on a carrying pole. One basket held various vegetables for offering and the other held a small table. He walked up to my bed and put down this load. After putting the little table on my stomach, he placed the offerings on it. He kneeled down and prostrated himself three times to me. Then he put the offerings and table back in the baskets and carried them away.

Soon I saw a fancy automobile pulling up in front of my quarters. A fat man and a thin man got out. Both were around fifty years old and wore nice suits. The fat man walked to my bed and motioned to me to enter the car. The thin man stood behind him and gestured not to go. I was debating what to do when a bright light appeared before my eyes. A bodhisattva dressed all in white drifted down from the sky and landed before me. "Don't go with him, child," she said with a smile. "You'll get better." I looked carefully and discovered that she was none other than my long-dead mother. "Mama," I cried loudly as I jumped toward her embrace. But, opening my eyes, I saw nothing but the dark interior of my living quarters. As I thought back over my dream in wonder, I heard the principal ask, "Old Liu, what's wrong?"

"There's nothing wrong."
"You let out a yell just now that gave me quite a scare."
"What time is it?"
"After twelve o'clock."
"After twelve? Why haven't the teachers come back to sleep yet?"
"They went to sleep in the office."
"Why did they want to sleep in the office?"
"Because you've been talking non-stop in your sleep. It scared them, so they left."
"Sir, weren't you afraid?"

"You gave me quite a start a minute ago. Of course I was frightened. But no matter how frightened I was, I couldn't leave you lying here all by yourself."

Perhaps it was because the principal's words had moved me, or perhaps the images in my dream had touched a sensitive spot in my heart: at any rate, I suddenly broke down crying. It may seem strange, but after this crying fit my illness gradually took a turn for the better. However, a period of exactly forty-seven days elapsed from the day I was stricken ill to the day I actually got out of bed. During this period I passed nothing but clotted blood and decomposed tissue in my stool. The stench of it nauseated me, but the goodhearted principal and the goodhearted janitress patiently disposed of it and washed me. I will never forget their kindness and goodness as long as I live!

Joy Sent from Above

Causes and conditions meet to form events;
No dharma [*fa*][1] can arise from cause alone.
Just look at the wintry river willows
Turn green after a touch of spring wind.

This *gātha* was part of a sermon which I delivered before a class during the 1962 ordination session at Ta-kang Mountain. Those who study Buddhism know that the totality of events and dharmas in this world and beyond it can be accomplished only when both fundamental cause and conditioning cause are present. If one is present without the other, nothing can be brought to completion. This is just as true of the dharmas that are part of this world as of those that are not of this world. One would be hard-pressed to point to all the numerous statements of this truth in Buddhist scriptures. There are people whose experience has not given them an appreciation of this truth and who cannot believe it unreservedly.

After my near fatal illness I was preoccupied with the idea of becoming a monk again. Actually I had harbored the same notion when I left the army, but one thing had been missing — the conditioning cause that would have made the fundamental cause, which was my wish, to bear fruit. This was because Wan-li-ch'iao was a remote mountain village of less than two hundred households. Although it was a small stop on the Hua-tung [Hua-lien and Tai-tung] rail line, there were seldom ten people at the station at one time except in the holiday season. There was no Buddhist temple or monastery; nor was there a Catholic or Protestant church. There was not even a single shrine to the God of the Earth. The inhabitants seemed to do little but get up at sunrise to work in the fields and return home at sunset to rest. Not only did they have little of what could be called religious belief, they had probably not even heard the names of Buddha and Christ. When the fashionably atheistic schoolteachers were not teaching, they were in the town of Feng-lin four miles away watching movies or doing other things. They never so much as touched on the subject of religion. During their occasional conversations with me they said that I was fine in every respect, except that I was too superstitious. Although the principal liked to dabble in reading *Lao-tzu*, *Chuang-tzu*, and books on Buddhism and Confucianism, he had regrettably not been able to delve deeply into them. Naturally the word faith could not be applied to his casual interest. How was a person living in such an environment to obtain any news about Buddhism? All this led me to suspect that there was no Buddhism on Taiwan. Nevertheless, my wish to become a monk again was never dampened by my environment. In other words, I would have renounced lay life as soon as the proper conditioning cause came along, even if there had not been any Buddhism on Taiwan. This wish, which seemed so much at odds with my surroundings, returned with great intensity after my recovery.

"Old Liu! Here's a Buddhist magazine for you to read." One day as I was pacing aimlessly in the courtyard beside my living quarters, the principal roused me by calling my name and handing me a magazine. Sure enough, it was an issue of the *Bodhi Tree* [*P'u-t'iShu*]. I looked at the title in joyful surprise and then looked at the principal in wonder. With a laugh he said, "In the past Śākyamuni found the truth under the *Bodhi Tree*; now, in the same way, you will find the truth in the *Bodhi Tree*." I asked him where he had bought it, and he replied that a student's parent had bought it for him to read. I walked into my room, moved a wicker chair to the window and sat down. I opened the magazine and read every line with great care. It was, to be sure, a Buddhist publication. When I read an article by Tung Cheng-yi called "Instructor at the Ta-hsien Monastery Recitation Session" and saw the names Chieh-teh, Hao-lin and Ching-nien, my heart pounded with excitement as I thought: "Chieh-teh! Wasn't he a proctor at T'ien-ning Monastery in Changchow? Hao-lin! Wasn't he my classmate at the T'ien-ning Buddhist Seminary? Ching-nien! Wasn't he my best friend when I was at Ling-yen Monastery?" Another thought suddenly arose: "Don't fool yourself. How could they have come across mountains and ocean to Taiwan?" But then I thought: "Wait a minute! It could be. I came to Taiwan; couldn't they have come here too?" I frantically dashed to the office, grabbed an envelope and a few sheets of paper, then returned to my room. Then, crouching over my desk, I rapidly wrote a five-page letter to Ching-nien and stuffed it into the envelope. As I prepared to write the address, something occurred to me which made my heart skip a beat: "Where should I send the letter? Where in that vast sea of people can the postman go to find Ching-nien?" I was stymied.

Suddenly a light bulb flashed in my mind. "The article doesn't mention his address, but maybe the editor of the magazine knows it. If he doesn't, maybe he can find out for me." Having made up my mind what to do, I proceeded at a flat-out run to the postal office, where I paid for a year's subscription by depositing twenty-four New Taiwan dollars under the account number of *Bodhi Tree*. I wrote a few sentences in the "remarks" section of the mail payment form asking Devotee Chu-p'ei, the editor and publisher, to find out Ching-nien's address for me and to send it along with the magazine. After a few days my copy of *Bodhi Tree* came in the mail, and inside it was a small note reading: "Dharma Master Ching-nien lives in Kuang-teh Monastery, Kang-hou Village, A-lien Township, Kao-hsiung County." I sent the letter I had written a few days before to this address and waited for the return letter as a farmer waits for rain clouds in a drought. The reader might think this was impetuous of me, and that I had no way of being certain that he was the Ching-nien who had been my friend at Ling-yen Monastery, since there are a good many people in this world with identical names.

This is a good point, but I had thought of it beforehand. Besides explaining what had happened after our parting at Ling-yen Monastery and telling about my experiences in Taiwan, I added the following note: "If the recipient is not the Dharma Master Ching-nien of my acquaintance, there is no need to answer this letter." However, buddhas and bodhisattvas never turn their backs on those who have taken pains. Five days after mailing my letter, I received an answering one from Kuang-teh Monastery. I opened it and, sure enough, it was he! It was written by my old friend, Dharma Master Ching-nien. Even now I remember the first two sentences: "Brother Chün, I can't tell you how happy I was to read your letter! I never dreamed that you would come to Taiwan, much less serve in the Nationalist army...."

After reading Dharma Master Ching-nien's letter, I was too happy to put my feelings into words. I was obsessed with the wish to go to Kao-hsiung County immediately and visit him at Kuang-teh Monastery, but my hopes were crushed when I received his second letter. Kuang-teh Monastery, which he presided over, was in fact a small rural temple. He received only five dollars a year for personal use. The food he ate was a boiled mixture of rice and yams. All this, plus his inability to communicate with the Taiwanese-speaking peasants, combined to fill his life with misery and depression. He wrote: "Once when I was sick, I did not even have enough money for medicine. I thought it would be better to die and be reborn in the West than to live in such misery. So I resolved to recite the Buddha's name singlemindedly, without eating or drinking, to see if I could not be reborn in the Western Paradise. After reciting for seven days, I was not reborn, but I did recover. Thus I could only accept the causes which act upon me and go on living."

Once I knew how things stood with him, I dared not follow my impulse to run and see him. This was not due to timidity or indecision, but because I feared that running to visit him would only burden him more and be of no benefit to me. So I sent him an offering of fifty dollars and continued to live quietly at the school, waiting for circumstances to set the mechanism of my fate in motion.

Twenty-some days later I received a letter sent by Dharma Master Hao-lin from Shih-p'u Monastery in Taipei. A certain matter had taken Dharma Master Ching-nien to Taipei, where he ate a meal one day at the same table with Hao-lin. Somehow the conversation got around to me. When Master Ching told him that I had gotten a discharge because of an arm injury, Master Hao was frantic with worry, supposing that I had lost my arm. His letter, filled with expressions of solicitude and warm friendship, moved me greatly. He told me to go to Taipei as soon as I received his letter and wrote: "Many of our classmates from the T'ien-ning Buddhist Seminary are living in the Inner Courtyard of Maitreya in Hsi-chih so they can be close to the Venerable Dharma Master Tz'u-hang. Come quickly! We will take care of everything for you." Of course I then made up my mind to quit my job and go to Hsi-chih outside of Taipei.

What an amazing thing circumstantial causes are! If a student's parent had not given a copy of the *Bodhi Tree* to the principal; if the principal had not given it to me; if Devotee Tung Cheng-yi had not written that article; if Devotee Chu-p'ei had not told me Dharma Master Ching-nien's address; if matters had not taken Ching-nien to Taipei; if he had not eaten at the same table with Hao-lin and somehow mentioned me; and if Hao-lin had not written to say that my classmates were living in close contact with the Venerable Dharma Master Tz'u-hang at the Inner Courtyard of Maitreya in Hsi-chih, my wish to become a monk again might never have been fulfilled. No wonder it says in the *Awakening of Faith*: "All dharmas have their fundamental and conditioning causes. Only when both are present can things be brought to completion. Look for example at the combustibility of wood, which is a fundamental cause of fire. If no one recognizes its combustibility and helps it along, it is not possible for wood to leap into flames by itself. Human beings are also this way: though they may have the fundamental cause which drives them to seek the truth, if they do not meet with buddhas, bodhisattvas, and men of true wisdom, and allow these beings to work upon their lives as conditioning causes, it is impossible for them to cut away the delusions of passion and enter nirvana of themselves. And if men are acted upon by external conditions but are not driven by a dharma of purity inside them to seek the truth, they too cannot turn away in disgust from the suffering of life and death in order to seek gladly after nirvana."

To Taipei by Air

After receiving Dharma Master Hao-lin's letter, I first wrote to say my injury was not as serious as he imagined and that, aside from wanting him to recommend a place where I could live, there was no need for my former classmates to trouble themselves for my sake. I then wrote a note to the principal asking for an extended vacation and hoping he would let me leave my job and go north immediately, so that my long-standing wish might be fulfilled. The principal read my note and put it in a drawer without saying a word. After work, when we had finished supper and returned to our living quarters, he finally had a long talk with me. He said, "You are a man of good character and wide learning. You are also responsible in your work. I was planning to wait until summer vacation to file a report about you to the county education commission and have them hire you as a Chinese teacher. Your handing me this request is tantamount to pouring cold water on my head. I don't understand why you have to go and become a monk. Old Liu, I hope you will reconsider."

"To be a monk is my only wish, and you can say it is my only calling. The times forced me to be a soldier, and circumstances also caused me to become a janitor. I didn't wish to be either: they were not my calling. But I try to live by the proverb that says, 'As long as you are a monk, just go on ringing the daily bells.' As a soldier I tried to do my duty as a soldier, and as a janitor I tried to fulfill the responsibilities of a janitor. Now that I have an opportunity to become a monk again, what more is there to consider?"

Seeing how strongly I was determined to go, the principal agreed to my request. However, on the day of my departure he said, "I've given you leave, but my superiors don't know about it, so I can keep your name entered as an employee. Leave your personal seal with me. If you wish to come back within the next three months, you can do so. Otherwise, I'll take care of all the paperwork for your resignation. During the three month period, I'll send you your regular salary." Then he grabbed my hand tightly and shook it. "Old Liu, with your will and determination, you are certain to become a great monk someday."

"Just as long as I am a monk, I don't care whether I become a great monk or just an ordinary little monk," I told him laughingly. When we had said our mutual goodbyes, my year as a janitor came to a close. I took a train from Wan-li-ch'iao to Hua-lien, where I stayed the night at a friend's house. Early the next morning I hurried to the Hua-lien airline office and bought a ticket to Taipei. After eating a bowl of soybean milk and two steamed buns, I rode in the airline's limousine to Pei-p'u Airport to wait for the 8:05 flight to Taipei.

I had never in my thirty-some years ridden in an airplane; nor had I even thought of riding in an airplane. I had always thought that only government officials, famous scholars and businessmen with bulging moneybags were the patrons of airlines, while the mass of people, eking out their hand-to-mouth lives, could have saved for a lifetime and not been able to afford an airplane ride. After being a poor monk for a good part of my life, a soldier for three years and a janitor for one, my total assets were between six and seven hundred dollars N.T. Naturally I had never seriously entertained the notion of riding in an airplane. But when I asked about it in Hua-lien, I was amazed to hear that $110 N.T. was enough to buy a ticket to Taipei. In a moment of delighted surprise I took out one sixth of my total assets and bought an airplane ticket, so that I could have the experience of flying just once.

After a short wait the airplane crawled out of its hangar like some strange, giant beast and stopped at one end of the runway. After the ground crew had rolled the steps into place and opened the door, the passengers climbed one by one into the fuselage. The kindly stewardesses showed each passenger where to sit. When everyone's seat belt was fastened tightly, the plane lurched into motion, started to skim down the runway and then lifted off. As its speed increased, it left the ground further behind. Soon it was flying over the Pacific. How quickly it all happened! We descended through the cloud cover, whizzed over a series of mountains and there we were, landing at Sung-shan Airport after only thirty-five minutes.

Some of the passengers were picked up by friends and relatives in cabs. The rest of us rode the airline bus to Kuan-ch'ien Avenue near the Taipei bus station. For some strange reason I had no sooner gotten off the plane than I felt faint, and my ears began tingling and aching. My eardrums felt as if they were about to burst. When I got off the bus in Taipei, I still felt faint and there was a feeling of pressure in my ears. At the same time my legs started to feel rubbery. So I did not proceed directly to Shih-p'u Monastery, but instead walked to the lobby of the train station and sat down to rest. After everything went back to normal, I finally got on a train for

Hsi-chih.

In the four years since I had left P'u-t'o Island and come to Taiwan, I had not so much as seen a single Buddhist temple or monastery. As I entered Ching-hsiu Monastery and saw the spotless halls, the thick foliage of the trees and shrubs in the courtyard and the pristine, solemn Buddha image, I could not keep hot tears from spilling down my cheeks. I put down my bag and made three heartfelt prostrations to the Buddha. I dried my eyes and was about to look for someone who could point out the road up the mountain, when suddenly I saw a tall, slender monk standing on the porch of the reception room to my right, his gaze fixed in my direction. I recognized him at once as Ho-yi (now known as Dharma Master Ch'ing-lin), but he looked on me as just another passer-by. This was no wonder, because we had been separated so long, and I had changed so much. How, in a moment's glance, could he see in me his classmate of yesteryear? Of course when I explained that I was Chen-hua, he quickly extended a friendly hand.

Short Stay at Ling-ch'uan

While I was talking with Ching-lin in Ching-hsiu Monastery, several other former classmates came down from the Inner Courtyard of Maitreya. At first they were as ignorant of my identity as Ch'ing-lin had been when he first caught sight of me, but once he had introduced me, everyone gathered around solicitously and subjected me to a barrage of questions. My classmates showed their sympathy for what I had been through, and some sighed at the lifetime that seemed to have elapsed since we had last been together.

I learned that Master Hao-lin had already told them the whole story of my coming to Taiwan as a soldier, and that, owing to the recommendation of Master Yen-ch'ih, the Inner Courtyard would send me to Keelung for a short stay in Ling-ch'uan Monastery on Yüeh-mei Mountain, where I would await the ripening of my affinity with Buddhism before joining the Venerable Dharma Master Tz'u-hang in the Inner Courtyard. "This is what the Venerable Dharma Master wishes," they told me.

Though they might have been stretching the truth to say that all this was the Dharma Master's idea, I was more than satisfied that they had found me a place to stay and had given me back my identity as a monk. I felt nothing but gratitude for the Venerable Dharma Master's compassion and my classmate's assistance. If my satisfaction was less than perfect, it was because I regretted not being able to get close to the Venerable Dharma Master. However, this regret disappeared not long afterward, because three months later I moved into the Inner Courtyard.

After a freewheeling conversation with my friends and a meal at Ching-hsiu Monastery, I followed everyone to the Inner Courtyard to pay my respects to the Venerable Dharma Master, whom I had looked up to for so long. I stayed the night and, rising early the next morning, changed into the clothes my friends had given me. I then went before the Buddha and repented of my sins, after which Dharma Master Yen-ch'ih accompanied me to Ling-ch'uan Monastery on Yüeh-mei Mountain.

Ling-ch'uan is a modest monastery set in a quiet, secluded area. Starting from the Ssu-chiao Pavilion on foot, one needs about forty minutes to reach the top. Though the place appeared rather decrepit and few monks were in evidence when I arrived, it had been a flourishing monastery in the days of its founder, Monk Shan-hui. Many great and pious monks from the mainland had stayed there when they visited Taiwan to discuss scriptures, preach the Dharma and benefit all those with ears to hear. When the mainland fell in 1949, many of the dharma masters who came to Taiwan with the government concealed their brilliance there, cultivating themselves in seclusion and waiting for better fortune. From this it is obvious that mainland monks who came to Taiwan had a special affinity with this monastery.

My classmate Yen-ch'ih accompanied me to Ling-ch'uan, where we met Abbot Wen-yin just as we walked in the front gate. Masters Yen and Wen were already acquainted. With a show of hearty welcome Master Wen led us to the guest department for tea and conversation. Though his Mandarin was far from being standard, I could catch the drift of what he said. My speech was unintelligible to him. Fortunately Master Yen, who spoke fluent Taiwanese, acted as a bridge between us.

During lunch Master Yen introduced me to two old bodhisattvas, Yün-feng and Ch'ang-ching, who had both come to stay at Ling-ch'uan Monastery before me. Both were aged and virtuous practitioners who had traveled to the mainland in search of instruction: they could recount the local traditions of each major public monastery; the rules of each sect; the methods of spiritual cultivation; and the paths to knowledge, with all the familiarity of people enumerating their family heirlooms. Yün-feng possessed especially broad knowledge and deep understanding. During my stay at Ling-ch'uan, I treated them as respected elders, and they felt I was worthy of learning what they had to teach. We got along wonderfully. What a pity that both of these old bodhisattvas departed peacefully from this world several years ago.

After lunch I saw Master Yen off and then walked once more around the grounds. Having returned to the guest hall and given my confused thoughts time to settle, I crossed my legs and sat for a while on my tatami.

Just them Master Wen-yin walked in and said, "You can stay in the guest hall for a few days, then I'll assign a job to you." I nodded my head in agreement. "Would you be willing to serve as verger [*hsiang-teng*] in the great hall after a few days rest?" he went on to ask. I nodded again, at which he smiled and walked out. I had wanted to ask him what a verger did, but I had been afraid that he would not understand my question. After supper I went to Bodhisattva Yün-feng's room to tell him what Master Wen-yin had said and inquire about the duties of a verger. He answered with a question: "You spent all that time in public monasteries on the mainland, and you still don't know what a verger does?"

"I've always kept to my own little corner, without paying attention to what everyone else does. Besides, I've never served as verger: How should I know what to do?"

"Hmph! You're not far from becoming a 'no-mind' [*wu-hsin*] hermit."[2]

I laughed in embarrassment, and the old bodhisattva laughed with me. Then he said, "Don't be fooled by the smallness of the shrine hall here; being a verger is not easy. When you get out of bed in the morning you have to sound the board for morning devotions and then ring the great bell. After you've rung the bell you light incense and change the offering water. When that's done you put the gong, chimes and wooden fish in their proper places. Then you attend devotions with the other monks. If too few people attend devotions, you must take over striking one of the instruments of worship. If nobody comes for morning devotions, you repeat Refuges vows and make offerings yourself. After breakfast you must if necessary dust, sweep or wash the Buddha niche, the offering tables and every corner of the shrine hall. When these things are done you can rest."

The old monk stopped for a moment, then went on to tell me: "All you do at noon is change the offerings. However, if anyone comes to burn incense or rid themselves of some affliction through prayer, you must come out and greet them. Your duties before and after evening devotions are pretty much the same as what you do in the morning. The only difference is that in the morning you ring the bell and in the evening you strike the drum. There are a great many small matters — too many to mention all at once. You'll just have to deal with them as they arise."

Then I asked him how to sound the board for awakening, how to ring the great bell and how to chant devotions. "All these things are just like on the mainland. Just watch a few times and you'll know how." Actually, a few years in the army had nearly erased my memories of how devotions were chanted, but I went on nodding to show that I understood.

On the day that I moved from the guest hall to the verger's quarters, Bodhisattva Yün-feng asked, "Did you save any money when you worked in that school?"

"I only saved six hundred and some dollars. I spent over a hundred of that for an airplane ticket to Taipei. I spent another hundred on miscellaneous purchases. Now I have less than four hundred dollars to my name."

"The monthly allowance here is only five dollars. That's hardly enough for toilet paper. My idea is that if you have the money, I can put it to work for you. The interest you'll earn every month will supplement your spending money."

"Where will you lend it? How much is the monthly interest?"

"I'll deposit it with San-kuang Moneylenders in Keelung. They pay six percent interest."

As soon as I heard this my reservations disappeared. "I'll invest three hundred dollars," I said.

"That's fine. If you put in three hundred dollars, you'll get eighteen dollars interest per month. That's more than three times your monthly allowance."

I handed three hundred dollars over to Bodhisattva Yün-feng with no further discussion, and he handed it over to San-kuang Moneylenders. In less than a month the owner of San-kuang Moneylenders disappeared with my three hundred, Yün-feng's three thousand, and tens of thousands of dollars belonging to many other people in his pocket. When this news reached Ling-ch'uan Monastery, Bodhisattva Yün-feng could not get over his regrets. He constantly told me how sorry he was. I comforted him, saying, "Bodhisattva, don't take it so hard, all right? Perhaps he ran off with our money because we owed him a debt from former lives. If not, he'll have to repay us sooner or later."

I comforted him this way because I knew that he was even sadder over the loss of his own money than the loss of my smaller sum. He was a thrifty monk who had scrimped and saved for years, probably so he could have the money to return home once the mainland was recovered. Now he had lost all his money, so of course he was heartbroken. I had no choice but to endure my own sadness in order to comfort him.

Kitchen Work at Hsi-chih

The loss of my money preyed on my mind for a time, but after a few days I put the matter behind me. Besides contentedly attending to my duties as verger, I spent my free time making prostrations to Buddha, meditating, reading scripture and practicing calligraphy. The days passed in peaceful ease. During this period former classmates living at the Inner Courtyard in Hsi-chih such as Ching-hai, Hung-tz'u, Yi-teh and Ching-lin as well as Hao-lin, who lived at Shih-p'u Monastery in Taipei, all came to see me. All expressed their sympathy and concern, but since they were nearly as poor as I, they could do no more than give me a few pieces of old clothing. I took a great deal of comfort in their gestures of concern, because spiritual encouragement is much more to be valued than material support. Aside from the fare, which was somewhat austere, the accommodations and interpersonal relations at Ling-ch'uan Monastery were actually better than I had expected. What was more, Masters Hsiu-ho and Hsiu-yen, who had studied at Ling-yin Monastery in Hsin-chu, had already moved to Ling-ch'uan Monastery. Both could speak Mandarin, and they were deeply interested in Buddhist studies. Our conversations helped me to dispel many unnecessary and unwholesome thoughts.

One day as I was busily sweeping the floor of the shrine hall, my former classmate Ch'ing-yüeh of the Inner Courtyard of Maitreya suddenly appeared on the porch. I dropped my broom, invited him to my quarters and had him sit down on my bed. When he entered my room, his gaze wandered from the bed to the desk to the walls as if he were looking for something. Then he asked in a slow, drawn-out voice: "Do you like it here, old buddy?"

"I'm a work-harried verger. What is there to like?" He stared at me soundlessly for such a long while that I started to wonder what this was all about. I was about to ask, "Why do you keep staring at me like that?" Suddenly he asked, "Do you know why I came here today?"

"You came to visit me, naturally."

"Can you think of anything else?"

"You want to enjoy yourself a bit while you're at it."

"Anything else?"

"You've got me."

"I figured you wouldn't be able to guess. I've come to ask you to go live in the Inner Courtyard."

"Live in the Inner Courtyard?"

"That's right. All your classmates welcome you, and the Venerable Dharma Master is in favor."

"Of course I want to live in the Inner Courtyard, but..."

"But what? Can't you bring yourself to leave this quiet, secluded verger's room?"

"It's not that I can't bring myself to leave here. It's that all of you have been studying the Dharma for all these years. How can I keep up with you?"

"Now don't be so modest. We're all classmates. How about this: Dharma Master Ch'eng-cheng, who cooks for the Inner Courtyard, has been feeling poorly of late. He wants to go to Hui-lung Monastery in T'a-liao-k'eng to nurse his illness. Everyone had the idea (perhaps this was Ch'ing-yüeh's own idea!) that you could come to the Inner Courtyard and serve as cook. At the same time you could sit in on the Venerable Dharma Master's lectures. Later, when we find someone else to do the cooking, you won't have to keep slaving in the kitchen. That is, you can take up permanent residence in the Inner Courtyard and study with your classmates. What do you think?"

"After beating about the bush all this time, it turns out that you've come to ask me to be rice steward [*fan-t'ou*] at the Inner Courtyard, right?"

"How could I ask an old classmate to become a rice steward? Nevertheless, I feel that this is a good opportunity for you to go live there."

"Do you mean to say that unless I take this opportunity, I'll never have a hope of living in the Inner Courtyard?"

"That's not what I meant at all. Don't you want to live together with your old classmates?"

"Too bad you're a monk. If you weren't, you'd make a fine diplomat."

"Enough, enough! Get down off your high horse. Go ahead and make a decision."

"Let me think about it, all right?"

"If you're going to go, go. What is there to consider?"

"Even if I don't take time to consider, I can't get up and leave with you right away."

"I'm not telling you to leave with me right now. If you decide, I'll have something to tell them when I go back. It doesn't matter if you leave ten days from now."

After giving it some thought, I finally quit my job as a verger at Ling-ch'uan Monastery and went to the Inner Courtyard of Maitreya to serve as rice steward. Cooking had always been my specialty, but when I entered the kitchen in the Inner Courtyard, I didn't even know how to begin. This is because the monks there were, with the exception of myself and Dharma Master Lü-hang, all southerners. Rice is the staple of southern cooking, while my specialty was wheat bread and noodles. Fortunately my classmates Yen-ch'ih and Kuan-yü gave me assistance and guidance from the sidelines, or I would not even have measured up as a rice steward.

At that time the Inner Courtyard, under the leadership of the virtuous and renowned Dharma Master Tz'u-hang, was filled with a morning-like atmosphere of growth and resurgence. Though the Venerable Dharma Master was a bit permissive with his disciples, most of them were able to supply their own motivation and watch over their own behavior, like Dharma Masters Tzu-li (Ch'eng-ju) and Wei-tz'u (Jih-chao), who now teach in the Philippines; Dharma Master Miao-feng, who is now spreading the Dharma in America; Dharma Master Ching-hai, who is studying in Thailand; Dharma Masters Liao-chung, Neng-kuo and Kuo-tsung, who are seeking knowledge in Japan; Masters Yin-hai, Huan-sheng, Hung-tz'u, Chieh-shih, Yen-ch'ih, Hao-lin, Ch'ing-lin, Yi-teh, Kuan-yü and Ch'ang-cheng, who are now in Taiwan; and Dharma Master Ch'ing-yüeh, who passed away the year before last. All of these are luminaries of the Buddhist religion and flowers of Buddhist learning. Some of them are good writers; some are good speakers; some are excellent cantors, suited to leading recitation sessions; some emphasize intellectual understanding, while some give more importance to religious practice; some like to stay in one place, and others are always on the move. Each one has his own strong points, and each uses his special talents to make contributions to the Buddhist religion. Besides all these there was Dharma Master Lü-hang, once a general, who recites the Buddha's name with earnestness and proselytizes enthusiastically. Living in such an environment brought both joy and agony to a thirty-two year old rice steward like myself. The joy came from being lucky enough to meet with such good teachers and saintly friends. The agony was due to the fact that I was nearly a middle-aged man. I could not come close to my fellow disciples in intellectual attainments or religious practice. However, I did not get carried away with myself for joy, nor did I give up on myself in agony. I rose at three o'clock every morning and stole quietly to the kitchen to wash my face. I bowed down in worship to the Buddha in the shrine hall and then read the sections of the *Sūrangama Sūtra* which the Venerable Dharma Master had lectured on the day before. At 4:30 I went to the kitchen, lit a fire to boil water, rinsed rice and made the morning porridge. I was busy until everyone sat down to breakfast, at which time I could go out and rest. After breakfast my fellows had free time. Some strolled in the courtyard, some read in their rooms and some sat talking in the gazebo out back. Meanwhile I was busy washing plates, cups, bowls, dishes, chopsticks, pots and pans. I was wiping tables; rearranging stools; and mopping the floor. By the time everything was in order it was almost time for the Master to lecture on scriptures. I followed the other monks to the cell where the Master was in sealed confinement. Immediately after the lecture I dashed back to the kitchen to begin sorting and washing vegetables for lunch.

After lunch and a nap I went to the Master's cell at two o'clock to hear a lecture on the *Sūrangama Sūtra*. I then ran back to the kitchen to cook supper and heat water for baths. The time after supper and before lights-out was my own, but fatigue from the day's labor made it impossible for me to sit under a lamp and read quietly. I spent half a year in the Inner Courtyard in just this way.

Living on Nuan-nuan Mountain

In February 1954 I left the Inner Courtyard of Maitreya to live in a thatched hut on Nuan-nuan Mountain, Keelung. Come to think of it, this too must be attributed to the power of causal affinity.

In 1953 at the time of the Buddha's birthday, a seven-day Buddha recitation session was held at Ch'ien-fo [Thousand Buddha] Monastery in Keelung. Knowing that Dharma Master Lü-hang was a Pure Land practitioner, the organizers sent someone to the Inner Courtyard of Maitreya expressly to ask Master Lü to preside over the recitation session. Although Master Lü was a confirmed Pure Land follower, he had become a monk late in life, and so knew nothing of the rules and regulations for running a recitation session. But since the organizers had asked him in all sincerity, he could hardly disappoint them. So he promised his services, at the same time enlisting Hung-tz'u and a few other dharma masters to keep time on percussion instruments and advise him where necessary. The day before he left for Keelung, Master Lü made a special request of me, saying, "If you can spare a few days, it would be nice if you would join in too, because you have lived on Ling-yen Monastery and are more familiar with recitation sessions." However, I did not dare agree to go, because finding someone to take over my duties was no easy matter.

On the third day of the session Master Lü went so far as to send a letter by way of Devotee Ku Ting-sheng (now Master Chih-ting, proctor at Shih-fang Ta-chüeh Monastery in Keelung), telling me to come immediately to Ch'ien-fo Monastery to help with the recitation session. Having no other choice, I had to ask a classmate to take my place for a few days while I went to Keelung with Ku Ting-sheng.

Most of the devotees taking part in the session at Ch'ien-fo Monastery were merchant seamen or relatives of merchant seamen such as Yü Tso-hou, who has since become a monk (his dharma name is Chih-chi and he is abbot of the Lotus Association in Keelung) and his wife Chu Nien-ssu (now Mistress Ch'ang-chih, temple manager of the Lotus Association). They and Ku Ting-sheng were initiators of this session. When I arrived there with Ku, Ku told Yü and the others that I struck him as having a deep commitment to the Path, because he found me at the Inner Courtyard sitting on a bed mending worn-out clothing. Moreover, Master Lü had told them I once lived at Ling-yen Monastery, which made them look on me as an experienced spiritual practitioner. Amitābha only knows how little spiritual work I have done!

It happened that a young woman became hysterical during the recitation session. She cried and screamed that she had seen Amitābha and that she was about to be reborn in the Western Paradise. Everyone was so startled they didn't have the slightest notion of what to do. Master Lü suggested sending her to a hospital, but the young woman would rather have died than allow herself to be taken out of the recitation hall. Her cries and screams grew even wilder. Then I thought of something. I told everyone to be silent, to avoid giving further stimulation to her deranged nerves. I called for half-cup of clean water, which I held before an image of Buddha as I devoutly recited the "Mantra of Great Compassion" [*Ta-pei chou*] twenty-one times. I then sprinkled half the water on her head and urged her to drink the rest. Truly, the power of the Dharma is beyond conception, and nothing stands in the way of compassion. In less than an hour the young woman was back to normal. This caused the young woman's family and the devotees at the session to regard me as a veritable bodhisattva! The young woman insisted on taking the primary Buddhist vows with me as her master, and more than ten other people wanted to take the Three Refuges vows under me. Being at my wit's end, I could only say, "If you keep saying you want to take the Refuges vows under me again, I'll return to Hsi-chih immediately." However, the young woman did ultimately become my Refuges disciple.

At the end of the session an old woman went together with a few devotees to present me with one hundred dollars. They said they wished to raise money to build a lay Buddhist center [*chü-shih lin*] in Keelung, and they wanted me to lead them. At the time I chuckled and said, "I'd rather live in a thatched hut in the mountains than spread the Dharma in the middle of a city." Unexpectedly, one of the older ladies kept my statement in mind. Not long after I returned to Hsi-chih, she came to the Inner Courtyard with two other devotees. Having found me she explained that while still in Shanghai she had promised herself to provide for a monk livingin a thatched hut. The turmoil on the mainland had driven her to Taiwan before she could fulfill her wish. Earlier, hearing me say that I wished to live in a thatched hut, she had wanted to tell me her idea, but there had not been enough time. She had come this time expressly to discuss this matter with me. If I was willing, she would have a thatched hut built for me and provide my living expenses for three years.

Then, seemingly afraid that I doubted her financial means, she went on to say, "My sons, daughters-in-law and grandchildren all stayed in Shanghai. My husband and I are alone in Taiwan. My husband works for the Merchants Steam Navigation Company. Though he has little faith in the

Buddha, he is not opposed to my faith. Don't you worry, Dharma Master: I'll have no problem providing for you for three years."

This is why I wrote above that my being able to live in a hut on Nuan-nuan Mountain should be attributed to the power of causal affinity. The old woman came to discuss this with me just when I was so upset over another matter that I wanted nothing more than to leave the Inner Courtyard right away.

Hearing her offer, I was convinced she had been sent to save me by a buddha or a bodhisattva, and so I agreed unreservedly to her proposal. But where should the thatched hut be built? The day after the old woman and the two devotees returned to Keelung, I went to look for a site in the area of Yüeh-mei, Pa-tu, Chi-tu and Nuan-nuan Mountains. With the help of Masters Yen-ch'ih and Ching-liang I obtained the permission of the abbot. Work on the hut was begun in January 1954. On February 15 of the same year I moved in. Almost all my classmates from the Inner Courtyard of Maitreya came for the housewarming. Some gave me money and some brought presents. I was overcome with gratitude. Having made the noonday offering, I fried up an assortment of vegetables and served them to my classmates. Everyone had a jolly meal and left in high spirits.

On the mainland I had often heard old practitioners say, "Do not become a hermit until you have broken through the first barrier; do not enter sealed confinement until you have broken through the second barrier." This means that one who wishes to live as a hermit or enter sealed confinement must first have true comprehension of the Buddhadharma. Otherwise one will either become deranged or lose heart — in either case one's aim will never be fulfilled. Amitābha! I was not only lacking in true comprehension of the Buddhadharma — I was without even a superficial understanding. All I did was get carried away by impulse and agree to someone's request. Not until I moved into the hut did I realize that it wasn't going to be as easy as I had thought. But my patron had already spent several thousands of dollars building the hermitage: I could not very well slink away after living there a few days. That is why I forced myself to live there for three years. During this time I was disturbed on many occasions by my own mind and body, by supernatural occurrences, and by human relations.

1. Disturbances of mind and body: In the *Tao-te Ching* of Lao Tzu it is written: "I am beset by great affliction because I have a body. Had I no body, what affliction would there be?" I paraphrase this as follows: "I am beset by great affliction because I have a mind. Had I no mind, what affliction would there be?" Of course Lao Tzu's "body" is not Vairocana's Dharma-body of Purity. It is, rather, a putrid bag of skin formed by a

transitory union of the elements. What I mean by "mind" is certainly not the enduring and wondrous mind of true suchness. It is instead the delusive consciousness which devises its own right and wrong when the moment of impulse arises. Though countless people in the past — rising and sinking as they writhed along the round of life and death — have already piled up mountains of bones and poured out rivers of blood for their exaggerated faith in this putrid bag of skin and this delusive consciousness, still countless people plunge ahead to follow them down the same road! What tragedy could be crueler than this? No wonder the sūtra says, "The body is a wellspring of sin, the mind is a thicket of evil."

I lived in the thatched hut, supported by money that people had earned with their own blood and sweat. By all rights I should have shaken off the tyranny of this mind and body, and gone about my work with intense effort. But things did not work out that way. When I tried to prostrate myself to the Buddha a few times more than usual, I fell into a faint. When I tried to meditate a bit more, my legs throbbed with pain. When I stayed awake a bit later than usual, my eyelids drooped disobediently. As soon as I managed to concentrate on a righteous thought, fleeting notions would sneak up and drive it away. Whenever I opened a sūtra and read a few pages, my mind would begin hopping about like a monkey. In short, neither my mind nor my body would do what they were told. After three years had passed, I was older, but I had accomplished nothing.

2. Supernatural occurrences: Keelung is famous for its frequent rainfall, and Nuan-nuan gets even more rain than Keelung. In winter a chill wind blows and dreary rain falls ceaselessly. A cloudless, sunny day is a rarity. Though my hut was in the vicinity of Chin-shen Cloister, it was some distance away. To make things worse, the two or three monks who lived in the temple often went away and did not return to the mountain at night. I was often the sole inhabitant on this desolate little mountain. Though not wholly immune to fear, I am not one to be afraid of things that go bump in the night. Though people often told me that the broken-down house on the slope below my hut was haunted, I did not give it a second thought. At about ten o'clock one night, when I had just finished evening prayers and set out food for hungry ghosts, I stood in the doorway reciting the Buddha's name. The light shining from the doorway revealed a man walking toward me from the direction of Chin-shan Cloister. "That's strange," I thought. "At this hour and in this rain, why would anyone be walking on the mountain?" When he was ten or so steps from my hut I asked, "Who is it?" The man stopped and, when I tried to get a better look, disappeared suddenly. All night I sensed someone walking about outside the hut. Next morning when I went down to buy groceries, I saw a man hanging from a

roadside tree halfway down the mountain. A police investigation revealed that he had hung himself at about ten o'clock the night before. The monks in Chin-shan Cloister feared that his unappeased ghost would remain to haunt the area, so they requested Dharma Master Chieh-teh and others to conduct a service to release the hungry ghost. Aside from this incident, I often heard people speaking in guarded voices outside the hut, or the sound of wild dogs fighting, but as soon as I opened the door to look out, everything was as still as an ancient grave.

3. Relations with others: My elderly patroness was a lay Buddhist who was strong in devotion but weak sometimes in judgement. Whenever she came up the mountain she would tell gossipy tales about this family or that. She would ramble on and on about her glorious past and trivial household matters. And there was another aspect of her temperament which left me more dumbfounded than angry. She felt nothing but animosity toward all the female believers who came to my hut, whether they were nuns or lay women, and whatever their age. Sometimes she even made snide, objectionable remarks that left me wondering whether to laugh or cry. For instance, she would say, "You female believers shouldn't come to see the Dharma Master. Don't you read in the papers about what happens between dharma masters and female believers?" If someone asked her: "You are a woman, why do you come to see the Dharma Master so often?" she would answer without hesitation: "I am an old woman. What could happen?" She was already an elderly woman of sixty-four, but this character trait had not mellowed in the slightest. This prompted some concerned friends to tell me that people had begun to talk about me. I brushed this aside with a laugh, not attempting to defend myself, because I felt that time is the best witness.

A student named Ch'en lived at the foot of Nuan-nuan Mountain. He was an intelligent boy who felt he had been born to accomplish something. Because he was an adopted son, his foster parents would not allow him to continue his schooling past junior high. Instead, they made him go to work in a mine. This turn of events caused him to look on the world with jaundiced eyes. Morning and evening he walked aimlessly near my hut. When I learned of his situation, I frequently gave him encouragement and material assistance, hoping he would work hard in the mine as his parents wished, while making every effort to study on his own. I never dreamed that he would take the twenty dollars I gave him one day and use it to buy a knife to kill himself with. Luckily he was found in time on a riverbank in Keelung, and his life was saved. However, I was subjected to extremely worrisome intrusions on my quiet life, because the papers reported that the student Ch'en had attempted suicide after his foster parents forbade him to become a monk and live with his master, a hermit on Nuan-nuan Mountain. The papers also reported that his master had given him the money to buy the vegetable knife with which he had tried to kill himself. Because of this, certain police officers had to go to the bother of running up to my hut several times to conduct an investigation. Although the truth eventually came out and I was absolved of all blame, I learned my lesson: never again would I dare to show indiscriminate compassion.

One evening at dusk a fine-looking young man came up the mountain. He walked into my hut, burned a stick of incense, bumped his forehead on the floor three times, and, turning toward me cried, "Master, I must seek release! I must seek release!" I thought he wanted to become a monk, so I advised him: "You look like you are able to accomplish things. At a time like this, you should consider how you can work for the benefit of your country, your family and yourself. Why do you wish to become a monk? Don't think for a minute that in times like these, when your country and its people are suffering such deep distress, that becoming a monk would free a young man like yourself from the obligation to save them ..."

He spoke abruptly before I had finished: "Master! You misunderstand me. The release I'm speaking of is not becoming a monk but committing suicide!"

"Why do you want to destroy yourself?" I asked in shock.

"Master, there are Oh-so-many reasons for wanting to destroy myself. It's too much to say all at once. To put it briefly, I feel that once I kill myself I'll be rid of all pain and far removed from my misery."

"From the looks of you, you don't seem to have drunk too much. Maybe you haven't been drinking at all. Why this drunken babbling? If it's really as you say; if suicide can release one from all pain and misery, then the men who go on living in this world are all superfluous. Friend! You are the one who doesn't understand the meaning of the word release. According to the Buddhadharma, people who kill themselves are not released from pain and suffering. Instead, they will descend to one of the three evil paths of destiny — purgatory, existence as a hungry ghost, or bestiality — and be subjected to extreme suffering. Why is this? Because all the thousands of different reasons for suicide boil down to the three poisons of covetousness, anger and delusion. These three poisons are the fundamental causes of the three evil paths of destiny, and the three evil paths are their effects. This is what is meant by 'Plant melons and melons will grow: plant beans and beans will grow.' If you think that suicide is a release, you obviously have not gained a clear understanding of cause and effect. I am a monk. When I see insects and worms about to die, I do what I can to save them: how much greater should my concern be for a man of my own country! I have no right to force my way of thinking on you. You are free to listen or not. But I hope with all my heart that you will use the courage it would take to commit suicide to walk forward on the broad and shining road toward goodness. Only by doing that will you truly be able to find release from pain and misery!"

The saying that "Words are the keys that open the heart" is true. The youth had been on the verge of letting the imps of Hell drag him away, but at last he realized how wrong he had been. However, after this disturbance, I could not regain my serenity for a long time.

NOTES

1. Dharma (*fa*) is a Buddhist technical term referring to the irreducible unit of reality which is beyond our ordinary mode of perception. Instead of viewing the world as consisting of persons and things, Buddhism speaks of dharmas which are forever changing, dependent on causation, and therefore having no self-nature. The common-sensical way of looking at the world results in the illusion of permanence which leads to attachment and clinging. The dharma-theory is developed by the Abhidharma school and is one of the most significant theories in Buddhist philosophy. A good discussion of this philosophy can be found in T. I. Stcherbatsky, *The Central Conception of Buddhism and Meaning of the Term "Dharma"* (London: Royal Asiatic Society, 1923).

2. No-mind or no-thought is used in Ch'an Buddhism to refer to the state of enlightenment. Whereas the ordinary man is always filled with thoughts and has a distracted mind, an enlightened person has no mind of his own for he does not discriminate. His mind is centered yet empty.

[illegible]

[illegible]

[illegible]

[illegible]

[illegible]

Chapter XV

TEACHERS AND TEACHINGS THAT I CANNOT FORGET

Tz'u-hang [Compassionate Ferry] Bodhisattva

Tz'u-hang Bodhisattva is another name for the pious and world-famed Venerable Master Tz'u-hang. On the fifth anniversary of his death, when his burial urn was opened, his corpse had still not decomposed. For this reason everyone called him Bodhisattva of Enduring Flesh [*Jou-shen P'u-sa*]. This is why I use "Bodhisattva" in the title of this section. Actually Tz'u-hang would have been worthy of the word Bodhisattva even if his corpse had altered.

The Bodhisattva's lay name was Ai. His soubriquet was Chi-jung and he was styled Yen-ts'ai. He was a native of Chien-ning County, Fukien. He was born in 1894 and died in 1954, having lived forty-three of his sixty years as a monk. The Bodhisattva's parents died when he was young. In such straitened circumstances, he was only able to go to a private schoolhouse to read the *Three Character Classic* [*San-tzu Ching*], another primer, and part of the *Analects* before he was forced to quit school and work as a tailor's apprentice. After he became a monk he traveled everywhere in search of instruction and got to know famous monks, but owing to a "natural endowment lacking in cleverness," he was unable to write smoothly or read sūtras with understanding, even after the age of thirty. But because his desire to learn was strong, he had the persistence to read one hundred times what others needed to look at only once. He overcame his lack of cleverness and went on to complete a massive work of 1,200,000 words. He spread the Dharma both here and overseas and became one of the greatest monks of our times.

In an article titled "Uphold the Three Noble Qualities of Dharma Master Tz'u-hang" (see the memorial collection published on the third anniversary of the master's passing), Master Tao-an writes movingly of the Bodhisattva's insatiable will to learn, his tireless zeal to teach and his love of giving.

First Master Tao-an writes of his insatiable will to learn: "In 1911 when Tz'u-hang was eighteen years old, he accompanied his tonsure master Tzu-chung to Neng-jen Monastery to receive ordination as a monk. His master was fond of him and tried to hold him back. This put Tz'u-hang in a difficult position, and he ran away several times before he was free of this entanglement. Then he was able to travel to Mt. Chiu-hua. He sought instruction at Chung-fa Monastery and T'ien-ning Monastery in Changchow; Chieh-chung Monastery in Soochow; Kuan-tsung Monastery on T'ien-t'ai Mountain; Hsiang-lin Monastery in Nanking; and Kao-min Monastery in Yangchow. He got to know such great masters as Ti-hsien, Tu-e, Yüan-ying and T'ai-hsü. In March of 1927, when he went to study at the Southern Min Buddhist Seminary in Amoy, he was still unable to write clearly. The late Dharma Master Ta-hsing, who was then dean of studies at the seminary, took him to task. Tz'u-hang told me that the dean reprimanded him with these words: 'On the outside you are impressive: you really look like someone. You are already over thirty. Why is it that you don't know the first thing about calligraphy?'"

"The master once told me the following: 'In 1929, when I served as abbot of Ying-chiang Monastery in Anhui, I was still unable to read Buddhist texts. I was the head of the whole monastery — the leader of a monastic community — but I couldn't get to the heart of Buddhist philosophy. I was terribly ashamed. I considered entering a seminary again, but I was getting on in years and knew so little. Three confused and muddleheaded months at Southern Min Seminary had taught me a lesson, and I did not care to sample the life at a seminary again. Though I was already thirty-five years old, my aspirations had not yet died. Just then Dharma Master Fa-hang and Devotee T'ang Ta-yüan began offering correspondence courses out of Wu-ch'ang Buddhist Seminary. When I finished jumping for joy, I immediately sent a money order to enroll for a course. I paid one and a half silver dollars for tuition and got an incomprehensible book called *Lecture Notes on the Consciousness Only School*. Though I couldn't read it, I couldn't very well give up and throw it away just like that. Besides, it was a matter of pride. I felt that since other people could write, teach, and sell such material, it would be terribly shameful if I couldn't even read it. I wouldn't give up, so wherever I went, the book went with me. I could not stop thinking about it. Later I took it to Hong Kong, Burma and Singapore. I felt compelled to read from it nearly every day, even on trains and ships. Then when I was in Singapore, I finally understood it all. That was how I laid a foundation for my studies in the Consciousness Only school.' With his insatiable will to learn, how could the master not succeed?"

Tao-an also wrote of the master's tirelessness in teaching others: "Master Tz'u-hang's imposing physique overflowed with vitality, and he possessed abundant spiritual energy. This, combined with his mighty resolve to save others, gave him a tireless will to teach and spread the Dharma. In all his travels abroad and in China, his zeal to teach never once diminished. He could lecture eight hours a day without rest, and when the lectures were over, he would immediately pick up his inkbrush and begin writing or editing. On the day of his passing he lectured all morning. Right after lunch he was back at work compiling an index to the Buddhist canon when he put down his brush and passed into nirvana. The number of his hearers and their level of knowledge had no effect on his determination to teach. If only a single person wished to hear an explanation of a sūtra, Tz'u-hang would go ahead and give a lecture anyway. Rarely in the course of many centuries does a man appear who can equal the master's great altruistic spirit. A look at his daily regimen will show us that his will to learn and teach was worthy of our emulation, whether we are young or old.

05:00-06:30.........worship and read scripture
07:00-08:00.........study English
08:00-10:00.........lectures
10:00-12:00.........editing
14:00-17:00.........lectures
17:00-18:00.........editing
20:00-21:00.........lecture
22:00-................worship, meditate, sleep

"His spirit of pure, unremitting effort is rare, even among pious Buddhist monks. I can only borrow Liang Ch'i-ch'ao's epitaph on Hsüan-tsang and apply it to him: 'A brave man should die on the battlefield; a scholar should die at the lectern.' To judge from his activities on the last day of his life, Tz'u-hang is worthy of being called a paragon among scholars."

Master Tao-an wrote the following about Tz'u-hang's compassion and love of giving: "Master Tz'u-hang's karma of human relations was such that when he needed money, his disciples did their utmost to provide for him. Thus he never had to worry over a lack of material offerings. Knowing his great love of almsgiving, some disciples redoubled their efforts to provide him with means, but some people took advantage of his generosity to get their hands on money. Master Tz'u-hang did not hold this against them. What he received with his right hand he soon handed out with his left. No sum of money remained in his keeping overnight. If a dollar came in, a dollar went out. If $10,000 came in, $10,000 went out. 'Empty-handed I came and empty-handed I shall go' was the attitude that he kept throughout his life. A few who knew of this attitude let covetousness get the better of them and even opened his letters secretly. When they learned that a certain disciple was about to send a sum of money, they waited for the messenger to come, and then said, 'Master, I'm broke. Please lend me that money.' Master Tz'u-hang was never miserly. He styled himself 'Tz'u-hang of the Universal Gate' [P'u-men Tz'u-hang]. Looking at his writings and his behavior, we knew that he was dedicated to making the truth once again manifest on this earth. It is written that of all the things we can offer to others, offering the Dharma is the most precious. Master Tz'u-hang was able to offer both the Dharma and material benefit to others. Was he not indeed a bodhisattva? He was especially concerned for young monks — more so than for his own life. From 1949 to 1950, when young monks streamed to Taiwan from the mainland with not a scrap to wear or a bite to eat, his passionate endeavors on their behalf kept him running about like an ant on a hot griddle. The august heavens do not turn away from earnest-hearted men: at last he was able to establish the Inner Courtyard of Maitreya, where he made places for over twenty young monks thirsty with desire for knowledge."

I have borrowed Master Tao-an's words because they reflect so well my own memories of the Bodhisattva. I once wrote a small memorial essay, the title of which reflects my feelings — "Seasons Pass Lightly; Our Master's Goodness Is Not Easily Forgotten." Now I will refrain from further verbosity and conclude with the Bodhisattva's own departing message:

To my followers, a word of advice
On the importance of constant reflection;
Wake up to what you do and think each day,
Keep account of every right and wrong.
When you have made peace with yourself,
North, south, east, west are all the same.
If one man has yet to cross the ford,
Never run away to save yourself.
Dharma-nature is still and void;
Cause and effect are never off a hair:
Whatever you do, you're doing to yourself,
No one can suffer in your place!
Flowers of illusion, reflections of moon on water,
Here is where to build your place of truth.
Everywhere tie threads that lead to Buddha;
Seize this moment to save yourself and others.

Guiding Master Yin-shun

During my years in Taiwan, aside from getting close to Tz'u-hang Bodhisattva, there has been Guiding Master Yin-shun. I got to know Tz'u-hang Bodhisattva at an earlier date, but my friendship with Guiding Master Yin-shun lasted a longer time. I assure the reader that I am not dropping the names of these two great men to elevate my own status. This is not my intention at all. I bring up the names of these two fine old men because both of them behaved toward me with amazing generosity when I became a monk in Taiwan. Since this little book of mine is entitled *In Search of the Dharma*, how can I leave out the two last, and really most important stops on the route of my lifetime travels? Actually, when I hear people say, "Goodness! You're a disciple of Dharma Master Tz'u-hang! You're a disciple of Dharma Master Yin-shun!" I feel very unworthy and deeply afraid that these two old gentlemen would be embarrassed to have such an incompetent disciple as I. Why do I say this? Because under Tz'u-hang I was nothing but a "rice steward" and under Yin-shun I was only an "escaped soldier." What qualifications did I have to be their disciple? But, all that aside, I did, after all, get close to them for a time, so I ought to talk about my friendships with them. I have already told of getting to know Tz'u-hang in the sections "Cook at Hsi-chih" and "Tz'u-hang Bodhisattva," so now I will talk about how I got to know Yin-shun.

Ever looking toward the lofty mountain
Trying to emulate that life of virtue,
Though I can never arrive there,
My heart is filled with longing.

These are lines from the *Book of Odes* which the Grand Historian Ssu-ma Ch'ien (145-90 BC) quoted at the beginning of his "Encomium on the Annals of Confucius." I use these sentences to describe how much I look up to Guiding Master Yin-shun. Originally, during my first two years in the hut on Nuan-nuan Mountain, I disagreed with Master Yin-shun's thought. (I was just following along with the crowd. If someone had really asked, "What exactly is wrong with his thought?" I could only have made an evasive reply.) It was probably the second half of 1956 when my former classmate Yin-hai sent me three books: *Recalcitrant Rocks Nod in Understanding* [*Wan-shih tien-t'ou*], *Use Buddhism to Study Buddhism* [*I fo-fa yen-chiu fo-fa*], and *Toward the Study of Nature as Void* [*Hsing-kung-hsüeh t'an-yüan*]. Because these three books were written by Guiding Master Yin-shun, I picked up *Recalcitrant Rocks Nod in Understanding* with the intention of "blowing aside the fur to expose blemishes." But in the end I not only failed to expose blemishes, I myself followed in the footsteps of the "recalcitrant rocks" mentioned in the title. Only after I had read the remaining two books did I succeed in ridding myself of preconceptions which were as foolish as those of a "frog in the bottom of a well." Only then did I know that Guiding Master Yin-shun was a person of oceanic wisdom rather than a run-of-the-mill expositor of sūtras. His prose, which moves like floating clouds and flowing water, his profound yet accessible reasoning, and his wonderful metaphors —all these make you able to express what you have wished say but could not. They give you understanding of truths which you had an inkling of but could not put your finger on. When these things happen you will give a heartfelt sigh of admiration and say, "No wonder everyone says he is a great scholar of Buddhism and calls him the guiding master of men and heavenly beings. The name truly fits with the reality."

Owing to this "affinity leading to a higher stage" [*tseng-shang yüan*], I wrote a brash letter of self-introduction to Guiding Master Yin-shun in January 1957, when I had completed my three year stay in the thatched hut. I first gave a rough account of how I became a monk, a soldier, and then a monk again, and went on to entreat his gracious permission to be with him and learn from him at the Fu-yen Retreat [Fu-yen ching-she]. Though a return letter came only a few days later, I was not honored with his acceptance. Then I sent another letter. In a second letter he granted my request, but I was only to "try a three month stay at first." Only after I had stayed three months, assuring myself that the Guiding Master had no intention of telling me to leave, did I put my mind at rest and get down to serious study of the scriptural readings the old gentleman had selected for his students.

In an article entitled "Idle Remarks on Fu-yen Retreat,"[1] Guiding Master Yin-shun writes, "For those of you who have come to this Retreat, the foremost thing is not to think of this as an ideal place. People around me say that I understand myself quite well. I am not a gifted person, and my karmic blessings are slight. I haven't had enough experience in teaching, either. Your staying here with me cannot be an ideal thing. However, I want you to know that there is something to be said for someone who is not very intelligent and lacking in karmic blessing like myself. When it comes to the Buddhadharma, I can put all else aside and get down to realistic, serious work instead of acting on impulse or chasing after external things, and thus neglecting my spiritual work. For the past twenty years I have harbored the wish to do this, and I have lived in accordance with this wish. Because of this, I do have some small measure of realization of the Buddhadharma; at the same time, the Buddhadharma has brought me great benefits. Nothing in this world comes with absolute ease; nor are there absolute difficulties. It is simply that 'out of familiarity springs the marvelous.' If you are willing to make an effort and learn devotedly, you will certainly succeed somehow, even if you are ignorant. Those of you who have deep potential for wisdom certainly ought to get a firm grasp of your gifts and put forth honest effort, and even those with less natural endowment should not worry: as long as you can settle your mind and keep learning, you will be better for it in the end. In my student days I met many brilliant fellow students. All of them were young and healthy, good at writing and speaking, and possessed of remarkable talents. But the affinities drawing them to external things were many, and the time spent on learning was little. They were busy serving as seminary deans and abbots, involved all day with social intercourse and the forming of new ties, so they did nothing with their time. The best of them turned out to be no more than monastic administrators. This shows that in studying the Buddhadharma, you have to put extraneous things aside and settle your mind. Only then, with perseverance, can you enter deeply into the Buddhadharma, and only then can you attain true benefit."

"My health has never been good, and my karmic blessings and circumstances have been very poor. I have led a plain, studious life for so many years that it has become part of my nature to love tranquility and shun activity. Of course you must not follow my negative example in this. In Buddhism there are many things just waiting to be done. In the future when you leave here you should resolve to do everything within your ability which will benefit the Buddhist religion and all living things. But during this present period of study, I only hope that you will, for a time, learn from me peace of mind, tranquility, and an approach to life which is not compelled by ambition."

The Guiding Master had this to say about his attitude toward teaching: "I have always had absolute respect for my students' freedom. This is because the Buddhadharma which I know and pass on to people is not all that perfect or ideal. And so I have never tried to teach everyone to learn things my way. Because I went to the Wu-ch'ang Buddhist Seminary in 1934 to study the Three Treatises School [*San-lun tsung*],[2] everyone says that I am a scholar of that school. Perhaps my innate predispositions are fairly close to the School of Void [*K'ung-tsung*],[3] but my studies certainly have not been limited to any sect or school. Even less have I sought, in directing people's studies, to control their thinking and make them like me. As for the scriptures I have selected for all of you to read during the next three years, in the first year there will be selections from three hundred sūtras, vinaya texts and philosophical discourses, representing Mahāyāna and Hinayāna, the School of Void and the School of Being [*Yu-tsung*];[4] in the second year the scope of our reading will, on one hand, continue with translated scriptures from India and, on the other hand, expand to include works by the founding fathers of Chinese schools. In the third year we will extend our reading to the works of Siamese, Japanese and Tibetan thinkers. In my lectures I will go over the important works dealing with the three major strands of Buddhist studies — such works as the *Lankāvatāra Sūtra*, *The Awakening of Faith*, *The Mādhyamika Śāstra* [*Discourses on Meditation on the Mean*], *Treatises on Consciousness Only*, and so on. Moreover, I also intend to lecture a bit on the three paths of Buddhist learning — discipline, meditation and wisdom. To sum it up, the Buddhadharma is one in essence though it has many manifestations. In the first stage of your studies, you should gain broad understanding by reading everything you can. Later you can enter deeply into the door of knowledge which you choose according to your individual predisposition and preference. It does not matter if this is the Madhyamika, the Conscious Only, the T'ien-t'ai or the Hua-yen School. However, at this stage, it is imperative that your studies embrace many facets, lest you someday be drawn into a sectarian mentality. Each Buddhist school has its good points, and each can contribute to the perfection of the others. This is just like many Chinese religions and philosophies: there are points at which they reach equivalent conclusions, and the boundaries between them are never very strict. So I say you should not indulge in sectarian thinking. There is only one Buddhist religion, but it was divided into schools in order to suit the innate capabilities of different people. In studying Buddhism the first thing is to 'vow to learn the gateways to the Dharma, though they be innumerable.' As for which gateway we should pass through in the end, that depends on our innate capabilities."

Guiding Master Yin-shun's teaching methods were as lively as his philosophy of teaching was free. We were not confined to a rigid schedule of lectures, recitations, quizzes and examinations as is the case at most Buddhist seminaries; nor were we given topics to discuss for a certain period of time as at academic institutions. Instead, he simply had the students adhere to the program of selected readings. On one hand we were to read conscientiously, and on the other we were to take notes faithfully. Every month or two he would read all the notebooks and at the end write the date in his own hand. That was all. However, this method was limited to the few of us who were more advanced in age. The younger students had to attend classes and take exams together with the nuns from the women's seminary set up in the same monastery.

Though my stay at Fu-yen Retreat lasted only one year and eight months, and I was neither able to complete the Guiding Master's selected readings nor listen to his lectures on important works of the three major strands of Buddhist studies (I had only heard lectures on half of the *Lankāvatāra Sūtra*, and half of the lectures on the path to Buddhahood before the Guiding Master took a position as abbot over two large monasteries in the Philippines), my determination to study hard was, nevertheless, awakened by my experience there. In the years since leaving Fu-yen retreat, no matter how difficult my circumstances or depressed my state of mind, I have always used my free time to delve into the sacred scriptures of the Tripitaka. I do not dare to indulge in the slightest thought of relaxing and giving up. I feel that given the compassionate light and intercession of the Three Treasures, as long as I have a breath left, no sacrifice will be great enough to discourage me from the task of spreading the Dharma and benefiting living things.

President Pai-sheng

Dharma Master Pai-sheng's reputation reached a pinnacle during his term as president of the Chinese Buddhist Association, and so I use the above title for this section. During his term as president of the Chinese Buddhist Association, he did three great things for Buddhism:

1. Regaining membership in the World Buddhist Friendship Organization. The *Yearbook of the Chinese Buddhist Association* has the following: "The Republic of China was one of the founding countries of the World Buddhist Friendship Organization, and we sent representatives to attend the first convention in Columbo in 1950 and the second convention in Japan in 1952. Although we did not attend the third convention held in Rangoon in 1954, at our cabled request the Association agreed to save our places. Because the Association invited Communist China to take part in the fourth convention called in Nepal in 1956, we voiced our objections by announcing that we would no longer send representatives to these conventions. The false representatives, aside from paying dues for each year since the founding of the Association, made a donation of 5,000 rupees. The Association went so far as to alter section 12 of the Charter, thus recognizing the Chinese Communists' seats as representing all of China. Our membership in the Association was lost at that time. And now the sixth convention will be held November 12-22, 1961 in Pnom Penh, Cambodia. The Chinese Buddhist Association has stated all the facts in a strong argument for its case and has already received an answering letter granting it renewed membership and a place in the coming convention. Moreover, the Executive Yuan, having agreed on an expenditure of $8,406.30 in New

Taiwan dollars — equivalent to US$300 — for 1961 membership dues, has already transferred the sum to our embassy in Rangoon for payment."

2. Ordination of American *bhiksus*: The twenty-eight year old *bhiksu* Shih Hsi-ti was born into a Christian family in California. Feeling that the teachings of Christianity were arrogant and failed to address practical need, he determinedly gave up his traditional faith and became a follower of southern Hinayāna Buddhism. Later, because of his admiration for Chinese Mahāyāna Buddhism, he came to Taiwan on April 2, 1961, and asked to receive Mahāyāna ordination. On the eighteenth of that month he was ordained in the Dharma of Mahāyāna by Dharma Master Pai-sheng, President of the Chinese Buddhist Association, at Lin-chi Monastery on Yüan Mountain in Taipei. On that day more than 2,000 government officials, well-known personages from all fields, and diplomats stationed in Taiwan came to observe the ceremony. On October 3 of that year, another *bhiksu* Pa-t'o-lo, from the state of Michigan, came to be ordained. Again he received this honor from Dharma Master Pai-sheng at Lin-chi Monastery. In November of that year the American *bhiksu* P'u-lai-shih came to take Bodhisattva vows, and this too was presided over by Master Pai. It would seem there was nothing so very amazing about these three foreign monks coming to China for ordination, but actually the influence which this had on the Buddhist religion was greater than the effect a Dharma Master could achieve by giving a hundred sūtra lectures in America.

3. Organizing a Chinese Buddhist delegation: On June 26, 1963, the Chinese Buddhist delegation led by Dharma Master Pai-sheng set out from Taipei's Sung-shan Airport. Thousands of well-wishers, while wishing them a pleasant and successful trip, disagreed among themselves as to the probable outcome of the mission. Some said that the delegation would not easily accomplish its task due to the weak lineup of delegation members. Others said that with Dharma Master Pai-sheng's reputation in Buddhist circles the past few years and the excellent speaking and writing abilities of Dharma Master Hsing-yün, the mission was bound to accomplish the hoped-for results. Some people said that success and failure are not only determined by the strength of a delegation's lineup, the eminence of its members, or their speaking and writing abilities: the important thing is whether the members of a delegation can work together harmoniously, and whether they can adapt to all sorts of circumstances. In the end the delegation was tremendously successful. In Thailand the king laid out a banquet in offering. In Malaysia, Singapore, the Philippines and Hong Kong they were either met by chief executives or welcomed enthusiastically by

government figures and overseas Chinese. According to the newspapers, India's Premier Nehru incurred strongly worded objections from the Chinese Communists for meeting with the delegation. From this we see that the strength of the delegation not only raised the international prestige of Chinese Buddhism, but also made for successful citizens' diplomacy.

These three things all occurred while Dharma Master Pai-sheng was serving as president of the Chinese Buddhist Association. Though we cannot say his achievements made a contribution to Buddhism that will never be rivaled, we should say that they were without precedent.

I have heard people say, "Dharma Master Pai-sheng's Shanghai polish is too thick; he lacks the self-cultivation and bearing of a pious monk." Perhaps in certain respects Dharma Master Pai-sheng falls a bit short in self-cultivation and bearing, but his dedication to the Dharma and to others goes beyond that of most so-called pious monks. On this point there is no need to bring forth a great deal of evidence. Just by looking at a passage from Devotee T'ang Hsiang-ch'ing's "In Honor of the Venerable Master Pai-sheng's Sixtieth Birthday," we can get a glimpse of his character: "I remember in 1949 when the mainland had just fallen to the Communists, crowds of monks fled to Taiwan. Most of the young monks who came here went to Yüan-kuang Monastery in Chung-li to study at the Taiwan Buddhist Seminary, which was run by the Venerable Dharma Master Tz'u-hang. As for older monks of established virtue, most lived at Shih-p'u Monastery through the generosity of Master Pai-sheng. For example, the Venerable Dharma Masters Chih-kuang, Nan-t'ing, Tao-yüan, Mo-ju and others stayed at Shih-p'u Monastery for quite a while when they first got to Taiwan. Venerable Master Pai's merit in paving the way for older monks who came to Taiwan stands side by side with Master Tzu-hang's merit for taking in young monks."

I knew of Dharma Master Pai-sheng while I was studying on the mainland, but the stinginess of fate denied us a meeting. Not until 1954 did I, through Dharma Master Lü-hang's introduction, pay my respects to this man of great virtue. Later Shih-p'u Monastery, which he presided over, engaged me as instructor for its first ordination session, and Lion's Head (Shih-t'ou) Mountain invited me to serve as monitor at its summer's end retreat. After that I served several times as secretary during his ordination sessions. Only then did true understanding grow between us. In the past ten years, he has been very solicitous and kind toward me. When we get together we talk without reservation of everything on our minds. For this reason, some people think I belong to the "Pai-sheng group"! Actually, my attitude in seeking the truth has always been to "accord with the Dharma, not with men." I have never thought about belonging to one group or another.

In spring of 1963,when Lin-chi Monastery in Taipei held an ordination ceremony, the ordinees spent over $10,000N.T. to present their ordaining master Pai-sheng with an aloeswood throne in honor of his birthday, and they asked me to write a eulogy to be carved on a marble slab and placed on the throne as a memorial. I wrote the following:

Great indeed is this monk;
In the Law's last age a flower remains
Bearing things that can't be borne
Doing things that can't be done.
His seed of goodness planted in the past,
With childlike innocence he finds the truth;
Seeking to remake himself
In a bodhisattva's mold.
Schools and teachings deeply known,
Are all at his command;
As a tiger growing horns
Can go wherever it pleases.
In the decade since his coming to Taiwan,
He has known no daytime rest,
Ordaining, renewing Buddhist knowledge,
Revitalizing, doing away with the old.
Each of his efforts have made
The Buddha's sun grow daily brighter.
Brilliant rays of light
Shine throughout the realm of dust.
Now in the year of *k'uei-mou*
On the sixtieth anniversary of his birth,
We reverently present this throne
To honor his longevity.

Honored Elder Tao-yüan

Honored Elder Tao-yüan, whose lay surname was Wang, is a countryman of mine, having been born in Chou-k'ou Village, Shang-shui County, Honan. The Honored Elder's mother passed away when he was young, and his stepmother would not tolerate him, so he and his sister were raised to maturity by their uncle's wife. In his twentieth year his sister and aunt, who were closer to him than anyone in the world, died one after another of illness. In his grief the Honored Elder suddenly realized the pain, emptiness and transience of human life. Without a moment's reluctance he cut off his locks and became a monk. At twenty-four he received all the precepts of ordination at Kuei-yüan Monastery in Han-yang County, Hupei. After a period of study, he returned to his home temple to help with administrative duties. At twenty-eight, hearing that Dharma Master Tz'u-chou, the great teacher of the School of Discipline [*Lü-tsung*], had opened a school for monks in Hsing-fu Monastery on Yü Mountain, Ch'ang-shou County, Kiangsu, he took leave of his teacher and went south to study there. Afterward he accompanied Dharma Master Tz'u-chou to Ling-yen Mountain, Soochow, where he helped set up a Pure Land place of truth. He assisted Dharma Master Tz'u-hang with running Ying-chiang Monastery in An-ch'ing and got to know the Venerable Master T'ai-hsü at the Wu-ch'ang Buddhist Seminary. Together with Dharma Master Pai-sheng he went into sealed confinement at Pao-t'ung Monastery on Hung Mountain. At the invitation of Dharma Master Ching-yen of K'ai-feng, Honan, he served as an instructor at the Honan Buddhist Seminary. He made pilgrimages to Chiu-hua and P'u-t'o Mountains, spent time with the Venerable Master Yin-kuang at Ling-yen Monastery, and got to know Dharma Master Yüan-ying in Shanghai. He assumed for a time the duties of Dean of Studies at the Dharma Realm Academy in Fa-hai Monastery, Fuchow, and assisted Dharma Master Tz'u-chou with lectures on the *Avatamsaka Sūtra* at Ching-lien Monastery in Peking. He served as the abbot of Tou-shuai Monastery on Sheng-fang Mountain in Fang-shan, Hopei. On six occasions he was the main lecturer at the Tz'u-hung Buddhist Seminary of Kuang-chi Monastery, Peking, as well as a professor during the ordination session at that monastery. When Yün-ch'uan Monastery on Ssu-erh Mountain in Chang-chia-k'ou was changed from a hereditary to a public monastery, he served as its first abbot. He once served as president of the Chahar Province branch of the Chinese Buddhist Association. Coming to Taiwan with Dharma Master Pai-sheng in 1949, he first lived at Shih-p'u Monastery to weather the turmoil of those times. Later he went to Ling-yin Monastery in Hsin-chu and Yüan-kuang Monastery in Chung-li at the invitation of Dharma Master Tz'u-hang, to assist in setting up classes and giving sūtra lectures. Then he founded the Pure Land Hai-hui Monastery on Cheng-tao Mountain, Pa-tu, and went on to serve several times as professor during ordination sessions at Ta-hsien Monastery in Tainan. He also served as ordaining master at Yüan-kuang Monastery on Shih-t'ou Mountain, at Kuan-yin Mountain in Taipei, and at Tung-shan Monastery in P'ing-tung. The breadth of his moral influence is without comparison. Within the next few years he will likely be chosen president of the Chinese Buddhist Association, at which time he will lead a delegation to attend the convention of the World Buddhist Friendship Association to be held in India. His dedication to our religion and to the Dharma justifies comparison with a countryman of his who lived 1,300 years ago — Hsüan-tsang.

While living in a hut on Nuan-nuan, I had the good fortune to make frequent visits to Hai-hui Monastery, which the Honored Elder had founded, and spend time at his side respectfully listening to his teachings. At that time he was nearly sixty years old and frequently ill, so by all rights he should have paid more attention to his diet, but the old gentleman's habits were unimaginably austere. One day I went with Elder Mo-ju to Hai-hui Monastery for a visit. At lunch there was an abundance of fine dishes. After we had eaten, Elder Mo-ju asked, "Do you usually eat meals like this?" The Honored Elder said, "I had these dishes prepared especially for you, classmate (they had been classmates at Yü Mountain in Ch'ang-shou). Usually I don't buy a piece of beancurd once in a fortnight!" At this I interrupted to ask, "Dharma Master, your ordinees are everywhere on Taiwan, and you have many Refuges disciples. They need only give a small sum in offering, and you will have enough to live on. Why must you be so hard on yourself?" He answered, "People make offerings in order to seek blessings. Their money should be used to build temples, print sūtras and give aid to suffering people. How can I use it for my own enjoyment?"

In the years 1955, 1959, 1961 and 1963 he served at Shih-p'u, Hai-hui and Lin-chi Monasteries either as professor during ordination sessions or as ordaining master. At the same sessions I served as either an instructor or secretary. During this period I came a step closer toward understanding this old gentleman. Previously I had only known that he was a Dharma Master devoted to Pure Land — a kindly, approachable man who demanded much of himself and lecturer who stuck to the text. Only after hearing him give a few lectures to ordinees during ordination sessions did I realize he was a beneficial friend for anyone to have — eloquent, mindful of the importance of monastic discipline and bearing, motivated by deep concern for others and possessed of independent judgement. Once during a session at Hai-hui Monastery, he lectured on "Discipline and Bearing of Novice Monks." When he spoke of the line that reads "The five vows of the householder only curb licentiousness; the ten vows for becoming a monk cut off lustful appetites," he said in a grave tone, "Buddhism in Taiwan was influenced by the Japanese occupation. There are those who, living in temples as abbots, get married and have children yet still feel that they are monks. This phenomenon of decline is characteristic of an age of Decay of the Dharma. However, Japanese followers of the Buddha can be forgiven such actions. It is a regrettable thing though, for monks of Taiwan to follow after them.

We know that the freedom of Japanese monks to marry started with Shinran. This came about because the younger sister of the emperor forced him to marry. If he had not submitted, all of Japan would have been forced into a great persecution.[5] Shinran weighed the alternatives and sacrificed himself. But after the marriage he withdrew from the monastery and organized the lay Buddhist Japanese Lotus Sect [*Jih-lien tsung*][6] to glorify the Pure Land. Then, owing to the emperor's support, this sect spread widely. The Eastern Temple of the Original Vow [Higashi Honganji] and Western Temple of the Original Vow [Nishi Honganji] of today are its two branches. Japanese monasteries number 50,000 in all, and of these, 30,000 belong to either one of these two branches. From this we can see how great the power of this sect is. The Meiji Restoration of 60 to 70 years ago, due to Japan's underpopulation, commanded that all monks in their prime must marry, while older monks could remain celibate. With time the older monks grew feeble and died away, while those who came to take their place were all married monks with offspring. But an evil ruler brought all this about by force. Why would monks of Taiwan, who are under no political pressure, want to marry and have children as Japanese monks do?"

He went on to say, "Before 1949 the status of monks in Taiwanese society was declining every day, and faith in Buddhism was dying. Many monks were returning to lay life, but no one was going the other way. Since 1949, when pious monks came to Taiwan and advocated ordination, there have been ordinations on eleven occasions [Tao-yüan himself has participated eight times], so things have taken a turn for the better. The renaissance of Buddhism in this province will depend on monks, especially male monks. That is because female believers are often not at the level of advancement that men are, and men are society's core of strength. But now that you are taking vows to become monks, you must abide by the precepts of purity and cleanliness. No longer can you be half-monks and half-laymen, eating meat and taking a wife! Otherwise, if you break your vows, Buddhism can never gain new strength."

At the pre-ordination ceremony, he instructed ordinees as follows: "In the search for Buddhahood, monastic life is fundamental, while secular life is expedient; monastic life is the thoroughgoing way, while secular life is a way that caters to the way of sentient beings. Only if we leave lay life, give up greed, and cut off the duties of affection can we transcend the profane and enter the saintly realm, far from the six paths of reincarnation in the bitter sea of life and death. The perfection of all this comes through the monastic life. Therefore all the buddhas of the three worlds have realized the Way by leaving the mundane world. Your determination to be monks comes as the result of a root of goodness built up over many lives. You should honestly repent of your sins, so that your mind and body are purified for the ten novice precepts which I will pass on to you tomorrow. The precepts possess four meanings:

1. "Precept-dharma " [*chieh-fa*] refers to the written text and the content of the precept.

2. "Precept-substance " [*chieh-t'i*] is something which, while having neither form nor characteristics, has nevertheless a real substance.

3. "Precept-conduct " [*chieh-hsing*] is behavior which manifests externally through the carrying out of the written precepts.

4. "Precept-phenomenon " [*chieh-hsiang*] is a manifestation in events which comes from the practice of holding to the precepts.

In discussing the four meanings, he repeatedly stressed the importance of "precept-substance, " saying: "Tomorrow when you receive the Three Refuges, you should practice meditation through visualization [*tsao-huan*] of the following: First, that you have resolved to receive the precepts and that, with respect to the 'realm of sentient and insentient beings' you are willing to cut all evil and cultivate all good, and you vow to save all living things. This can move the very earth to tremble under your feet. At the same time, clouds formed by the merit of the precepts will wreath and curl upward. Second, meditate that the clouds of merit extending across the great void come together in a canopy of jewel-like light which spreads out in the sky above your head. Third, meditate on the canopy of merit slowly descending, flowing into the top of your head, entering your inmost mind, and spreading throughout your body. What is this? This is the 'precept-substance.'"

Because the old gentleman spoke these words of instruction in a pleasantly clear voice and with utmost sincerity, many ordinees were so moved that they could not stop the tears from pouring down their cheeks. And so I feel that not only is he the most distinguished among the northern monks in Taiwan, but that he is one of the outstanding elders of Buddhism in free China. Now, in our age of declining Dharma and strong demonic hindrances, we especially need such a great man to live long among us, dispelling evil with righteousness and holding firmly to the Buddhadharma.

To Fellow Followers of the Way

The account of my search for knowledge should actually draw to a close right here, since after my departure from Fu-yen Retreat in Hsin-chu I was so presumptious as to travel everywhere in Taiwan in the name of "proselytizing the Dharma"! Since then, though my virtue and knowledge are sadly lacking, and my achievements in spreading the Dharma are nothing to rave about, I have been asked by the Chinese Buddhist Association to serve on their "committee for spreading the Dharma"; the Taiwan provincial branch of the Chinese Buddhist Association has issued a citation praising me for enthusiasm in spreading the Dharma; and I have even been awarded the title of Venerable Dharma Master! Think for a moment: For this committee position, this citation and this title I have chased after external affinities from morning till night. I had felt there were not enough hours in the day to begin with: where would I find leisure to even think about searching or studying? There is one warning I wish to give fellow seekers (that is, all young monks and nuns who are now seeking knowledge of Buddha-truth) and kindred-minded persons (that is, monks and nuns who aspire to spreading the Dharma and helping others): before your virtue and knowledge are sufficient, never, under any circumstances, let yourself be carried away by the high-sounding words "proselytizing the Dharma," to the point that you leave everything else and run off to spread the word. You should know that if seeking knowledge of the Buddha's truth is not easy, spreading the Dharma is even more difficult!

But Taiwan is a subtropical island, and everything seems to mature quickly here. In the northern part of the mainland there is only one harvest of wheat and one of assorted grain crops per year, while in Taiwan rice is harvested twice, yams once, and turnips or other vegetables once. On the mainland a youngster of eight or nine still has trouble with numerals, while seven- and eight-year-old children in Taiwan can become little calligraphers. There are even cases of three-year-old tots who do computation in their heads (see *Central Daily*, March 26, 1965). Young monks who graduated from mainland Buddhist seminaries did not presume to think of themselves as "Dharma Masters," even after several years of additional study, but in Taiwan if a monk has merely put in time for a couple of years in a Buddhist seminary he acts as if his eyes have moved to the top of his head, or proclaim in a voice thick with self-satisfaction: "I am a Dharma Master now too!" Whereupon he will run all about the island in the name of spreading the Dharma. And what will be the result? Nothing more than harm to himself and to others!

Well then, how can it be done without harm to oneself and others? Guiding Master Yin-shun, in an article entitled "On the Cultivation of Monks," said, "Persons whose talents suit them for spreading the Dharma do not simply possess knowledge about Buddhism, because spreading the Dharma is not only the imparting of knowledge. For the monk who is himself a religious teacher, if he truly wants to be able to attract a wide following and give them the benefit of the Buddhadharma, he must, aside from knowledge of Buddhism, possess high character and rigorous spiritual discipline. Only then can he help his followers to strengthen their faith and go on to guide them as they enter deeply into the Buddhadharma."

Then he went on to say: "First, today is a time when knowledge is highly developed. If Buddhists want to win out over evil practices and heterodox religions so that the Dharma banner may be raised high, then they must enter deeply into the Buddhadharma: only then can they convert people through the expedient skill of deep ideas expressed simply, making nonbelievers believe and believers grow in faith. People's innate abilities are different. Of course, there are many different doors to the truth: sometimes words are not needed, and one can move others by example. But in view of the broad spectrum of human types and the currents of our times, a proselytizer for Buddhism must have clear and deep comprehension of the vast, profound Buddhadharma. Not only can he give well-thought-out, rigorous expression to its deep implications, but he can also provide a concise conceptual framework so that people have a correct, overall idea of the Buddhadharma. Only in this way can modern people easily accept it...."

"Second, a religious teacher who wishes to convert others should, aside from possessing profound understanding of the Buddhadharma, have wide acquaintance with general worldly knowledge. This does not mean that we should devote our minds solely to studying all sorts of modern knowledge. In the history of Chinese Buddhism such great masters as Tao-an and Hui-yüan had good grounding in Chinese scholarship. Only because of this were they able, after becoming monks and studying Buddhism, to guide the intellectuals of the time toward the Buddhadharma. In India such great masters of discourse as Aśvaghoṣa, Nāgārjuna, Aśanga and Vasubandhu were all famous scholars in their day and were all very learned in the Upanishads and the Vedas. Only because of this could they accommodate worldly learning within the Buddhadharma and criticize the learning of their time. Through comparison of one with the other, the profundity and loftiness of the Buddhadharma were made apparent, thus making it easy for people to accept and believe. If we look at ministers and priests in other religions, they must, in addition to having the general knowledge of a college graduate, have undergone several years of religious education before they can consider being an evangelist or missionary. This has proved to be remarkably effective. Although they use material goods to lure new converts, the good training of missionaries also has its advantages. Don't think that the rise of Ch'an in the T'ang dynasty was due solely to emphasis on the spiritual work of the individual, without the need to understand anything else. In truth, Ch'an practitioners strove energetically to take positive action, placing little value on hearing and thinking about scriptural teachings, and this was precisely because practical teaching at that time was extremely developed and widespread. How much truer this is now! At that time the rival teachings were Confucianism and Taoism. Ch'anists knew something about them. How about modern worldly scholarship? In these times we cannot give all our energies and abilities to studying the philosophy of Buddhadharma: if we are lacking in worldly knowledge, yet wish to benefit others by spreading the Dharma, we will certainly be faced with a difficult task."

Finally he said, "Some enthusiastic Buddhists, hoping that the Buddhadharma can take deep hold in folk culture, have suggested some very simple truths and very simple spiritual exercises for ordinary people, or perhaps the use of music and slide shows. Of course this is a wonderful convenience for guiding new believers. But, taking the long view, if we want people in the society to have correct understanding and believe in the Buddhadharma, we must win over the intellectuals. And so, simply relying on popularized preaching will not accomplish our goal of revitalizing Buddhism."

And so, for fellow students and kindred-minded souls who aspire to spread the Dharma, the passages quoted above can serve as a mirror by which we can get a clearer picture as we try to help ourselves by helping others, rejuvenate what is declining, and save Buddhism from its terrible fate. Take a good look! Have you become fully aware that "today is a time of expanding knowledge"? Look and see if you have the ability to "overcome evil practices and heterodoxy, and raise high the Dharma banner." Look and see if you possess a "deep understanding of the Buddhadharma, as well as broad acquaintance with general worldly knowledge." If you have taken a hard look and you find your qualifications and abilities sufficient, then by all means strengthen your resolve to work at the task of spreading the Dharma. Otherwise, the best thing is to cultivate yourself in seclusion for a few more years before you consider it again.

Some people may ask: "Since you understand what is involved, why didn't you cultivate yourself in seclusion for a few more years before running all over the place in the name of "proselytizing the Dharma"?

The answer is simple: I was carried away by those high sounding words! Now, in order to avoid being a "blind man riding a blind horse who leads others into a pit of fire," I tell all of you with utmost sincerity — don't ever walk in my footsteps!

Always Remember the Teachings Left Us by the Buddha

A filial son or daughter will always keep firmly in mind his or her parents' last words, no matter how much time has elapsed since their deaths. In the same way, a true disciple of the Budddha should think constantly of the teachings he left us, etching them deeply on his mind. Recently while reading the *Record of the Pointing Finger and the Moon* [*Chih-yüeh lu*], I noted that every time a Ch'an patriarch passed on the Dharma, he would solemnly say to his chosen disciple: "Long ago the Tathāgata imparted the Dharma-eye to Mahākāśyapa. It was entrusted by each generation to the next until it came to me. Now I give it to you: guard it and keep it well." Though nowadays the patriarchate is not "entrusted by each generation to" the next, the responsibility to "hold firmly to the Dharma and extend the Buddha's life-in-wisdom" is one we cannot decline. And so we must make the teachings left us by the Buddha into a daily guide and use this to spur our conduct, both in mind and body, that we may remain on the track laid down by the teachings. Only then will we keep from being like an old cow, left unwatched, which "intrudes upon the grain sprouts in other men's fields."

The teachings left by the Buddha are as vast as the sea (the Tripitaka and the Twelve Branches of the Mahāyāna canon are all his teachings)! But if we can only remember and carry out what is said in the *Sūtra of the Buddha's Last Instructions* [*Fo i-chiao ching*], we will obtain inexhaustible benefit. If you do not believe me, please quiet your mind and try reading the passages below:

Treasure and revere monastic discipline: "Monks, after my life is extinguished, you should honor and revere the precepts as a benighted man who finds the light or a poor man who comes upon treasure. Know that these precepts shall be a great teacher for all of you. If I were still of this world, that would be no different from the presence of these...."

"You must not take part in worldly affairs, carry official messages, use spells or magic herbs, cater to the wealthy or fraternize with the disrespectful and arrogant. You should make your mind upright and seek deliverance through correct thought...."

"If you can hold to the precept of celibacy, you can possess the dharma of goodness. If you are not celibate, then goodly merit cannot arise. Know that this precept is where to find the merit that puts mind and body at rest...."

Control the mind: "Monks, if you know how to obey the precepts you should curb the five faculties of sense, lest they turn into the five desires. Be like the cowherd who watches his charges with staff in hand, keeping them under control, lest they intrude upon the grain sprouts in other men's fields.... The mind rules over these five faculties of sense, so you should control your mind. So fearsome is the mind that neither poisonous snake, nor fierce beast, nor vengeful outlaw, nor great fire raging out of control is sufficient to compare with it. And so, monks, you should strive rigorously to bring the mind to submission."

Guard against sleep: "Monks! In the daytime practice the dharma of goodness devotedly, never missing a minute. Nor should you give up your efforts in the early [*ch'u-yeh*] and late [*hou-yeh*] parts of the night.[7] In the middle of the night [*chung-yeh*] recite scriptures as you rest. Do not let the conditioned cause of sleep make your life pass to no purpose!"

"Know that the world of men is aflame with the fire of transience. Seek now to deliver yourself — do not retreat into sleep. The passions wait to fall upon men like murderous outlaws — they are more destructive than mortal enemies. How can you allow yourself to sleep and lose your vigilance? The poisonous snakes of passion sleep in your mind. Like black lizards they sleep in your chamber. You should pull them out and cast them away with hooks made by observance of precepts. Once the sleeping snakes are out you can slumber peacefully. He who sleeps while they still remain is shameless...."

Do away with anger and hatred: "You monks, even if a man comes before you and wants to tear you limb from limb, you should restrain your mind from hatred and guard against speaking abusively. By giving rein to rage, you will impede your advancement and lose the benefit of merit already gained!..."

"Why is this so? The harm of anger and rage ruins the dharma of goodness and sullies your good name. Men of your generation and of later generations will not wish to know of you. Be advised that anger is worse than fierce fire. Guard against it constantly, do not let it in. There is no greater spoiler of merit than anger!..."

Refrain from deceit and deviousness: "Monks! Since the Buddha laid his hand on your head, you should have given up self-adornment. You wear a rag-robe[8] and carry an alms bowl and beg for what you need to live. Knowing this, when conceit and deviousness do arise, you must extinguish them immediately.... A convoluted, devious mind is at odds with the Way, so you should examine it and make it straight. Know that convoluted thought is merely trickery. Those who enter the Way do not dwell in this!..."

Have few wants and know contentment: "You monks should know that men of many wants suffer more, because they often seek their own gain. Men of few wants seek nothing and want nothing, and so they avoid this hardship. The man of few wants does not use devious means to cater to the wishes of others, and he is not pulled one way and another by his faculties. The mind of the man who wants little is tranquil, and he dreads nothing. In everything there is sufficiency — never a sense of lack. To escape from the sea of bitterness, one must meditate on being easily satisfied. If one knows contentment, he will find that wealth and happiness lie safely hidden therein. The man who is easily contented can feel comfortable though he sleeps on the ground, while he who is not would not find heaven to his liking...."

Zealous efforts: "Monks! If you make zealous effort, then nothing is too difficult. So I say that all of you should put forth zealous effort. A trickle of water flowing long enough can pierce stone. If the practitioner's mind lapses often into inactivity, this is like one who, trying to start fire with bow and drill, rests before the tip is hot. He may want fire, but it will not come about this way."

Gather your thoughts: "Monks! In seeking good friends and helpful associates, nothing is more important than remembering to be mindful. Deadly passions cannot enter where there is mindfulness. And so all of you ought to hold your thoughts to one thing. If you lose your grip, your merit will be lost as well. If your power to dwell on one thing is strong, though you go among the five bandits of sense desire you will not be harmed...."

Practice samādhi: "Monks! Once you have gathered your thoughts together, your mind will be in samādhi. The mind in samādhi can understand the phenomena of worldly birth and death. And so all of you should cultivate the various types of samādhi. If you achieve samādhi, then your mind will not be scattered. Just as the farmer who cares about water will do a good job of building dikes and banks, the practitioner will do a good job at meditation so that the water of wisdom will not leak away...."

Cultivate wisdom: "Monks! With wisdom there is neither covetousness nor attachment. If you look constantly inward without interruption, you can obtain release through my Dharma. If you do not do this you are not a man of our faith, yet you are not a layman. I would not know what to call you. Actual wisdom is a trusty ship to carry us across the sea of old age, infirmity and death. It is also a bright lamp in the darkness, a medicine for all afflictions and a sharp axe to cut the tree of passions. And so all of you should study, meditate on and cultivate wisdom for your own benefit...."

Think of the Dharma you have received: "Monks! You should be single-minded in gaining the many forms of merit. Relinquish all indulgence as if leaving a mortal enemy. The benefit preached by the World-Honored One is ultimate: you should practice it devotedly. Whether you are in the mountains, in a desolate marsh, under a tree or in a quiet room, think intently on the Dharma you have received. Find the strength in yourself to practice it zealously. Don't live to regret too late that you have lived for nothing! I am like a conscientious physician who knows your illness and prescribes medicine. If you do not take it, the doctor is not to blame. Again, I am like an excellent guide leading a person toward the good path. If he hears but does not walk upon it, the guide is not at fault."

Transience of worldly phenomena: "Monks! Do not be filled with grief! I have lived on this earth for a *kalpa*, and there must come a time when my life is extinguished. Coming together never to separate is something that cannot happen. Whether it is helping oneself or helping others, the Dharma is sufficient. I could offer no more than this were I to remain another lifetime. Those who can be saved, whether in heaven or on earth, are already saved. Those who are not saved have already initiated the conditioning causes of salvation. If all my disciples practice it and pass it onward, then this will be the constant living presence of Tathāgata's Dharma-body. You should know that the world is transitory; where there is coming together, there must be separation. Do not be filled with sadness; this is just the way worldly phenomena are. You ought to make intense effort to seek early deliverance. Vanquish the oppressive darkness with light of wisdom. The reality of this world is a tottering, fragile thing: nothing is strong enough to last. The extinguishing of my life will be like the falling away of a terrible affliction. This body ought to be relinquished as a thing of sin and evil; it is falsely termed a body. It founders in the sea of old age, infirmity and death. Could a wise man be anything but overjoyed to see it done away with, just as when a mortal enemy is killed?"

When honored Anirudha said, "The moon may turn hot; the sun may turn cold; but the four noble truths taught by the Buddha can never be altered," he might well have been speaking of the above passages from the Buddha's teachings. We ought to receive them with joy and never lose them. We should find strength in ourselves to cultivate them with intense effort. Only by doing this will we do justice to the Honored One's "last instructions."

Practice the Deeds of Samantabhadra

At the Flower Garland Meeting,[9] Samantabhadra Bodhisattva told young Sudhana and all the great bodhisattvas present the following: "If all the Buddhas of the ten directions preached one after the other of the Tathāgata's virtue for as many *kalpas* as there are infinitesimal specks in all the inexpressibly many Buddha lands, they could not exhaust them. To enter the door to this virtue, one should practice ten great vows."

The ten great vows are what we recite every day in our morning devotions: "First, to worship and revere all Buddhas; second to praise the Tathāgata; third, to make extensive offerings; fourth, to repent of karmic hindrance; fifth, to rejoice in the welfare of others; sixth, to ask that the Wheel of the Dharma be set in motion; seventh, to call upon the Buddha to abide in this world; eighth, to pursue the Buddha-truth; ninth, to follow along with living things; and tenth, to transfer one's own merit to the salvation of all living things." These ten, from worship to transfer of merit, are all fully explicated in the chapter entitled "The Vows of Samantabhadra Bodhisattva."[10] For example, in the passage on worship and reverence toward all Buddhas we find: "Samantabhadra Bodhisattva said to Sudhana: young man, to worship and revere all Buddhas means that I, through the power of my vows, believe from the depths of my mind in all the innumerable World-Honored Buddhas in the entire Dharma-realm and in all the ten directions of every Buddha land — past, present and future — as if they were in front of my eyes, and I worship and revere all of them constantly with pure karma of body, speech and intention. Each Buddha manifests as many bodies as there are particles of infinitesimal dust in all the inexpressible Buddha lands. Proceeding through each manifestation, I will worship all Buddhas, who equal in number the infinitesimal particles of dust in all the inexpressible Buddha worlds. When the void has been exhausted, my worship will be at an end. Because the void can never be exhausted, my worship and reverence are without end. In the same way when the universe of living beings, the karma of living beings, and the afflictions of living beings have been exhausted, my worship will be at an end. But since the universe of living beings and their afflictions cannot be exhausted, my worship and reverence will never come to an end. Let each reverent thought follow the last without interruption; let the good karma of body, speech and intention be untiring."

The section on the fourth vow, repentance for karmic hindrances, has the following: "And now, young man, I will speak on repentance for karmic hindrances: The bodhisattva thinks to himself — for countless kalpas in the past I have, owing to covetousness, anger and infatuation, acted with body, mouth and mind to lay down limitless evil karma. If such evil karma possessed substance and form, then even the infinity of empty space would not be able to contain it. Now I, with pure karma of body, speech and intention do make sincere repentance before all Buddhas and bodhisattvas in all lands — as numerous as infinitesimal specks — of the Dharma realm, vowing never again to lay down such karma but to abide permanently in the virtues of pure discipline..."

Fig.9 Chen-hua, the author, serving as the catechist at the ordination held in the winter of 1978 at Sung Shan Monastery, Taipei, hands the staff to an ordinee

The section on the eighth vow, to follow the Buddha's example and pursue constantly the study of truth, says: "And now, young man, I will speak of following the Buddha's example and constantly pursuing the study of truth. In this toiling troubled world Vairocana, from when he first vowed to be enlightened, has exerted himself with tireless zeal and bestowed his body of inexpressible wonder upon us: his peeled-off skin became paper, his bones were splintered into pens; his blood was drained from puncture wounds as ink for writing a pile of scriptures as high as Sumeru — the central mountain of the world. Out of devotion to the Dharma, he thought nothing of giving the life of his body. How much less important should a royal throne, or cities, or settlements, or palaces, or parks or any transient entities be to us? Because of this, we should follow his example and pursue the study of truth."

The passage on the ninth vow — to always follow along [*shun*] with living things — says: "And now, young man, I will speak of following along with living things. In the entire Dharma-realm, in the ten directions on land and sea, there are living things differing in many ways. They are oviparous, viviparous, spawned in damp, spontaneously generated, born and abiding in one of the four elements, or perhaps born or abiding in the void or on trees and plants. They have various modes of birth, various appearances, various shapes, various expressions, various lifespans, various group characteristics, various names, various natures, all sorts of knowledge and opinion, all sorts of desires and joy, all sorts of intentions and behavior, all manners of behavior, all kinds of clothing, all kinds of food and drink. They live in all sorts of villages, camps, settlements, cities and palaces. They include the eight classes of supernatural beings, the human and non-human, the legless and the two-legged, the four-legged and the multi-legged, those with form and those that are formless, those that have thought and those that lack it, and those that do not have thought and those that do not lack it. I will follow along and comply with these many kinds. I will meet their needs in many ways and give them many sorts of offerings. As I respect my parents and serve my teachers, elders, arhats and even Tathāgata, in the same way I will serve them. No act of compliance to a living thing is without merit. Be a doctor to the sick; show the true way to the lost; give light to the benighted; help the poor find hidden treasure: in such a way the bodhisattva impartially saves and benefits all living things. Why? If the bodhisattva can follow along with living things, then he will be following along with and making offerings to all Buddhas. If he honors and meets the needs of all living things, he will be honoring and meeting the needs of Tathāgata. If he makes living things happy, then he makes all Tathāgatas happy. Why? Because all Tathāgata Buddhas have compassionate mind as their substance...."

The passage on the tenth vow—to transfer one's merit to others—says: "And now, young man, I will speak of the transfer of merit to others. All merit, beginning with worship and proceeding to compliance with living things, is directed toward all living things in the Dharma realm as vast as empty space, in hopes that they have lasting joy without suffering, that their desires to do evil will come to no result, that the dharma of goodness they have cultivated will quickly come to completion, and that the doors to all evil destinies will be closed to them, while the true road to nirvāna will be pointed out. I will suffer in the stead of living things which are oppressed by the bitter fruits of accumulated evil karma, that those living things may all obtain release and reach the ultimate stage of perfect bodhi-wisdom. In this way the bodhisattva practices transfer of merit...."

The text then goes on to speak of the benefit and merit of reciting the ten great vows regularly: "If bodhisattvas accord with and commit themselves to these vows, they can help all living things toward completion; they can be one with unexcelled and complete enlightenment; they can fill in the vast sea of Samantabhadra Bodhisattva's vows....If a person holds to regular reading and reciting of these vows with deep faith, then he can soon rid himself of the five karmas leading to the hell of uninterrupted suffering.[11] All afflictions of mind and body, all forms of suffering, and all evil karmas as numerous as infitesimal dust-specks will thus disappear....If a person recites these vows, his life on earth will be without obstacle, like the moon breaking through wisps of clouds. All Buddhas and bodhisattvas will praise him; all men and *devas* should revere him; all living things should support him with offerings. This good man will have been born in human form to good purpose. Having perfected all the virtues of Samantabhadra Bodhisattva, like Samantabhadra he will soon perfect a marvelous physical appearance possessing the thirty-two qualities of a great hero.[12] Whether born as a man of *devas*, he will belong to the nobility. He will be able to destroy all evil destinies, to stay far from evil friends, to conquer and triumph over all heterodox paths and to be released from all afflictions....Again this man, at the moment before death when all his faculties scatter, when his relatives are resigned to his departure and all the strength of his presence fades, then his palace and cities with their surrounding lands; his elephants, horses and carriages; his valuables and treasures —all these things will no longer follow him. Only this king of vows will not depart from him. It will go before him as a constant guide, and in an instant he will be reborn in the world of bliss....When he arrives there, he will see Amitābha!...Young man, if you heed and believe in this great king of vows, if you hold firmly to chanting it and if you preach of it to many people, you will obtain merit such that only the Buddha, the World-Honored One, can know."

Because the merit and benefit of holding to and chanting the Vows of Samantabhadra are so great, I often saw Pure Land practitioners on the mainland chanting them morning and evening as their regular devotions. For this reason I regularly recited it for two years, but being unable to recite it from memory, I could not continue to chant it while in the army. Only later, when I went to the Ling-ch'uan Monastery in Keelung, did I make this chapter part of my regular devotions. While at Hsi-chih, Nuan-nuan, and Hsin-chu I seldom let a day go by without chanting it. Though trivial matters have kept my head swimming for the past several years, each morning after rising and washing I chant it devoutly as a prayer for the day. In chanting the ten great vows I am not thinking to "attain to the limitless virtue of Tathāgata" but only hoping, with the sublime power of these ten great vows, to be "reborn in the world of bliss" at the "last moment, when all faculties have scattered."

Turn Toward the Buddha-Way

Some people may ask: "So you intend only to recite the name of Amitābha and chant the vows of Samantabhadra so you can be reborn in the Western Paradise. Is that the extent of it?" No. My goal in seeking rebirth in the Western Paradise is to borrow the help of favorable circumstances in order to find Buddhahood more quickly and fulfill my wish of helping others and myself. I do not hope to run off to the Western Paradise and enjoy Dharma-bliss with no thought of coming back. That is why every time I chant sūtras or recite the Buddha's name or bow down to him, I often make this wish: "Your disciple Chen-hua makes obeisance with all his heart to all Buddhas in the entire Buddha-realm. I ask that the Buddha will intercede for me, his disciple, and grant that my sins will be absolved, my blessings and wisdom will increase, my bodily needs will be met, my body and mind will be at peace and, knowing beforehand that the time has come, without torment of painful illness and free from all covetousness, with my thoughts in the undisturbed state of samādhi, I will be born into the Pure Land. After rebirth in that land I will realize perfect bodhi-wisdom before going forth to the lands of the ten directions to save all living things." There are numberless doors of spiritual cultivation. If one can follow one's own innate nature and interests to "learn what the Buddha learned, practice what the Buddha practiced, and do the spiritual work the Buddha did" as far as one's lot permits, one can arrive at the plane of "witnessing what the Buddha witnessed." Why insist stubbornly on a certain method?

For this reason Guiding Master Yin-shun, at the opening of the chapter entitled "Pay Reverent Homage to the Three Refuges" in his famous *The Way to Buddhahood*, writes, "To seek Buddha-truth is to learn from the Buddha. We take the Buddha as an ideal, as a paragon, and learn from him ceaselessly. Reaching the same level with him means the attainment of Buddhahood."

He goes on to say: "The Buddha is the awakened one, the mightily compassionate one, the perfectly virtuous one, the ultimate sage. For an ordinary mortal who is ignorant and unblessed to attain this ultimate fruit of spiritual cultivation is not an easy matter. One must practice the proper teachings and follow the right path to Buddhahood; only then can one begin with what lies at hand and proceed onward, moving from the shallow to the deep, until the goal of Buddhahood is reached."

Now then, what are the proper teachings? What is the right path?

He writes: "In order to accommodate different innate capacities, the Buddhadharma has different paths: the path of good works, the path of wisdom, the difficult path and the easy path, the worldly path, the disciple's path, and the bodhisattva path. In reality there is but one path; all these are nothing other than doors leading to Buddhahood. These are the proper teachings, as well as the right path to Buddhahood for the 'ignorant, unblessed mortal' of whom I speak."

Though the paths of good works and wisdom, the difficult and the easy paths are all proper teachings, in spiritual practice one follows them by "beginning with what lies close at hand and proceeding onward, moving from the shallow to the deep." One must move forward by following a logical order and doing first things first, instead of "overstepping the ranks" and "asking for everything at once." For this reason the Guiding Master wrote one chapter each on the five stages of the path to Buddhahood: "Reverence to the Three Refuges"; "Heed and Turn Toward the Dharma"; "The Common Truth of the Five Vehicles"; "The Common Truth of the Three Vehicles"; and "The Unique Truth of Mahāyāna."

All merit rests in the Three Refuges: "All merit is produced by the Three Refuges. Thus the first step in spiritual work is to pay homage to the Three Refuges. However, this being done, we must still rely on our own hard work. Dependence on what has been done will lead to vacillation and the abandoning of further effort: do not let it happen! We all know about the famous disciple Ananda. Falling back on his status as the Buddha's personal disciple, he was unwilling to do serious work. Once, entering a city to beg for food, he was ensnared by a female hermit. Luckily Mañjuśrī, acting on the Buddha's instructions, arrived just in time to rescue him. Otherwise, the result would have been too terrible to contemplate. No wonder that when he saw the Buddha he "made tearful obeisance" and said repentantly: "I regret that I did not heed you from the beginning, for my spiritual power is not yet whole." He also said, "Since my resolve to leave lay life and follow the Buddha, I have leaned upon his lordliness. I have thought: 'No need to trouble myself—Tathāgata will be stow samadhi upon me.' I did not realize that what the body does outwardly can never take the place of what the mind does inwardly."

Thus the *gātha* at the end of "Pay Reverent Homage to the Three Refuges" tells us: "When a man devotes his life/ To the limit of his strength/ An answering accord will await him/ He will find refuge with the truth." "To the limits of his strength" means we should use what abilities we have to cultivate ourselves zealously in accordance with the right Dharma. Do not think only to lean on the Buddha's lordliness and neglect the truth that "what the body does outwardly can never take the place of what the mind does inwardly."

After paying homage to the Three Refuges, the next step is to listen to the Dharma. Why? The first *gātha* in "Heed and Turn Toward the Dharma" says: "By listening we know of all dharmas/ By listening we block many evils/ By listening we cut off the meaningless/ By listening we find nirvāna." He then explains: "This *gātha* from the scriptures praises the merit of listening to the Dharma. We can say that all merit in the Buddhadharma comes from listening to the Dharma. Speaking of listening to the Dharma, Nāgārjuna Bodhisattva said that 'we hear it from three places': First, we hear the Dharma from the Buddha; second, we hear the Dharma from the Buddha's disciples; third, we hear the Dharma from the scriptures. Hearing the Dharma from the Buddha or his disciples is hearing spoken instructions in person, and so the sūtra says: 'This alone is the true substance of the teachings; it is silence expressed in sound.' But since Śākyamuni entered nirvāna, we can only hear of the Dharma from his disciples. Although the Buddhas of the ten directions — the Buddha of Medicine in the East, Amitābha in the West, and the rest — preach the Dharma even now, we of this time and place cannot hear their preaching for ourselves till we reach a certain stage of spiritual cultivation. Hearing of the Dharma from the sūtras is 'taking the Dharma as one's teacher' — it is understanding the Buddhadharma through reading sūtras and discourses. Thus listening to the Buddha's disciples and reading his written teachings are both called heeding the Dharma. Learning about the Buddhadharma begins with this."

Again he says, "Roughly speaking, listening frequently to the Dharma brings four kinds of merit: First, by listening to the right Dharma, we can know all dharmas. What are all dharmas? They are dharmas of goodness, dharmas of evil, dharmas of defilement, dharmas of non-defilement and many others. After listening we know which of these we ought to gather unto ourselves through spiritual work and which we ought to let go of. Again, *fa*, our word for dharma, also means conformity to method. If we listen to the Buddhadharma, we know many methods which we can follow in cultivating goodness. Second, by listening to the right Dharma, we can block out the many sorts of evil. We may have evil thoughts in our minds or evil acts in body and speech. If we listen to the right Dharma and acquaint ourselves with evil causes and effects, then we can extinguish evil thinking. Third, by listening to the right Dharma we can get to the root of all sorts of meaningless things in our lives. Some believers in heterodox religions, though their purpose is to seek deliverance, mistakenly enter the path of ascetic practices — fasting, sleeplessness, nakedness — thinking that these practices bring enlightenment. They practice austerities and teach their disciples to do the same. The Buddha called such austerities meaningless because they are foolish, self-defeating acts. Having heard the right Dharma preached by the Buddha, one will naturally stay away from austerities and follow the right path of spiritual work. Fourth, by listening to the right Dharma and cultivating the self accordingly, one can attain the release of nirvana. In view of this, cannot all merit of the Buddhadharma be gained from listening?"

We see from this the importance of listening to the Buddhadharma. Without it, there would certainly be no means to gain all the merit of the Buddhadharma, and there would be no avenue of deliverance from life and death. One would not even be able to recite "Amitābha" a single time. After we know that all the merits of the Buddhadharma are to be obtained by listening to the right Dharma, we ought to go from listening to thinking, from thinking to practice, and from practice to attainment. But how can we accomplish this transition? As we move forward we must follow the stages of the common truth of the Five Vehicles [*wu-ch'engkung-fa*], the common truth of the Three Vehicles [*san-ch'eng kung-fa*], and the unique truth of Mahāyāna [*ta-ch'eng pu-kung fa*].

What is the common truth of the Five Vehicles? It is the "initial resolve which leads to improvement and the proper door for attaining birth as a man or *deva*. Within the Buddhadharma it is the path for men livingat the lowest of three levels. That is, it underlies the holy Dharma of transcendence, and from this it gets its name. It ensures that when cultivating the transcendent Dharma of the Three Vehicles, though one does not seek the karmic rewards of being a man or a *deva*, one already has a sufficiency of merit required for birth as a man or *deva*."

What is the common truth of the Three Vehicles? "It is the dharma of transcendence. It is built upon a foundation of the common truth of the Five

Vehicles. Only those who have achieved merit allowing rebirth as a man or a *deva* can work toward this transcendent truth."

What is the unique truth of Mahāyāna? "The unique truth of Mahāyāna lies beyond the dharma that embraces the vehicles of the human condition, of divinity [*devas*], and of discipleship [*śrāvaka*] and private enlightenment [*pratyeka buddhas*]; it is a further illumination of the conditioning acts and karmic merit of Buddhas and bodhisattvas. It is different from the Lesser Vehicle, so it is called the Great Vehicle. It includes something more than the dharmas of men, of *devas*, of disciples and privately enlightened Buddhas." Thus it is called "unique." In sum, "This is the real hope which Tathāgata had for others when he came forth to preach the Dharma." It is the "unique Dharma-gate to Buddhahood." And if we follow the "unique Dharma-gate to Buddhahood" as we move forward, we can surely attain the ultimate fruit of Buddhahood and reach our final goal in studying Buddhism. I would like to end this account with this final wish:

I will follow sentient beings
Through the endless kalpas of the future,
Ever practicing the conduct of
Samantabhadra Bodhisattva,
To realize perfect and unequaled enlightenment.

NOTES

1. Yin-shun's complete work is entitled *Miao-yün chi*.

2. "Three treatises" (*San-lun*) refer to the three important Mahāyāna treatises: Mādhyamika-śāstra (*Chung-lun*), Dvādśanikāya-śāstra (*Shih-erh men lun*), and the Śata-śāstra (*Pai-lun*). The first two were written by Nagārjuna who lived during the second century A.D. and the last by his disciple Aryadeva. All three were translated into Chinese by the famous translator Kumārajīva (344-413, var. 409).

3. *K'ung-tsung* is another name for the Madhyamika school. It is so named because of the school's central teaching of śūnyatā (*k'ung*) or the unsubstantiality of all phenomena.

4. *Yu-tsung* is another name for the Dharma-laksana (*Fa-hsiang*) or Wei-shih school founded by Hsüan-tsang (ca. 596-664). The school teaches that all things in the world are composed of one hundred dharmas which alone

are real.

5. Shinran (1173-1262) was the favorite disciple of Hōnen (1133-1212) and the founder of the True Pure Land school in Japan. It has generally been asserted that Shinran started the tradition of married clergy in Japanese Buddhism. As to how he came to get married, there are different stories. According to one, it was Fujiwara Kanezane the regent (not the emperor, as asserted here), who told Hōnen that "he wished his daughter to marry a priest who would thus become a householder and combine religion with a layman's life." Hōnen was not shocked at the suggestion and suggested Shinran as a suitable candidate. Shinran hesitated for a year and then became Kanezane's son-in-law. His wife was known as Tamahi no Miya (Princess Burning Crystal) and they had six children. Charles Eliot, *Japanese Buddhism* (London: Routledge & Kegan Paul Ltd., 1935), p. 270. According to another story, Shinran got married "at the express request of Hōnen in order to demonstrate that monastic discipline was not essential to salvation and that the family rather than the monastery should be the center of the religious life." *The Buddhist Tradition*, edited by Wm. Theodore deBary (New York: The Modern Library, 1969), p. 332. DeBary also mentions that letters written by Shinran's wife, recently found in Echigo, cast doubt on her Fujiwara origin. But in any event, Shinran was not forced into marriage either by Fujiwara or by Hōnen. Giving up celibacy was a logical consequence of his theology which emphasized the absolute reliance on Amida's grace.

6. By "Jih-lien" Tao-yüan means the Japanese Pure Land School or the (True Pure Land School), for "Lotus" symbolizes "Pure Land." I do not think it refers to Nichiren which is also written with the same two characters.

7. In Ch'an monasteries the twenty-four hours of a day and night are divided into six periods: *ch'u-jih* begins at 6 a.m., *chung-jih* at 10 a.m., *hou-jih* at 2 p.m., *ch'u-yeh* at 6 p.m., *chung-yeh* at 10 p.m., and *hou-yeh* at 2 a.m. Each lasts four hours.

8. *Huai-sse i* is the name given to the monk's robe. It is so named because it is of a brown color which is described as a neutral color through the dyeing out of other colors. The robe is stitched together out of several pieces of cloth, for originally it was supposed to be made out of discarded rags.

9. Depending on the translations, the *Flower Garland Sūtra* (*Avatamsaka Sūtra*) is divided into eight or nine meetings (*hui*). "There exists three Chinese translations of this sūtra: the first in 60 *chüan* by Buddhabhadra, made during the period 418-420; the second in 80 *chüan* by Sikshananda during 695-704; and the third in 40 *chüan* by Prajñā during 795-810. The last is essentially a translation of the *Gandavyūha* or that portion of the whole sūtra which describes the journey of the youth Sudhana in search for the truth." Kenneth Ch'en, *Buddhism in China, A Historical Survey* (Princeton University Press, 1964), pp. 313-314.

10. This chapter, "P'u-hsien hsing-yüan p'in," is found in *Flower Garland Sūtra*. But it is so popular that it is often printed and circulated among Buddhist believers by itself.

11. The karma which makes a person fall into the Avici hell (the lowest of the eight hells) results in five kinds of uninterrupted (*wu-chien*) suffering. For this reason, the Avici hell is also called the uninterminable hell. The term "uninterrupted" is used because: 1) there is no gap between the creation of bad karma and the suffering after death, 2) there is no interruption in one's suffering, 3) there is no interruption in time, 4) one's life continues in this state without interruption, 5) one's body is co-extensive with the vast hell, and there is not any space between one's body and the hell.

12. These are the thirty-two laksanas or physical marks of a cakravarti or "wheel king," especially of the Buddha. They are "level feet, thousand-spoke wheel-sign on feet, long slender fingers, pliant hands and feet, toes and fingers finely webbed, full-sized heels, arched insteps, thighs like a royal stag, hands reaching below the knees, well-retracted male organ, height and stretch of arms equal, every hair-root dark colored, body hair graceful and curly, golden-hued body, a 10-foot halo around him, soft smooth skin, the 'seven places,' i.e., two soles, two palms, two shoulders and crown well rounded, below the armpits well filled, lion-shaped body, erect and full shoulders, forty teeth, teeth white and even and close, the four canine teeth pure white, lion-jawed, saliva improving the taste of food, tongue long and broad, voice deep and resonant, eyes deep blue, eyelashes like a royal bull, a white urna or curl between the eyebrows emitting light, an usnisa or fleshly protuberance on the crown." William Edward Soothill and Lewis Hodous, *A Dictionary of Chinese Buddhist Terms* (Taiwan: Buddhist Culture Service, 1962 reprint), p. 60.

GLOSSARY

A-mi-t'o ching 阿彌陀經
A-yu-wang ssu 阿育王寺
chai-t'ang 齋堂
Chang Chi 張繼
ch'ang-shan 長衫
ch'ang-sheng wei 長生位
cheng-fa 正法
cheng-ke 正科
Chi-ch'an 寄禪
Chi-kung tien 濟公殿
Chi-ming ssu 雞鳴寺
Ch'i-hsia ssu 棲霞寺
chi-pao hang-shu 七寶行樹
"chi-pei cha" 七杯茶
"chi-pei chiu" 七杯酒
chia-fang 架房
chia-feng 家風
chia-hsiang 加香
chia-sha 袈裟
ch'iao chien-ch'ui 敲犍椎
Chieh-chung ssu 戒幢寺
chieh-fa 戒法
chieh-fei 戒費
chieh-hsiang 戒相
chieh-hsing 戒行
Chieh-kung Ch'ih 戒公池
chieh-pa 戒疤
chieh-shih 戒師
chieh-t'i 戒体
chieh-tieh 戒牒
Ch'ien-fo ssu 千佛寺
chien-hsiang 監香
Chien-yueh 見月

Chih-chi 智積
Ch'ih Chin-kang Shen 持金鋼神
chih-ke 知客
Chih-kuang 智光
chih-shan 知山
Chih-tu 智度
Chih-yueh lu 指月錄
Chin-shan ssu 金山寺
chin-shih 進士
Ching-an 敬安
ching-chin 精進
Ching-fan ssu 淨梵寺
Ch'ing-liang ssu 清涼寺
ching-nien 淨念
Ch'ing-yun 清雲
Chu-sheng ssu 祝聖寺
Chu-shih-lin 居士林
ch'u-ti 初地
ch'u-yeh 初夜
chu-yuan 助緣
ch'uan-fa 傳法
ch'uan-hsien 傳賢
chuang-chu 莊主
Chueh-yuan 覺園
Chun-shan 峻山
Chung-feng Ming-p'en 中峰明本
Ch'ung-fa ssu 崇法寺
Chung lun 中論
Chung-nan Shan 終南山
chung-yeh 中夜
fa 法
fa-chuan ssu-shu 法眷私屬
Fa-hsiang 法相
Fa--hua ssu 法華寺
Fa-yu ssu 法雨寺

fan-t'ou 飯頭
fang-pien fa-men 方便法門
Fo-ch'i yi-kuei 佛七儀軌
Fo i chiao ching 佛遺教經
fu-ssu 副寺
Fu-yen ching-she 福嚴精舍
hai-ch'ing 海青
Hai-hui ssu 海會寺
Han-shan ssu 寒山寺
Ho-hsuan 鶴軒
ho-shang pao-chang 和尚保長
hou-yeh 後夜
hsiang-fa 像法
Hsiang-kuang 香光
Hsiang-lin ssu 香林寺
hsiang-pa 香疤
hsiang-teng shih 香燈師
Hsiang-yen 香嚴
hsiao kuai-kuai 小乖乖
Hsien-ch'in ch'ung-pao ch'an-ssu 顯親崇報禪寺
hsien-hsiu ke 先修科
hsin-so 心所
hsin-wang 心王
Hsing-k'ung hsueh t'an-yuan 性空學探源
hsing-t'ang 行堂
Hsing-yun 星雲
Hsiu-hsi chih-kuan tso-ch'an fa-yao 修習止觀坐禪法要
huai-sse i 壞色衣
Hui-chi ssu 慧濟寺
Hui-chu ssu 慧居寺
hui-hsiang 迴向
Hui-o (Eigaku) 慧諤
Hung-hua She 弘化社
I fo-fa yen-chiu fo-fa 以佛法研究佛法
i-hsin pu-luan 一心不亂

i-tan ch'ien 衣單錢
Jih-lien tsung 日蓮宗
Jou-shen p'u-sa 肉身菩薩
Ju-lin wai-shih 儒林外史
Jui-yun ssu 瑞雲寺
kai-shin 開示
kan ching-ch'an 趕經懺
Kao-feng Yuan-miao 高峰原妙
Kao-min ssu 高旻寺
kao sheng-ssu-chia 告生死假
Ku-lin ssu 古林寺
kua-t'a 掛褡
kua-tan 掛單
k'ua-tzu 侉子，誇子
kuan-fang 關房
Kuan-tsung ssu 觀宗寺
Kuan-wu-liang-shou ching 觀無量壽經
Kuan kung (Kuan Yu) 關公 (關羽)
Kuang-chi ssu 廣濟寺
Kuei-chu 規矩
k'ung-ch'eng-chi 空城計
kung-chung 供眾
K'ung-tsung 空宗
Leng-yen ching 楞嚴經
Leng-yen chou 楞嚴咒
Liao-jan 了然
Li chiao 理教
Lien-ch'ih yen 蓮池庵
Lien-ch'ih ta-shih 蓮池大師
Lin-chi ssu 臨濟寺
Ling-ch'uan ssu 靈泉寺
Ling-ku ssu 靈谷寺
ling-t'ang 靈堂
Ling-yen hsiao-chih 靈巖小志
Ling-yen Shan 靈岩山

lo-han-chi 羅漢期
Lu-hang 律航
Lung-ch'ang ssu 隆昌寺
Lung-t'u kung-an 龍圖公案
ma-liu-tzu 馬騮子
ma-ma hu-hu 馬馬虎虎
Mi-yun 密雲
miao-chan tsung-ch'ih pu-tung tsun 妙湛總持不動尊
Miao-chen 妙真
miao-chu 廟祝
Miao-jou shang-jen 妙柔上人
Miao-yun chi 妙雲紀
mo-fa 末法
Mo-ju 默如
Nan-t'ing 南亭
nien-fo san-mei 念佛三昧
Nien-fo t'ang 念佛堂
Niu-t'o Ma-mien 牛頭馬面
Pa-chih T'ou-t'o 八指頭陀
pa-shih 八識
Pa-t'o-lo 跋陀羅
pai-ching t'ai 拜經台
Pai-fa ming-men lun-chieh 百法明門論解
Pai-fa ming-men lun-shu 百法明門論疏
Pai lun 百論
Pai-sheng 白聖
Pao Ch'eng 包拯
Pao-hua Shan 寶華山
Pao kung 包公
Pao-kung an 包公案
Pao-kuo yung-tso ch'an-ssu 報國永祚禪寺
pao-shen 報身
pao-tzu 包子
pi-ch'iu chieh 比丘戒
pi-kuan 閉關

P'i-lu ssu 毘盧寺
P'in-shan 品山
P'u-hsien hsing-yuan p'in 普賢行願品
P'u-lai-shih 浦萊士
P'u-men Tzu 普門子
p'u-sa chieh 菩薩戒
P'u Ta-fan 濮大凡
p'u-t'i hsin 菩提心
P'u-t'i shu 菩提樹
P'u-t'o Shan 普陀山
p'u-tu yen-kou 普度餕口
san-ch'eng kung-fa 三乘共法
san-fo 三佛
"san-hua" 散花
san-i 三衣
San-kuo yen-i 三國演義
San-lun tsung 三論宗
san-mei 三昧
san-t'an cheng-shou 三壇正授
San-tzu ching 三字經
sha-mi chieh 沙彌戒
shan chih-shih 善知識
shan-ken 善根
Shan-tao ssu 善導寺
shang kung 上供
shang-p'in 上品
shang-tso 上座
"Shao hsiao-kuo-tzu" 燒小鍋子
she-li-tzu 舍利子
Sheng-ch'uan ssu 聖泉寺
sheng-wen 聲聞
Shih-erh-men lun 十二門論
Shih-fang ta-chueh ssu 十方大覺寺
Shih Hsi-t'i 釋西諦
shih-kung 師公

Shih-p'u ssu 十普寺
Shih-t'ou Shan 獅頭山
Shu-t'ang 樹唐
Su-tsai Chih Chia 素菜之家
sui-hsi 隨喜
ta-ch'eng pu-kung fa 大乘不共法
Ta-ch'eng pai-fa ming-men lun 大乘百法明門論
ta fo-ch'i 打佛七
Ta-hsien ssu 大仙寺
Ta-hsing 大醒
Ta-hsiung pao-tien 大雄寶殿
ta hui-hsiang 大迴向
Ta-ming-wang 大明王
Ta-pei chou 大悲咒
ta p'u-fo 大普佛
ta-shih yin-yuan 大事因緣
T'ai-hsu 太虛
T'ai-pai Shan 太白山
tai-shu 代數
tai-yeh wang-sheng 代業往生
"T'an chi-chi" 嘆七七
T'an-hsu 倓虛
"T'an k'u-lou" 嘆骷髏
tang-chia 當家
t'ang-chu 堂主
t'ang-li 堂裡
Tao-an 道安
tao-chang 道場
Tao-sheng 道生
"tao-t'ou ching" 倒頭經
Tao-yuan 道源
T'ao Yuan-ming 陶淵明
Te-sen 德森
T'i-hsien 諦閑
T'ien-ning ssu 天甯寺

T'ien-t'ung ssu 天童寺
t'ien-yen-t'ung 天眼通
To-pao 多寶
tsao-ke 早課
Tsao-wu 早悟
tseng-shang yuan 增上緣
tso-kuan 作觀
t'u-chih 徒侄
Tu-e 度厄
tun-cheng 頓証
tun-hsiu 頓修
tun-wu 頓悟
T'ung-chieh lu 同戒錄
Tung-lin 東林
tung-pan t'ang 東板堂
Tung-yueh miao 東嶽廟
Tz'u-hang 慈航
tz'u-shu 次數
wai-liao 外寮
"Wan-shih tien-t'ou" 頑石點頭
wai-fu ssu 外副寺
wai-hu 外護
wang-seng wei 往生位
wei-no 維那
Wei P'u-chi 韋普濟
wo-wo-t'ou 窩窩頭
wu-ch'eng kung-fa 五乘共法
wu-chien 無間
wu wu-chien yeh 五無間業
wu-ch'u 五趣
wu-hsin 無心
Wu-liang-shou ching 無量壽經
wu-sheng jen 無生忍
ya-yang-seng 啞羊僧
Ye-she tsun-che 耶舍尊者

Yi-meng man-yen 一夢漫言
Yin-kuang 印光
Yin-kuang fa-shih wen-ch'ao 印光法師文鈔
yin-kuo 因果
yin-li shih 引禮師
Yin-shun 印順
Ying-ch'en hui-i lu 影塵回憶錄
Ying-chiang ssu 迎江寺
ying-fu seng 應赴僧
ying-yuan 應院
Yu-fo ssu 玉佛寺
yu-ke 預科
Yu tsung 有宗
yuan-chueh 緣覺
Yuan-chueh ching 圓覺經
Yuan-ying 圓瑛

INDEX